Library of
Davidson College

# THE SOVIET IMPACT ON COMMODITY MARKETS

The Soviet Union is a dominant factor in many commodity markets both as exporter and leading producer as well as importer and major consumer. Foreign trade monopoly combined with the dominant market share provides the Soviet Union with an effective instrument of economic and political pressure in relations with other countries. This volume is an attempt to assess the Soviet commodity power not only in particular commodity markets but also in a larger system of economic and political relations between nations.

An in-depth study of this broad issue requires an intimate knowledge of particular commodity markets, familiarity with the Soviet economy of mineral and agricultural resources as well as an understanding of the Soviet role in the international economic and political relations. Such a diversity of expertise which is required to assess the Soviet commodity power in the international system called for a team of scholars in which particular participants would contribute their specific knowledge.

This collective work deals with the general issues such as the Soviet commodity power, Soviet terms of trade and the Soviet attitude towards international commodity agreements, and comprises studies evaluating the Soviet role in specific markets of natural resources: oil and gas, copper, manganese and chromite, bauxite and aluminium, gold and platinum, coal and asbestos, grain and cotton.

# THE SOVIET IMPACT ON COMMODITY MARKETS

Edited by
M.M. Kostecki

St. Martin's Press   New York

©M.M. Kostecki 1984

All rights reserved. For information, write:
St. Martin's Press, Inc., 175 Fifth Avenue, New York, NY 10010
Printed in Hong Kong
First published in the United States of America in 1981
ISBN 0-312-74839-6

**Library of Congress Cataloging in Publication Data**
Main entry under title:

Soviet impact on commodity markets.

   Includes bibliographical references.
   1. Soviet Union—Address, essays, lectures.
2. Raw materials—Soviet Union—Addresses, essays,
lectures. 3. Commodity exchange. I. Kostecki, M.M.
HF3626.5.S683   1981     332.63′28′0947   81-9223
ISBN 0-312-74839-6              AACR2

963 CL14 D1.4

# Contents

| | |
|---|---|
| *The Contributors* | vii |
| *List of Tables* | ix |
| *List of Figures* | xii |
| *Abbreviations* | xiii |
| *Acknowledgements* | xiv |
| Introduction   *M.M. Kostecki* | 1 |
| 1  Soviet Commodity Power in International Economic Relations   *Raymond Vernon* | 6 |
| 2  Long-Term Commodity Agreements and the USSR   *Marie Lavigne* | 15 |
| 3  Exports of Primary Commodities and the Soviet Terms of Trade   *Zdeněk Drabek* | 26 |
| 4  The Soviet Union and World Trade in Oil and Gas   *J.B. Hannigan and C.H. McMillan* | 68 |
| 5  Soviet Coal Exports   *Svjetlana Adler and Harriet Matejka* | 100 |
| 6  The USSR and the International Aluminium Market   *Carmine Nappi* | 116 |
| 7  The Role of the Soviet Union in Metals Markets: A Case Study of Copper, Manganese and Chromite   *Walter Labys* | 135 |
| 8  The Soviet Impact on World Trade in Gold and Platinum   *Michael Kaser* | 156 |
| 9  The Soviet Impact on International Trade in Asbestos   *Petr Hanel* | 173 |
| 10  The Soviet Union in International Grain Markets   *M.M. Kostecki* | 194 |

| 11 | The USSR as a Major Factor in International Cotton Markets  *Lewis Fischer* | 218 |

*Notes* 237
*Selected Bibliography* 259
*Index* 267

# The Contributors

Svjetlana ADLER
Research Fellow
The Graduate Institute of International Studies
University of Geneva

Zdeněk DRABEK
Professor of Economics
Department of Economics
University College of Buckingham

Lewis FISCHER
Professor of Agricultural Economics
Department of Agricultural Economics
McGill University

Petr HANEL
Associate Professor of Economics
Department of Economics
University of Sherbrooke, Quebec

John B. HANNIGAN
Research Fellow
Institute of Soviet and East European Studies
Carleton University, Ottawa

Michael KASER
University Lecturer
St. Antony's College
Oxford University

Michel KOSTECKI
Associate Professor of Economics
Institute for Applied Economics
Ecole des Hautes Etudes Commerciales
University of Montreal

Walter LABYS
Professor of Resource Economics
West Virginia University
and Visiting Scholar
Energy Laboratory
Massachusetts Institute of Technology

Marie LAVIGNE
Professor of Economics
Director
Centre d'Economie Internationale des Pays Socialistes
Université de Paris I (Panthéon – Sorbonne)

Harriet MATEJKA
Associate Professor of Economics
The Graduate Institute of International Studies
University of Geneva

Carl McMILLAN
Professor of Economics
Director
Institute of Soviet and East European Studies
Carleton University, Ottawa

Carmine NAPPI
Associate Professor of Economics
Director
Institute for Applied Economics
Ecole des Hautes Etudes Commerciales
University of Montreal

Raymond VERNON
Clarence Dillon Professor of International Affairs
Centre for International Affairs
Harvard University
Cambridge, Massachusetts

# List of Tables

| | | |
|---|---|---|
| 3.1 | Volume, Price and Terms of Trade Indices in Soviet Foreign Trade: 1975 and 1976 | 34 |
| 3.2 | Indices of Soviet Net Barter Terms of Trade with the World, the West and CMEA: 1960–1980. | 36 |
| 3.3 | Aggregate Soviet Export and Import Price Indices with Four Main Trade Regions and Terms of Trade 1970–1977 Based on Prices in Roubles or SDRs | 39 |
| 3.4 | Unit Value Indices for Soviet Foreign Trade: 1960–1978 | 40 |
| 3.5 | Price Changes in Soviet Trade with the World, Eastern Europe, and non CMEA Countries: 1975–1977 | 42 |
| 3.6 | Unit Value Indices for Soviet Exports of Eight Primary Products: 1959–1976 | 46 |
| 3.7 | Quantity Indices for Soviet Foreign Trade, National Income and Gross National Product: 1960–1978 | 48 |
| 3.8 | Aggregate Soviet Export and Import Quantity Indices with Four Main Trade Regions and Gross Barter Terms of Trade, 1970–1977 | 49 |
| 3.9 | Windfall Gains to the Soviet Union from Trade with MDC and CMEA Countries | 52 |
| A.1 | Soviet Trade with the CMEA Six | 60 |
| A.2 | Soviet Trade with the OCPEs | 62 |
| A.3 | Soviet Trade with the MDCs | 64 |
| A.4 | Soviet Trade with the LDCs | 66 |
| 4.1 | Output and Reserves of Petroleum and Natural Gas by Region and by Country – 1979 | 69 |
| 4.2 | USSR Trade in Petroleum and Natural Gas (1950–1980) | 72 |
| 4.3 | Soviet Shares of World Trade and Regional Markets in Crude Oil, Oil Products and Natural Gas in the Postwar Period | 80 |
| 5.1 | Soviet Production of Solid Fuels: 1950–1981 | 102 |

## List of Tables

| | | |
|---|---|---|
| 5.2 | Soviet Production, Trade and Consumption of Solid Fuels: 1950–1979 | 103 |
| 5.3 | Soviet Hard Coal Exports: 1950–1981 | 104 |
| 5.4 | The Direction of Soviet Hard Coal Exports: 1950–1980 | 108 |
| 5.5 | 1981–85 Production Plan Broken Down by Coal Basin | 112 |
| 5.6 | The USSR's Coal Demand and Production | 113 |
| 6.1 | Geographical Distribution of the International Production of Bauxite, Alumina and Aluminium | 120 |
| 6.2 | Geographical Distribution of International Aluminium Consumption | 122 |
| 6.3 | International Aluminium Trade: 1972–1980 | 124 |
| 6.4 | Soviet Bauxite and Alumina Imports: 1964–1975 | 126 |
| 7.1 | Comparison of the USSR and World Copper Market | 140 |
| 7.2 | Destinations of USSR Exports of Refined Copper | 142 |
| 7.3 | Copper Production by Countries | 144 |
| 7.4 | Comparison of the USSR and World Manganese Ore Market | 146 |
| 7.5 | Destinations of USSR Exports of Manganese Ore | 149 |
| 7.6 | Comparison of the USSR and World Chromite Market | 152 |
| 8.1 | Author's Estimates of Soviet Gold Production by Field: 1970–1990 | 160 |
| 8.2 | Production and Trade in Gold: 1975–1981 | 162 |
| 8.3 | Production and Trade in Platinum-Group Metals: 1975–1980 | 163 |
| 8.4 | Alternative Estimates of Soviet Gold Sales to the West: 1974–1981 | 164 |
| 8.5 | Estimates of the Soviet Hard-Currency Balance of Payments: 1970–1980 | 168 |
| 9.1 | The Soviet Share in World Production of Asbestos: 1953–1990 | 176 |
| 9.2 | USSR: Asbestos Production by Principal Mines and Mills: 1968–1990 | 177 |
| 9.3 | World Consumption of Asbestos in 1974 | 179 |
| 9.4 | Soviet Exports of Asbestos to COMECON Countries | 181 |
| 9.5 | Imports of Asbestos and Evolution of Market Shares | 182 |
| 9.6 | Summary of Forecasts of US and Rest of World Asbestos Demand | 191 |
| 10.1 | Major Grain Producers and Traders | 195 |
| 10.2 | Soviet Production and Trade of Grain | 196 |

| | | |
|---|---|---|
| 10.3 | Composition of Soviet Grain Imports by Type of Grain: 1960–1979 | 197 |
| 10.4 | Dependence on Grain Trade: USSR and Major Exporters | 200 |
| 10.5 | Utilisation of Grain in the Soviet Union | 203 |
| A.1 | USSR Exports of Grain by Country of Origin | |
| 11.1 | Cotton: Production Trend in the Largest Producer Countries | 219 |
| 11.2 | World Cotton Consumption 1971/72–1980/81: | 222 |
| 11.3 | Exports of Cotton 1971/72–1980/81: | 224 |
| 11.4 | Imports of Cotton 1971/72–1980/81: | 226 |
| 11.5 | Exports of Cotton from USSR, by Country of Destination | 230 |
| 11.6 | Distribution of Soviet Cotton Exports by Regions | 233 |
| 11.7 | Imports of Cotton into USSR by Country of Origin | 233 |
| 11.8 | Cotton Prices in Selected Countries | 234 |
| 11.9 | Value of Cotton Exports and Grain Imports – Soviet Union | 235 |

# List of Figures

| | | |
|---|---|---|
| 5.1 | Export Trend, 1950–1990 | 107 |
| 9.1 | The Evolution of Soviet Production Consumption and Exports of Asbestos | 178 |
| 9.2 | The Evolution of the USSR's Share of the Asbestos Market | 183 |
| 9.3 | The Evolution of Import Prices: Japan, India, Western Europe | 186 |
| 10.1 | Soviet Grain Imports and Exports | 198 |
| 10.2 | Soviet Grain Production and Imports | 206 |
| 10.3 | Evolution of Soviet Terms of Trade | 207 |
| A–1 | Trend of Soviet Grain Production 1956/57–1980/81 | 214 |
| A–2 | Trend of Coarse Grains Imports over Time 1960–1979 | 215 |
| A–3 | Trend of Wheat Imports over Time 1960–1979 | 216 |
| 11.1 | Exports of Cotton, 1971–72 to 1979–80 | 227 |
| 11.2 | Imports of Cotton, 1971–72 to 1979–80 | 228 |
| 11.3 | Exports of Cotton from USSR by Destination 1965–1979 | 229 |
| 11.4 | Imports of Cotton into USSR: Selected Major Suppliers 1965–1979 | 232 |

# Abbreviations

| | |
|---|---|
| CMEA | Council for Mutual Economic Assistance (also referred to as COMECON) |
| CPE | Centrally Planned Economy |
| CWB | Canadian Wheat Board |
| DFTT | Double Factoral Terms of Trade |
| ECE | Economic Commission for Europe |
| EEC | European Economic Community |
| f.o.b. | free on board |
| GBTT | Gross Barter Terms of Trade |
| IBA | International Bauxite Association |
| ICA | International Commodity Agreement |
| IPC | Integrated Programme for Commodities |
| ISA | International Sugar Agreement |
| ITT | Income Terms of Trade |
| LDCs | Less Developed Countries |
| LME | London Metal Exchange |
| MDCs | More Developed Countries |
| MFN | Most-Favoured Nation |
| MTE | Market Type Economy |
| NBTT | Net Barter Terms of Trade |
| NRPs | Natural Resource Products |
| OAPEC | Organization of Arab Petroleum Exporting Countries |
| OCPEs | Other Centrally Planned Economies |
| OPEC | Organization of Petroleum Exporting Countries |
| SDRs | Special Drawing Rights |
| SFTT | Single Factoral Terms of Trade |
| UNCTAD | United Nations Conference for Trade and Development |
| VT | Vneshnyaya Torgovlya |
| VTSS | Vneshnyaya Torgovlya Sovyetsogo Soyuza |
| WMPs | World Market Prices |

# Acknowledgements

A major portion of this volume is based on papers presented at a conference at the Ecole des Hautes Etudes Commerciales of the University of Montreal, Canada. I would like to express my appreciation to the director of the Centre for International Business Studies Professor Jean-Emile Denis for his encouragement in the preparation of this project. I have also an enormous debt of gratitude to Mrs Sylvia Toledano who administered this complex undertaking and Mrs Sybil Denis who emended the English and improved the clarity in many of the following chapters.

Publication of this volume is rendered possible through grants from Alcan Aluminium Ltd. Ecole des HEC and the Social Sciences and Humanities Research Council of Canada.

With these expressions of gratitude go our personal affirmations of responsibility for this book.

# Introduction

## M.M. Kostecki

The objective of this volume is to assess the role of the Soviet Union in the international trade of basic minerals and agricultural commodities. The long-term trends in Soviet trading patterns, their implication for international commodity markets as well as for a broader system of international economic and political relations are here of major concern.

This collective work is divided into two distinct parts. The first part deals with general topics such as Soviet commodity power, Soviet terms of trade and the Soviet attitude towards international commodity agreements. The second part comprises studies evaluating the Soviet role in specific markets of natural resources: oil and gas, coal, alumina and bauxite, platinum and gold, copper, manganese and chromite, asbestos, grain and cotton. It would be next to impossible, in a single volume, to deal with all the commodities in which the Soviets are important traders. Nevertheless, even the limited sample of 13 commodity markets discussed below provides extensive evidence of the USSR's major role in international commodity trading during the past three decades.

The Soviet Union is generally thought to be comparatively less powerful in the economic than in the military or political spheres. However, if there is one economic area where a strong Soviet impact is internationally felt it is certainly that of natural resources. The USSR does seem to have the potential to influence other nations by means of its central position in international commodity markets. This ability is referred to as Soviet commodity power.

The aspect of this Soviet commodity power surveyed in this volume is, essentially, its economic features. Commodity trading is, first of all, a money-making operation and Soviet trade in commodities is, at least in the Western markets, remarkably business-like.

Only through market power can economic pressure be exerted on commodity trading. Assessment of the USSR's place in market structures, its market power and role in international price formation are, thus, central topics of the commodity studies presented below. In numerous commodity markets the Soviets are sometimes shown reaping large benefits from their price-making power and exhibiting great skill in maximising their short-term gains from trade. During the seventies, there was also considerable long-term improvement in Soviet terms of trade. However, that improvement may most probably be explained by the general commodity boom with its rising commodity prices rather than the impact of Soviet trading strategies alone.

The Soviet concern with improving terms of trade has also frequently been at odds with immediate balance-of-payments considerations. For example, during the early 1980s Moscow was forced to sell commodities (gold, oil, gas, timber, diamonds, etc.) at low prices in sluggish international markets in order to cover the cost of its essential imports. Hard currency shortages may become even more of a determining factor in Soviet commodity exports as cheap Western credit becomes more limited in the future.

Another way of looking at Soviet commodity power is to consider it in terms of the Soviet potential to deprive the West of access to essential raw materials (strategic commodity power). Do the Soviets really have the means to cripple Western industry by depriving it of supplies of some of the thirty or so critical materials upon which modern industrial activities depend? The problem has been raised in the case of minerals such as manganese and chromite (which are crucial to steel production) and a number of others with important industrial applications (e.g. nickel, copper, titanium, vanadium and lead).

Several of the authors in this volume consider that the Soviet potential to exercise strategic power does not exist to any substantial degree (and certainly not for chromite, manganese and copper). Note, however, that the situation might change if the USSR formed a common front with several other exporters from the Third World. Considerations of this type might have important implications for the geopolitical strategies of the Soviet Union. Zimbabwe and South Africa, which share with the USSR important portions of international markets for several strategic commodities, seem to provide the most logical targets for the Soviet Union's efforts to increase its sphere of political influence.

Obviously, vulnerability to strategic blackmail may be considerably reduced by adequate stockpiling or material substitution. For example, it should be noted, that, in the rare cases when the Soviets clearly aimed at using commodity power for strategic purposes (e.g. the reduction of manganese supplies to the West during the Korean War), that strategy had little effect on Western industries.

The question of strategic commodity power has become a central issue in the recent debates over Soviet gas supplies to Western Europe. Here, the first and most obvious concern is that, through increased dependence on Soviet deliveries of natural gas, oil and other essential raw materials, the West Europeans could be manoeuvred into economic dependence on the USSR. More reasonably, the question is probably not whether Western Europe should or should not use Soviet gas but rather how much it should use. West Europeans, if politically minded, would diversify their sources of energy supply so that their dependence on any single supplier is kept within proper bounds. To rely excessively on a single source of supply is to beg for blackmail.

Still another way of looking at Soviet commodity trading is to consider it in the perspective of *trade for political objectives* (political commodity power). There is no doubt that the political character of a USSR trading partner at times influences the terms on which Soviet raw materials may be bought. In other words, through concessionary sales of raw materials (e.g. sales below the international market price) the Soviets manage not only to increase a given partner's dependence on their supplies (by that token also probably increasing their strategic commodity power) but also to obtain specific political gains. In that context, exporting raw materials on terms particularly favourable to the partner country may be a way of subsidising political support abroad.

The issue is of special importance for the COMECON area, the main receiver of Soviet commodity exports. The impressive strength of Soviet political commodity power within the COMECON area may be largely explained by the following three factors. First of all, several COMECON countries are almost totally dependent on USSR supplies of essential raw materials. In many cases this dependence involves long-term commitment because of technological features which would often make it difficult for COMECON industries to replace Soviet supplies by imports from other countries.

Secondly, in the past the Soviets were willing to accept "barter deals" with their allies even for commodities which might have been easily sold for hard currency in Western markets. Although, in economic terms, such bilateral arrangements might then have been to the advantage of the USSR's COMECON partners, allowing them to pay for Soviet commodities with low quality industrial and consumer products difficult to sell in the West, this form of bilateralism certainly reinforced the Soviets' political hold on the countries concerned.

Finally, it is frequently claimed that the Soviets have supplied the COMECON member countries with commodities at preferential prices as compared to world market prices. At least until very recently, East European countries, drawing upon cheap Soviet petroleum and other essential raw materials, seemed to be accepting economic subsidisation in exchange for political allegiance. However, this popular view meets with at least one important objection. Given the essentially bilateral character of trade within the COMECON area, it is very difficult to make conclusive price comparisons of the type suggested above. Indeed, if the aforementioned subsidy effect does arise it is primarily a consequence of the combined factors of: pricing practices in intra-bloc trade, the structure of the exports and imports concerned and alternative trade opportunities with the hard currency area. Elements of this sort may not always be evaluated in an objective manner. Moreover, it is very doubtful whether official COMECON statistics tell the whole truth about intra-COMECON trading. For example, an honest assessment of who gains what from intra-COMECON trade is hardly conceivable without taking into consideration military equipment and the price that the East European countries have to pay for it. Note that proponents of the so-called "exploitational" vision of Soviet trade policy in COMECON suggest that the Soviets are more than well paid for the raw materials they export to the COMECON countries.

It is shown below that Soviet trade in many essential commodities has undergone significant changes since 1980. Indeed, in recent years the Soviets have started progressively to cut their exports of oil, gas and other raw materials to COMECON countries and have adjusted their prices upwards to meet those of the international market. This seems to imply that Soviet commodity exports are under increasing pressure. Several commodity studies in this volume suggest that the development of Soviet commodity exports is highly dependent on Soviet access to Western technology and Western assistance in exploiting new projects. The Soviet Union has been borrowing enormous sums in the West to finance, among others, such projects as the natural gas pipeline from Siberia to Western Europe. Soviet loans for the pipeline alone totalled more than $2 billion in 1982 and the USSR has been asking for additional credits since then. Under the weight of this debt burden the USSR may be forced to make even further cuts in its deliveries of essential raw materials to the COMECON countries in order to increase its sales for hard currency. At the same time, however, several East European countries appear to be headed for costly economic dependence on the USSR, in a period when Soviet economic problems and the expense of maintaining large military forces could be overwhelming. What impact these policies will have on Western commodity markets is difficult to assess in general terms. Some insights in that direction with reference to specific commodity groups, are presented below and new trends in Soviet natural resources policy indicated. Clearly, the Soviet role in the international markets of several major commodities will change considerably during the 1980s and Soviet impact on market conditions will probably be strongly felt. However, one of the objectives of this volume is to emphasize the significance of Russia's commodity trading in the context of its more general political and economic relations with other international powers. In the economic sphere, natural resources are Moscow's strongest card *vis-à-vis* both the West and its political allies in COMECON. Soviet commodity power might thus easily become an increasingly significant factor in future international relations and we hope that this collective book will provide the reader with a useful overview of the major issues involved.

# 1 Soviet Commodity Power in International Economic Relations

Raymond Vernon

THE ISSUE

The debate over the size of the Soviet Union's "commodity power" has been with us for a long time. The question can hardly be avoided. A nation of 265 million people with a gross national product exceeded only by that of the United States has centralized its decisions on the production, export, and import of its commodities. Few other countries leave such decisions wholly to the vagaries of the market place. But the Soviet Union stands out in two respects. Apart from the People's Republic of China, it is by a considerable margin the largest of the nations that have made the choice to centralize. And its centralizing controls, with no important exceptions, are the most rigorous on earth.

Assume, then, that the Soviet Union has centralized its buying and selling of commodities for the purpose of maximizing its power outside of the home economy. Has that step in fact endowed the USSR with any significant amount of power? And if so, to what end will such power be used?

Judging from the expressions of concern of observers outside the USSR, one can distinguish three possibilities. First, the Soviet Union might see some advantage at times in upsetting – or in threatening to upset – the international economic system of the non-Soviet world, as a tactical step in the rivalry between competing ideologies. Second, the USSR might see possibilities for using its commodity power to influence the political behaviour of individual nations. Third, commodity power might be used by the USSR to capture the lion's share of the economic gains that arise from ordinary international trade. How seriously is one to take any of these alternatives?

## UPSETTING THE SYSTEM

The fundamental fact that needs to be remembered in exploring all of these alternatives is that, measured against world aggregates, the Soviet Union is a dominant seller of only a few commodities, such as chromite, manganese and platinum, and a dominant buyer of practically nothing. Yet the experience of the past few years, notably in petroleum and in grains, suggests that the position of a country does not need to be overwhelming in order to create a measurable short-term effect on world markets.

The reason for the Soviet Union's ability to affect some commodities in which it does not appear to have a dominant position is evident. In the short run, the price elasticities of supply and demand for many products, including oil and grains, are very low; increased prices neither reduce consumption very much nor generate very large increases in production. Moreover, the Soviet Union projects an image abroad of imperturbability regarding its needs to buy or to sell the products concerned, while the sellers and buyers that it confronts scramble to persuade their respective governments that the prospective sales or the prospective purchases are a matter of life or death. In such circumstances, the bargaining position of the USSR may be strong, at least in the short run.

The corollary to this general observation is that the USSR may be capable of influencing inflationary and deflationary movements in countries with open economies, out of all proportion to the size of the country's place in world markets. Whether the USSR actually realises that potential depends in part on how the inflationary and deflationary waves in those economies are generated. Some economists view short-term ripples in the world price of any given commodity, whatever the commodity's importance, as largely irrelevant to the world's inflationary cycles. These are thought to be determined by other kinds of factors, notably the supply of money. Changes in the supply of money in turn are regarded as stemming from factors that have little to do with the decisions of any one buyer or seller with regard to a commodity or two.

However, other economists, including myself, are prepared to entertain the possibility that a change in the price of some key factor such as oil or grain can trigger a series of price increases over a broad front. Short-term disequilibria, such as were experienced in grain in 1972 and in oil at various times in the 1970s, provoke an inflationary push in all other commodities, until eventually the relative prices of the various products are brought into line again. If the object of a purposeful intervener were simply to generate inflation in world markets and if the expectations of the rest of the world were ripe for a follow-up, according to this argument, it would need no very large intervention in the market to produce the amplifying response.

I doubt that the USSR has ever used its commodity power with any such general purpose in mind. That would be ascribing to the USSR more subtlety of purpose and more control in the execution of buying and selling strategies than seem warranted. And from the lack of exploration of this possibility on the part of other contributors to this volume, I detect a general assent that this contingency carries a low probability in their minds as well.

INFLUENCING INDIVIDUAL NATIONS

It is another matter altogether when one considers the possibility that the USSR may be hoping to use its commodity power to influence the political behaviour of other nations.[1] In the Soviet view, trade and politics are inseparable in foreign policy. Accordingly, if intent could determine effect, there would be no question that the trade of the Soviet Union represented an instrument for the exercise of political power.

To be sure, the USSR is not alone in linking trade to politics. In some degree, all nations conduct their foreign trade with an eye to politics. For instance, since the end of World War II, the United States and Western Europe have maintained special restrictions on their trade with Eastern Europe, based upon political and security considerations. With these same considerations in mind, the West also imposed embargoes or restrictions from time to time on other countries, such as Southern Rhodesia and Cuba. Moreover, both the United States and Europe in other ways have linked the nature of their trade regime to their political objectives. The United States has used the General Agreement on Tariffs and Trade to support its aspirations for the development of an open interdependent trading world; and Europe has used the European Community as its vehicle for reducing the risk of conflict among its members and for maintaining special links with former colonies and with selected countries in the Mediterranean area.

Still, the USSR can be distinguished from Europe and the United States in the way it has used trade for political ends. The USSR conducts its foreign trade on the principle that no trade is justified unless it makes a contribution to the nation's objectives. The economies of Western Europe and North America conduct their trade on the principle that any trade is permissible unless it is explicitly adjudged harmful to the nation's objectives. In practice, the two courses of action converge toward one another; yet the remaining gap between them is vast. In the case of the market economies, if the trade benefits some significant group within the economy, that is usually enough to protect the trade from arbitrary cut-off for political purposes; US sales of grain to the USSR represent a striking case in point. In the case of the USSR, the state's screening of its trade for the achievement of the state's objectives appears much more rigorous.

What is more, as part of its control system over international trade, the USSR prefers where it can to develop deals in which payments are explicitly matched with receipts. The various means by which that is achieved are of course well-known and fully documented.[2] In some cases, the matching is achieved by deals with individual firms in the West, deals in which the firm eventually receives payment for its sales in the form of specified products; in other cases, the matching is done by government-to-government agreements that specify, in greater or lesser degree, the goods that are to be exchanged.

*A priori*, agreements of this sort executed under the USSR's system of trade controls offer some potential for the USSR to exercise coercion. Just how much coercion, however, depends critically on a number of factors regarding the relative situation of the two trading partners. A nation that badly needs the imports or exports it undertakes—that is, a nation that would assume a high cost if it failed to undertake the trade—can hardly be said to have much commodity power. Moreover, a nation that hopes to exercise commodity power by withholding its exports must be able to count on the inelasticity of supply from other sellers; if other sellers are prepared to fill a void created by the power-seeking seller, the seller's objective will be thwarted. (A parallel statement, of course, can be made for the power-seeking buyer.) Finally, the country seeking market power must confront trading partners on the other side of the transaction whose discretionary power in the market is limited; if the buyer is as centrally organised as the seller and also has as much choice as the seller about the size and timing of its purchases, than the capacity of each to manipulate the other is indeterminate.

On these criteria, the USSR appears to be a strong candidate for the exercise of political power. Various CMEA countries look to the Soviet Union as their principal source of raw materials, a relationship that the USSR has fostered in some instances at considerable cost to its economy. Cuba relies on the USSR to absorb its sugar; in the short run, the costs would be staggering for Cuba if the USSR were to suspend its purchases of sugar, whereas the inconvenience to the USSR would be slight. (Ironically, the US embargo in this case increases Cuba's perception of its costs and hence enhances the power of the USSR.)

In other cases, the coercive power of the USSR may be less clear. Germany's importation of Soviet gas will carry little coercive power as long as Germany's gas users are in a position to turn easily to alternative sources of fuel. In still other cases, the coercive capabilities of the USSR can only be marginal. US reliance on Soviet chromium and platinum, for instance, presumably bestows little coercive power on the USSR, inasmuch as the United States draws on a number of other sources and has the option of expanding its strategic stockpiles if the problem seems serious enough.[3]

Nevertheless, the power of the USSR is not to be belittled. In any given commodity, one can usually find a country with a higher level of aggregate purchases or sales than the Soviet Union; but not, as a rule, under a central control.

Finally, the USSR stands out from most other nations in the degree of secrecy surrounding its demand and supply situation in individual commodities. Lacking information, the USSR's trading partners find it difficult to evaluate the USSR's bargaining strengths and bargaining weaknesses. Once the USSR begins to show its hand, the risk of exaggerating its strength is relatively high.

It is a serious question, therefore, whether the USSR is in a position to use its commodity power in order to extend its influence beyong the CMEA. On this score, the various commodity studies that follow should cast a little light.

## CAPTURING THE GAINS FROM TRADE

The bilateral approach to international trade places large countries in a position not only to influence the political behaviour of some of their trading partners but also to capture the lion's share of the gains from trade. Although the suspicion has often been voiced that the Soviet Union may have been motivated partly by that objective in choosing the bilateral balancing approach, the evidence on that score is equivocal; some bilateral relationships, as we have suggested earlier, seem costly to the USSR in economic terms.

Here and there, however, the possibility persists; it is especially plausible for transactions in which the USSR has agreed to provide raw materials to foreign buyers in compensation for their supplying the capital equipment that will produce the materials. In this case, the USSR is in a position to mobilise all its oligopoly strength, such as it is, to shift the risks onto the buyer. But a great deal more analysis of such deals will be needed before the USSR's power in this regard can be assessed. The papers in this volume can only be seen as an opening salvo in the exploration of that issue.

Another way in which the USSR might conceivably be expected to try to enlarge its share of the gains from trade would be to form an international cartel in the products that it exports or to join one that already exists. In a sea of uncertain conjectures, this is one possibility on which the signals are fairly clear. The USSR is no joiner. In part, this may be because of the identity of the countries it would have to join: for gold, South Africa; for asbestos, Canada; for cotton, the United States. In part, too, it may be because of the USSR's overwhelming penchant for secrecy and control. In any case, in the range of alternative possibilities to be considered, this one takes a low priority.

Finally, we are left with the possibility that the USSR might exercise its oligopoly or oligopsony power as best it can in open world markets. This is the kind of question with which economists and commodity analysts feel most at home. And it is on this issue that the chapters which follow cast the clearest light.

## THE FUTURE STRUCTURE OF MARKETS

Yet one is entitled to wonder if studies of individual commodity markets can go very far in answering the central questions of this volume. Such studies, after all, are based largely on history. And history in this case may be providing an imperfect guide for the future. Some changes in the organisation of the world's commodity markets in recent years suggest that the power of a country organized on the lines of the USSR may increase in the future.

In oil and the various non-ferrous metals in particular, some portentous changes in market structure have been taking place over the past several decades. Those changes can be described in three rather distinct stages: a period of control by the multinationals in the period immediately following World War II; a second period in which that control was weakening, accompanied by some decline in the degree of concentration of the industry in world markets; and finally, a period in which state-owned enterprises appeared as sellers, leading to a market that was more diffuse and more fragmented than in the past.

With the end of World War II, a very considerable part of world production and trade in each of these industrial raw materials was concentrated in a handful of large western firms, operating in a market structure that protected their oligopoly rents and promised a certain stability. In oil, seven leading international companies controlled nearly 90 per cent of the internationally traded product;[4] in aluminium six firms controlled about 85 per cent of the world's smelting capacity.[5] Only in iron ore was the world industry reasonably diffused in structure; in this case, the different national steel industries had few interlocking links. But even in this case, the principal producers of some important countries, including the United States and Japan, managed to maintain some strong links to their foreign sources of ore, using vertical integration, long-term contracts, and monopsony arrangements to maintain control.[6]

During the first period in which the big multinational enterprises typically were in control, their profit-making objectives were largely expressed in efforts to achieve stability and security of supply. As long as they were left in tolerably peaceful possession of their mines and oilfields and as long as their contractual arrangements were not being disturbed by demands for renegotiations or threats of nationalisation, host countries heard very little from the enterprises. One index of the strength of these enterprises lay in the fact that when the USSR was involved in the export of any commodity in which the multinationals dominated, the Soviet sellers rarely showed any disposition to play an independent role in the market. In tin and aluminium they coordinated their sales with that of the Western leaders,[7] while in oil they tended to shade their prices with care, cutting them only enough to secure the necessary market penetration.[8]

The "commodity power" of the multinationals was not exposed to any real test until the second period, when the host countries decided to try to overturn existing arrangements. Incidents of that sort occurred continuously in oil and occasionally in the nonferrous metals from the 1950s on. When they did, it grew clear that the power of the companies and their governments was quite circumscribed after all. In the early 1950s, to be sure, in response to Mossadeq's takeover of Iranian oil, the oil companies did succeed in preventing the Iranians from assuming an independent position in world oil markets by mobilising the economic and political power of Britain and the United States. But that situation was exceptional, being based mainly on the fact that Iran's geographical position made control of the area appear critical in the pursuit of the cold war.[9] There were numerous other occasions both before and after the Mossadeq affair in which the willingness and ability of the United States to support its multinational oil companies were put to the test. The earlier oil nationalisations in Bolivia and Mexico and the subsequent ones in Indonesia, Peru and elsewhere, provided such occasions. The support that the oil companies were able to muster on these occasions was characteristically sporadic, episodic and ineffectual.[10]

In copper, iron ore and bauxite, the story was very much the same.[11] All that the companies could do in response to expropriation and threats of expropriation was to turn to safer areas for their subsequent expansion.[12] This response on the part of the multinational companies did represent commodity power in a sense; but its coercive effect was largely negated by the fact that the state-owned enterprises that absorbed the properties of the multinationals were free to borrow in world capital markets.

With the decline in the power of the multinationals during the second and third stages, the markets for many non-agricultural commodities have taken on some new characteristics. As in the past, these markets continue to be fairly concentrated in structure, in the sense that a considerable part of the production lies in the hands of a few sellers and a considerable part of the consumption is accounted for by a few buyers. The threat of instability, therefore, continues to hang over these markets, as it has in the past. What has changed, however, has been the nature of the equilibrating mechanisms that once operated in these markets. As long as the multinationals dominated, they acted as intermediaries in the system. In that role, they matched supply with demand in their vertically integrated structures, they swapped supplies and markets with one another to cover temporary imbalances,[13] and they resorted to various institutional devices to avoid periods of overproduction or shortage for world markets as a whole.[14]

With the decline in the power of the multinationals, governments and their enterprises have assumed a greater measure of power in such decisions. But the ability or willingness of governments to coordinate such decisions among themselves have, on the whole, been considerably less than the ability and willingness of the multinationals to perform those roles.[15]

Governments, therefore, appear to be in the position of having more responsibility for deciding to whom they shall sell and from whom they may buy. At the same time, however, they are exercising that responsibility in markets which have been changing in character. With weaker coordinating devices among the producers, the markets are more prone to the appearance of transitory surpluses or shortages than in the past; and with weaker means for swapping among producers, they are less effective in balancing supplies and markets at any moment in time. Balance will be achieved after the fact; but it is likely to entail more frequently than in the past external adjustments in the marketplace rather than internal adjustments within the multinational systems. In practice, this could mean more frequent breaches of contract as well as more vigorous swings in spot prices.

As tendencies of this sort grow in any market, there is a presumption that a purposeful seller or a purposeful buyer, bent on using their buying or selling power for specific ends, will encounter more opportunities for the exercise of that power. If sudden shortages and surpluses prove more common in these markets, the purposeful seller that can fill the shortage and the purposeful buyer that can absorb the surplus presumably find a larger stage for their operations.

What this change suggests is that, in a new era of less stable commodity markets, the commodity power of the Soviet Union could well increase. But that expectation needs to be tested against the background that is presented in the studies that follow.

# 2 Long-Term Commodity Agreements and the USSR

## Marie Lavigne

To analyse Soviet attitudes towards multilateral commodity agreements is a study in paradoxes. To evaluate Soviet experience of participation in negotiating or implementing such arrangements is research in the unexplored. For these reasons, this contribution is bound to be short and controversial. No clear evidence is to be provided, except on one fact: the desire of the Soviet Union to keep a low profile on this issue.

In principle the Soviet Union has to favour International Commodity Agreements (ICAs). This was asserted very early, at the first meeting of the UNCTAD by V.S. Patalichev, chairman of the Soviet delegation.[1] He recalled that in line with traditional Soviet policy towards the developing countries, the best type of arrangement would be the bilateral long-term agreement providing for an expansion of mutual trade in commodities exported by both parties. However, the Soviet Union was not against multilateral agreements, and was prepared to support recommendations for price-stabilising international agreements for such commodities as vegetable oil, cotton, bananas, citrus fruit, zinc, lead, copper, petroleum. Finally, the Soviet delegate expressed his opposition to compensatory financing devices in case of price fluctuations, considering them much less adequate than price-stabilising agreements. Such devices were advocated by France, and supported by many Third World delegations. Using tactics which would be often repeated, the Soviet delegation tried to show that in fact such a proposal was quite demagogical, politically biased, and that it had to be reassessed within the whole context of the relations between the former colonialist powers and the Third World.

Thus, as early as 1964, the uneasiness of the Soviet position was quite perceptible. It became the more so in the following decade, with the world crisis, the emergence of the North-South dialogue, the steps taken by the UNCTAD for integrating and managing the ICAs. Fortunately perhaps for the Soviet Union and the socialist community, the conflicts between the main producers and consumers of commodities – as well as among each of these groups – prevented most of the ICAs from becoming operational. The weakest points in the Soviet position are not highlighted by current practice, except for one: the case of sugar.

## 1. THE SOVIET ATTITUDE TOWARDS MULTILATERAL COMMODITY AGREEMENTS: A STUDY IN PARADOXES

The ambiguous position of the Soviet Union is due to the fact that some of its political and economic interests require a participation in the ICAs while other different political and economic considerations tend to prevent it from playing an active role in the ICAs.

**1. The Soviet Union cannot remain indifferent to efforts to stabilise international commodity markets**

The first reason is a political one.

Attempts to regulate commodity markets are not new. Having begun before World War II, they resumed soon afterwards, with the wheat, sugar and tin negotiations (1949–1956). They entered a new phase with the UNCTAD project for an integrated programme aimed at the stabilisation of markets for 18 major commodities, in 1976.

The Soviet Union has always supported the main actions of UNCTAD and may even claim that it fathered the organisation, when in 1962 it advocated the calling of an international conference on trade and development. Beginning in 1974–1975, the Soviet Union, and the other European socialist countries, have been exposed to attacks and various claims from the "77" group. Nevertheless they endorsed most of the proposals made at the IVth UNCTAD, and particularly the idea of an integrated programme "which would...take into account international primary commodity agreements already in force or in the process of elaboration."[2]

Apart from the political context, a very obvious economic reason compels the Soviet Union to take part in many of the ICAs which are either in operation or projected. It is a significant importer or exporter for a wide range of commodities. To remain outside of market regulation would mean to abdicate a part of its international stance.

Let us give some examples. After having been an exporter of wheat in the 1960s and early 1970s, the Soviet Union is now a significant importer (slightly less than 15 per cent of world imports in 1979–1980). The same evolution is characteristic for sugar of which the Soviet Union was an exporter in the 1960s (4.6 per cent of world exports in 1962–1968) but a net importer in the 1970s (with about one sixth of world imports in 1975–1979). The Soviet Union accounts for over 7 per cent of world imports of rubber and cocoa, a small share (under 3 per cent) of tin imports, even less (1–1.5 per cent) of coffee imports. Its share in world exports of cotton is over 20 per cent.

Thus, for almost all commodities already covered by an international agreement, or for which negotiations are underway with some chance of success, the USSR can claim quite real interests.

Finally, while the very idea of interfering with the market may seem contrary to the capitalist approach, every move to plan foreign trade relations should be in line with the methods of a planned system. This was acknowledged by the socialist group at the IVth UNCTAD: "as planned-economy countries, they are genuinely interested in the normalization of the international commodity trade and in limiting the effect of unrestrained market forces on the course of that trade."[3]

## 2. The Soviet Union has to be very cautious in its approach to the whole ICA system

Several strong political reasons make the Soviet Union reluctant to become deeply involved in the ICAs.

First, while the Soviet Union is bound to support the developing countries, it has felt compelled to state, from the very beginning, that it is not responsible for the disorganisation of the markets. The socialist group at the UNCTAD (with the exception of Romania, always closer to the "77") constantly maintains that the former colonialist countries bear the main responsibility for the troubles and the difficulties of the developing countries. Its members also underline the destabilising policy of the multinational companies in the field of price fixing or investment.[4]

If members of the socialist group feel the need to clear themselves of all responsibility it is because they appear formally, in the United Nations system, to belong to the "rich nations" group. And here again the socialists put up constant resistance, especially as China and Romania deliberately stress the fact that they belong to the group of the poor nations. For instance, the socialist group (all Eastern European countries except Romania, with the USSR, and paradoxically, Mongolia) declared in its 1980 comment on UNCTAD's contribution to the elaboration of the new international strategy for development: "one would increase the efficiency of the role of UNCTAD...by giving up present attempts to join unfairly together the socialist and industrialised capitalist countries in the same group, called the "developed countries" group, and to extend to the socialist countries the types of relations, arrangements and situations stemming from the practice of the world capitalist economy."[5]

Although the CMEA countries are identified in the UNCTAD negotiations as "group D," it is true that they are often considered, the Soviet Union in particular, as sharing the same interests as the "other" developed or rich countries. For intance, the "Manila Declaration" of the "77" (February 1976), which remains up to now the most extensive list of claims addressed by the Third World to the socialist countries, contains a whole set of requirements directed to them in the same form as to the capitalist countries. The Soviet Union is very sensitive on this issue.

While pleading for special treatment, to be derived from systemic criteria and not from purely statistical considerations, the Soviet Union has still another political issue in view. It cannot accept a form of regulation which would encompass all trade in a particular commodity, since commercial relations within the CMEA are already subject to an internal regulation for prices and quantities based upon bilateral agreements and multilateral rules. This is why, in all ICA negotiations, the Soviet Union always insists that intra-CMEA trade in the particular commodity under review be excluded from the discussion. But this in turn conflicts with another politically sensitive issue. The Soviet Union has always condemned "closed regional groupings" (alluding to the EEC) and denied that CMEA had such a character. In recent negotiations (post-1976) it has regularly objected to the fact that EEC representatives, in compliance with the common trade policy, intervened on behalf of EEC members. There is a paradox in defending this position while at the same time setting aside intra-CMEA relations. In some cases intra-CMEA flows are indeed very important, as for sugar.

The special status of CMEA is a political issue with economic implications. There are more specific economic problems in the ICA case.

The financial and commercial interests of the Soviet Union are not one-sided. As a producer, it would be bound to support, along with Third World suppliers, stable high prices. As a consumer, its interests are opposite and lean decidedly in the direction of the "rich" countries. This is why the USSR regularly underlines the point that commodity prices must be "economically justified, remunerative and fair to producers and consumers," so as to "make it possible for all main producer and consumer countries and exporters and importers of given commodities or groups of commodities to gain access to these markets under conditions of equality, non-discrimination and mutual respect for the interests of all countries."[6]

Such requirements are purely political, because they are impossible to satisfy. In fact, the contradiction in the Soviet interests would induce the USSR to avoid participating in ICAs were it not for the political reasons mentioned in the first section. The Soviet Union actually considers the ICAs a second-best arrangement compared to long-term bilateral agreements. These lead to "co-ordination of trade with economic development programmes in a situation where planning and programming are the key to economic management".[7] What is not stressed, but underlies this argument, is the fact that bilateral agreements provide the possibility of selecting, among the developing countries, those which are ideologically closer to the socialist system.

Another very substantial point is the fact that the ICAs are costly. The Soviet Union does not wish (let us add that many developed countries share the same view) to get entangled in heavy financial commitments. In negotiations, the USSR is generally opposed to any additional contributions. In general, it maintains a very restrictive position on buffer stocks, viewing them only as auxiliary devices, "to the extent that it is feasible and expedient". The negative experiences of former agreements are quoted to justify this position.[8] A Soviet article published in 1981 tries to discredit the buffer system with another argument. The capitalist countries, the authors write, fear that their supplies in raw materials might be disrupted due to some actions of developing countries. They favour buffer stocks because it gives them some control over their supplies. This is why they advocate large buffer stocks, and large gaps between maximum and minimum prices.[9]

To sum up: the Soviet Union has to be present to ICAs, but does not want to be tied by them in any way. In the Soviet literature a few articles have been published in the past five years about the ICAs and the UNCTAD position. But a non-informed reader would never guess that the socialist countries are members of some ICAs and take part in the negotiations. The whole question of ICAs is always presented as the conflicting area of industrialised and developing countries relations. When statistical data are given, no figures are provided for the relevant exports, imports, or output of the socialist countries.

## II. THE SOVIET PARTICIPATION IN NEGOTIATING OR IMPLEMENTING ICAs: A MOST INCONSPICUOUS STANCE

When the UNCTAD adopted the Integrated Programme for Commodities (IPC) in 1976 and decided to convene a conference on a Common Fund in the framework of Resolution 93 (IV), several ICAs had already been formed and some of these were still in operation. So far, there has been only one case of a successful agreement (rubber). Negotiations continue without results up to now for half a dozen commodities, and there remain about eight commodities for which the prospects of an agreement are very remote.

The USSR has not played an active role in any of the past agreements or the present negotiations. Nevertheless, some logical lines can be derived from its behaviour.

### 1. Pre-IPC agreements

The case of sugar is the most significant as far as the role of the USSR is concerned in "classical" international agreements.

Let us briefly review the four other cases, before concentrating on the International Sugar Agreement.

*(a) Wheat*

Before World War I, Russia was the main exporter of this commodity. And during the years of Stalinist industrialisation, it had again to rely on wheat as the most important single item to bring in hard currency, even during periods when the Soviet people were starving. When it joined the International Wheat Agreement in 1962 it sat among the exporters, although it was already an occasional importer.

The USSR formally withdrew from the Agreement in 1977,

although, in fact, the Agreement had ceased to operate in 1968. Already in 1967, the Soviets had refused to take part in the food aid programme which was associated with the new International Grains Agreement. The Soviet Union can only be very critical of the positions of the main exporters, which are mostly, with the exception of Argentina, developed countries. Nevertheless, it is a member of the Interim Committee on Wheat installed in 1978. As a big importer in the 1970s and probably in the 1980s, the Soviet Union is certainly interested in an efficient agreement favourable to buyers, and especially in a clause which would forbid embargo measures as is suggested in a 1980 article.[10] On the other hand, it did not really suffer from the "free market rules" which operated at the time of the big deals of 1972. And the bilateral long-term agreements signed in 1975 and 1983 with the United States, in 1980 with Argentina and in 1981 with Canada correspond much more to Soviet views on the best ways to regulate commodity markets. (*see* Chapter 10.)

*(b) Coffee*

The USSR has never been a member of the coffee agreements concluded since 1962. This may be explained by the very small Soviet share in world coffee imports and by the character of the agreements' membership. The main producers are the Latin American countries with which the Soviet Union has not developed substantial flows of trade and which therefore are of less importance to the USSR than other areas. Besides, in the context of the IPC, the structure of the coffee agreement is quite specific, relying on quotas, and the new 1981 agreement has not been renegotiated in the UNCTAD framework—this may also explain the Soviet attitude towards it.

*(c) Tin*

The Soviet Union, like the other East European countries, is a member of the International Tin Council, and has participated in most of the first five agreements since 1956. Tin is the only non-ferrous metal for which the import dependence for all the socialist group is important. The Soviet Union took part in the compromise reached for the renewal of the sixth International Tin Agreement in June 1981. Although it has remained largely silent in the discussions, it has displayed a generally reserved attitude towards the claims of the producing countries, Poland and Hungary appearing by comparison much more favourable.

*(d) Cocoa*

Although the first Cocoa Agreement was concluded in 1972 before the IPC, it has never worked and neither has the second, because the world price has always remained over the trigger price of the Agreement. The Soviet Union took part in the negotiations which led to the third agreement signed in 1980. It is a significant importer (7.8 per cent of world imports in 1976–1979). But in the domestic policy of the Soviet Union, chocolate is not a priority good. Although the demand is very strong even at a very high domestic price (relative to the prices of other food commodities and compared with relevant Western prices), the Soviet Union does not wish to expand the supply of the domestic market, and tries to buy the cheapest types of cocoa beans. This explains its very discreet position in the negotiations, supporting the producers but without arguing against the claims of the consumers for the lowest range of prices. The Soviet Union found itself in a very curious situation in June 1981, when it seemed that neither the USA nor the EEC states would ratify the new Agreement: the socialist countries would then have represented two thirds of the consumers. Finally the EEC joined the Agreement; and favourable pact prospects raised prices,[11] which might not have been in the USSR's best interests.

*(e) Sugar*

The first International Sugar Agreement was signed in 1953; it was renewed in 1958. Then a major event occured: the socialist revolution in Cuba in 1959, followed in 1960 by the crisis between Cuba and the United States and the exclusion of Cuba from the benefit of the American Sugar Act. From then on, the USSR and the other socialist countries agreed to become the main buyers – on preferential terms – of Cuban sugar, which determined the structure of the sugar market up to the present times, given Cuba's position as the main world exporter (with a share comprised of between 22 per cent and 25 per cent of world exports). By 1961, the ISA was no longer in operation.

The ISAs of 1968 and 1977 were very favourable to Cuba – and to the socialist camp. But they did not operate satisfactorily, and even ceased functioning altogether in the 1973–77 period. One cannot attribute their failure only, or even mainly, to the behaviour of the socialist countries. But these countries certainly contributed to the disorganisation and occasional crises of the sugar markets.

For the socialist community, including Cuba, the ISA is a part of a very complex sugar policy, and also interferes with a specific COMECON problem: the need to support the Cuban economy in a hostile environment, while maintaining its main sugar-growing orientation. This has had the following consequences:
– internal relations between Cuba and its European partners are not negotiable and remain outside the sphere of the ISA. Thus, Cuba can export non-limited quantities to COMECON countries. Moreover, the USSR obtained in 1968 and in 1977 a special right to re-export definite quantities of sugar even outside the COMECON, not taking into account its exports to socialist countries.
– sugar is the only currency earner for Cuba (in a still remote future, it will perhaps be supplemented by nickel). Even with very favourable terms in its sugar trade with COMECON, Cuba exerts a permanent pressure on the free sugar market and also tries to obtain quotas exceeding its real capacities, thus adding uncertainty to the already difficult conditions of the market.
– Eastern Europe has a share of less than 20 per cent of world sugar production. The Six (without the USSR) achieve self-sufficiency; the rate of the USSR is 68 per cent in the 1976–78 period. The requirements of their domestic market and the fluctuations in Cuba's supply induce important disruptions on the free world market.[12]

But it would not be fair to attribute to the Soviet-COMECON policy the sole, or even the main, responsibility in the disruptions. One should not forget the other "special systems" (EEC, USA) as well as the role of the free-market operators.[13]

## 2. The Post-IPC period

The Soviet Union and the other socialist countries took part in the consensus for the establishment of a Common Fund which was reached in 1980. But like most of the UNCTAD members, they have not yet confirmed their participation. While supporting the consensus because of the great importance attached to it by the developing countries, they remained critical of the buffer stock method, and asserted their preference for long-term contracts with administered prices. Finally they protested against the high costs which they had to incur in comparison with the countries of group B (developed countries).[14]

Whether or not the Fund becomes operative will depend on the number of working agreements: negotiations are currently under way for a range of goods. The Soviet Union has participated in many of them, always with the same strategy – keeping informed, and never exposing itself.

*(a) Natural rubber*

As an importer (7.15 per cent of world imports) the Soviet Union took part in the meetings on the natural rubber agreements (reached in 1979), which it signed in 1980. As usual, the USSR criticised the excessive size of the buffer stock, and the range of prices which allows far too large fluctuations.[15]

*(b) Cotton*

The case of cotton is interesting as the only one where the Soviet Union appears as an exporter: 20 per cent of world exports in 1976–79 (7 per cent when taking into account its exports towards non-socialist countries). The Soviet Union is rather pessimistic on the possibility of an agreement. It nevertheless came out in strong support for the proposals of the "Izmir group" – representing the main producers – although these proposals provided for a buffer stock along with a system of national stocks internationally coordinated. At the same time, the Soviet Union expressed its preference for multilateral obligations of producers and consumers to sell and buy cotton within the range of "just and reasonable" minimum and maximum prices. On this particular point the Soviet proposal was in open – and one may almost say unusual – conflict with the US position.[16] (*See* Chapter 11.)

*(c) Copper*

This commodity is important in the same sense as sugar because it involves large intra-CMEA flows, and is also a currency earner for the USSR and Poland. During the negotiations, which came to a standstill in 1980, the Soviet Union reasserted its traditional themes about the special status of trade between socialist countries. It supported as usual the proposals of developing countries (in this case, Peru), including a buffer stock, but mentioned that it would be "too burdensome if other stabilisation measures were not included in the agreement" (Statement at the 6th meeting, March 1979). It also praised the experience of "long-term contracts on a compensatory basis" between the socialist countries of Eastern Europe and countries outside the system.

*(d) Jute*

As for copper, the Soviet Union repeatedly stressed the advantages of long-term contracts in current use by the socialist countries with their suppliers, and on the whole approved of the position of the developing countries (namely the claim of Bangladesh, their main supplier, for the headquarters of the Agreement to be located in Dacca).

*(e) Other commodities*

The prospects for an agreement are very remote for all the other commodities. The Soviet Union usually attended the first meetings, and often dropped out afterwards (for phosphate, manganese), or did not participate actively (for iron ore, tea, timber).

Let us finish with tungsten, which does not belong to the commodities encompassed by the IPC, but is particularly interesting because of the stature of the two main producers – USSR and China. In 1979 the Tungsten Committee initiated negotiations for an agreement. The meetings failed to reach an accord between producers and consumers. The remarkable point was the similarity of views between China and the USSR on the main features of the proposed agreement.

The pattern of Soviet behaviour in the International Commodity Agreements is in the last analysis logical. Most of these agreements have not worked or are doomed to fail. The Soviet Union does not consider itself responsible for the situation which necessitated the search for international coordination. It does not want to be held responsible for the failure of the agreements themselves. And, finally, from the point of view of the USSR, all that happens here provides examples of capitalist contradictions – even if, as Lenin said, one has to howl with the wolves.

# 3 Exports of Primary Commodities and the Soviet Terms of Trade

Zdeněk Drabek

INTRODUCTION

The period of the 1970s has witnessed a considerable price explosion in the world commodity markets with significant distributional effects on world income particularly through changes in relative prices. The well-known OPEC-inspired increases in prices for oil have meant that oil exports have become an important factor of growth in the oil producing countries. The question arises, therefore, whether the Soviet Union, with its vast natural resource endowment, has been able to benefit from these changes through its participation in the international division of labour; if so, it would also be desirable to know something about the extent of these gains. This chapter represents an attempt to provide an answer to this question and, in addition, to suggest the likely Soviet attitudes towards exports of primary commodities in the future.

Soviet exports have been dominated throughout history by exports of natural resource products (NRPs) and this pattern continues even nowadays (see Tables A.1 to A.4 in the Appendix). At present, the Soviet Union sells about two-thirds of its exports in the form of NRPs, with the rest being accounted for by exports of manufactures.[1] This dependence on NRPs is particularly pronounced in the case of exports to More Developed Countries in the West (MDCs) where the share of NRPs in exports exceeds 90 per cent. Only in trade with Less Developed Countries (LDCs) is the pattern reversed; in 1977 the share of NRPs was some 17 per cent of the total exports to LDCs. But by then, the share of LDCs in total Soviet exports was only 16 per cent.

If the general dependence on NRPs in Soviet exports is heavy, the concentration within the NRP group is even greater. There are at present 9 commodities which provide the bulk of export earnings and in 1976, for example, these commodities accounted for 39 per cent of total Soviet exports. The commodities include: petroleum and petroleum products (27.3), coal (2.9), natural gas (2.6), iron ore (1.7), rolled ferrous metals (4.3), non-ferrous metals (2.6), logs (1.7), sawn timber (2.2) and cotton fibres (2.7).[2] Clearly, by far the greatest "hard" and "soft" currency earners are petroleum and petroleum products.

At the same time, the Soviet Union is a massive importer of NRPs, i.e. mainly food and grain and flour. The share of NRPs in total Soviet imports accounted for just under a half in 1977. Clearly, imports for LCDs and Other Centrally Planned Economies (OCPEs), are dominated by NRPs, but the Soviet Union also remains heavily dependent on Western supplies of NRPs (about half of total Soviet imports were from MDCs in 1977). Only in the case of imports from CMEA is the share relatively low – about a quarter. In sum, even though the Soviet Union remains a net exporter of NRPs, its dependence on NRPs is still considerable and most of these NRPs have to be purchased in the world markets (56 per cent of total Soviet imports of NRPs in 1977).

Gains from trade can be defined in terms of changes in export and import prices and can therefore be evaluated on the basis of changes in terms of trade. The development of Soviet terms of trade has recently again attracted considerable attention both in the East and in the West.[3] In the West, the studies of Soviet terms of trade include particularly: Hewett (1980), United Nations (1978), Tiraspolsky (1978), Hanson (1981), Vanous (1981), Stankovsky (1981), Dietz (1979), Kohn (1979) and Kohn and Lang (1977). In view of the abundance of the literature, no attempt will be made in this study to generate yet another set of estimates of Soviet terms of trade. Instead, I shall concentrate on identifying the main differences among relevant estimates and, most important, the main trends in the development of the indices.

I shall concentrate only on the most recent studies of terms of trade. Nevertheless, the reader in the development of Soviet terms of trade in historical perspective may wish to consult Marer (1972), Hewett (1974) and Dohan (1973). I shall further avoid any assessment of the official Soviet and other East European estimates which has been adequately treated in Hewett (1980a). Further, I shall concentrate (exclusively) on those studies which estimate a time series of the indices rather than on estimates for particular years.

## METHODOLOGY OF ESTIMATING TRADE GAINS FROM THE SOVIET UNION'S CHANGING TERMS OF TRADE

The most recent literature concerning the estimates of Soviet terms of trade has been concentrated almost exclusively on computation of Net Barter Terms of Trade (NBTT). Formally, NBTT is defined as a ratio of prices of exports ($P_x$) and prices of imports ($P_M$) or, more precisely,

$$\text{NBTT} = \frac{P_x}{P_M} \times 100 \tag{1}$$

This definition of terms of trade has been adopted in Hewett (1980), Vanous (1981), Hanson (1981), Tiraspolsky (1978), Dietz (1979) and Stanovsky (1981). The only exceptions among these studies are Hewett (1980a) and Vanous (1981) who also estimated the Soviet terms of trade by means of Gross Barter Terms of Trade (GBTT) defined as the ratio of import volume ($Q_M$) and export volume ($Q_x$), i.e.

$$\text{GBTT} = \frac{Q_M}{Q_x} \times 100 \tag{2}$$

Both NBTT and GBTT represent the purchasing power of exports in terms of imports. However, while NBTT represent the purchasing power of *one* unit of exports for a unit of imports, GBTT represent the purchasing power of *total* real exports in terms of total real imports. If trade is balanced in a given period, i.e. total exports are equal to total imports ($P_x.Q_x \times P_M.Q_M$), it follows that given changes in the $P_x/P_M$ ratio must be exactly compensated by changes in $Q_M/Q_x$ ratio. In other words, NBTT will be exactly equal to GBTT. If trade is not balanced, NBTT and GBTT will differ.

Since the main reason for computing the terms of trade of a particular country is to estimate gains from trade, let us first define the latter concept before proceeding any further. Trade gains are often defined for this purpose as the difference between the resource cost of producing exports and the potential resource cost of producing imports.[4] Using this definition for the present purposes, one of the reasons for changes in gains from trade is a change in the purchasing power of export changes. In this respect, both NBTT and GBTT are suitable indicators of gains from trade.

However, by emphasising NBTT, the observers of Soviet foreign trade have also stressed a particular aspect of trade gains resulting from changes in terms of trade. Since NBTT refer to the purchasing power of *one unit* of exports while actual gains from trade should be derived from all units of exports, NBTT represent, in effect, a concept of potential gains from trade. In other words, they indicate how well off the country might have been rather than how well off it has been.[5] In contrast, GBTT measure *de facto* costs of total real imports, i.e. what quantity of real imports can be obtained for a given quantity of real exports. It has been suggested that for the above reason the terms of trade which matter to the planners in the CPEs are GBTT.[6]

It should further be noted that NBTT will understate or overstate the two gains to the economy if, together with changes in terms of trade, there are changes in productivity in export industries ($PP_x$) leading to changes in factor costs. In order to allow for changes in $PP_x$, economists compute what is known as Single Factoral Terms of Trade (SFTT) defined as

$$\text{SFTT} = \frac{P_x}{P_M} \times PP_x \times 100 \qquad (3)$$

Moreover, since there also may be simultaneous changes in productivity abroad ($PP_M$) leading to changes in costs of foreign factors, it may sometimes be useful to compute Double Factoral Terms of Trade (DFTT) defined as:[7]

$$\text{DFTT} = \frac{P_x}{P_M} \times \frac{PP_x}{PP_M} \times 100 \qquad (4)$$

According to my knowledge, neither SFTT nor DFTT have been computed for the Soviet Union; we need not, therefore, discuss the issue any further. However, the reader should keep in mind that, for example, an improvement in export costs by say 20 per cent which is accompanied by a fall of 10 per cent in export prices relative to import prices makes the country still better off. In view of the differences in efficiency between CPEs on the one hand and MTEs on the other and among CPEs themselves, the omission of SFTT among various estimates of Soviet terms of trade is far from innocuous.[8]

Unfortunately, the limitations of NBTT do not rest with the above elements. Under conditions of disequilibrium in product and factor markets there are unique possibilities for changes in gains from trade due to changes in terms of trade.[9] First, it is possible to increase gains from trade by minimising the ratio of factor cost and foreign trade prices on the export side and maximising it on the import side. In other words, the minimisation of the ratio means maximising the accounting profits from exports. This type of gain obviously arises because (at least some) foreign trade decisions in CPEs are made outside the efficiency calculus and the above method increases the gains from trade measured in terms of domestic (rather than foreign) prices.

Second, it is often argued that the price of capital is kept artificially low in the CPEs. If true, this could mean that surpluses and deficits are repaid in the CPEs at rates below the equilibrium rate. The actual costs of financing trade deficits and surpluses would be, therefore, lower than they would be in the absence of disequilibrium which, in turn, would represent an extra "gain" ("loss") to the deficit (creditor) country.

Finally, NBTT may also understate the true gains to a country under the conditions of highly elastic export supply. In specific terms, if our terms of trade deteriorate as a result of reduced prices for our exports, it may be that the decline in export prices is more than compensated for by an increase in export volumes or a result of increased competitiveness of our exports. Thus, it is possible to compute the so-called Income Terms of Trade (ITT) whereby NBTT are weighted by export volumes (X), i.e.:

$$\text{ITT} = \frac{P_x}{P_M} \times X \times 100 \qquad (5)$$

Once again ITT have not been computed for the Soviet Union but I mention them here because a similar concept based on modified ITT will be used later in this paper to compute the windfall gains to the Soviet Union.[10]

## STATISTICAL PROBLEMS OF COMPUTING SOVIET TERMS OF TRADE

From issues of interpretation we shall now turn to issues of a technical nature. In general, computations of NBTT and GBTT involve the following statistical problems: (1) choice of weights, (2) representativeness of samples and (3) separation of inflationary effects from changes in terms of trade. All these problems have been faced by researchers computing Soviet terms of trade.

The computation of terms of trade involves computation of price indices which, in turn, involves decisions about the choice of weights. In general, the price indices can be computed according to the following three formulae which give rise to three different types of indices:

$$\text{Laspeyres Price Index (LPI)} \text{ (i.e. base-year quantity weights)} = \frac{\sum_{i=0}^{N} P_i^{t+1} Q_i^t}{\sum_{i=0}^{N} P_i^t Q_i^t} \quad (6)$$

$$\text{Paasche Price Index (PPI)} \text{ (i.e. current-year quantity weights)} = \frac{\sum_{i=0}^{N} P_i^{t+1} Q_i^{t+1}}{\sum_{i=0}^{N} P_i^t Q_i^{t+1}} \quad (7)$$

Fischer Price Index (FPI) (i.e. the geometric mean of Laspeyres and Paasche Price Indices)

$$= \frac{\sum_{i=0}^{N} P_i^{t+1} Q_i^t}{\sum_{i=0}^{N} P_i^t Q_i^t} \times \frac{\sum_{i=0}^{N} P_i^{t+1} Q_i^{t+1}}{\sum_{i=0}^{N} P_i^t Q_i^{t+1}} \quad (8)$$

where
 P = price of commodity exported (imported)
 Q = quantity exported (imported)
 i = ith commodity
 t, t+1 = time periods

There are statistical criteria for the choice of weights and, in addition, the choice among the individual indices also depends on the purpose for which these are intended. All the criteria have been discussed in detail in Hewett (1974). What is important to mention here, however, is that the various results reported in the following section are based, in fact, on all these three indices, which affect the degree of comparability. Following the traditional approach, all the studies use the Unit Value Index (UVI) as the estimator or price index.[11]

The representativeness of the samples used in the computation of Soviet terms of trade causes a particularly difficult problem. In addition to the general problem of selection of "representative" commodities, as well as the associated problems resulting from changes in commodity structure of trade, the specific problems in choosing the "representative" sample arise from a reduction of information in the Soviet Union's officially published trade returns. Thus there has been a "steady decline" in the provision of trade data in the official Soviet statistics, a difficulty which is complicated further by the fact that some of the recently "missing" commodity items refer, in fact, to one of the most important traded commodities.[12]

The third general problem, which some may argue is much more eminent in the computation of Soviet (and other CPEs) terms of trade than in the case of MTEs, arises from changes in the quality and weight of commodities due to changes in technical progress. On the one hand, it is possible that gains from trade may be reduced due to deterioration in quality of imports even if NBTT and GBTT remain constant over time.[13] On the other hand, technical progress affecting weight of commodities (for example, introduction of electronics) leads to distortions of UVI. Of all the studies reported below, only Vanous (1981) attempts to allow for changes in quality and weights of commodities.[14]

Fourth, a certain proportion of Soviet (and other CPEs') trade with the CMEA is settled in hard currencies which also presumably implies strict use of world prices. This obviously complicates the construction of price indices since, as we shall see below, intra-CMEA prices differ from world prices and since trade flows are predominantly settled in non-convertible currencies.[15]

Finally, the reader may have noticed that no mention has been made up to now of any official Soviet indices of terms of trade as published in the official Soviet sources. The Soviet Union published the overall world export and import price indices as well as aggregate price indices with socialist and capitalist countries. However, the problem with this published information is that: (1) the data are not sufficiently disaggregated particularly for the problem at hand in this study and (2) there is very little information about the method of construction and the commodity coverage of the price indices.

There are also further specific problems with the officially published Soviet indices of terms of trade. First, data published in Soviet sources are sometimes contradictory as can be seen from Table 3.1. The case in point is the distribution of price increases in 1975 and 1976 which affects, correspondingly, the distribution of real trade flows. Interestingly enough the aggregate terms of trade show very small differences. The discrepancy between these officially published statistics remains a mystery. According to Dietz (1979) the discrepancy, which, incidentally, also pertains to a comparison between the official (VTSS) indices and Western estimates reported in the next section, is unlikely to be due to different methodology.

One explanation for the discrepancies has been recently suggested in Polish sources, attributing the difference to the mechanism of price increases which was agreed upon by CMEA members in January 1975, on the one hand, and to the method of statistical reporting of price changes in trade returns, on the other. Be that as it may, the indices are suspect, at least with regard to 1975 and 1976.

There are also additional problems of inconsistency of official Soviet (volume) indices, problems arising from unannounced revisions of the quantity indices and problems which have been attributed to changes in sampling procedures.[16] For example, the official volume indices for 1971 which are reported by Hewett (1980) show that total volumes are inconsistent with the underlying indices for trade with socialist countries and capitalist countries.[17]

Last but not least, the research on the evolution of current price indices and indices of terms of trade has been seriously hampered by a considerable reduction in the volume of information provided in the official Soviet trade returns. The Soviet Union, together with a number of other CPEs, has eliminated from its trade statistics various items. The elimination has led to a reduction in the officially reported coverage of Soviet foreign trade, preventing computation of consistent series of unit value indices. For this reason, consistent trade series have to be compiled from non-primary sources and even estimated. It is for these reasons that the data on which the following analysis is based could not be updated in time for publication of this study.

Table 3.1 Volume, Price and Terms of Trade Indices in Soviet Foreign Trade: 1975 and 1976
(Annual growth rates given as percentages)

|  | Total | | CMEA(8)[a] | | | | Rest of world[b] | | | |
|---|---|---|---|---|---|---|---|---|---|---|
|  | Exports VTSS[c] | Imports VTSS[c] | Exports VT[d] VTSS[c] | | Imports VT[d] VTSS[c] | | Exports VT[d] VTSS[c] | | Imports VT[d] | |
| Volumes | | | | | | | | | | |
| 1975 | 2.9 | 18.4 | 10.9 | 1.6 | 17.3 | 9.0 | −4.4 | 4.1 | 19.5 | 27.8 |
| 1976 | 7.8 | 6.3 | −6.3 | 2.3 | −5.1 | 2.1 | 25.5 | 14.7 | 17.6 | 10.2 |
| Prices | | | | | | | | | | |
| 1975 | 12.6 | 19.6 | 21.6 | 32.7 | 16.5 | 25.3 | 4.3 | −5.8 | 22.7 | 13.9 |
| 1976 | 8.2 | 1.3 | 19.2 | 9.2 | 13.6 | 5.6 | −5.5 | 6.8 | −16.2 | −1.7 |
| Terms of Trade | | | | | | | | | | |
| 1975 | −5.9 | | 4.4(VTSS) | 5.9(VT) | | | | −16.4(VTSS) | | −17.3(VT) |
| 1976 | 6.8 | | 4.9(VTSS) | 3.4(VT) | | | | 6.8(VTSS) | | 8.7(VT) |

*Notes:*
(a) CMEA Europe plus Mongolia and Cuba
(b) Derived from data on overall trade and CMEA trade
(c) Vneshnyaya Torgovlya: Statisticheskii Sbornik (VTSS) (Yearbook)
(d) Vneshnyaya Torgovlya (VT) (Journal)

*Source:* Based on Dietz (1979), Tables 3 and 3A.

## EVOLUTION OF CHANGES IN THE SOVIET UNION'S UNIT VALUES AND TERMS OF TRADE: 1970–1979

The purpose of this section is to analyse the movement in Soviet terms of trade over the period of 1970–1979. In doing so, we shall also examine the pattern of changes in export and import volumes as well as unit values. Both the volumes and unit values will be examined on aggregate and more detailed levels. As indicated earlier, several estimates will be reported. To the extent that these estimates should differ, we shall confine ourselves to a simple identification of the nature of the differences without any further detailed analysis. The reason for this approach is quite simple. Discrepancies among individual indices can be due to various causes, as we have shown earlier and, consequently, all of them can contribute to these discrepancies.

In order to see the changes in what may be called "potential gains from trade",[18] I have compiled a table showing the development in Soviet NBTT with the World, the West and the member countries of the Council for Mutual Economic Assistance (CMEA). The table includes various Western estimates and a brief description of the methodology of each estimate is presented in the table. It is quite apparent that, in analysing the Soviet gains from trade, we are going to face a number of difficulties. Thus, the estimates reported in Table 3.3 differ between estimates based on official data at one extreme (Hewett, Tiraspolsky and Hanson)[19] and estimates based on adjusted trade data (Vanous, 1981a) at the other. Needless to say, however, the discrepancies are not great, at least with regard to the estimates of overall Soviet terms of trade with the "World".

The important common feature of all these estimates is the *improvement in Soviet NBTT*, and only the extent of this improvement is unclear. The improvement in Soviet NBTT over the examined period ranges between some 12 per cent and (around) 20 per cent. The improvement in NBTT was more or less continuous throughout the examined period and, in addition, it originated not only in trade with the West but also with the CMEA.

However, in examining the contribution of individual markets to the improvement in the overall Soviet NBTT in Table 3.2, it is not at all clear whether the improvement in overall terms of trade over the 1970–1976 period was mainly due to an improvement in NBTT with the West or with the CMEA. Using Hewett, Tiraspolsky and Hanson's estimates based on official trade returns, the major con-

Table 3.2 Indices of Soviet Net Barter Terms of Trade with the World, the West and CMEA (1970=100)

| | World | | | | | West | | | | | CMEA | | |
|---|---|---|---|---|---|---|---|---|---|---|---|---|---|
| | Hewett (1980b) 1 | Hewett (1980b) 2 | Tiraspolsky 3 | Vanous (1981a) 4 | Hewett (1980b) 5 | Ericson and Miller 6 | Tiraspolsky 7 | Vanous (1981a) 8 | Hanson 9 | Hewett (1980b) 10 | Tiraspolsky 11 | Vanous (1981a) 12 | Hanson 13 |
| 1960 | 113 | N.A. | N.A. | N.A. | N.A. | N.A. | N.A. | N.A. | N.A. | N.A. | N.A. | N.A. | N.A. |
| 1965 | 105 | 106 | N.A. | N.A. | 111 | N.A. | N.A. | N.A. | N.A. | 111 | N.A. | N.A. | N.A. |
| 1970 | 100 | 100 | 100 | 100 | 100 | N.A. | 100 | 100 | 100 | 100 | 100 | 100 | 100 |
| 1971 | 100 | 105 | 104 | 103 | 108 | 100 | 108 | 109 | 105 | 98 | 101 | 102 | 102 |
| 1972 | 98 | 103 | 103 | 103 | 101 | 111 | 101 | 108 | 110 | 101 | 105 | 101 | 99 |
| 1973 | 105 | 110 | 109 | 102 | 119 | 130 | 119 | 122 | 115 | 102 | 107 | 105 | 104 |
| 1974 | 104 | 109 | 108 | 108 | 116 | 170 | 118 | 149 | 114 | 102 | 104 | 114 | 103 |
| 1975 | 98 | 102 | 102 | 106 | 94 | 145 | 96 | 142 | 93 | 106 | 109 | 118 | 109 |
| 1976 | 104 | 108 | 109 | 115 | 102 | 153 | 104 | 164 | 101 | 109 | 114 | 118 | 114 |
| 1977 | 110 | 114 | N.A. | 117 | 111 | 154 | N.A. | 170 | 110 | 114 | N.A. | 123 | 119 |
| 1978 | 112 | 117 | N.A. | N.A. | 117 | N.A. | N.A. | N.A. | 119 | 113 | N.A. | N.A. | 121 |
| 1979 | N.A. | N.A. | N.A. | N.A. | N.A. | N.A. | N.A. | N.A. | 141 | N.A. | N.A. | N.A. | 123 |
| 1980 | N.A. | N.A. | N.A. | N.A. | N.A. | N.A. | N.A. | N.A. | | | | | |

*Notes:*
1. UVI based on official data on total exports and total imports from *Vneshnyaya Torgovlya*, Hewett (1980a), Table 5. Close approximation on Paasche indices.
2. UVI estimated by Hewett (1980a), Table 5, as the weighted average capitalist and socialist (official Soviet) indices.
3. Tiraspolsky (1978), Table 8, Estimated as UVI obtained as the ratio of value indices and volume indices (computed as Laspeyres indices).
4. Vanous (1981a), Table 15, Based on aggregation of 7 commodity group price indices. Price indices for manufactures deflated by a factor of 1.01–1.03 per annum in order to take into account "improvement in quality and reduced unit weight as a result of technological improvements". The aggregation-based UVI (Laspeyres indices) are estimates of price formula. The aggregate regional export price indices were of Paasche type. Based on prices in roubles and SDRs.
5. As in column 1. "Capitalist countries" include all countries except: (1) CMEA, i.e. Bulgaria, Czechoslovakia, GDR, Hungary, Poland, Romania, Mongolia (since 1962), Cuba (since 1972) and Vietnam (since 1978); (2) China, North Korea, North Vietnam and Laos (since 1978).
6. Hewett (1980a). Based on UVI. The UVI obtained by dividing quantity indices into indices of total value of convertible currency merchandise exports and imports. The NBTT are the export UNI divided by import UVI.
7. Tiraspolsky (1978), Table 9; no definition of capitalist countries.
8. Vanous (1981a), Table 15, The "West" includes North America, Western Europe, Turkey, Japan, Australia and New Zealand.
9. Hanson (1982), Table 9, No definition of the "West" based on official indices.
10. Hewett (1980a), Table 5, for Definition of CMEA see column 5.
11. Tiraspolsky (1978), Table 9.
12. Vanous (1981a), Table 15: CMEA includes Bulgaria, Czechoslovakia, GDR, Hungary, Poland, Romania.
13. Hanson (1981), Table 4, No definition of CMEA, based on official statistics.

tribution came from the improvement of NBTT with CMEA. In contrast, using the estimates of Ericson and Miller and Vanous, the Soviet Union experienced a far greater improvement in NBTT with the West. How can we reconcile this rather fundamental discrepancy?

Perhaps the most plausible explanation of the discrepancy is the inclusion of Less Developed Countries (LDCs), in the region "the West" in the estimates based on official data.[20] Since LDC exports to the Soviet Union are primarily Natural Resource Products (NRPs) and their imports from the Soviet Union mainly manufactures (i.e. a pattern precisely opposite to the pattern in trade with More Developed Countries (MDCs), it would be highly desirable to further disaggregate the regional pattern of terms of trade. A set of estimates computed in Vanous (1980) is reproduced in Table 3.3. It shows export and import UVI and terms of trade with the CMEA Six (i.e. 6 European CMEA member countries), OCPEs MDCs and LDCs. His estimates indeed suggest the considerable influence of NBTT improvement with MDCs on the aggregate NBTT with the West. In fact, it appears that the Soviet Union experienced a considerable deterioration in NBTT with LDCs as well as with OCPEs, the latter being also primary NRP exporters, and importers of manufactures.[21]

Unfortunately, even this finding is not entirely without some ambiguity. According to Hewett (1980b) the contribution of the "socialist market" (i.e. CMEA *and* other socialist countries) to the overall improvement of terms of trade in the 1970s was greater than that of CMEA itself. Hewett's estimates are shown in Table 3.4. Moreover, the estimations of the official Soviet data of NBTT with CMEA by Kohn (1979) suggest another source of the discrepancy between the movement in NBTT with the West and with CMEA countries respectively. More precisely, they both suggest that, at least for 1975, the NBTT index with CMEA understates the "true" NBTT.[22]

In sum, the Soviet Union has clearly benefited from the rapid price increases in world markets in terms of increasing the purchasing power of one unit of their exports. The inflation affected both export prices and import prices but the increase in export prices was much more significant (Tables 3.3 and 3.4). The phenomenon is obviously not surprising as far as Soviet trade with market economies is concerned since that part of Soviet trade is conducted at world market prices. As far as Soviet trade with CMEA is concerned, however, the "transmission instrument" for the inflationary rise of

Table 3.3 Aggregate Soviet Export and Import Price Indices with Four Main Trade Regions and Terms of Trade 1970–1977 Based on Prices in Roubles or SDRs

| Year | CMEA Six[a] | OCPEs[a] | MDCs[a] | LDCs[a] | World |
|---|---|---|---|---|---|
| | | Exports | | | |
| 1970 | 100 | 100 | 100 | 100 | 100 |
| 1971 | 101.1 | 102.6 | 113.9 | 104.5 | 104.1 |
| 1972 | 102.4 | 103.5 | 108.8 | 104.1 | 104.0 |
| 1973 | 102.3 | 107.0 | 135.2 | 110.0 | 110.7 |
| 1974 | 107.7 | 137.1 | 231.8 | 138.9 | 138.4 |
| 1975 | 147.5 | 148.1 | 244.7 | 147.3 | 164.6 |
| 1976 | 163.3 | 165.0 | 267.0 | 150.7 | 181.1 |
| 1977 | 176.1 | 176.3 | 292.0 | 162.7 | 194.1 |
| | | Imports | | | |
| 1970 | 100 | 100 | 100 | 100 | 100 |
| 1971 | 99.5 | 102.6 | 104.6 | 102.8 | 101.2 |
| 1972 | 100.4 | 103.7 | 100.5 | 107.5 | 101.3 |
| 1973 | 101.1 | 121.1 | 110.5 | 144.4 | 108.8 |
| 1974 | 102.6 | 163.5 | 155.4 | 182.2 | 128.1 |
| 1975 | 129.9 | 209.6 | 172.3 | 187.1 | 155.3 |
| 1976 | 139.0 | 209.4 | 163.0 | 202.1 | 157.8 |
| 1977 | 143.3 | 223.3 | 171.6 | 241.5 | 165.6 |
| | | Terms of Trade | | | |
| 1970 | 100 | 100 | 100 | 100 | 100 |
| 1971 | 101.5 | 100.0 | 108.9 | 101.6 | 102.8 |
| 1972 | 102.1 | 99.8 | 108.2 | 96.8 | 102.7 |
| 1973 | 101.2 | 88.4 | 122.3 | 76.2 | 101.7 |
| 1974 | 104.9 | 83.9 | 149.2 | 76.2 | 108.0 |
| 1975 | 113.6 | 70.7 | 142.0 | 78.8 | 106.0 |
| 1976 | 117.5 | 78.8 | 163.9 | 74.6 | 114.8 |
| 1977 | 122.9 | 78.9 | 170.2 | 65.8 | 117.2 |

(a) For abbreviations see page xiii

*Source:* Vanous (1981a), Table 10, p. 699.

prices in the intra-CMEA trade was the introduction of the new "sliding price" formula of 1975 which formally links the intra-CMEA prices to world market prices (WMP).[23]

Given the róle of NRPs in Soviet exports, the major contribution to the improvement in the Soviet terms of trade in the 1970s came

Table 3.4 Unit Value Indices for Soviet Foreign Trade: 1960–78

| | Unit Value Indices (1970 = 100) | | | | | | | | | | Terms of Trade (1970 = 100) | | | | |
|---|---|---|---|---|---|---|---|---|---|---|---|---|---|---|---|
| | Exports | | | | | Imports | | | | | | | | | |
| Year | Total A | Total B | Soc. Ct. | CMEA | Cap. Ct. | Total A | Total B | Soc. Ct. | CMEA | Cap. Ct. | Total A | Total B | Soc. Ct. | CMEA | Cap. Ct. |
| 1960 | 106 | nd | nd | nd | nd | 94 | nd | nd | nd | nd | 113 | nd | nd | nd | nd |
| 1961 | 106 | nd | nd | nd | nd | 96 | nd | nd | nd | nd | 111 | nd | nd | nd | nd |
| 1962 | 106 | nd | nd | nd | nd | 95 | nd | nd | nd | nd | 111 | nd | nd | nd | nd |
| 1963 | 105 | 106 | 113 | 114 | 93 | 94 | 93 | 92 | 94 | 97 | 112 | 113 | 123 | 121 | 95 |
| 1964 | 105 | 107 | 113 | 115 | 95 | 100 | 99 | 96 | 98 | 106 | 105 | 109 | 118 | 117 | 90 |
| 1965 | 103 | 103 | 109 | 108 | 92 | 98 | 97 | 95 | 97 | 101 | 105 | 106 | 114 | 111 | 91 |
| 1966 | 97 | 98 | 103 | 103 | 88 | 98 | 97 | 94 | 95 | 104 | 100 | 100 | 109 | 108 | 84 |
| 1967 | 98 | 97 | 103 | 103 | 88 | 97 | 95 | 94 | 95 | 99 | 101 | 102 | 110 | 108 | 89 |
| 1968 | 98 | 98 | 103 | 100 | 90 | 95 | 95 | 94 | 93 | 98 | 102 | 103 | 110 | 108 | 92 |
| 1969 | 98 | 97 | 103 | 102 | 86 | 98 | 97 | 95 | 96 | 99 | 99 | 100 | 108 | 106 | 87 |
| 1970 | 100 | 100 | 100 | 100 | 100 | 100 | 100 | 100 | 100 | 100 | 100 | 100 | 100 | 100 | 100 |

# Exports of Primary Commodities

| Year | | | | | | | | | | | | | | | |
|---|---|---|---|---|---|---|---|---|---|---|---|---|---|---|---|
| 1971 | 102 | 105 | 104 | 102 | 107 | 102 | 100 | 101 | 104 | 99 | 100 | 105 | 103 | 98 | 108 |
| 1972 | 101 | 104 | 106 | 104 | 100 | 103 | 101 | 102 | 103 | 99 | 98 | 103 | 104 | 101 | 101 |
| 1973 | 111 | 113 | 108 | 107 | 121 | 105 | 103 | 103 | 105 | 102 | 105 | 110 | 105 | 102 | 119 |
| 1974 | 118 | 121 | 108 | 107 | 142 | 114 | 111 | 103 | 105 | 122 | 104 | 109 | 104 | 102 | 116 |
| 1975 | 133 | 136 | 139 | 129 | 131 | 136 | 133 | 128 | 122 | 140 | 98 | 102 | 109 | 106 | 94 |
| 1976 | 144 | 146 | 154 | 141 | 138 | 138 | 135 | 134 | 129 | 136 | 104 | 108 | 113 | 109 | 102 |
| 1977 | 156 | 158 | 163 | 153 | 152 | 142 | 139 | 139 | 134 | 138 | 110 | 114 | 117 | 114 | 111 |
| 1978 | 160 | 163 | 173 | 161 | 149 | 142 | 139 | 147 | 142 | 128 | 112 | 117 | 118 | 113 | 117 |

*Source*: Hewett (1980b), Table 5. All indices were obtained by dividing indices of total value (using total values reported in various years of VTSS) by the quantity indices in this table. The quantity indices are close to Laspeyres and discussed in the Data Appendix of Hewett (1980b). The "A" variant of the indices for total imports and exports is taken directly from Vneshnyaya Yorgovla. As discussed in the text, this index does not appear to be a true average of the socialist and capitalist indices and, for this reason the "B" variant as an alternative index was constructed. It is a weighted average of the socialist and capitalist indices, where the weights are the value of trade in 1970.

Table 3.5 Price Changes in Soviet Trade with the World, Eastern Europe, and Non-CMEA Countries 1975–1977

|  | Exports |  |  |  |  | Imports |  |  |
|---|---|---|---|---|---|---|---|---|
|  | Price Changes (in percent) |  |  |  |  | Price Changes |  |  |
|  | Shares 1974 | 1975 | 1976 | 1977 | Shares 1974 | 1975 | 1976 | 1977 |
| *Total trade*[a] |  |  |  |  |  |  |  |  |
| Machinery | 22.9 | 7.8 | 17.4 | 8.6 | 34.4 | 23.6 | 15.4 | 10.7 |
| Fuels | 30.2 | 30.4 | 14.0 | 15.4 | 3.7 | 27.9 | 4.9 | — |
| Ores, metals | 17.9 | 23.5 | −1.8 | −3.7 | 12.6 | 26.0 | −14.0 | — |
| Chemicals and building materials | 4.8 | 15.5 | −2.0 | 1.5 | 7.4 | 1.8 | −0.8 | 14.3 |
| Agriculture and foods | 21.2 | 2.7 | 1.9 | 14.2 | 26.5 | 15.9 | −2.8 | 4.9 |
| Industrial consumer goods | 2.9 | 5.9 | 5.2 | 4.4 | 15.4 | 9.2 | 2.0 | −3.3 |
| Total | 100.0 | 16.7 | 8.8 | 11.6 | 100.0 | 18.2 | 3.5 | 6.8 |
| *Trade with CMEA (6)*[a] |  |  |  |  |  |  |  |  |
| Machinery | 32.5 | 3.0 | 19.6 | (15.0) | 55.4 | 21.6 | 9.2 | (2.5) |
| Fuels | 21.4 | 83.5 | 10.3 | (16.9) | 2.5 | 107.5 | 6.1 | — |
| Ores, metals | 24.3 | 45.3 | −0.1 | (5.1) | 2.4 | 47.2 | 6.2 | (5.1) |
| Chemicals and building materials | 4.3 | 32.6 | 3.7 | (7.3) | 4.4 | 21.7 | −2.7 | (−3.1) |
| Agriculture and foods | 14.4 | 40.9 | 5.8 | (8.4) | 11.1 | 32.2 | 2.4 | (11.7) |
| Industrial consumer goods | 3.1 | 7.7 | 7.3 | (2.7) | 24.1 | 22.6 | −0.4 | (3.3) |
| Total | 100.0 | 39.0 | 8.8 | (11.6) | 100.0 | 25.9 | 5.6 | 5.0 |

from the dramatic increase of the relative NRP prices. The empirical evidence to document this point is rather sketchy but the pattern can be observed from the following Table 3.5. The table shows the relative changes in prices of Soviet exports and imports classified according to six commodity groups and two major trading areas (CMEA and other countries). The figures are not entirely consistent with the estimates reported in Table 3.3 and 3.4. However they are

Table 3.5 Prices Changes in Soviet Trade with the World, Eastern Europe, and Non-CMEA Countries 1975–1977 *(Continued)*

|  | Exports |  | Imports |
|---|---|---|---|
|  | Price Changes (in percent) |  | Price Changes |
|  | Shares 1974 | 1975 1976 1977 | Shares 1974 | 1975 1976 1977 |

*Trade with all other countries*

| | Shares 1974 | 1975 | 1976 | 1977 | Shares 1974 | 1975 | 1976 | 1977 |
|---|---|---|---|---|---|---|---|---|
| Machinery | 13.4 | 7.7 | 13.7 |  | 21.5 | 27.5 | 23.6 | — |
| Fuels | 23.3 | 5.3 | 17.1 |  | 4.9 | −1.9 | 4.2 | — |
| Ores, metals | 14.1 | −6.5 | −5.0 |  | 21.2 | 24.2 | −16.0 | — |
| Chemicals and building materials | 5.2 | 3.4 | −8.8 |  | 10.1 | −4.7 | 0.1 | — |
| Agriculture and foods | 26.2 | −16.6 | −0.6 |  | 32.3 | 8.2 | −5.3 | — |
| Industrial consumer goods | 2.0 | 6.0 | 4.5 |  | 10.0 | −14.7 | 5.9 | — |
| Total | 100.0 | −1.4 | 9.1 |  | 100.0 | 10.1 | 2.1 | — |

(a) CMEA(6) = Bulgaria, USSR, German Democratic Republic, Hungary, Poland, Romania

*Note:* Figures in parentheses estimated from changes in Soviet prices by commodity groups in foreign trade with Hungary (from Hungarian sources). In calculating the CMEA(6) total export and import shares of Soviet trade were used.

*Source:* Dietz (1979), Table 5, p. 278.

quite closely related to the official (VT) indices reported in Table 3.1. They are also more consistent with Hewett's indices than with those estimated by Vanous.[24]

Thus, according to Dietz (1979), export prices of both machinery and industrial consumer goods were rising in the period of 1975–1977 at a considerably slower pace than export prices of the most important NRP commodity, namely fuels. The export prices of other

NRPs, such as ores, metals, food and other agricultural products, had a rather different and divergent pattern of development, a point to which we shall return later. In contrast, the increases in import prices of machinery and industrial consumer goods were lagging behind the increases of export prices of fuels.[25]

The next question is whether the inflationary price developments in world markets have been "passed on" to intra-CMEA prices and, if so, whether the price increases were consistent between both markets. Clearly, as the agreement on the sliding price formula came only in 1975, its effect was delayed by two years (1973 and 1974) and the gap which opened was quite considerable. In 1975, the gap between WMPs and intra-CMEA prices was dramatically reduced at a stroke and the period between 1975 and 1976 was characterised by a divergent pattern of price changes leading to a reduction of the discrepancy. (Compare UVI for imports and exports as between these two regions in Tables 3.3, 3.4, and 3.5.)

However, it appears that the price increases for Soviet exports to the CMEA area still remain well *below* the prices the Soviets have been able to charge to their Western partners in MDCs (i.e. WMPs) or the prices (again WMPs) which the Soviet Union has been charged by LDCs. Given the structure of Soviet exports to MDCs and Soviet imports from LDCs, the development of the export price index to MDCs and the import price index from LDCs reflects primarily changes in NRP prices. As can be seen from Table 3.3, these increases are well above the increases in the export (i.e. mainly NRPs) price index to CMEA.[26]

The differentiating pricing policy favouring the CMEA partners of the Soviet Union is also confirmed by a separate estimate reported in Table 3.6. The table shows price indices (i.e. UVI indices) for 8 key NRP groups which dominate Soviet primary product exports to the West and to CMEA. These 8 commodity groups together with natural gas represented 39 per cent of all Soviet exports and about 80 per cent of all exports of fuels, minerals, raw metals and metals and agricultural raw materials.[27] According to this estimate it appears that the Soviet Union has agreed to keep the price increases (particularly for fuels) below the increases witnessed in the world market. The conclusion is further confirmed in studies such as Vanous (1981b) and Hewett (1980a).

What is, however, unclear is the extent to which the level of the CMEA prices differs from that of world prices. Comparisons of the two price levels cannot be undertaken without a considerable degree of ambiguity, due to the presence of (disequilibrium) the overvalued exchange rate of the rouble. Yet, such a comparison would be extremely useful since differences in prices obtained by the Soviet Union in different markets would indicate the opportunity costs of trading with given partners. We shall return to this point in the next section. It may suffice to say at this stage that even the "sliding price" formula did not immediately generate the "maximum" effect. According to this formula, the Soviet Union would have gained 40 per cent improvement in terms of trade with CMEA in 1975 and no change in 1976 (i.e. the "low" year 1970 was taken off the official base). However, it appears the Soviet negotiators have agreed to lower increases below what the price rules would have allowed.[28]

As we have seen earlier, it is often argued that GBTT are a much more meaningful measure of gains from trade to the planners in CPEs than NBTT. The Soviet GBTT are shown in Tables 3.7 and 3.8, using once again two different estimates (low and high). As both tables show, the 1970s was a period of rapid expansion of *real* foreign trade flows. Both exports and imports grew considerably faster than the Soviet national income (for using Western concepts, GNP). This rapid growth of trade was accompanied by a dramatic *geographical diversion* of exports to and imports from the West with a significant decline in the real share of CMEA countries in total trade turnover of the Soviet Union. For various reasons, this process was to some extent halted in around 1977, when the trade links with CMEA began to re-intensify.[29]

At the same time, the real expansion of exports was relatively slower than that of real imports so that GBTT improved. This improvement constituted some 9 to 15 per cent between 1970 and 1977, depending on the estimate used.[30] This improvement in GBTT has been characteristic in trade with all trade partners except, most likely, with LDCs. However, the main gains as measured by GBTT were derived from trade with MDCs, while the CMEA did relatively better in this respect.[31]

All the estimates reviewed in this section suggest the following:
1) The Soviet Union has experienced a considerable improvement in terms of trade – irrespective of whether the NBTT or GBTT concept is being used.
2) Since the prices which the Soviet Union has had to pay for imports have been rising, the improvement in NBTT was due to faster growth of export prices.
3) The main reason for the dramatic improvement in NBTT was the change in the relative price of fuels in terms of other commodities.
4) Even though there has been an improvement in terms of trade

Table 3.6 Unit Value Indices for Soviet Exports of Eight Primary Products: 1959–1976

|   | 1959 | 1960 | 1961 | 1962 | 1963 | 1964 | 1965 | 1966 | 1967 | 1968 | 1969 | 1970 | 1971 | 1972 | 1973 | 1974 | 1975 | 1976 |
|---|------|------|------|------|------|------|------|------|------|------|------|------|------|------|------|------|------|------|
| (a) Exports to the West |
| 1 | 138.0 | 117.0 | 109.0 | 105.0 | 101.0 | 112.0 | 109.0 | 104.0 | 102.0 | 94.0 | 95.0 | 100.0 | 141.0 | 126.0 | 120.0 | 205.0 | 330.0 | 313.0 |
| 2 | 130.0 | 105.0 | 95.0 | 95.0 | 94.0 | 89.0 | 85.0 | 88.0 | 95.0 | 101.0 | 97.0 | 100.0 | 136.0 | 128.0 | 243.0 | 592.0 | 558.0 | 625.0 |
| 3 | 250.0 | 250.0 | 229.0 | 163.0 | 143.0 | 124.0 | 116.0 | 101.0 | 98.0 | 98.0 | 93.0 | 100.0 | 114.0 | 99.0 | 92.0 | 112.0 | 183.0 | 192.0 |
| 4 | 52.0 | 72.0 | 66.0 | 69.0 | 63.0 | 79.0 | 95.0 | 67.0 | 59.0 | 55.0 | 64.0 | 100.0 | 79.0 | 79.0 | 91.0 | 218.0 | 107.0 | 128.0 |
| 5 | 83.0 | 55.0 | 35.0 | 37.0 | 43.0 | 56.0 | 62.0 | 101.0 | 120.0 | 79.0 | 77.0 | 100.0 | 98.0 | 86.0 | 120.0 | 165.0 | 158.0 | 169.0 |
| 6 | 66.0 | 65.0 | 72.0 | 84.0 | 81.0 | 85.0 | 82.0 | 78.0 | 84.0 | 99.0 | 93.0 | 100.0 | 108.0 | 101.0 | 142.0 | 206.0 | 175.0 | 163.0 |
| 7 | 77.0 | 85.0 | 94.0 | 77.0 | 85.0 | 90.0 | 97.0 | 97.0 | 89.0 | 84.0 | 91.0 | 100.0 | 108.0 | 97.0 | 136.0 | 258.0 | 166.0 | 184.0 |
| 8 | 88.0 | 97.0 | 97.0 | 100.0 | 100.0 | 99.0 | 95.0 | 95.0 | 98.0 | 105.0 | 102.0 | 100.0 | 106.0 | 115.0 | 109.0 | 200.0 | 137.0 | 150.0 |
| 9 | 106.0 | 93.0 | 89.0 | 87.0 | 87.0 | 88.0 | 87.0 | 90.0 | 94.0 | 95.0 | 93.0 | 100.0 | 121.0 | 112.0 | 176.0 | 366.0 | 339.0 | 368.0 |
| Exports to CMEA (includes Cuba, not Mongolia or Vietnam) |
| 1 | 118.0 | 117.0 | 115.0 | 112.0 | 112.0 | 109.0 | 105.0 | 99.0 | 99.0 | 100.0 | 99.0 | 100.0 | 103.0 | 110.0 | 110.0 | 232.0 | 236.0 |
| 2 | 159.0 | 146.0 | 138.0 | 125.0 | 130.0 | 132.0 | 121.0 | 108.0 | 105.0 | 106.0 | 103.0 | 100.0 | 103.0 | 111.0 | 109.0 | 123.0 | 228.0 | 250.0 |
| 3 | 120.0 | 120.0 | 121.0 | 120.0 | 120.0 | 121.0 | 111.0 | 101.0 | 100.0 | 100.0 | 100.0 | 100.0 | 101.0 | 103.0 | 98.0 | 106.0 | 138.0 | 131.0 |
| 4 | 126.0 | 125.0 | 130.0 | 126.0 | 131.0 | 132.0 | 117.0 | 102.0 | 102.0 | 102.0 | 100.0 | 100.0 | 101.0 | 101.0 | 99.0 | 102.0 | 169.0 | 150.0 |

|   |   |   |   |   |   |   |   |   |   |   |   |   |   |
|---|---|---|---|---|---|---|---|---|---|---|---|---|---|
| 5 | 122.0 | 124.0 | 118.0 | 115.0 | 113.0 | 109.0 | 111.0 | 110.0 | 110.0 | 107.0 | 97.0 | 100.0 | 110.0 | 134.0 | 137.0 | 132.0 | 170.0 | 173.0 |
| 6 | 84.0 | 79.0 | 89.0 | 82.0 | 81.0 | 84.0 | 88.0 | 91.0 | 95.0 | 96.0 | 97.0 | 100.0 | 98.0 | 105.0 | 106.0 | 133.0 | 127.0 | 138.0 |
| 7 | 96.0 | 95.0 | 97.0 | 97.0 | 77.0 | 96.0 | 98.0 | 99.0 | 98.0 | 97.0 | 99.0 | 100.0 | 107.0 | 113.0 | 113.0 | 117.0 | 204.0 | 206.0 |
| 8 | 103.0 | 105.0 | 104.0 | 105.0 | 106.0 | 105.0 | 104.0 | 106.0 | 101.0 | 103.0 | 102.0 | 100.0 | 103.0 | 102.0 | 101.0 | 105.0 | 132.0 | 134.0 |
| 9 | 127.0 | 123.0 | 122.0 | 118.0 | 119.0 | 120.0 | 112.0 | 104.0 | 103.0 | 103.0 | 100.0 | 100.0 | 103.0 | 108.0 | 107.0 | 113.0 | 180.0 | 181.0 |

*Exports to other Countries*

|   |   |   |   |   |   |   |   |   |   |   |   |   |   |   |   |   |   |   |
|---|---|---|---|---|---|---|---|---|---|---|---|---|---|---|---|---|---|---|
| 1 | 92.0 | 90.0 | 87.0 | 84.0 | 82.0 | 89.0 | 87.0 | 85.0 | 71.0 | 95.0 | 95.0 | 100.0 | 138.0 | 121.0 | 117.0 | 197.0 | 320.0 | 291.0 |
| 2 | 138.0 | 137.0 | 131.0 | 135.0 | 129.0 | 98.0 | 85.0 | 80.0 | 87.0 | 90.0 | 93.0 | 100.0 | 120.0 | 99.0 | 148.0 | 392.0 | 369.0 | 432.0 |
| 3 | 0.0 | 1.0 | 46.0 | 0.0 | 38.0 | 0.0 | −186.0 | 0.0 | 0.0 | 161.0 | 33.0 | 100.0 | 64.0 | 45.0 | 155.0 | 112.0 | 187.0 | 180.0 |
| 4 | 105.0 | 44.0 | 107.0 | 104.0 | 102.0 | 96.0 | 106.0 | 86.0 | 74.0 | 71.0 | 73.0 | 100.0 | 87.0 | 87.0 | 106.0 | 152.0 | 139.0 | 252.0 |
| 5 | 41.0 | 44.0 | 34.0 | 24.0 | 22.0 | 30.0 | 33.0 | 34.0 | 35.0 | 61.0 | 115.0 | 100.0 | 87.0 | 86.0 | 82.0 | 115.0 | 47.0 | 31.0 |
| 6 | 96.0 | 303.0 | 89.0 | 100.0 | 45.0 | 59.0 | 114.0 | 111.0 | 86.0 | 88.0 | 96.0 | 100.0 | 111.0 | 118.0 | 116.0 | 175.0 | 206.0 | 205.0 |
| 7 | 95.0 | 96.0 | 110.0 | 245.0 | 249.0 | 66.0 | 66.0 | 68.0 | 76.0 | 75.0 | 88.0 | 100.0 | 104.0 | 95.0 | 89.0 | 261.0 | 201.0 | 189.0 |
| 8 | 98.0 | 99.0 | 110.0 | 108.0 | 107.0 | 106.0 | 108.0 | 96.0 | 101.0 | 109.0 | 104.0 | 100.0 | 69.0 | 112.0 | 104.0 | 181.0 | 127.0 | 146.0 |
| 9 | 104.0 | 102.0 | 104.0 | 108.0 | 104.0 | 87.0 | 85.0 | 78.0 | 80.0 | 88.0 | 97.0 | 100.0 | 118.0 | 100.0 | 118.0 | 249.0 | 215.0 | 252.0 |

(a) Commodity labels: 1-Coal, 2-Petroleum and Petroleum Products, 3-Iron Ore, 4-Rolled Ferrous metals, 5-Non-Ferrous Metals, 6-Timber, 7-Logs, 8-Cotton, 9-Weighted Average (weights = 1970 values)

*Source:* Hewett (1979), Table A-11 (Appendix)

Table 3.7 Quantity Indices for Soviet Foreign Trade, National Income and Gross National Product: 1960–1978

Quantity Indices (1970 = 100)

| Year | Total A | Total B | Exports Soc. Ct. | Exports CMEA | Exports Cap. Ct. | Total A | Total B | Imports Soc. Ct. | Imports CMEA | Imports MDCs +LDCs | Marxian National Income | GNP |
|---|---|---|---|---|---|---|---|---|---|---|---|---|
| 1960 | 41 | nd | nd | nd | nd | 51 | nd | nd | nd | nd | 50 | 61 |
| 1961 | 44 | nd | nd | nd | nd | 52 | nd | nd | nd | nd | 54 | 64 |
| 1962 | 52 | nd | nd | nd | nd | 58 | nd | nd | nd | nd | 57 | 67 |
| 1963 | 54 | 54 | 54 | 54 | 53 | 64 | 64 | 71 | 67 | 52 | 59 | 67 |
| 1964 | 57 | 56 | 57 | 58 | 54 | 66 | 67 | 73 | 69 | 55 | 64 | 73 |
| 1965 | 62 | 62 | 61 | 62 | 64 | 70 | 71 | 77 | 73 | 59 | 69 | 77 |
| 1966 | 71 | 71 | 68 | 68 | 76 | 69 | 69 | 73 | 71 | 62 | 74 | 82 |
| 1967 | 77 | 78 | 74 | 73 | 84 | 75 | 76 | 83 | 81 | 64 | 81 | 86 |
| 1968 | 85 | 85 | 83 | 84 | 88 | 84 | 85 | 89 | 92 | 76 | 88 | 91 |
| 1969 | 94 | 94 | 89 | 90 | 104 | 90 | 91 | 92 | 94 | 89 | 92 | 93 |
| 1970 | 100 | 100 | 100 | 100 | 100 | 100 | 100 | 100 | 100 | 100 | 100 | 100 |
| 1971 | 106 | 103 | 104 | 104 | 101 | 104 | 106 | 106 | 105 | 106 | 106 | 104 |
| 1972 | 109 | 106 | 104 | 106 | 111 | 122 | 125 | 122 | 119 | 131 | 110 | 106 |
| 1973 | 124 | 121 | 112 | 114 | 138 | 140 | 143 | 130 | 127 | 168 | 120 | 114 |
| 1974 | 153 | 148 | 137 | 136 | 170 | 157 | 160 | 145 | 139 | 189 | 126 | 118 |
| 1975 | 157 | 154 | 139 | 151 | 181 | 186 | 190 | 159 | 163 | 246 | 132 | 120 |
| 1976 | 169 | 167 | 144 | 155 | 210 | 197 | 202 | 164 | 166 | 271 | 140 | 125 |
| 1977 | 185 | 183 | 156 | 167 | 233 | 201 | 206 | 179 | 182 | 254 | 146 | 130 |
| 1978 | 194 | 190 | 163 | 175 | 242 | 230 | 236 | 205 | 209 | 293 | 153 | 134 |

Source: Hewett (1980b), Table 1, For methodology see note to Table 3.4.

# Exports of Primary Commodities

Table 3.8 Aggregate Soviet Export and Import Quantity Indices with Four Main Trade Regions and Gross Barter Terms of Trade, 1970–1977

| Year | CMEA Six | OCPEs | MDCs | LDCs | World |
|---|---|---|---|---|---|
| *Exports* | | | | | |
| 1970 | 100.0 | 100.0 | 100.0 | 100.0 | 100.0 |
| 1971 | 106.0 | 107.6 | 101.2 | 95.2 | 103.6 |
| 1972 | 108.0 | 104.0 | 104.0 | 105.0 | 106.2 |
| 1973 | 118.6 | 112.0 | 130.6 | 147.6 | 124.7 |
| 1974 | 132.9 | 120.2 | 123.7 | 131.2 | 129.3 |
| 1975 | 132.3 | 126.7 | 120.6 | 126.7 | 128.5 |
| 1976 | 132.0 | 139.9 | 134.9 | 133.9 | 133.8 |
| 1977 | 142.5 | 150.3 | 142.1 | 181.1 | 149.6 |
| *Imports* | | | | | |
| 1970 | 100.0 | 100.0 | 100.0 | 100.0 | 100.0 |
| 1971 | 110.0 | 89.4 | 97.9 | 107.9 | 105.1 |
| 1972 | 128.2 | 88.9 | 134.6 | 109.5 | 124.4 |
| 1973 | 134.1 | 102.8 | 165.9 | 106.6 | 136.1 |
| 1974 | 140.4 | 115.5 | 153.5 | 112.7 | 138.4 |
| 1975 | 145.9 | 140.4 | 229.5 | 144.8 | 165.4 |
| 1976 | 147.3 | 152.3 | 258.9 | 120.0 | 171.7 |
| 1977 | 161.9 | 164.7 | 230.7 | 109.8 | 173.1 |
| *Gross Barter Terms of Trade* | | | | | |
| 1970 | 100.0 | 100.0 | 100.0 | 100.0 | 100.0 |
| 1971 | 103.8 | 83.1 | 96.7 | 113.3 | 101.4 |
| 1972 | 118.7 | 85.5 | 129.4 | 104.3 | 117.1 |
| 1973 | 113.1 | 91.8 | 127.0 | 72.2 | 109.1 |
| 1974 | 105.6 | 96.1 | 124.1 | 85.9 | 107.0 |
| 1975 | 110.3 | 110.8 | 190.3 | 114.3 | 128.7 |
| 1976 | 111.6 | 108.9 | 191.9 | 89.6 | 128.3 |
| 1977 | 113.6 | 109.6 | 162.4 | 60.6 | 115.7 |

Source: Vanous (1981a), Table 12, p. 703.

with all trade partners except LDCs and OCPEs, the most dramatic improvements in NBTT and GBTT took place in trade with MDCs (i.e. the West). In comparison with the West, CMEA losses due to deteriorating terms of trade were not as severe.

5) There are disagreements among various scholars as to the magnitude of total gains in NBTT and GBTT. It appears, however,

that the Sovit Union's gains from the improvement of NBTT were at least 12 per cent between 1970 and 1978, the lowest of all the estimates quoted.

## WINDFALL GAINS AND TERMS OF TRADE OF THE SOVIET UNION

In this section, an attempt will be made further to quantify the gains which the Soviet Union enjoyed due to the improvement in terms of trade. Following our definition of terms of trade adopted previously and the distinction among various elements of gains from trade, we shall concentrate here on those gains which occurred only due to the changes in the purchasing power of exports. Several relevant aspects are, therefore, not considered.

First to be excluded are the gains arising from rising (falling) efficiency in production of exportables. It may be that Soviet export production costs have been rising rapidly, in which case, given the improvement in its terms of trade, the Soviet Union would have been able to pass these increases on to its customers. If export production efficiency had been on the rise, the true gains from trade would have been even *greater* than indicated by the improvement in NBTT.

Second, gains from trade, arising due to changes in efficiency of production abroad are not considered.

Third, gains from trade arising under specific conditions of central planning are also excluded.[32]

We have seen earlier that in evaluating the gains from trade due to changes in purchasing power of exports in market-type economies (MTEs), the usual procedure is to analyse the movements in NBTT. GBTT are not frequently used since they do not so much reflect changes in price movements as in the balance of payments and capital movements. In the case of the Centrally Planned Economies (CPEs), however, NBTT are not necessarily the most useful concept and, as we suggested earlier, GBTT matter more to the planners. This is because plans of material supplies are worked in physical terms, so that extra (unplanned) exports required to balance trade in the event of terms-of-trade deterioration could have severe repercussions on domestic allocations. In addition, any disequilibrium on current accounts has to be eliminated by movements of commodities (and services) in the light of the inconvertibility of East European (and Soviet) currencies.

## Exports of Primary Commodities

As far as the Soviet planners are concerned, therefore, the question arises how increases in foreign trade prices have been financed. In theory there are a number of alternatives. Namely: (1) an increase in the growth of export volumes of countries with deteriorating terms of trade (i.e. import volumes of the Soviet Union), (2) reduction of export volumes for a given flow of imports, (3) various methods of price fixing in bilateral negotiations between the Soviet Union and its CMEA partners, or, barring these, (4) the costs of the price increases in the case of, say, fuels are borne by the Soviet Union in the form of increased trade surpluses (reduced trade deficits).

Let us start by quantifying the additional import capacity generated by the improvement in Soviet terms of trade. The extra import capacity can be estimated by applying a concept similar to that of ITT which I described previously. The results which are reported in Table 3.9, column 1, show the total additional import capacity (i.e. additional import possibilities) due to the improvement in terms of trade in comparison to 1970. The figures in column 1 were obtained by deflating nominal exports in SDRs by NBTT indices and deducting the resulting amounts from the nominal exports. The difference between these two amounts which is reported for each year of the 1970–1977 period represents export proceeds which are available for imports over and above the proceeds needed to purchase the actual imports in each year at 1970 prices. The figures in column 2 were computed in the same way but they refer to trade with CMEA. Columns 3 and 4 refer to total merchandise, imports from MDC and CMEA respectively. The data used are valued in Special Drawing Rights (SDRs), a method which has some advantages over the use of foreign exchange roubles.[33] The SDR-based data were also used in computing the estimates in columns 1 and 2. Finally, the figures in columns 5 and 6 show the proportion of actual imports which were made possible due to the improvement in Soviet terms of trade with the two regions respectively.[34]

It is quite apparent from the table that the Soviet Union has been able to generate a massive additional import capacity as a result of improved terms of trade. For the period as a whole, i.e. for the period of 1970–1977, almost one quarter of total imports from the West could be financed from windfall gains due to improved terms of trade and, by 1977, the share reached almost 37 per cent (Column 5).[35]

Since the price re-alignment in the intra-CMEA market did not

Table 3.9 Windfall Gains to the Soviet Union from Trade with MDC and CMEA Countries (Millions of SDRs)

|  | Additional Import Capacity due to Improved Terms of Trade | | Actual Merchandise Imports | | Share of Additional Import Capacity in Actual Merchandise Imports (per cent) | |
|---|---|---|---|---|---|---|
| | MDC 1 | CMEA 2 | MDC 3 | CMEA 4 | MDC 5 | CMEA 6 |
| 1970 | — | — | 2822.3 | 6633.7 | — | — |
| 1971 | 225.4 | 107.0 | 2889.9 | 7258.5 | 7.8 | 1.5 |
| 1972 | 205.3 | 153.7 | 3818.8 | 8541.0 | 5.4 | 1.8 |
| 1973 | 770.8 | 97.2 | 5173.6 | 8992.0 | 14.9 | 1.1 |
| 1974 | 2262.7 | 451.8 | 6734.3 | 9555.7 | 33.6 | 4.7 |
| 1975 | 2088.2 | 1578.4 | 11158.6 | 12568.5 | 18.7 | 12.6 |
| 1976 | 3361.3 | 2168.9 | 11911.3 | 13584.6 | 28.2 | 16.0 |
| 1977 | 4095.0 | 3160.6 | 11174.9 | 15390.8 | 36.6 | 20.5 |
| 1978 | — | — | — | — | — | — |
| 1979 | — | — | — | — | — | — |
| 1971–1977 | 13008.7 | 7717.6 | 55683.7 | 82524.6 | 23.4 | 9.4 |

*Sources:* Columns 1 and 2: Exports in SDRs deflated by indices of NBTT and the resulting value deducted from the nominal value of exports. The NBTT indices taken from Table 3.3 above and export values from Vanous (1981a), Table 1, p. 688, Table 3, p. 690.
Column 3: Vanous (1981a), Table 8, p. 696
Column 4: Vanous (1981a), Table 6, p. 695
Column 5: (Column 1: Column 3) × 100
Column 6: (Column 2: Column 4) × 100

take place until 1975, the effect of improved terms of trade on Soviet windfall gains from trade with CMEA countries was also delayed. On the whole, the additional import capacity due to improved terms of trade was considerably smaller in trade with CMEA in comparison to gains from trade with the West – just over 9 per cent over the examined period. However, due to the rapid improvement in NBTT between 1974 and 1977, the windfall gains also increased dramatically in those years (Column 6).

The extra import capacity generated from the improvement in terms of trade with the West did not remain unutilised since the Soviet Union started to import on a massive scale from that area. The impact of this import drive on trade balances can be observed from a comparison of NBTT and GBTT in tables 3.3 and 3.8 and 3.4 and 3.7 respectively. If GBTT exceeds NBTT, this reflects a rising trade deficit (falling trade surplus) and vice versa. Using, for example, Table 3.3 and 3.8, NBTT exceeded GBTT in only three years: 1971, 1974 and 1977. Large Soviet borrowing in the West, especially in 1975 and 1976 resulted in GBTT exceeding NBTT and in a substantial deterioration in the trade balance (See Appendix).

The implication of all this is that, in the absence of the improvement in terms of trade, the Soviet Union would have had to borrow an additional 13 Billion SDRs in order to sustain the actual level of imports. The contribution to balance of payments with the convertible currency area was therefore considerable. Moreover, according to one estimate, this contribution represented about 50 per cent of the increased import capacity over the examined period due to the continued effect of increased borrowing; improved terms of trade and increased gold prices.[36] Of the remaining 50 per cent, 34 per cent was due to increased borrowing, the rest to increased gold prices.[37]

The utilisation of the extra import capacity due to improved terms of trade with CMEA countries was much less significant. GBTT exceeded NBTT only in the period of 1971–1974, presumably in connection with increased imports of machinery to finance various fuel and raw materials investment prospects. However, the significant improvement in NBTT in 1975–1977 was not accompanied by rapid expansion of Soviet imports from these countries and, as a result, the Soviet Union cumulated substantial trade surpluses (See Appendix).

Given the commodity structure of Soviet foreign trade, the contribution of primary commodities (i.e. NRP's) to these gains has been considerable. Yet, as we can see from Table 3.7, it was essentially only three commodity groups (i.e. coal, petroleum and petroleum products and natural gas which is not shown) which were primarily responsible for the increase in export prices. Other NRPs did much worse as far as concerns the prices which the Soviet Union was able or willing to charge for them.

The contribution of the above commodity groups to windfall gains from trade with CMEA was much more muted. Nevertheless, of the remaining 6 commodity groups, the Soviet Union was able to increase prices faster to its CMEA partners than to its Western partners in the case of rolled ferrous metals, non-ferrous metals and logs.

In practice, however, it is virtually impossible to estimate precisely the contribution of primary commodities to windfall gains by areas. For one thing, the gains have been substantially mitigated by the willingness of the Soviet Union to run foreign trade surpluses with CMEA countries which cannot be used to finance deficits in trade with other areas.

Secondly, the improvement in terms of trade reflects not only an increase in the relative price of exports in terms of imports but, most likely also an increase in the relative price of NRPs in terms of non-NRPs (i.e. mainly manufactures). Hence, changes in terms of trade reflect not only changes in absolute prices of exports and imports but changes in relative prices of NRPs and non-NRPs exported and imported.

The contribution of NRPs to an improvement in NBTT becomes, therefore, muted once the country in question exports and imports both NRPs and non-NRPs. In such a case, the changes in NBTT between areas depend on the commodity structure of trade which, as we have seen earlier, differs considerably as between intra-CMEA trade and East-West trade.[38]

Moreover, the contribution of NRPs to windfall gain may be distorted further through forms of discriminating pricing policies. Since the intra-CMEA trade is conducted on a bilateral basis it is possible for Soviet negotiators to trade smaller price increases for their primary commodity exports in return for the CMEA countries' acceptance of higher export prices of manufactures. It was indeed observed by Dietz (1979), whose results are reported in Table 3.5, that the increase in export prices in machinery sales to CMEA, which had been traditionally lagging behind import prices, showed a sudden reversal in 1976 and 1977 in favour of the USSR.[39]

# FUTURE ROLE OF THE SOVIET UNION IN WORLD COMMODITY MARKETS

In this final section I shall outline the main elements of the Soviet response to external disturbances which should provide some indication of Soviet intentions in world commodity markets in the near future.

One of the main conclusions of the above empirical analysis was that the USSR experienced a considerable improvement in NBTT in the range of 10 to 17 per cent, with further improvement most likely in 1978 and 1979. The gains from trade (defined in terms of NBTT changes) were materialized mainly with the West (MDCs), i.e. with the convertible currency areas while in trade with Less Developed Countries (LDCs) and Other Centrally Planned Economies (OCPEs), the Soviet Union experienced a deterioration in NBTT. In trade with European members of CMEA (i.e. CPEs) NBTT also improved; the Soviet gains were moderate at first but increased rapidly in the second half of the 1970s. The assymetry between the evolution of NBTT with CPEs and with MDCs was mainly due to the effect of the so-called "sliding price formula" introduced by the CMEA countries in establishing intra-CMEA prices.

These changes in terms of trade took place at a time of rapid expansion of Soviet trade, particularly that of Soviet imports from MDCs which, between 1970 and 1976, had already increased by a phenomenal rate of some 250 per cent in real terms. Most importantly the Soviet trade account with MDCs turned into substantial trade deficits and, consequently, into balance of payment deficits. Similar trade imbalances were characteristic of trade with OCPEs. In contrast, the Soviet Union generated considerable trade surpluses with CPEs and LDCs.

In general, trade imbalances must be treated by CPE planners separately as between imbalances resulting from trade with MDCs (and to a large extent with LDCs) on the one hand and those which result from trade with CPEs and OCPEs on the other. The trade with MDCs and LDCs is conducted primarily in terms of convertible currencies which permit the financing of imbalances through multilateral transfers. In contrast, trade among CPEs (and OCPEs) is conducted primarily in terms of inconvertible currencies which do not allow such multilateral payments.[40] On the contrary, imbalances in bilateral trade have to be adjusted typically via trade, i.e. real or nominal flows.

The question now arises how the USSR responded to what became a chronic external disequilibrium throughout the 1970s. The question can be analysed by looking first on the response of the Soviet Union to the change in the aggregate world demand or, in other words, by looking at the Soviet export performance. Alternatively, the Soviet planners could have responded to the extreme disequilibria by adopting certain policy measure(s) which would affect imports either directly or indirectly or, to put it differently, direct inport controls or domestic expansion.[41]

In its "deficit" trade (i.e. with MDCs) the Soviet Union was unable to match the growth of imports. The real growth of exports was persistently slower. At the same time, the Soviet planners did not adopt measures which would check the expansion of real imports until 1977. In contrast, the USSR was much more successful in dealing with trade imbalances (surpluses) with OCPEs. While imports grew at a faster rate than imports from any other area except MDCs, Soviet exports grew almost at the same rate. Thus, the USSR was much more successful in the less competitive markets of OCPEs than with MDCs.

In the case of its "surplus" trade, two pictures emerge. First, the Soviet CPE surpluses were financed to some extent by expanding real imports from the area even though the expansion was not sufficient to eliminate the trade imbalances completely. In contrast, the import-financing of Soviet trade surpluses with LDC was not pursued. On the contrary, real imports continued to grow at a relatively slower pace than exports and the resulting trade surpluses were then used to finance deficits with MDCs (Hewett (1979, p.43)).[42]

Nevertheless, it became clear that the Soviet Union was unable to finance the rising overall imports with the convertible currency area by increased export earnings. Hence, other sources became increasingly important, particularly those resulting from the improvement in terms of trade. Thus, according to my estimates above, the Soviet Union was able to finance almost a quarter of its total imports from MDCs "without moving a finger" – i.e. from the improvement of terms of trade. This improvement in NBTT, represented about 50 per cent of increased import capacity over the examined period; the other sources of financing accounted for much less; namely 34 per cent in the case of foreign borrowing and 16 per cent in the case of increased gold prices.

At the same time domestic aggregates appear to have been virtually unaffected by changes in terms of trade. The rate of growth of output has been falling rather than rising as it might have been expected. There was a change in composition of final demand, a shift to consumption in 1975–1976 and back to investment in 1977 but it would be difficult to attibute these changes to external factors.[43]

In spite of the dramatic improvement in Soviet NBTT and the resulting windfall gains, the Soviet Union had to draw, of course, on foreign borrowing, gold sales and sales of arms, to finance its trade deficits with the West. It is clear, however, that these sources of financing will not be used to the same extent in the future. After the dramatic fall in gold prices and a considerable reduction in Soviet reserves, the "gold financing" of payments deficits must become rather doubtful and similar scepticism must be raised with regard to future Western loans in the aftermath of the Polish crisis. Clearly, even if the loans are available, the USSR will be unlikely to have the same access to cheap sources of finance as in the past.

One "solution" is obviously a slowdown of imports which the planners may contemplate in view of the relatively small size of the foreign-trade sector in the Soviet economy and this has already taken place to some extent. However, there may be several constraints on the planners' behaviour. The Soviet imports include a significant proportion of commodities for which the possibilities of substitution from alternative sources of supply are limited or, in some cases, non-existent. These commodities include imports of food, feedstuffs and technology.

There are also some opportunities to finance Soviet deficits with MDCs by surpluses with LDCs but these opportunities are limited since LDCs willingness and capacity to absorb Soviet goods are extremely limited (perhaps except Soviet fuels and other so-called "hard" goods). There is also, undoubtedly, going to be increased pressure on the Soviet planners to direct some resources from CMEA to alternative uses such as exports of oil to the West but here the hands of the planners are tied and the degrees of freedom to manoeuvre are small.

The third and most likely option for the Soviet planners is a general promotion of exports in high demand both in convertible and non-convertible currency areas (such as oil, gas and a number of other NRPs). There is already some evidence that this will indeed be the path the Soviet planners will want to take. The evidence is provided particularly by various compensation deals between the Soviet Union and a number of Western countries about deliveries of natural gas and oil. Moreover, in a separate study of Soviet responses to external disturbances I have undertaken elsewhere (Drabek (1981)), I have estimated the allocations of Western technology according to end-using sectors.[44] The results of the estimations suggest that Western technology tended to be allocated preferentially not only into sectors producing traded commodities but, even more importantly, into sectors in which the Soviet Union has a comparative advantage and products of mining. It appears therefore that the interest of Soviet planners to participate actively in world commodity markets is unlikely to decline in the future.

## SUMMARY AND CONCLUSIONS

The purpose of this study was to assess the evolution of Soviet terms of trade, the windfall gains arising from changing terms of trade and the implication for future Soviet import demand for and exports of primary commodities. On the basis of various estimates we have concluded as follows:

1. Overall NBTT improved considerably during the 1970s. Only in trade with LDCs and OCEPs did NBTT deteriorate.
2. While there is no doubt about the improvement in NBTT, there is not a general agreement about the magnitude of this improvement and the estimate may fall between 12 and 20 per cent over the period of 1970 and 1978.
3. The improvement in NBTT with CMEA and MDCs, the two most important partner areas, also varied substantially. The improvement in NBTT with MDCs was far greater than the improvement in NBTT with CMEA.
4. Perhaps the most important reasons for the discrepancy in changes in NBTT was the delay in introducing the link between WMPs and prices ruling on the CMEA market and, in addition, discriminatory pricing practices conducted by the Soviet Union. The latter seem to favour its CMEA trading partner area.
5. As in the case of world trade, the commodity group which has been primarily responsible for the improvement in NBTT was fuels. Prices of other NRP commodities also exported by the USSR were increasing at modest rates in comparison to the inflation of fuel prices.
6. The improvement in NBTT has generated a massive import capacity which has become additionally available to the Soviet planners. The increase in the impact capacity so generated over

the period of 1970–1977 was almost one quarter of total imports from the West (i.e. MDCs) but considerably less (9 per cent) in the case of imports from CMEA.
7. There has been a response by Soviet planners to changes in terms of trade. The response took essentially the form of closing the "foreign trade gap" and thus to restore external balance. In trade with CMEA, however, the Soviet Union has been prepared to finance a part of the improvement in NBTT by running trade surpluses.
8. Judging from the available evidence, there appears to have been virtually no internal adjustment to the external disturbances. There has been no expansion in total output and, consequently, aggregate demand which would be required in MTEs to sustain a given target on the external account. On the contrary, the real trade flows have been growing faster in comparison to GNP.
9. There is also no evidence of the "substitution effect" of rising NBTT. An examination of the sectoral pattern of allocations of hard currencies for purchases of Western technology reveals that, if anything, the planners promoted further expansion of the primary sector (mainly fuels).

If the analysis of the adjustment process is correct, it is very unlikely that a major expansion of Soviet primary exports can be expected in the short-to-medium run as a result of rising output. However, it is also quite unlikely that there will be any significant withdrawal of the Soviet Union as an important exporter of primary commodities. The pattern of allocation of Western technology would definitely suggest the opposite, at least as far as exports of fuels are concerned.

To a large extent, the Soviet options are limited. While domestic adjustment would require expansion of income and hence import demand and *output*, the expansionary path is constrained by limits on production and, mainly by full employment of resources. Moreover, adjustments on the external account will have to come mainly from expansion of imports from CMEA, and, at least, sustained growth of exports to the West. In some respects there is more leeway in trade with the West since trade surpluses can be used for amortisation of past debts. Should imports from the CMEA not expand adequately, however, (there is always the problem of quality of East European manufactures!) Soviet exports of NRPs (i.e. "hard" goods) to CMEA may not be expanded, in which case more may be available for shipments to the West.

## APPENDIX

Table A.1 Soviet Trade with the CMEA Six (in millions of current SDRs)

| Year | Machinery and Equipment for Investment | Arms | Fuels | Non-Food Raw Materials | Grain and Flour | Other Food | Industrial Consumer Goods | Total |
|---|---|---|---|---|---|---|---|---|
| | | | | Exports | | | | |
| 1970 | 1416.1 | 744.3 | 1015.7 | 2888.3 | 305.4 | 235.5 | 153.1 | 6758.4 |
| 1971 | 1660.1 | 662.6 | 1167.5 | 2947.9 | 431.1 | 208.6 | 163.5 | 7241.3 |
| 1972 | 1895.5 | 660.9 | 1301.5 | 3047.4 | 225.1 | 165.0 | 178.6 | 7474.0 |
| 1973 | 2250.1 | 729.8 | 1442.6 | 3194.3 | 223.4 | 161.7 | 199.0 | 8200.9 |
| 1974 | 2672.8 | 866.0 | 1739.3 | 3551.7 | 310.1 | 241.0 | 291.7 | 9672.6 |
| 1975 | 2879.3 | 1099.5 | 3473.5 | 4840.4 | 271.8 | 234.1 | 386.1 | 13184.7 |
| 1976 | 3454.4 | 1230.5 | 4118.4 | 5133.2 | 57.5 | 138.6 | 430.3 | 14562.9 |
| 1977 | 4117.5 | 1418.3 | 5195.4 | 5438.3 | 224.3 | 137.5 | 531.0 | 16962.3 |
| 1978 | (4480.0) | n.a. | 6268.3 | n.a. | (5.0) | n.a. | n.a. | 18828.4 |
| Est. 1979 | (4800.0) | n.a. | (7200.0) | n.a. | n.a. | n.a. | n.a. | 20609.7 |

*Exports of Primary Commodities* 61

## Imports

| Year | | | | | | | | |
|---|---|---|---|---|---|---|---|---|
| 1970 | 2926.7 | 294.7 | 159.4 | 1068.4 | 35.2 | 581.3 | 1568.0 | 6633.7 |
| 1971 | 3079.6 | 307.3 | 193.4 | 1111.9 | 33.4 | 676.1 | 1856.8 | 7258.5 |
| 1972 | 3735.3 | 398.4 | 227.2 | 1335.2 | 20.7 | 823.1 | 2001.1 | 8541.0 |
| 1973 | 4197.2 | 485.2 | 233.9 | 1279.8 | 48.5 | 760.5 | 1986.9 | 8992.0 |
| 1974 | 4413.4 | 531.3 | 217.2 | 1342.5 | 29.5 | 958.6 | 2063.2 | 9555.7 |
| 1975 | 5729.8 | 510.3 | 464.5 | 1811.6 | 184.7 | 1278.3 | 2589.3 | 12568.5 |
| 1976 | 6316.5 | 707.2 | 452.3 | 1997.3 | 94.3 | 1268.3 | 2748.7 | 13584.6 |
| 1977 | 7266.9 | 878.2 | 457.1 | 2200.9 | 29.3 | 1479.1 | 3079.3 | 15390.8 |
| Est. 1978 | (10130.0) | n.a. | 552.2 | n.a. | (45.0) | n.a. | n.a. | 18639.9 |
| 1979 | (10600.0) | n.a. | (500.0) | n.a. | n.a. | n.a. | n.a. | 19427.1 |

## Trade Balance

| Year | | | | | | | | |
|---|---|---|---|---|---|---|---|---|
| 1970 | −1510.6 | 449.6 | 856.3 | 1819.9 | 270.2 | −345.8 | −1414.9 | 124.7 |
| 1971 | −1419.5 | 355.3 | 974.1 | 1836.0 | 397.7 | −467.5 | −1693.3 | −17.2 |
| 1972 | −1839.8 | 262.5 | 1074.3 | 1712.2 | 204.4 | −658.1 | −1822.5 | −1067.0 |
| 1973 | −1947.1 | 244.6 | 1208.7 | 1914.5 | 174.9 | −598.8 | −1787.9 | −791.1 |
| 1974 | −1740.6 | 334.7 | 1522.1 | 2209.2 | 280.6 | −717.6 | −1771.5 | 116.9 |
| 1975 | −2850.5 | 589.2 | 3009.0 | 3028.8 | 87.1 | −1044.2 | −2203.2 | 616.2 |
| 1976 | −2862.1 | 523.3 | 3666.1 | 3135.9 | −36.8 | −1129.7 | −2318.4 | 978.3 |
| 1977 | −3149.4 | 540.1 | 4738.6 | 3237.1 | 195.0 | −1341.6 | −2648.3 | 1571.5 |
| Est. 1978 | (−5650.0) | n.a. | 5716.1 | n.a. | (−40.0) | n.a. | n.a. | 188.5 |
| 1979 | (−5800.0) | n.a. | (6700.0) | n.a. | n.a. | n.a. | n.a. | 1182.6 |

*Source*: Vanous (1981a)

Table A.2 Soviet Trade with the OCPEs (in millions of current SDRs)

| Year | Machinery and Equipment for Investment | Arms | Fuels | Non-Food Raw Materials | Grain and Flour | Cuban Sugar | Other Food | Industrial Consumer Goods |
|---|---|---|---|---|---|---|---|---|
| | | | | Exports | | | | |
| 1970 | 576.7 | 106.5 | 201.7 | 418.7 | 122.7 | — | 94.7 | 87.5 |
| 1971 | 578.3 | 209.4 | 229.1 | 433.8 | 104.4 | — | 114.3 | 107.2 |
| 1972 | 623.7 | 128.8 | 229.2 | 416.9 | 78.7 | — | 148.0 | 106.8 |
| 1973 | 659.8 | 124.8 | 339.9 | 416.2 | 104.2 | — | 158.9 | 123.3 |
| 1974 | 831.8 | 110.9 | 540.7 | 630.8 | 167.1 | — | 230.8 | 139.4 |
| 1975 | 940.1 | 148.4 | 739.6 | 627.8 | 186.3 | — | 223.5 | 153.6 |
| 1976 | 1263.6 | 136.4 | 870.7 | 805.7 | 220.8 | — | 242.2 | 172.8 |
| 1977 | 1407.4 | 205.6 | 1129.2 | 824.8 | 265.7 | — | 265.3 | 163.3 |
| 1978 | (1660.0) | n.a. | 1241.4 | n.a. | (220.0) | — | n.a. | n.a. |
| Est. 1979 | (2050.0) | n.a. | (1550.0) | n.a. | n.a. | — | n.a. | n.a. |

# Exports of Primary Commodities

## Imports

| Year | | | | | | | |
|---|---|---|---|---|---|---|---|
| 1970 | 85.6 | — | 0.0 | 302.5 | — | 94.4 | 115.3 |
| 1971 | 67.1 | — | 0.0 | 366.4 | — | 121.8 | 158.1 |
| 1972 | 67.3 | — | 0.0 | 339.9 | — | 129.4 | 241.2 |
| 1973 | 68.7 | — | 1.6 | 407.3 | — | 134.6 | 277.2 |
| 1974 | 130.8 | — | 0.3 | 540.1 | — | 212.1 | 331.1 |
| 1975 | 210.2 | — | 1.1 | 633.6 | — | 218.1 | 394.4 |
| 1976 | 340.0 | — | 0.8 | 669.0 | — | 206.8 | 427.7 |
| 1977 | 443.2 | — | 0.8 | 682.6 | — | 282.8 | 417.2 |
| Est. 1978 | (550.0) | — | 1.0 | n.a. | — | n.a. | n.a. |
| 1979 | (600.0) | — | (0.0) | n.a. | — | n.a. | n.a. |

## Trade Balance

| Year | | | | | | | |
|---|---|---|---|---|---|---|---|
| 1970 | 491.1 | 106.5 | 201.7 | 116.2 | 122.7 | 404.8 | 0.3 | −27.8 |
| 1971 | 511.2 | 209.4 | 229.1 | 67.4 | 104.4 | 206.1 | 0.3 | −50.9 |
| 1972 | 556.4 | 128.8 | 229.2 | 77.0 | 78.7 | 146.1 | 18.6 | −134.4 |
| 1973 | 591.1 | 124.8 | 338.3 | 8.9 | 104.2 | 358.9 | 24.3 | −153.9 |
| 1974 | 701.0 | 110.9 | 540.4 | 90.7 | 167.1 | 678.6 | 18.7 | −191.7 |
| 1975 | 729.9 | 148.4 | 738.5 | −5.8 | 186.3 | 1493.7 | 5.4 | −240.8 |
| 1976 | 923.6 | 136.4 | 869.9 | 136.7 | 220.8 | 1553.1 | 35.4 | −254.9 |
| 1977 | 964.2 | 205.6 | 1128.4 | 142.2 | 265.7 | 1861.5 | −17.5 | −253.9 |
| Est. 1978 | (1100.0) | n.a. | 1240.4 | n.a. | (220.0) | 2352.4 | n.a. | n.a. |
| 1979 | (1450.0) | n.a. | (1550.0) | n.a. | n.a. | (2250.0) | n.a. | n.a. |

*Source*: As for Table A.1.

Table A.3 Soviet Trade with the MDCs (in millions of current SDRs)

| Year | Machinery and Equipment for Investment | Arms | Fuels | Non-Food Raw Materials | Grain and Flour | Other Food | Industrial Consumer Goods | Total |
|---|---|---|---|---|---|---|---|---|
| | | | *Exports* | | | | | |
| 1970 | 91.0 | 13.1 | 706.4 | 1324.9 | 22.7 | 156.3 | 79.0 | 2393.4 |
| 1971 | 85.7 | 10.4 | 984.3 | 1349.6 | 81.5 | 154.2 | 92.4 | 2758.1 |
| 1972 | 99.0 | 10.3 | 886.0 | 1451.5 | 24.7 | 123.5 | 114.2 | 2709.2 |
| 1973 | 168.1 | 13.3 | 1535.0 | 2055.1 | 120.6 | 167.6 | 167.8 | 4227.5 |
| 1974 | 184.9 | 14.9 | 3201.1 | 2770.5 | 277.7 | 224.2 | 188.3 | 6861.6 |
| 1975 | 300.7 | 18.0 | 3929.6 | 2309.5 | 28.0 | 231.1 | 243.3 | 7060.2 |
| 1976 | 33.2 | 19.8 | 5248.9 | 2551.3 | 0.2 | 203.2 | 265.0 | 8621.6 |
| 1977 | 287.2 | 23.3 | 6194.5 | 2899.6 | 26.3 | 163.7 | 333.8 | 9928.4 |
| 1978 | (315.0) | n.a. | 6189.1 | n.a. | (10.0) | n.a. | n.a. | 9665.3 |
| Est. 1979 | (350.0) | n.a. | (9900.0) | n.a. | (0.0) | n.a. | n.a. | 13896.3 |

## Exports of Primary Commodities

|  |  |  | Imports |  |  |  |
|---|---|---|---|---|---|---|
| 1970 | 1104.1 | — | 7.8 | 1154.0 | 122.7 | 106.3 | 327.4 | 2822.3 |
| 1971 | 1032.5 | — | 9.5 | 1256.8 | 182.0 | 98.2 | 310.9 | 2889.9 |
| 1972 | 1247.0 | — | 7.7 | 1339.4 | 817.8 | 108.0 | 298.9 | 3818.8 |
| 1973 | 1605.1 | — | 12.2 | 1821.9 | 1267.6 | 226.5 | 240.3 | 5173.6 |
| 1974 | 2109.8 | — | 18.3 | 3515.3 | 496.0 | 242.3 | 352.6 | 6734.3 |
| 1975 | 4128.3 | — | 36.4 | 4372.1 | 1751.7 | 333.9 | 536.2 | 11158.6 |
| 1976 | 4745.8 | — | 50.2 | 4021.2 | 2142.9 | 416.9 | 534.3 | 11911.3 |
| 1977 | 4967.4 | — | 33.9 | 3853.6 | 1156.9 | 649.8 | 513.3 | 11174.9 |
| 1978 Est. | (5305.0) | — | 58.5 | n.a. | (1605.0) | n.a. | n.a. | 12201.4 |
| 1979 | (6200.0) | — | (70.0) | n.a. | (2400.0) | n.a. | n.a. | 14727.8 |

*Trade Balance*

| 1970 | −1013.1 | 13.1 | 698.6 | 170.9 | −100.0 | 50.0 | −248.4 | −428.9 |
| 1971 | −946.8 | 10.4 | 974.8 | 92.8 | −100.5 | 56.0 | −218.5 | −131.8 |
| 1972 | −1148.0 | 10.3 | 878.3 | 112.1 | −793.1 | 15.5 | −184.7 | −1109.6 |
| 1973 | −1437.0 | 13.3 | 1522.8 | 233.2 | −1147.0 | −58.9 | −72.5 | −946.1 |
| 1974 | −1924.9 | 14.9 | 3182.8 | −744.8 | −218.3 | −18.1 | −164.3 | 127.3 |
| 1975 | −3827.6 | 18.0 | 3893.2 | −2062.6 | −1723.7 | −102.8 | −292.9 | −4098.4 |
| 1976 | −4412.6 | 19.8 | 5198.7 | −1469.9 | −2142.7 | −213.7 | −269.3 | −3289.7 |
| 1977 | −4680.2 | 23.3 | 6160.6 | −954.0 | −1130.6 | −486.1 | −179.5 | −1246.5 |
| 1978 Est. | (−4990.0) | n.a. | 6130.6 | n.a. | (−1595.0) | n.a. | n.a. | −2536.1 |
| 1979 | (−5850.0) | n.a. | (9830.0) | n.a. | (−2400.0) | n.a. | n.a. | −831.5 |

*Source*: As for Table A.1.

Table A.4 Soviet Trade with the LDCs (in millions of current SDRs)

| Year | Machinery and Equipment for Investment | Arms | Fuels | Non-Food Raw Materials | Grain and Flour | Other Food | Industrial Consumer Goods | Total |
|---|---|---|---|---|---|---|---|---|
| | | | | Exports | | | | |
| 1970 | 674.1 | 891.3 | 73.0 | 235.3 | 17.5 | 113.9 | 34.6 | 2039.7 |
| 1971 | 689.7 | 779.5 | 97.3 | 249.7 | 44.6 | 130.8 | 38.6 | 2030.2 |
| 1972 | 740.8 | 1063.0 | 86.6 | 230.4 | 8.5 | 57.6 | 41.6 | 2228.5 |
| 1973 | 814.5 | 1934.8 | 76.8 | 396.8 | 5.8 | 45.9 | 36.1 | 3310.7 |
| 1974 | 745.2 | 1825.1 | 324.8 | 599.5 | 34.0 | 141.9 | 45.5 | 3716.0 |
| 1975 | 923.9 | 1847.5 | 388.0 | 473.9 | 12.6 | 105.4 | 54.9 | 3806.2 |
| 1976 | 1010.3 | 2214.8 | 392.6 | 367.7 | 0.3 | 67.5 | 62.8 | 4116.0 |
| 1977 | 1189.5 | 3737.5 | 527.1 | 413.9 | 8.8 | 57.5 | 75.0 | 6009.3 |
| 1978 | (1315.0) | (3700.0) | 431.7 | n.a. | (6.0) | n.a. | n.a. | 6362.6 |
| Est 1979 | (1650.0) | (3600.0) | (600.0) | n.a. | n.a. | n.a. | n.a. | 7018.3 |

## Exports of Primary Commodities

### Imports

| Year | | | | | |
|------|------|------|------|------|------|
| 1970 | 1.5 | — | 67.4 | 657.8 | 0.0 | 410.8 | 135.4 | 1272.9 |
| 1971 | 2.8 | — | 134.1 | 630.4 | 25.0 | 458.1 | 161.5 | 1411.9 |
| 1972 | 6.0 | — | 208.5 | 607.9 | 0.0 | 487.0 | 189.0 | 1498.4 |
| 1973 | 11.7 | — | 344.7 | 783.8 | 0.0 | 598.0 | 221.9 | 1960.1 |
| 1974 | 11.8 | — | 489.7 | 1011.7 | 105.0 | 718.1 | 277.8 | 2614.1 |
| 1975 | 19.0 | — | 677.8 | 933.9 | 345.2 | 1154.7 | 317.7 | 3448.3 |
| 1976 | 18.4 | — | 639.3 | 767.9 | 292.6 | 1093.8 | 275.0 | 3087.0 |
| 1977 | 23.4 | — | 722.1 | 1000.2 | 56.9 | 1291.6 | 280.8 | 3375.0 |
| 1978 Est | (35.0) | — | 808.9 | n.a. | (240.0) | n.a. | n.a. | 3145.8 |
| 1979 | (40.0) | — | (800.0) | n.a. | n.a. | n.a. | n.a. | 3543.9 |

### Trade Balance

| Year | | | | | |
|------|------|------|------|------|------|
| 1970 | 672.6 | 891.3 | 5.6 | −422.5 | 17.5 | −296.9 | −100.8 | 766.8 |
| 1971 | 686.9 | 779.5 | −36.8 | −380.7 | 19.6 | −327.3 | −122.9 | 618.3 |
| 1972 | 734.8 | 1063.0 | −121.9 | −377.5 | 8.5 | −429.4 | −147.4 | 730.1 |
| 1973 | 802.8 | 1934.8 | −267.9 | −387.0 | 5.8 | −552.1 | −185.8 | 1350.6 |
| 1974 | 733.4 | 1825.1 | −164.9 | −412.2 | −71.0 | −576.2 | −232.3 | 1101.9 |
| 1975 | 904.9 | 1847.5 | 89.8 | −460.0 | −332.6 | −1049.3 | −262.8 | 357.9 |
| 1976 | 991.9 | 2214.8 | −246.7 | −400.2 | −292.3 | −1026.3 | −212.2 | 1029.0 |
| 1977 | 1166.1 | 3737.5 | −195.0 | −586.3 | −48.1 | −1234.1 | −205.8 | 2634.3 |
| 1978 Est | (1280.0) | (3700.0) | −377.2 | n.a. | (−236.0) | n.a. | n.a. | 3216.8 |
| 1979 | (1610.0) | (3600.0) | (−200.0) | n.a. | n.a. | n.a. | n.a. | 3474.4 |

*Source*: As for Table A.1

# 4 The Soviet Union and World Trade in Oil and Gas*

## J.B. Hannigan and C.H. McMillan

The Soviet Union occupies a salient position in world output and reserves of hydrocarbons. At the end of the 1970s, it remained the world's leading producer of petroleum, accounting for nearly one-fifth of world production. Moreover, despite the depletion of some of its historic fields, it was estimated in 1979 to dispose of 10 per cent of the world's proven reserves, which placed it alongside Kuwait and second only to Saudi Arabia in this measure of output potential.

Soviet predominance is still greater in the case of natural gas. With the rapid development of its natural gas resources over the preceding decade, and the boost provided by the exploitation of huge deposits in Western Siberia, the USSR by 1979 produced 27 per cent of world output, second only to the United States. Possessing an estimated 41 per cent of the world's proven gas reserves, however, the USSR stood far ahead of other nations in production potential. Table 4.1 shows the relative position of the USSR in terms of both world output and reserves of oil and gas.

Although the Soviet economy, with its continental dimensions and resource-intensive pattern of development, takes a major share of Soviet oil and gas output, there remains an important exportable surplus. In 1979, the USSR ranked as the world's second largest exporter of crude oil (after Saudi Arabia) and second largest exporter of natural gas (after the Netherlands). Its impact on international markets for oil and gas was not, however, commensurate with these

---

*This chapter draws upon reports prepared by the authors in a series on "The Soviet Union's International Energy Arrangement". Research for this series is funded by a generous grant from the Federal Department of Energy, Mines and Resources.

Table 4.1 Output and Reserves of Petroleum and Natural Gas by Region and by Country – 1979 (as a percentage of total world output and reserves)

|  | Petroleum[a] | | Natural gas[b] | |
|---|---|---|---|---|
|  | Output | Reserves | Output | Reserves |
| *Middle East* | 34 | 56 | 2 | 23 |
| Kuwait | 4 | 10 | negl. | 2 |
| Iran | 5 | 9 | 1 | 15 |
| Iraq | 5 | 5 | negl. | 1 |
| Saudi Arabia | 15 | 25 | negl. | 3 |
| *Western Hemisphere* | 24 | 14 | 46 | 16 |
| Canada | 2 | 1 | 5 | 3 |
| Mexico | 2 | 5 | 1 | 2 |
| USA | 13 | 4 | 38 | 8 |
| Venezuela | 4 | 3 | 1 | 2 |
| *Africa* | 10 | 9 | 2 | 7 |
| Algeria | 2 | 1 | 1 | 4 |
| Libya | 3 | 4 | negl. | 1 |
| Nigeria | 4 | 3 | negl. | 2 |
| *Western Europe* | 4 | 4 | 13 | 5 |
| Netherlands | negl. | negl. | 6 | 2 |
| Norway | 1 | 1 | 1 | 1 |
| United Kingdom | 2 | 2 | 3 | 1 |
| *Asia – Pacific*[c] | 5 | 3 | 4 | 6 |
| Indonesia | 3 | 1 | 2 | 2 |
| *USSR* | 19 | 10 | 27 | 41 |
| *Others*[d] | 4 | 4 | 6 | 2 |

a) World petroleum output and reserves in 1979 were estimated at 3,123 million metric tons and 87,894 million metric tons, respectively.
b) World natural gas output and reserves in 1979 were estimated at 1,489 billion cubic metres and 73,848 billion cubic metres, respectively.
c) excludes China.
d) primarily Eastern Europe and China.

*Sources:* Reserves figures for petroleum are from *Oil and Gas Journal*, (December 31, 1979): 70–71; output figures for petroleum are from United Nations, *1979 Yearbook of World Energy Statistics*. Reserve and output figures for natural gas are from *Petroleum Economist*, (August 1980): 337.

rankings. We shall seek to explain this apparent paradox through an examination of Soviet trade in these commodities.

We shall also examine trends and prospects. With the maintenance of the Soviet net export position in petroleum in question, and giant gas export deals coming into play, the first half of the 1980s appears destined to be a turning point. The analysis will therefore focus on whether, as gas replaces oil as the principal Soviet energy export, the USSR is likely to play a more important role in world trade in natural gas than it has in petroleum in the post-war period.

## SOVIET TRADE IN OIL AND OIL PRODUCTS

### (a) Soviet Oil Exports in Historical Perspective

Well before the October revolution, Tsarist Russia occupied a major position in world production of petroleum. Moreover, relatively limited domestic demand left a large exportable surplus; and at the turn of the century Russia was the world's leading exporter of petroleum, accounting for some 30 per cent of world exports.[1]

The historic Baku oil fields had already begun to decline before the revolution. Industrialisation, before and after the revolution, contributed to the growth of domestic demand for oil. As a result of these trends, the country's net export position weakened. By the end of the inter-war period (1939), Soviet exports of crude oil and oil products had dropped to below two per cent of output and comprised less than one per cent of world exports.[2]

The situation did not change immediately after the war. In the late 1950s, Soviet energy policy began to stress the substitution of liquid for solid fuels – the latter, in particular coal, having until then borne the brunt of domestic energy needs in the Soviet industrialisation drive.[3] The rapid development at this time of the rich Volga-Urals fields greatly facilitated this shift. In the late 1960s, the opening up of giant, new fields in Western Siberia gave another boost to capacity. Between 1955 and 1975, Soviet production of crude oil increased dramatically, from 71 mmt to 491 mmt.[4]

Despite the growth in domestic requirements, this rapid expansion of productive capacity generated an important export capability. Between 1955 and 1975, Soviet exports of crude oil increased from 3 mmt to 93 mmt and exports of oil products from 5 mmt to 37 mmt. The country had again become a major oil exporter.

An important share of oil exports was directed to the Soviet Union's allies in Eastern Europe, with which the USSR was economically associated in the Council for Mutual Economic Assistance (CMEA). Like the USSR, these countries were shifting increasingly to liquid fuels in their industrialisation strategies. The exception was Romania which, as an historic producer of petroleum, had earlier based its industry on hydrocarbons. Poor in oil and gas resources, these countries turned inevitably to Soviet sources of supply and their imports of Soviet oil grew rapidly in the course of the 1960s.[5] Table 4.2 records the growth of Soviet oil exports and the rise in the share going to the CMEA countries. Except in the case of Romania, Soviet oil in turn made up the bulk of the oil imports of the European CMEA countries (an average of 87 per cent in 1975–79).

Soviet exports to the rest of the world are divided in Table 4.2 among the other (non-CMEA) socialist countries and Finland, the developing countries and developed capitalist countries (following closely Soviet yearbook terminology). Over time, several of the more important, "other socialist" importers of Soviet oil became members of the CMEA: Cuba, in 1972, and Vietnam, in 1978. Yugoslavia is now the major importer in the "other socialist" category. Among the developing countries, India has consistently been the most important importer by far of Soviet oil, accounting in 1979 for 56 per cent (by value) of Soviet exports to the Third World.[6]

It should be noted here that the Soviet Union also purchases some oil from the Third World, notably several Middle Eastern countries. These "imports" are in fact purchases on the Soviet account which are redirected to other destinations. They serve to supplement Soviet export capabilities, providing a convenient means for the Soviet Union to meet some of its international commitments.[7] The volume of these imports is not great, however (some 7mmt in 1979), and hence the difference between Soviet gross and net oil exports is minimal.

With some relatively minor exceptions, Soviet oil trade with CMEA, other socialist countries, Finland and developing countries falls within the framework of bilateral clearing arrangements.[8] The special terms of the barter-like arrangements under which oil is exported to these destinations contrast with the normal commercial terms under which Soviet oil is exported to the developed capitalist markets. It is important to stress, therefore, that the Soviet oil export market is divided into two segments: a "barter" segment, in which special price and payments terms apply, and a "non-barter" segment,

Table 4.2 USSR Trade in Petroleum and Natural Gas (1950–1980)*

| | 1950 | 1955 | 1960 | 1965 | 1970 | 1975 | 1976 | 1977 | 1978 | 1979 | 1980 |
|---|---|---|---|---|---|---|---|---|---|---|---|
| *Crude Petroleum* (mmt) | | | | | | | | | | | |
| Exports[a] | 0.3 | 2.9 | 17.8 | 43.4 | 66.8 | 93.1 | 110.8 | 112.8 | 114.9 | 117.0 | n.a. |
| CMEA[b] | 0.3 | 1.7 | 6.2 | 18.3 | 34.4 | 64.0 | 68.8 | 72.4 | 75.2 | 77.7 | 79.2[e] |
| Other Socialist plus Finland[c] | — | 0.6 | 3.4 | 6.0 | 12.7 | 7.7 | 10.1 | 11.7 | 11.1 | 11.6[e] | n.a. |
| Western Europe[d] | — | 0.3 | 6.2 | 12.1 | 17.5 | 12.2 | 22.5 | 25.1 | 25.6 | 24.5 | 23.1[k] |
| Other Developed Capitalist[f] | — | — | 1.2 | 2.3 | 0.5 | 0.1 | 0.3 | 0.1 | 0.1 | n.a. | — |
| Developing[g] | — | 0.2 | 0.2 | 4.1 | 2.0 | 2.0 | 1.9 | 3.2 | 2.9 | 3.1[e] | n.a. |
| Destination Unknown | — | 0.1 | 0.1 | 0.5 | — | 7.1[m] | 7.7[m] | — | — | — | — |
| Imports[h] | 0.3 | 0.6 | 1.2 | — | 3.5 | 6.5 | 6.4 | 6.6 | 8.7 | 7.0 | n.a. |
| OAPEC | n.a. | n.a. | 0.7 | — | 2.1 | 6.5 | 6.4 | 6.4 | 8.7 | n.a. | n.a. |
| Other | n.a. | n.a. | 0.5 | — | 1.4 | — | — | 0.2 | — | n.a. | n.a. |
| *Petroleum Products* (mmt) | | | | | | | | | | | |
| Exports[a] | 0.8 | 5.1 | 15.4 | 21.0 | 29.0 | 37.3[n] | 37.7[n] | 33.3 | 40.1 | 41.0 | n.a. |
| CMEA[b] | 0.4 | 0.5 | 3.1 | 4.3 | 6.2 | 7.8 | 9.3 | 8.4 | 9.8 | 12.5 | n.a. |
| Other Socialist plus Finland[c] | 0.2 | 2.0 | 4.7 | 4.6 | 5.0 | 7.0 | 5.9 | 5.0 | 5.3 | 5.5 | n.a. |
| Western Europe[d] | — | 1.4 | 5.9 | 7.2 | 11.9 | 20.1 | 17.3 | 17.0 | 22.5 | 19.1 | n.a. |
| Other Developed Capitalist[f] | — | — | 0.2 | 1.6 | 2.2 | 2.0 | 2.7 | 0.8 | 1.0 | 0.8 | n.a. |
| Developing[g] | 0.2 | 0.2 | 1.1 | 1.8 | 1.7 | 2.5 | 2.6 | 2.1 | 1.5 | 3.1 | n.a. |
| Destination Unknown | — | 1.0 | 0.4 | 1.5 | 2.0 | — | — | — | — | — | — |

| of which[i] | | | | | | | | | | | |
|---|---|---|---|---|---|---|---|---|---|---|---|
| Gasoline | 0.3 | 1.4 | 2.8 | 2.4 | 4.0 | 6.0 | n.a. | n.a. | n.a. | n.a. | n.a. |
| Kerosene | 0.2 | 1.3 | 1.1 | 1.2 | 1.6 | 2.6 | n.a. | n.a. | n.a. | n.a. | n.a. |
| Diesel oil | 0.1 | 1.5 | 5.2 | 7.4 | 11.4 | 15.9 | n.a. | n.a. | n.a. | n.a. | n.a. |
| Residual fuel | 0.1 | 0.6 | 5.8 | 11.4 | 12.0 | n.a. | n.a. | n.a. | n.a. | n.a. | n.a. |
| Imports[h] | 2.3 | 3.8 | 3.2 | 1.9 | 1.1 | 1.1 | 0.6 | 0.6 | 0.6 | 0.7 | n.a. |

### Total Crude and Product

| | | | | | | | | | | | |
|---|---|---|---|---|---|---|---|---|---|---|---|
| Exports | 1.1 | 8.0 | 33.2 | 64.4 | 95.8 | 130.4 | 148.5 | 148.2 | 153.3 | 158.4 | n.a. |
| Imports | 2.6 | 4.4 | 4.4 | 1.9 | 4.6 | 7.6 | 7.0 | 7.2 | 9.3 | 7.7 | n.a. |
| Net Exports | −1.5 | 3.6 | 28.8 | 62.5 | 91.2 | 122.8 | 141.5 | 141.0 | 144.0 | 150.7 | n.a. |

### Natural Gas (bcm)

| | | | | | | | | | | | |
|---|---|---|---|---|---|---|---|---|---|---|---|
| Exports[a] | 0.1 | 0.1 | 0.2 | 0.4 | 3.3 | 19.3 | 25.8 | 33.1 | 40.3 | 49.6 | 57.3[k] |
| CMEA[b] | 0.1 | 0.1 | 0.2 | 0.4 | 2.3 | 11.3 | 13.4 | 14.7 | 15.8 | 23.2 | 29.8 |
| Other Socialist plus Finland[c] | — | — | — | — | — | 0.7 | 0.9 | 0.9 | 1.1 | 1.9 | 2.8 |
| Western Europe[d] | — | — | — | — | 1.0 | 7.3 | 11.5 | 17.5 | 23.4 | 24.5 | 24.7 |
| Austria | — | — | — | — | 1.0 | 1.9 | 2.8 | 2.8 | 3.2 | 3.4 | 3.0 |
| FRG | — | — | — | — | — | 3.1 | 4.0 | 5.3 | 8.6 | 10.1 | 11.8 |
| France | — | — | — | — | — | — | 1.0 | 2.1 | 2.8 | 2.7 | 2.8 |
| Italy | — | — | — | — | — | 2.3 | 3.7 | 7.3 | 8.8 | 8.3 | 7.1 |
| Imports[j] | — | — | — | — | 3.6 | 12.4 | 11.8 | 12.7 | 9.7 | 6.3 | 3.2[p] |
| Afghanistan | — | — | — | — | 2.6 | 2.8 | 2.5 | 2.4 | 2.5 | 2.2 | 2.5 |
| Iran | — | — | — | — | 1.0 | 9.6 | 9.3 | 10.3 | 7.2 | 4.1 | 0.7 |
| Net gas exports | 0.1 | 0.1 | 0.2 | 0.4 | −0.3 | 6.9 | 14.0 | 20.4 | 30.6 | 42.4 | 54.1 |

*Notes: see pp. 74–75*

Table 4.2  Notes

*Analysis of Soviet trade in oil and gas poses problems in terms of the availability and consistency of statistics. Beginning in 1967, the Soviet Union amalgamated the previously separate categories of "crude oil" (CTN 21) and "oil products" (CTN 22) when reporting imports and exports by country. In 1977, the Soviet Union stopped reporting any data on the volume of oil and gas trade; even at the most aggregate levels. Only value figures are now given for trade in these commodities. For disaggregated data, and post-1967 volume figures, we have consequently turned to the official statistics of the Soviet Union's foreign trade partners, and to statistical yearbooks published by international organizations like the United Nations and the Organization for Economic Cooperation and Development.

Notes and Sources for Table 4.2

a) Data for 1970–76 are from *Vneshniaia Torgovlia SSSR*; 1977–79 figures are totals of the regional breakdowns based on partner trade statistics.
b) CMEA includes the six Eastern European countries, Mongolia, Cuba from 1972 and Vietnam from 1978. Sources include *Vneshniaia Torgovlia SSSR*; United Nations, *World Energy Supplies* and *1979 Yearbook of World Energy Statistics*; National Foreign Assessment Center (Washington, D.C.), *International Energy Statistical Review*; and numerous press reports.
c) "Other socialist" includes Yugoslavia, China, People's Democratic Republic of Korea, and Vietnam and Cuba prior to their joining CMEA. Data for 1950–65 are from *Vneshniaia Torgovlia SSSR*; and for 1970–78, United Nations, *1979 Yearbook of World Energy Statistics*; 1979 is an authors' estimate. Data for Finland come from *Vneshniaia Torgovlia SSSR*; the Finnish foreign trade yearbook, *Ulkomaankauppa: Vuosijulkaisu, Osa 1*; OECD, *Statistics of Foreign Trade, Series C, Trade by Commodities, Market Summaries: Imports*; and United Nations; Economic Commission for Europe, *Annual Bulletin of Gas Statistics for Europe*.
d) OECD Europe less Finland, Turkey and Yugoslavia. Data are from *Vneshniaia Torgovlia SSSR* for 1950–65 and for 1970–79 from individual country foreign trade yearbooks and OECD, *Statistics of Foreign Trade, Series C, Trade by Commodities, Market Summaries: Imports*.
e) Authors' estimate based on numerous press reports.
f) Primarily North America and Japan, data for which come from *Vneshniaia Torgovlia SSSR* for 1950–1965; and from United Nations, *1979 Yearbook of World Energy Statistics*.

g) United Nations classification of "Developing Market Economies" less Cuba. Data for 1950–65 are from *Vneshniaia Torgovlia SSSR*; and for 1970–78, United Nations, *1979 Yearbook of World Energy Statistics*.
h) Data for 1950–65 are from *Vneshniaia Torgovlia SSSR*; and for 1970–78, from United Nations, *1979 Yearbook of World Energy Statistics*.
i) Data for the breakdown of petroleum products exports are from *Vneshniaia Torgovlia SSSR*.
j) Data on total imports and breakdown for 1970–76 are from *Vneshniaia Torgovlia SSSR*; and for 1977–79, from National Foreign Assessment Center (Washington, D.C.). *International Energy Statistical Review*; United Nations, *1979 Yearbook of World Energy Statistics*; and numerous press reports.
k) This is a preliminary figure based upon reports in *Petroleum Economist*, (June 1981), p. 272; and August 1981, p. 356.
m) The large volume of crude oil exports, the destination of which is unknown, results from the difference in the total of the regional breakdowns, derived from the sources noted above, and the total figure for crude oil exports reported in the official Soviet foreign trade yearbook. Although the same method and sources were used for 1970 data, no discrepancy emerged. While difficult to explain, the 1975–76 residuals would thus seem attributable to non-reporting of crude oil imports from the Soviet Union in those years rather than to generally divergent recording practices.
n) The figures do not sum exactly for the reason mentioned in note (m). In contrast to the figures for crude oil exports in 1975–76, the difference here is slight. This tends to reinforce the notion that the "mirror statistics" problem is not prevalent.
p) Total and regional breakdowns are from *Petroleum Economist*, (August 1981): 337.

where world market price and payments terms apply. The diversion of a major share of Soviet oil exports to the barter segment severely restricts the share available for the world market.

Table 4.2 can be used to develop this point further, in quantitative terms. Soviet petroleum exports to the West European countries, and to the other "developed capitalist" countries (North America, Japan), are conducted under conditions broadly set in international markets for crude and products. The share of Soviet crude oil exports to these countries in the latter half of the 1970s varied between 14 and 24 per cent, closer to 21 per cent in most of these years. They only slightly exceeded 25 mmt, whereas total Soviet crude oil exports were well over 100 mmt. The table also reveals that the share of Soviet exports of petroleum by-products to hard-currency markets was considerably higher than the share of crude exports. Ranging between approximately 18 and 24 mmt annually, exports to these markets typically comprised some 50–60 per cent of total Soviet products exports. The bulk of these exports were in the form of diesel fuel and residual fuel oil.

Western Europe receives the bulk of Soviet crude oil and products exported outside the CMEA. Excluding Finland, Western Europe in 1979 took 96 per cent of the combined value of Soviet crude and products sold to the developed capitalist countries. The remainder went to Japan and the United States. Again excluding Finland, the major West European importers of Soviet petroleum are, according to Soviet trade statistics: West Germany (19.3 per cent by value of 1979 exports to the developed capitalist countries), France (16.2 per cent), the Netherlands (13.0 per cent), Italy (12.5 per cent), Sweden (7.7 per cent), Great Britain (5.2 per cent) and Belgium (4.1 per cent).

With a few relatively minor exceptions, the remaining export destinations shown in Table 4.2 make up the soft-currency, or "barter" segment of the Soviet export market, where exports are settled under terms specified in bilateral, intergovernmental trade agreements.[9] This is the dominant segment of the Soviet export market, accounting for 79 per cent Soviet exports of crude and 51 per cent of Soviet exports of products, in 1979. We have included Finland in this group, with the "other socialist" countries, because its trade with the USSR since 1950 has been conducted under the aegis of a succession of bilateral clearing agreements.[10] The treatment of Finland is important, since it is a major importer of Soviet petroleum. In 1979, Finland imported 7.4 mmt of Soviet crude and 3.1 mmt of Soviet oil products.

The growth of Soviet exports after 1960 was greatly facilitated by the development of the internal pipeline system and the construction of the "Druzhba" pipeline, which provided a more direct and much cheaper transport link between the Volga-Urals fields (and later the West Siberian fields) and Eastern Europe. Completed in 1963 (and extended in 1968), the Druzhba system also allows oil to be piped to ports on the Baltic, where it is transhipped to Western European markets.

**(b) The Soviet Union and World Oil Markets**

Exports to the developed capitalist countries are handled, as is all Soviet trade in oil and oil products, by the All-Union Foreign-Trade Association, Sojuznefteexport. Currently the largest Soviet foreign trade organization in terms of annual turnover, Sojuznefteexport was founded in 1931, the heir to earlier state oil monopolies. Sojuznefteexport has developed a clientele of Western oil firms, state and private, with which it deals on a long-term contractual basis. In its more important West European markets, it has established its own companies. Wholly owned by Sojuznefteexport, these subsidiaries have assumed an increasing share of its commercial activities. As of 1981, the following subsidiary companies were in operation: Nafta in Britain, and Nafta B in Belgium, DFN in Denmark, Suomen Petrooli and Teboil in Finland, Nafta (It) in Italy and Sovoil in Switzerland. Several of those which have been longer established (in Finland, Belgium and Great Britain) have their own retail networks (service stations). At the end of 1978, Sojuznefteexport was reorganized into four specialized "firms" (*firmy*), each responsible for a geographic area. Those dealing with the developed capitalist countries are Euronafta (for Western Europe) and Dalnafta (for the Far East and America).

Sojuznefteexport's activities in Western Europe were already significant before the Second World War. While exports of oil and oil products were only 6.1 million tons in the peak pre-war export year of 1932, they nevertheless constituted an estimated 20 per cent of Europe's import requirements for oil products. Import dependence on the USSR was much higher than the average for several countries: 68 per cent for Italy, 30 per cent for Sweden, 35 per cent for Belgium and 26 per cent for Denmark.[11] Moreover, Soviet oil marketing subsidiaries abroad were already active in the pre-war period, operating in some important West European markets (Germany and Sweden) where after the war they ceased to function.

The reappearance of Russia, in new Soviet guise, on world oil markets in the early 1930s, gave rise to Western fears of disruptive Soviet oil "offensives". While operations on these markets are shrouded in commercial secrecy, such concerns appear in retrospect to have been much exaggerated. The two, alleged, Soviet oil "offensives" (in the early 1930s and early 1960s) were not Soviet attempts to disrupt international markets, but rather to break into markets dominated by the major Western oil companies. In the 1930s, the USSR had to use aggressive marketing tactics to sell its oil, because the Western majors refused to market Soviet oil. In the 1960s, Soviet discounts were a means of reestablishing its pre-war export position. Its actions were analogous to those of the Western "independents", and its discounts were not the largest offered at the time.[12]

The USSR was able to profit greatly from the 1973 Arab oil embargo, prompted by Western support of Israel in the Yom Kippur War, and the OPEC-imposed increase in the world price of oil. The volume of Soviet oil exports to the West expanded more rapidly in 1973 than in preceding years, while hard-currency earnings nearly doubled.[13] The jump in the world price also enabled the USSR to improve its terms of trade with Eastern Europe, although with a lag, and not to the extent that the shift in world price relationships could have justified. Although not a member of OPEC, the USSR was able to use subsequent OPEC price hikes to increase the value of its own hard-currency exports and to raise the price of oil shipments to its CMEA partners.

Table 4.2 shows Soviet exports of crude and products to Western Europe to have increased through 1978, on the basis of higher domestic output and in the context of substantially increased world market prices. As a result, oil exports in that year accounted for 47 per cent of Soviet hard currency earnings (compared with 29 per cent in 1972).

It should be noted that there were also certain drawbacks for the USSR in the restructuring of the world petroleum market after 1973. It became more difficult for the USSR and the other CMEA countries to obtain oil from OPEC sources (notably Iraq and Iran) on a barter basis.[14] OPEC assertiveness and the rise in the world price of oil also served to increase East European dependence on more stable and lower priced Soviet supplies. While increased East European energy dependence may offer certain political advantages to the USSR, CMEA requirements constrain its ability to take advantage of tight international markets to expand hard-currency exports.

There is little evidence that the USSR has sought to disrupt international markets, or has even attempted to capture a target share of them. Instead, it has sought as necessary and when possible to use oil, an important traditional export, to earn hard currencies to pay for the import of commodities needed to fulfil domestic development plans. To this end, it has sought to break into and make use of, rather than to disrupt, established international markets. The economic motives underlying Soviet oil export policy have not, however, ruled out the occasional use of oil as an instrument of Soviet diplomacy, especially in the Third World.[15]

The USSR has not, in fact, been in a position to break – much less to make – the rules of the game. Soviet export activity declined after 1932, and in the early post-war years, the USSR was even a net oil importer (see Table 4.2). Even when it did reassert itself after 1960, the Soviet Union's supplies to hard-currency markets were marginal, constrained by the factors outlined above. The USSR has accordingly acted as a price-taker rather than as a price-maker on these markets, operating within market parameters to its own best advantage.

Table 4.3 is intended to help place Soviet exports in this perspective. It shows the Soviet share of world exports of oil and oil products, and of their regional components, in selected years since 1960. Total Soviet crude oil exports to hard-currency markets in 1979 were 24.6 mmt, its share of these combined markets constituting a marginal two per cent. In terms of Western Europe alone, the Soviet share was a somewhat more significant four per cent. Moreover, the Soviet share of West European imports of oil products was 16.5 per cent. It should also be noted that the Soviet share of the import markets of some West European countries is well above the average (e.g., 63 per cent of Iceland's and 29 per cent of the Netherlands' total oil product imports came from the USSR; and 20 per cent of Austria's and 13 per cent of Denmark's total crude oil imports came from the USSR).

### (c) The USSR and World Trade in Oil in the 1980s

More recently, a very different kind of concern has emerged with regard to potential Soviet actions in the world market for petroleum. Concern has shifted from fear of disruptive Soviet behaviour in supplying the market to fear of potentially destabilising behaviour on the demand side. The earlier concerns were generated by the major

Table 4.3 Soviet Shares of World Trade and Regional Markets in Crude Oil, Oil Products and Natural Gas in the Postwar Period

| Region and year[a] | | Crude oil (million metric tons) | | | Oil products (million metric tons) | | | Natural gas (billion cubic metre) | | |
|---|---|---|---|---|---|---|---|---|---|---|
| | | World exports to[b] | Soviet exports to[c] | Soviet share | World exports to[b] | Soviet exports to[c] | Soviet share | World exports to[d] | Soviet exports to[c] | Soviet share |
| World | 1960 | 382.0 | 17.8 | 4.7% | n.a. | 15.4 | n.a. | n.a. | 0.2 | n.a. |
| | 1965 | 666.4 | 43.4 | 6.5% | 238.2 | 21.0 | 8.8% | 15.2 | 0.4 | 2.6% |
| | 1970 | 1,170.5 | 66.8 | 5.7% | 332.5 | 29.0 | 8.7% | 44.7 | 3.3 | 7.4% |
| | 1975 | 1,416.9 | 93.1 | 6.6% | 302.2 | 41.6 | 13.8% | 122.0 | 19.3 | 15.8% |
| | 1979 | 1,702.2 | 117.2 | 6.9% | 315.7 | 41.2 | 13.1% | 196.4[e] | 49.6 | 25.3% |
| CMEA | 1960 | 6.4 | 6.2 | 96.9% | 3.2 | 3.1 | 96.9% | 0.2 | 0.2 | n.a. |
| | 1965 | 18.9 | 18.3 | 96.8% | 4.9 | 4.3 | 87.8% | 0.4 | 0.4 | n.a. |
| | 1970 | 39.4 | 34.4 | 87.3% | 7.3 | 6.2 | 84.9% | 2.8 | 2.3 | 82.1% |
| | 1975 | 75.9 | 64.0 | 84.3% | 9.4 | 7.8 | 83.0% | 11.5 | 11.3 | 98.3% |
| | 1979 | 99.1 | 77.7 | 78.4% | 13.3 | 12.5 | 94.0% | 23.6 | 23.2 | 98.3% |
| Other Socialist + Finland | 1960 | 4.3 | 3.4 | 79.1% | n.a. | 4.7 | n.a. | —[f] | — | — |
| | 1965 | 7.3 | 6.0 | 82.2% | n.a. | 4.6 | n.a. | — | — | — |
| | 1970 | 18.8 | 12.7 | 67.6% | 9.3 | 5.0 | 53.8% | — | — | — |
| | 1975 | 17.0 | 7.7 | 45.3% | 8.6 | 7.0 | 81.4% | 0.7 | 0.7 | 100% |
| | 1979 | 23.6 | 11.6 | 49.2% | 5.9 | 5.5 | 93.2% | 1.9 | 1.9 | 100% |
| Western Europe | 1960 | 168.7 | 6.2 | 3.7% | n.a. | 5.9 | n.a. | — | — | 0% |
| | 1965 | 317.9 | 12.1 | 3.8% | 95.0 | 7.2 | 7.6% | 0.9 | — | 0% |
| | 1970 | 588.3 | 17.5 | 3.0% | 117.1 | 11.9 | 10.2% | 13.6 | 1.0 | 7.4% |
| | 1975 | 572.8 | 12.2 | 2.1% | 113.0 | 20.1 | 17.8% | 62.1 | 7.3 | 11.8% |
| | 1979 | 624.4 | 24.5 | 3.9% | 115.5 | 19.1 | 16.5% | 106.5 | 24.5 | 23.0% |

# The Soviet Union and World Trade in Oil and Gas

| | | | | | | | | |
|---|---|---|---|---|---|---|---|---|
| Other | 1960 | 108.8 | 1.2 | 1.1% | n.a. | 0.2 | n.a. | n.a. |
| Developed | 1965 | 172.7 | 2.3 | 1.3% | 84.1 | 1.6 | 1.9% | 13.4 |
| Capitalist | 1970 | 284.0 | 0.5 | 0.2% | 145.2 | 2.2 | 1.5% | 24.6 |
| | 1975 | 477.9 | 0.1 | negl. | 113.5 | 2.0 | 1.8% | 33.4 |
| | 1979 | 602.3 | 0.1 | negl. | 119.7 | 0.8 | 0.6% | 54.8 |
| Developing | 1960 | 92.0 | 0.7 | 0.8% | n.a. | 1.1 | n.a. | n.a. |
| Countries | 1965 | 145.8 | 4.1 | 2.8% | 44.1 | 1.8 | 4.1% | 0.4 |
| | 1970 | 224.9 | 2.0 | 0.9% | 51.8 | 1.7 | 3.3% | 0.5 |
| | 1975 | 264.6 | 2.0 | 0.8% | 59.3 | 2.5 | 4.2% | 2.0 |
| | 1979 | 334.1 | 3.1 | 0.9% | 64.2 | 3.1 | 4.8% | 2.1 |

*Notes:*

a) The regions are the same as for Table 4.2. Note particularly that the CMEA excludes the USSR.

b) The regional sub-totals do not add up exactly to the figure for total world exports because of rounding and because total world exports include those to the Soviet Union, but the Soviet Union is not included in any of the regional categories.

c) The regional sub-totals may not add up exactly to the figure for total world exports because of rounding and because the destination of some Soviet exports is unknown (see Table 4.2).

d) The regional sub-totals do not add up to the total figure for world exports because of roundings, differences resulting from conversion from measures of calorific content to volume, and because Soviet imports of natural gas are not included in any of the regional categories but are included in the figure for total world exports.

e) This figure is from *Petroleum Economist*, (August 1981): 337.

f) "—" represents none or none recorded in sources used.

*Sources:* Except where otherwise indicated, data on world exports of crude oil, oil products and natural gas are from United Nations, *World Energy Supplies*, various years, and the *1979 Yearbook of World Energy Statistics*. Data on Soviet exports and their breakdown by various regional destinations are from Table 4.2.

Western oil companies, who feared Soviet competition in the provision of oil to the world market. The new concerns have been sparked by Western governments, anxious about the political as well as economic implications of possible Soviet competition in the demand for oil on world markets. The new concerns centre on the slackening rate of growth of Soviet oil production in the late 1970s and increases in the ratio of Soviet output to proven reserves, which indicate a sharpening of this decline in the 1980s. They also focus attention on the rapid growth of demand for petroleum in the CMEA in the 1960s and 1970s, the important historic role of the USSR as supplier to the CMEA countries and the gradual decline in this role after 1970 (Table 4.3), as the CMEA countries sought to develop non-Soviet sources of supply. Together, these trends suggested 1) that after meeting its own and its CMEA partners' needs, the USSR should have less petroleum to export to other markets, and 2) that in the longer run, the CMEA as a whole and even the USSR itself might become net importers of oil. In the second event, the USSR and its allies would lose their position of relative independence from world markets for oil. Moreover, they would be converted from marginal net suppliers of oil to important new contenders for increasingly scarce world market supplies.

This prospect, and in particular the spectre of the USSR competing with the Western powers for OPEC oil, was raised most dramatically by the US Central Intelligence Agency in several well-publicised (and now much criticised) evaluations made public in 1977.[16] This is not the place to embark on a detailed review of the CIA reports and the critical literature which they have prompted.[17] The CIA position has since been modified.[18] Moreover, it has not been shared by other US government intelligence agencies, much less by those farther afield. Recently (September 1981), the US Defense Intelligence Agency issued a report containing a comparatively positive prognosis for Soviet oil production in the 1980s (while presenting a problematic outlook for the Soviet economy as a whole).[19]

Given the wide range of Western estimates of future Soviet oil balance,[20] it seems possible for the purposes of this chapter to concentrate on Soviet official projections. While they may prove overly optimistic, they are more conservative than several Western estimates.

The Soviet eleventh Five-Year-Plan (1981–85) essentially re-establishes the tenth plan targets for oil output, which were not met. If now achieved, these would entail an average annual rate of growth over the plan period in the range of 0.6 – 1.4 per cent. Compared with past rates of growth, the plan projects a levelling-off of Soviet production through 1985; but does not anticipate the peaking and rapid decline of output foreseen by the CIA.

What does this modest planned growth in the first half of the 1980s imply for Soviet exports? Oil export plans have not been made public, and projections of trends are compounded by uncertainties with regard to Soviet consumption of oil over the plan period. Official oil consumption estimates are also not available, and therefore must be deduced from planned rates of growth of national income. The Soviet planned rate of growth of oil output is well below the planned rate of growth of national income for 1981–85. It is unlikely that measures to conserve oil and to substitute other fuels can reduce the rate of growth of domestic oil consumption below the rate of growth of the economy as a whole.[21] The Soviet exportable surplus thus seems certain to erode if Soviet growth projections are fulfilled.

In an appendix we present several possible export outcomes, given a range of projected Soviet rates of growth of production and consumption, based for the most part on official plan targets for 1981–85. These calculations generally indicate that exports will decline over the period. In only one of the cases, where the higher rate of planned growth in oil production is achieved (1.4 per cent) and a well below plan (2.0 per cent) rate of growth in national income is attained, could the current (1979–80) levels of oil exports be maintained through 1985.

While the targeted range of growth in national income (3.4 – 3.7 per cent) is conservative by the standards of previous plans, the prospect of its fulfillment is still open to serious question.[22] A 2 per cent rate of growth would represent a very considerable plan failure, however. (In the tenth five-year-plan period, annual rates of growth of 3.8 per cent were achieved, compared to a targeted range of 4.4 to 5.1 per cent). It is, moreover, unlikely that the growth of national income would fall so short of plan targets without the planned rate of growth of oil production being affected. The Soviet exportable surplus therefore seems destined to decline.

If Soviet oil exports fall in 1981–85, how will the reductions be allocated? In a celebrated statement to the 34th Session of the CMEA, in June, 1980, Soviet Premier Kosygin promised that the 1980 level of Soviet oil supply to the CMEA countries would be maintained over the 1981–85, five-year-plan period (i.e., approximately 80 mmt per year).[23] While the East European CMEA countries have set very conservative five-year-plans for the period, designed to function within this supply constraint, unforeseen political and economic crises, such as the present situation in Poland, may compel the Soviet Union to raise exports to Eastern Europe above the 1980 level.

If the 1980 level of supply to Eastern Europe is maintained, then the brunt of any decline in overall oil exports must inevitably fall on Western markets. The appendix calculates the effect on residual exports to the West given various possible rates of growth of Soviet production and consumption. We see that within the targeted range of Soviet planned production and consumption, exports to the West could fall to zero by 1984 if commitments to the soft-currency markets are maintained. Given these commitments, only if an optimistic average annual rate of growth of oil output were attained while national income grew at a lower rate than planned, could annual oil exports to Western markets in the five-year period remain at roughly the 1980 level.

Would the USSR permit exports to the West to drop dramatically over the next five years? Such a drop would certainly entail a major loss in hard-currency earnings (which stood at $7.8 billion in 1979). Some decline in the volume of exports could be offset by increases in the world price of oil. This has been the thrust of recent Soviet oil export policy to the West. (For example, from 1978 to 1979 the volume of Soviet oil exports to hard-currency markets fell from 49.2 to 44.5 mmt while earnings increased by $2.7 billion.) The relative decline in the world price of oil in 1981 makes the maintenance of this strategy by no means certain, however.

These many uncertainties at the current juncture make it exceedingly difficult to predict the extent to which the volume of Soviet exports outside the CMEA will fall in 1981–85. The prospect of the serious erosion of its major source of hard currency earnings will certainly put pressure on the USSR to pursue policies of energy conservation and substitution. The development of gas exports to hard-currency markets gains urgency in these circumstances (see below).

Beyond 1985, many variables could ease the Soviet export squeeze. Some Western analysts are optimistic about the discovery of important new fields in Western Siberia, while others are more cautious in their assessment of the probabilities.[24] In any case, new fields could not be brought on stream immediately, and would probably only affect production trends after 1990. On the demand side, however, measures to improve the efficiency of oil use will have had more time to take effect by the late 1980s; and programmes already launched to develop alternative energy sources (especially nuclear power) will by then be well underway. Similar policies should ease the pressure of East European demand.

In sum, trends indicate a further weakening, through at least 1985, in the already declining Soviet position on the supply side of the international market. Without further offsetting increases in the world price of oil, the USSR faces the prospect of a serious loss in hard-currency earnings from oil exports in the next few years. Unless Soviet oil output drops sharply, however (a projection which even the CIA has now backed away from), the USSR does not seem destined to lose its overall net export position.

It is conceivable, under planned rates of growth and realistic, associated levels of oil consumption, that the CMEA countries as a group could slip into a small net import position in the mid-1980s (see Appendix). In the longer run, programmes now intensively underway to restrict regional oil consumption, and to increase future output of oil and alternative sources of energy, may bring a return to at least the net export position enjoyed by the CMEA at the end of the 1970s.

## THE SOVIET UNION AND WORLD TRADE IN NATURAL GAS

Over the 1960s and 1970s, the planned substitution of gas for oil in domestic use has enhanced Soviet oil export capability. While this strategy continues to be operative, natural gas has increasingly assumed as well an important direct role in Soviet fuels exports, a role which is destined to develop still more rapidly in the 1980s.

The Soviet natural gas industry does not have the long history of its petroleum counterpart. Prior to the 1950s, almost all gas produced domestically was "associated gas", a by-product of the exploitation of the Baku oil fields. Even in 1955, when total gas production was 9 bcm, one-third of this was still associated gas. Nevertheless, much of the associated gas at Baku was wastefully flared.[25]

The beginnings of a Soviet natural gas industry really date from the mid-1950s, with the decision to develop natural gas reserves in the North Caucasus (Stavropol and Krasnodar) and the Ukraine (Shebelinka). By the mid-1960s, production of natural gas had begun in Central Asia and the Volga Urals as well. The industry expanded rapidly in all of these regions throughout the 1960s, while its production potential continued unabated with the discovery of new, gigantic fields in West Siberia. Between 1955 and 1975, Soviet gas output rose from 9.0 bcm to 289.3 bcm, an average annual rate of growth over the entire period of 19 per cent. Around 60 per cent of the increase in volume came after 1965.

Foreign trade permitted domestic consumption of gas to outpace production. Gas exports did not begin in significant quantity until the late 1960s, and the Soviet Union was a net importer of gas from 1970 to 1973. Imports of natural gas were the result of two, long-term agreements concluded in the mid-1960s with Afghanistan and Iran. In return for Soviet industrial assistance, including material and technical assistance in the development of their natural gas resources and pipeline systems, these countries agreed to export specified amounts of gas to the USSR over a twenty-year, renewable period. These agreements formed an integral part of Soviet energy-development policy, which envisaged the supply to neighbouring parts of the USSR of relatively cheap Afghan and Iranian gas, in order to release additional quantities of Soviet gas for use in the industrial centres of European Russia and for export.[26]

A great upsurge in Soviet natural gas potential came with the opening up, beginning in the late 1960s, of giant gas fields in the northwestern part of Siberia. By 1975, these fields accounted for 14 per cent of total Soviet output, and this proportion has continued to increase rapidly since.

The major development of the Soviet gas industry coincided with the decline in the traditional sources of Soviet oil, and the migration of oil production activities northeastward to Siberia. The increasing shift in the locus of gas production activities to Siberia, however, faced Soviet planners with economic, technical and logistic difficulties similar to those encountered in the case of oil. The Siberian environment in which the most important Soviet gas reserves are now located is no less remote and inhospitable than that in which an increasing share of Soviet oil must be extracted.

The growth of domestic production was such that by 1974, Soviet exports of natural gas exceeded imports. This net export position has not only been sustained since, but has grown rapidly (table 4.2). An essential element in both domestic development and trade in gas has been the construction of an extensive, internal pipeline network, with links to foreign sources of supply in the Middle East and to export markets in Eastern and Western Europe. To date, Soviet gas trade has been almost exclusively by pipeline, with LNG shipments an exception.[27] The giant LNG export projects – North Star and Yakutia – proposed in the 1970s (and based on Western, especially American, technical and capital inputs) ran foul of US congressional restrictions and were never consummated. A recent Soviet-Japanese agreement, however, foresees the export of Soviet LNG from Sakhalin to Japan, beginning in 1988.[28]

Soviet trade in natural gas is the monopoly of a specialised, all-union foreign trade association subordinate to the Ministry of Foreign Trade, Sojuzgazexport. Like Sojuznefteexport, its petroleum counterpart, Sojuzgazexport has been sub-divided, since 1978, into constituent firms. Integas is responsible for trade in natural gas with Eastern Europe while Eximgas is responsible for trade with the rest of the world; Spetsgas handles trade in liquefied and special gases; and Transitgas arranges the transport of natural gas in foreign trade. Since gas pipelines have been so fundamental to Soviet gas trade, a vital role has been played by Soviet organizations specialising in their construction. Neftekhimpromexport, subordinate to the State Commitee for Foreign Economic Relations, is the organisation generally responsible for the construction of oil and gas pipelines abroad, and played a leading part in the construction of pipelines in Iran and Afghanistan for the import of gas from these countries. Soyuzintergazprom has been the vehicle for the development of pipeline links with the East European CMEA countries, and coordinated the joint construction of the Soyuz pipeline.

Soviet gas exports to Europe through the new pipeline facilities began in the late 1960s, with deliveries to Poland (beginning in 1966), to Czechoslovakia (1967) and to Austria (1968).[29] At this time, negotiations on gas exports were opened with Italy, West Germany and Japan; and discussions were undertaken within the CMEA with regard to the joint development of Soviet gas resources and pipeline capacity.

These negotiations were for long-term supply arrangements based on the so-called "compensation" format which had already been employed in the Soviet import agreements with Afghanistan and Iran.[30] In the case of gas exports, however, the Soviet role was reversed, with the USSR now seeking importer assistance in the development of its gas reserves and pipeline facilities in return for long-term supply commitments.

Compensation agreements calling for Western deliveries of large-diameter steel pipes in exchange for Soviet natural gas were concluded with Austria and Italy in the late 1960s. The most important gas-for-pipe deals with Western firms were concluded with Mannesmann of West Germany. Three successive agreements (in 1970, 1972 and 1974) together provided for total Soviet deliveries to Germany of about 275 bcm of natural gas extending from 1973 to the end of the century.

Initially, these long-term deals put a downward pressure on the price of imported gas in Western Europe. The principal existing supplier – the Netherlands – was even forced to reduce its price. Once in place, these agreements called for the renegotiation of prices on a regular basis, and the Soviet Union was able to exact significant price increases for its gas exports to Western Europe, especially in 1979–80.

The most important step in the export of Soviet gas to the CMEA countries came with the signing in 1974 of a multilateral agreement for development of the Orenburg natural gas fields and joint construction of a pipeline ("Soyuz") to deliver the gas to Eastern Europe. All six East European CMEA countries participated in the project, and deliveries to them through the new pipeline began in 1979. Under the compensation format of the agreement, 15.5 bcm of Soviet gas will be delivered to the six annually over a twenty-year period.[31]

Table 4.2 shows the rapid growth of Soviet exports of natural gas after 1975 on the basis of these various arrangements. All Soviet exports to date have been directed to Europe. The growth of exports to Western Europe is particularly marked, with nearly three-fourths of these in 1979 going to West Germany and Italy. Exports to the CMEA countries jumped after 1978, as the new Soyuz pipeline became operational in successive stages.

Soviet exports of natural gas to Western Europe were also scheduled for a significant increase, in 1981, when a trilateral "swap" agreement involving the Soviet Union, Iran and a West European consortium of gas utilities headed by Germany's Ruhrgas was to have become operative. Under the agreement (signed in 1975) the Soviet Union was to have exported 11 bcm of Soviet natural gas annually to Western Europe, while being compensated by offsetting shipments of Iranian gas. The latter would serve to increase supplies of Iranian gas to the Soviet Caucasus. Before it could be fully implemented, however, the agreement fell victim to the collapse of the Shah's government, and was unilaterally abrogated by the new revolutionary regime in 1979.[32]

Following Iran's withdrawal from the trilateral agreement, and as it became apparent that the situation in Iran would not permit its renegotiation in the foreseeable future, the remaining parties began to explore alternatives. Since early 1980, negotiations have been conducted by the Soviet Union with banking and industrial interests in a number of West European countries.[33] In return for Western material, technical and financial assistance in the further development of northwest Siberian gas deposits, and in the construction of a new pipeline (possibly a dual line) from these fields to Western Europe, the Soviet Union could supply the West European countries with between 30–60 bcm of natural gas annually over a twenty-year period, depending upon the pipeline capacity built. The projected supplies would increase the 1980 level of Soviet exports to Western Europe by 120–240 per cent.

The negotiations have encountered numerous problems, technical, commercial, financial and political; and their outcome remains in doubt. At the time of writing (September, 1981), there are signs that Soviet talks with the FRG, the principal West European national participant, have reached tentative agreement. It is possible, therefore, that the other pieces may now fall into place.

The details of the project (sometimes referred to as the Yamal, or Yamburg pipeline) remain unclear, however, especially with regard to the price and credit terms. The Soviet Union is apparently seeking to tie the price of gas to the fob price of crude oil, while the West Europeans are demanding a price linked to the closest substitute fuel, residual fuel oil. To finance purchases in the West for the pipeline, the Soviet Union sought a 7.75 per cent interest rate on combined official and private credits raised for the project. This would involve substantial interest rate subsidies by Western governments, but these may be at least partially made up in the price of Western materials and equipment.

The agreement would propel the USSR to a still more prominent position in international trade in natural gas. In 1980, the USSR surpassed the Netherlands in exports, and became the world's largest exporter of natural gas. (If present trends hold, it will overtake the United States by 1985 to become the world's leading producer as well.) Soviet exports reached 57.3 bcm in 1980 (Table 4.2), and constituted 28.4 per cent of total world exports (via pipeline and LNG).[34] They made up nearly 100 per cent of East European imports (Hungary imports small quantities of gas from Romania) and about 23 per cent of the West European import market, excluding Finland (Table 4.3).

It is this last share that will increase dramatically, as imports from the Netherlands (Western Europe's current major source of supply) taper off as projected, and if the northwest Siberian project is consummated. Soviet gas would then account for 50-60 per cent of total West European gas imports by the end of the 1980s.[35]

Will rapidly expanding hard currency earnings from gas exports compensate for lost earnings as oil exports decline? Too many "ifs" prevent any very conclusive answer to this question. However, if the 1979 relationship between oil and natural gas prices holds, and if Soviet hard-currency oil exports gradually decline to zero, then hard-currency gas exports would have to increase by 600 per cent over the 1979 level (to 175 bcm) to generate hard-currency revenues equal in purchasing power to those earned from oil exports in that year. This means that if the price index for Soviet oil and gas exports increases at the same rate as the overall price index for world imports (agricultural and manufactured products), then the Soviet Union will have to export to hard-currency markets 175 bcm of gas to offset the loss of hard-currency earnings from oil. Only then will the USSR be able to maintain the *real* value of its hard-currency earnings.[36]

It is unlikely that gas export hard-currency earnings could increase sufficiently to compensate in real terms for a loss of all hard-currency oil revenues. The 1980 volume of gas exports to hard-currency purchasers (24.7 bcm) plus the exports envisaged via the projected northwest Siberian pipeline (30–60 bcm) would yield a level of only some 55–85 bcm by the late 1980s.[37] It will take another project (or series of projects) of at least the same magnitude to achieve the necessary offset. Moreover, only when the hard-currency costs of pipeline construction are fully paid off will the increased gas exports resulting from the project yield a net gain to the balance of payments.

## COMPARATIVE SOVIET CAPABILITIES IN WORLD OIL AND GAS TRADE

This chapter has sought to provide the reader with an overview of Soviet participation in international trade in two, closely interrelated, energy-bearing commodities: oil and gas. We have tried in particular to identify important, long-term trends and to analyse in some detail prospects for Soviet trade in these commodities in the 1980s. We expect the Soviet Union to remain a net exporter of both gas and oil over the decade, and to continue to import only small amounts of the two commodities from the Middle East. The most dramatic change anticipated will be the further decline in the volume of oil exports to the West and the ascendancy of gas exports in Soviet foreign energy relations.

In conclusion, let us review the results of our analysis in terms of comparative Soviet export capabilities in oil and gas and the contrasting characteristics of world trade in the two commodities. We shall argue that the potential Soviet role in international trade in gas is far greater than in oil, where its impact was never more than marginal and is now diminishing. Even at their zenith, oil exports provided the USSR with negligible commodity power on international markets. Their primary effect was indirect, and on the demand side. They served, by rendering the CMEA largely self-sufficient, to limit CMEA purchases of oil on international markets.

Soviet supplies of oil and oil products to world markets have been conducted within the established market framework. Their principal impact on the institutional structure of the market was also indirect. As observers are fond of pointing out, Soviet re-entry into the international arena contributed in the early 1960s to a weakening in the international price and helped to convince oil exporting countries in the Third World of the need to establish OPEC.[38] The USSR has remained outside OPEC, however, while operating under (and generally profiting from) the conditions set by the organisation. In its operations on the world oil market, the USSR has maintained a relatively low profile by acting not very differently from one of the large, Western "independent" oil companies.

Concerns that the levelling-off of Soviet oil production could have a disruptive effect on the world market for oil seem unfounded at this juncture. The contraction of Soviet oil exports to the West, initiated in 1979, is likely to continue to be gradual and the quantities involved are marginal in terms of world supply. In the early 1980s they are occurring at a time when the world market is slack and world prices are softening. Moreover, as detailed in the Appendix, declines in Soviet exports to the West are being offset by reduced East European imports of OPEC oil. The CMEA as a whole therefore seems likely to remain a modest net exporter of oil through 1985. In these circumstances, economic pressures for a conceivable Soviet "grab" for Middle Eastern oil are neither very strong nor very immediate.[39]

In contrast to oil, Soviet export operations in natural gas have been far more "visible," generally conducted under the aegis of well-publicised international agreements. To understand this, it is important to bear in mind some fundamental differences in international trade in the two commodities.

International trade in gas remains much smaller than that in oil, relative to the size and growth of world reserves. Transport problems and attendant costs have impeded the development of gas trade. Unlike trade in oil, which is conducted primarily by relatively cheap tanker transport, international trade in gas is principally by pipeline. While for oil, tanker transport is cheaper than pipeline transport, LNG transport costs are higher than the costs of transport by gas pipeline.

The result has not only been to retard the development of gas trade, but to reduce its flexibility and to segment the potential market. It is in fact questionable whether one should speak of a world "market" for gas, in the absence of a unified market structure. Gas is exported under the aegis of large-scale, bilateral agreements, often providing for the construction of costly pipeline systems as well as for long-term trade in the commodity.

It is partly for these reasons that, despite the dominance of a few exporters, world trade in gas is not governed, as is oil, by a producer cartel. The OPEC countries themselves do not have the producer potential for such a role. They accounted in 1980 for an estimated 77 per cent of world (and 90 per cent of non-socialist) oil reserves, but only 38 per cent (60 per cent of non-socialist) reserves of natural gas.[40]

Because of transport costs, most gas produced is in fact not exportable, and currently only 37.5 per cent of proven gas reserves are available for export.[41] Over half of these are located in the Soviet Union. The other major potential gas exporting country – Iran – is farther removed from major markets and, as we saw, was forced to collaborate with the USSR in order to break into the European market. Moreover, under the revolutionary Islamic regime, Iran has abandoned its strategy for developing gas exports.

It is these circumstances which both enhance and inhibit the potential Soviet role in international trade in gas. The Soviet Union already dominates the East European market for gas and occupies an increasingly important share of West European imports. Current plans for further Soviet export development and the prospective decline in sources of supply within Western Europe indicate a dominant Soviet role in this market by the end of the decade, with Algeria as its principal potential competitor.

The potential Soviet impact on world trade in gas is, however, limited by the segmented nature of this trade, which restricts Soviet influence to specific markets. While the Soviet Union has been able to exert some power over the price of imported gas in Western Europe, its range of influence even there is limited by the terms of alternative sources of supply and close substitute fuels. Moreover, Soviet gas is, as we have stressed, not sold like oil at the spot price for cash payment, but is supplied under the complex terms of long-term agreements, from which the price of gas cannot easily be separated.

Because of the characteristics of the product and the structure of the market, gas does not offer the USSR the flexible instrument of international policy provided by oil, despite greater gas export capability. Like gold, "black gold" could easily be sold on world markets to earn convertible currencies as required. It could also be readily diverted from one market to another to serve a variety of foreign policy objectives. Gas exports lack this flexibility, which is an important source of oil's power as an export commodity.

How might the Soviet Union use the leverage gained through its expanded role as natural gas supplier to Eastern and Western Europe, and what are the limits on its power in this regard? These are questions of great current interest and discussion, and ones which the authors have sought to address at some length elsewhere.[42] For the purposes at hand, it may be noted that Soviet supplies of natural gas still serve a relatively small share of total energy consumption in both areas (5 per cent in Eastern Europe and 2 per cent in Western Europe in 1979). Moreover, the increased dependence on Soviet natural gas is accompanied by decreased dependence on Soviet oil. Finally, there are important economic and political constraints on Soviet ability to use any apparent leverage gained from gas exports.

The "compensation" agreement under which most Soviet gas is exported exemplify the degree of interdependence which is involved in the growth of Soviet exports. The Soviet Union has relied heavily on partner financial, material and technical assistance in the development of its gas export capability. While the Soviet Union built its own fleet of oil tankers, and constructed an oil pipeline system to serve European consumers in the face of restrictions, it is far more dependent on Western technology for the continuing exploitation of its gas export potential. Present Soviet reliance on Western supplies of pipe, compressor units and pipelaying equipment is the result of the magnitude of its requirements for transport development and the extremely difficult environmental conditions in which the development must occur.

We have emphasised throughout this chapter the importance of hydrocarbon exports to Soviet foreign trade policy. Oil, a traditional Russian export, has been a major source of hard-currency income to finance the import requirements of Soviet industrial development plans. Its function in this respect has recently been supplemented significantly by the growth of gas exports. Further growth in gas will help to offset the decline, since 1978, in the volume of Soviet oil exports to hard-currency markets. As we have shown, however, the Soviet Union's combined hard-currency revenues from oil and gas exports are unlikely to remain – at least over the coming decade – at the levels in real terms which they attained in 1980. This negative trend in its hard-currency balance of payments will constrain the Soviet Union's actual ability to wield any potential leverage gained from its increased share of European imports of natural gas.

# APPENDIX

**Projected Soviet Oil Exports in the 1981–85 Plan Period**

In the accompanying tables we present various scenarios of the potential for Soviet oil exports to hard-currency markets in the period 1981–85. The calculations use official Soviet plan targets for the period, and official Soviet statements regarding oil exports to the CMEA over 1981–85, to draw out the trade implications of the eleventh Soviet five-year-plan.

The following assumptions have been made for each of the four scenarios presented.
1) Except where indicated, plan targets are met.
2) The annual average rate of growth in Soviet oil consumption will be the same as the annual average rate of growth in the national income, i.e., a national oil consumption/national income elasticity coefficient of unity. This assumption is based upon estimates that over the period 1975–79 the average income elasticity of consumption was between 1.1 (based on United Nations data) and 1.3 (based on the authors' calculations). With oil conservation and substitution programmes underway, the coefficient is likely to fall somewhat during 1981–85, but not below unity.
3) Soviet imports of oil will remain at the modest 1979 level of 8 mmt.
4) Soviet oil exports to the soft-currency markets (CMEA, other socialist and Finland) will remain at estimated 1980 levels of 110 mmt, based on Soviet statements to the 1980 & 1981 sessions of the CMEA (see text).

The four scenarios shown below employ 0.6 and 1.4 per cent as the projected annual rates of growth in oil production, according to the upper and lower limits of official Soviet five-year-plan targets. Each of these limits is then matched with planned and below-plan rates of growth of national income. The below plan rates of growth reflect the expectations of several western assessments of Soviet five-year-plan prospects.

The two extreme cases are presented in Scenarios 2 and 3. Scenario 2 shows that if officially planned rates of growth in national income (3.4 – 3.7 per cent) are met, and the lower level of growth in oil production is achieved, the exportable surplus available for hard-currency markets will disappear by 1984. The other extreme, Scenario 3, where the higher rate of growth in oil production is combined with below-plan rates of growth in national income (2.0–2.5 per cent), shows that the exportable surplus available to hard-currency markets would remain around 50 mmt per year throughout the entire 1981–85 period, that is, approximately at 1980 levels. The mid-range scenarios (1 and 4) result in reduced exportable surplus to hard-currency markets of between 4–24 mmt in 1985.

In the extreme case of Scenario 2, where the exportable surplus to hard-currency markets disappears by 1984, the USSR would remain faced with difficult adjustments. It would have to curtail its domestic consumption of oil, lower its exports to soft-currency markets, increase its imports of oil, or attempt some combination of these. If confronted with these alternatives, and the USSR chooses only to increase its oil imports, these would have to rise to as much as 19 mmt by 1985 in order to maintain CMEA commitments and meet projected domestic consumption levels. At current (1981) prices for OPEC oil, this would entail a hard-currency expenditure of $4.5–4.9 billion in 1985. (In comparison, hard-currency earnings from oil exports were $7.8 billion in 1979). The resultant burden on the Soviet Union's hard-currency balance of payments would make this a most unattractive option. If the USSR wanted instead to reduce its oil exports to soft-currency markets, it would have difficulty in that much of this trade is conducted under five-year trade agreements, wherein export volumes may have been set for the entire term. Thus, the most probable outcome under Scenario 2 conditions is that domestic oil consumption will slow, thereby constraining overall growth in national income.

What are the implications of these various scenarios for the net oil export position of the CMEA as a bloc? Should the conditions of Scenario 2 prevail, the CMEA would turn into a net oil importing region by 1985. Assuming that East European oil imports from extra-CMEA sources remained at estimated 1980 levels, the CMEA sources remained at estimated 1980 levels, the CMEA would have net imports of around 20–25 mmt. (In 1979, the region's net oil exports were about 40 mmt.) Indications are, however, that the East European countries have reduced their imports of oil from OPEC during 1981, and are likely to continue this trend over the 1981–85 period. Any decline in Eastern Europe's oil imports from non-Soviet sources would offset the decline in Soviet exports to the West.

Under Scenarios 1 and 4, the CMEA could also become a small (under 5 mmt) net importer of oil, but only in the unlikely event that

Eastern Europe's imports from OPEC were maintained at 1980 levels through 1985. On the other hand, should the conditions of Scenario 3 be met, the CMEA would remain a net exporting region; and if the downward trend in Eastern Europe's imports from OPEC continued, the CMEA's net position would actually improve.

Scenario 1 Planned Rates of Growth of National Income with Upper End of Targeted Rate of Growth in Oil Production Achieved

| Year | AARG* in Oil Production of 1.3 percent | AARG in Oil Consumption of 3.4–3.7 percent | Imports | Exportable Surplus Total | Soft-currency Markets | Hard-Currency Markets |
|---|---|---|---|---|---|---|
| 1981 | 611 | 465–467 | 8 | 152–154 | 110 | 42–44 |
| 1982 | 620 | 481–484 | 8 | 144–147 | 110 | 34–47 |
| 1983 | 629 | 497–502 | 8 | 135–140 | 110 | 25–30 |
| 1984 | 637 | 514–520 | 8 | 125–131 | 110 | 15–21 |
| 1985 | 646 | 532–540 | 8 | 114–122 | 110 | 4–12 |

Scenario 2 Planned Rates of Growth of National Income with Lower End of Targeted Rate of Growth in Oil Production Achieved

| Year | AARG in Oil Production of 0.6 percent | AARG in Oil Consumption of 3.4–3.7 percent | Imports | Exportable Surplus Total | Soft-Currency Markets | Hard-Currency Markets |
|---|---|---|---|---|---|---|
| 1981 | 607 | 465–467 | 8 | 148–150 | 110 | 38–40 |
| 1982 | 611 | 481–484 | 8 | 135–138 | 110 | 25–28 |
| 1983 | 615 | 497–502 | 8 | 121–126 | 110 | 11–16 |
| 1984 | 619 | 514–520 | 8 | 107–113 | 110 | (–3)–3 |
| 1985 | 623 | 532–540 | 8 | 91–99 | 110 | (–19)–(–11) |

Scenario 3  Below Plan Rates of Growth of National Income with Upper End of Targeted Rate of Growth in Oil Production Achieved

| Year | AARG in Oil Production of 1.4 percent | AARG of Oil Consumption of 2.0–2.5 percent | Imports | Exportable Surplus Total | Soft-Currency Markets | Hard-Currency Markets |
|---|---|---|---|---|---|---|
| 1981 | 611 | 459–461 | 8 | 158–160 | 110 | 48–50 |
| 1982 | 620 | 468–473 | 8 | 155–160 | 110 | 45–50 |
| 1983 | 629 | 478–485 | 8 | 152–159 | 110 | 42–49 |
| 1984 | 637 | 487–497 | 8 | 148–158 | 110 | 38–48 |
| 1985 | 646 | 497–509 | 8 | 145–157 | 110 | 35–47 |

Scenario 4  Below Plan Rates of Growth of National Income with Lower End of Targeted Rate of Growth in Oil Production Achieved

| Year | AARG in Oil Production of 0.6 percent | AARG of Oil Consumption of 2.0–2.5 percent | Imports | Exportable Surplus Total | Soft-Currency Markets | Hard-Currency Markets |
|---|---|---|---|---|---|---|
| 1981 | 607 | 459–461 | 8 | 154–156 | 110 | 44–46 |
| 1982 | 611 | 468–473 | 8 | 146–151 | 110 | 36–41 |
| 1983 | 615 | 478–485 | 8 | 138–145 | 110 | 28–35 |
| 1984 | 619 | 487–497 | 8 | 130–140 | 110 | 20–30 |
| 1985 | 623 | 497–509 | 8 | 122–134 | 110 | 12–24 |

# 5 Soviet Coal Exports

## Svjetlana Adler and Harriet Matejka

In the early 1970s oil, which was transported over long distances, and coal, which was locally mined, were the two chief sources of primary energy in the industrial countries. Since the end of 1973, however, the price of petroleum has increased six times and other sources of energy have been substituted for oil. As a result, the pattern of consumption in the industrial countries has become more evenly distributed among five sources of primary energy: coal, oil, gas, nuclear power and renewable energy, of which hydro-power is the most important. Simultaneously, attention has been focused on coal reserves located far from the industrial centres which, because of the price rise, can now be profitably developed despite the transport costs involved. A substantial and, perhaps, major part of these is to be found in the Soviet Union.

This chapter examines the prospects for Soviet coal output and exports. After a review of the Soviet Union's present levels of coal production and consumption, the direction and evolution of Soviet exports are discussed. Then the USSR's major coal basins and their projected development are briefly described and the forecasts for Soviet coal production to 1985 and 1990 analysed. Finally, the projected Soviet coal export potential is considered and the conclusion drawn that actual exports are unlikely either to reach this potential or substantially to exceed 40 million tons in 1990.

### I
### 1950–1980

PRODUCTION AND CONSUMPTION

The USSR is the world's largest coal producer in terms of tonnage. It is, however, only the second largest producer, after the United

States, in terms of heating value, owing to the substantial share of low-grade hard coal and of lignite in the composition of its production. The breakdown of its output between coal, lignite and brown coal, and between primary and secondary production is shown in Table 5.1. As may be seen, some three-quarters of its primary production consists of hard coal compared with 95 per cent in the case of the United States.[1] The remaining primary production of the Soviet Union is composed of lignite and peat, in that order.

The Soviet Union's policy with respect to coal has changed twice since the end of the Second World War. In the early 1950s, coal accounted for over 70 per cent of the Soviet Union's total fuel production as measured in standard fuel units. In the years that followed, although coal production expanded steadily the emphasis shifted to oil and natural gas so that, by the mid 1970s, hydrocarbons accounted for some 70 per cent of total fuel production and coal for only 30 per cent. However, 1975 brought an increase in world oil prices and the recognition that coal reserves were immensely greater than those of petroleum and natural gas. This prompted a second policy reversal favouring the maintenance – and perhaps slight increase – of the share of coal in fuel production.

Policy changes prior to 1975 are reflected in the variations in the rate of increase of coal production shown in Table 5.2. The total output of solid fuels rose by 83 per cent between 1950 and 1960 (despite a small dip that year) but by only 17 per cent between 1960 and 1970 and 10 per cent between 1970 and 1975. The pattern was the same but the rates of increase more rapid in the case of hard coal whose production rose by 92, 22 and 12 per cent in the three periods respectively. As for the output of lignite and brown coal, it rose by 68 per cent from 1950 to 1960, by as little as 8 per cent in the 1960s.

As in the case of production, the rate of expansion of consumption declined from 1950 to 1980. The increase in consumption was 69 per cent between 1950 and 1960, falling back to 13 per cent from 1960 to 1970, still further to 10 per cent between 1970 and 1975 and, finally, to only 4 per cent between 1975 and 1979. While consumption rose more slowly than production during the twenty years from 1950 to 1970, its rate of increase subsequently drew even with that of production. Thus, although the policy switch in favour of coal was followed by a decline in the rise of both production and consumption, the fact that consumption continues to keep pace with production may be an indication that the policy change is beginning to take effect.

Table 5.1 Soviet Production of Solid Fuels, 1950–1981 (Quantities in thousand metric tons)

|  | Primary | | | Secondary | | | |
|---|---|---|---|---|---|---|---|
|  | Total | Coal | Lignite and Brown Coal | Total | Hard Coal Briquettes | Coke Oven Coke | Lignite and Peat Briquettes |
| 1950 | 297.089 | 185.225 | 111.864 | 27.728 | — | 27.728 | — |
| 1951 | 321.728 | 202.464 | 119.264 | 30.692 | — | 30.692 | — |
| 1952 | 338.075 | 215.009 | 123.066 | 33.733 | — | 33.733 | — |
| 1953 | 369.022 | 224.315 | 134.707 | 36.908 | — | 36.908 | — |
| 1954 | 392.209 | 243.681 | 148.528 | 40.320 | — | 40.320 | — |
| 1955 | 442.036 | 276.615 | 165.421 | 43.593 | — | 43.593 | — |
| 1956 | 473.943 | 304.002 | 169.941 | 46.629 | — | 46.629 | — |
| 1957 | 518.361 | 328.502 | 189.859 | 48.634 | — | 48.634 | — |
| 1958 | 535.237 | 338.900 | 196.337 | 50.893 | — | 50.893 | — |
| 1959 | 547.023 | 348.945 | 198.078 | 53.403 | — | 53.403 | — |
| 1960 | 543.749 | 355.918 | 187.831 | 56.233 | — | 56.233 | — |
| 1961 | 535.662 | 355.815 | 179.847 | 58.604 | — | 58.604 | — |
| 1962 | 528.294 | 363.430 | 164.864 | 66.600 | 1.281 | 60.929 | 4.390 |
| 1963 | 563.497 | 369.302 | 194.195 | 69.507 | 1.366 | 63.876 | 4.265 |
| 1964 | 583.502 | 381.266 | 202.236 | 72.478 | 1.402 | 66.282 | 4.794 |
| 1965 | 590.837 | 397.646 | 193.191 | 73.980 | 1.394 | 67.462 | 5.124 |
| 1966 | 616.213 | 406.567 | 209.646 | 75.075 | 1.385 | 68.493 | 5.197 |
| 1967 | 615.759 | 414.087 | 201.672 | 76.684 | 1.435 | 69.897 | 5.352 |
| 1968 | 601.247 | 416.224 | 185.023 | 78.481 | 1.472 | 71.505 | 5.504 |
| 1969 | 608.265 | 425.795 | 182.470 | 80.309 | 1.478 | 73.533 | 5.298 |
| 1970 | 634.860 | 432.715 | 202.125 | 82.617 | 1.448 | 75.404 | 5.765 |
| 1971 | 645.854 | 441.416 | 204.438 | 86.017 | 1.444 | 78.329 | 6.244 |
| 1972 | 664.827 | 451.119 | 213.708 | 87.794 | 1.488 | 79.773 | 6.533 |
| 1973 | 673.164 | 461.223 | 211.941 | 89.546 | 1.474 | 81.401 | 6.673 |
| 1974 | 670.305 | 473.394 | 196.931 | 90.949 | 1.363 | 82.641 | 6.945 |
| 1975 | 698.691 | 484.675 | 214.016 | 91.880 | 0.720 | 83.453 | 7.617 |
| 1976 | 687.108 | 494.377 | 192.731 | 92.954 | 0.854 | 84.400 | 7.700 |
| 1977 | 704.481 | 499.768 | 204.713 | 94.555 | 0.855 | 86.000 | 7.700 |
| 1978 | 691.807 | 501.536 | 190.271 | 94.002 | 0.700 | 86.400 | 7.302 |
| 1979 | 700.000 | 495.000 | 205.000 | 94.650 | 0.650 | 86.500 | 7.500 |
| 1980 | 718.000[a] | 492.900[c] | 225.100[d] | | | 87.000[e] | |
| 1981 | 704.000[b] | | | | | | |

Sources: *World Energy Supplies 1950–1974* (New York: United Nations, Department of Economic and Social Affairs, 1976—Statistical Papers, Series J, no. 19) p. 191; *1979 Yearbook of World Energy Statistics* (New York: United Nations, Department of International Economic and Social Affairs, 1981–Series J, no. 23) pp. 383–418.

Notes:

a) *Economicheskaya Gazetta,* February 1982, p. 2.
b) *Pravda,* January 24, 1982, p. 1.

Table 5.2 Soviet Production, Trade and Consumption of Solid Fuels (quantities in thousand metric tons of coal equivalent)

|      | Production | Imports | Exports | Consumption |
|------|------------|---------|---------|-------------|
| 1950 | 220.469    | 9.068   | 1.730   | 227.807     |
| 1951 | 238.268    | 8.217   | 1.330   | 245.155     |
| 1952 | 252.145    | 9.033   | 1.510   | 259.668     |
| 1953 | 268.118    | 9.234   | 3.900   | 273.452     |
| 1954 | 293.782    | 10.239  | 5.250   | 298.772     |
| 1955 | 332.302    | 9.069   | 5.768   | 335.602     |
| 1956 | 344.738    | 6.931   | 7.441   | 344.228     |
| 1957 | 375.551    | 3.757   | 10.748  | 368.559     |
| 1958 | 385.992    | 4.436   | 12.126  | 378.302     |
| 1959 | 393.001    | 4.951   | 13.288  | 384.664     |
| 1960 | 393.485    | 5.368   | 14.696  | 384.156     |
| 1961 | 389.613    | 5.316   | 17.831  | 377.098     |
| 1962 | 392.602    | 5.482   | 22.340  | 375.745     |
| 1963 | 410.069    | 5.689   | 24.778  | 390.979     |
| 1964 | 425.445    | 5.695   | 27.227  | 403.912     |
| 1965 | 429.534    | 7.396   | 25.800  | 411.130     |
| 1966 | 444.499    | 7.889   | 25.435  | 426.953     |
| 1967 | 450.987    | 8.416   | 25.637  | 433.767     |
| 1968 | 446.831    | 7.520   | 24.692  | 429.660     |
| 1969 | 456.233    | 7.819   | ˙26.895 | 437.157     |
| 1970 | 450.460    | 7.782   | 24.289  | 433.954     |
| 1971 | 458.325    | 9.220   | 24.732  | 442.813     |
| 1972 | 469.991    | 10.349  | 24.282  | 456.059     |
| 1973 | 474.806    | 10.713  | 24.523  | 460.996     |
| 1974 | 477.277    | 10.346  | 25.478  | 462.145     |
| 1975 | 490.294    | 10.670  | 24.914  | 476.050     |
| 1976 | 505.674    | 10.206  | 26.363  | 489.517     |
| 1977 | 514.850    | 9.786   | 27.427  | 497.209     |
| 1978 | 511.208    | 10.532  | 25.583  | 496.157     |
| 1979 | 511.021    | 10.675  | 24.834  | 496.862     |

*Source: World Energy Supplies 1950–1974,* 1976, p. 159; *1979 Yearbook of World Energy Statistics,* 1981, p. 314.

*Note:* No figures for bunkers or additions to stocks are available for the USSR.

---

Notes: Table 5.1 (continued)

c) Figures prepared for the ECE's Coal Committee, seventy-seventh session, 21–24 September 1981.
d) Difference between the total figure and the figure for coal.

Table 5.3 Soviet Hard Coal Exports, 1950–1981 (thousand metric tons)

|  | Total | Centrally Planned Economies | Western Europe | Japan | Other |
|---|---|---|---|---|---|
| 1950 | 1.100 | 55[a] | 36[b] | 59 | 950 |
| 1951 | 700 | 167[a] | 328[b] | — | 205 |
| 1952 | 700 | 253[a] | 364[b] | 30 | 53 |
| 1953 | 3.000 | 2.148[a] | 480[b] | 211 | 161 |
| 1954 | 3.900 | 2.624[a] | 786[b] | 92 | 398 |
| 1955 | 4.310 | 2.330 | 1.710 | 70 | 200 |
| 1956 | 5.670 | 2.930 | 2.490 | 70 | 180 |
| 1957 | 8.770 | 5.640 | 2.600 | 390 | 140 |
| 1958 | 12.150 | 8.170 | 3.460 | 440 | 80 |
| 1959 | 13.300 | 8.710 | 4.160 | 380 | 50 |
| 1960 | 14.700 | 9.250 | 4.830 | 540 | 80 |
| 1961 | 17.850 | 11.350 | 5.190 | 910 | 400 |
| 1962 | 22.350 | 14.700 | 6.280 | 1.140 | 230 |
| 1963 | 24.780 | 15.200 | 8.480 | 960 | 140 |
| 1964 | 27.230 | 17.310 | 8.415 | 1.090 | 415 |
| 1965 | 25.800 | 16.540 | 7.550 | 1.230 | 480 |
| 1966 | 25.435 | 15.955 | 7.510 | 1.590 | 380 |
| 1967 | 25.640 | 15.080 | 7.550 | 2.380 | 630 |
| 1968 | 24.690 | 13.950 | 7.980 | 2.730 | 30 |
| 1969 | 26.895 | 14.940 | 8.080 | 3.200 | 675 |
| 1970 | 28.240 | 16.420 | 8.305 | 2.855 | 660 |
| 1971 | 24.860 | 15.150 | 6.710 | 2.450 | 550 |
| 1972 | 24.410 | 14.820 | 6.490 | 2.490 | 610 |
| 1973 | 24.510 | 14.540 | 6.610 | 2.830 | 530 |
| 1974 | 26.210 | 15.000 | 7.400 | 3.230 | 580 |
| 1975 | 26.140 | 15.250 | 6.980 | 3.300 | 610 |
| 1976 | 26.900 | 15.140 | 7.940 | 3.230 | 590 |
| 1977 | 28.190 | 16.000 | 8.000 | 3.140 | 1.100 |
| 1978 | 26.700 | 15.700 | 7.300 | 2.500 | 1.200 |
| 1979 | 26.500[d] | 16.000 | 7.000 | 2.300 | 1.200 |
| 1980 | 26.000[cd] | 16.300[c] | 6.500[c] | 2.000[c] | 1.200[c] |
| 1981 | 21.000[c] |  |  |  |  |

Sources: *Foreign Trade of the USSR, 1918–1966* (Moscow: Ministry of Foreign Trade, Finansi i Statistika, 1969) pp. 126–127. *World Energy Supplies*, 1955–1958, pp. 47–51; 1958–1961, pp. 47–51; 1961–1964, pp. 41–45; 1964–1967, pp. 41–45; 1968–1971, pp. 43–47; 1971–1975, pp. 50–55; 1973–1978, pp. 114–119. *1979 Yearbook of World Energy Statistics*, p. 411.

# EXPORTS

The 5 per cent difference between domestic production and consumption goes for export. It is composed essentially of hard coal but also includes a few million tons of coke. In 1980, it is estimated that 26 million metric tons of coal and 5.7 million metric tons of coke were exported.[2]

Despite the small percentage of its production which goes for export, the Soviet Union ranked as the world's fourth largest exporter of hard coal after the United States, Australia, and Poland until 1980. Its exports account for some 14 per cent of the world total, more than twice the average share of the exporting countries in world exports of hard coal. But to assume on the strength of this fact that the Soviet Union has price-making power on the coal market would be to ignore the pattern of Soviet hard coal exports shown in Tables 5.3 and 5.4, and its implications.

The Soviet Union does not sell in a single market. It sells 60 per cent or more of its exports to other centrally planned economies or to developing countries on a series of separate markets established by the bilateral balancing agreements made necessary by the inconvertibility of partner currencies. Only the remaining 35–40 per cent is sold on a market unified by a multilateral payments system. While the Soviet Union may well enjoy monopoly power in the trade it conducts on a bilateral balancing basis, the same does not seem true for other forms of coal trade where the Soviet market share dwindles to average.

After the Second World War, Soviet exports were resumed and rose rapidly with the end of the Korean war, as Table 5.3 and Figure

---

*Notes:*

a) These figures may be incomplete. The identified Centrally Planned Economies during 1950–1954 were Bulgaria, the German Democratic Republic, Hungary and Poland, together with Czechoslovakia in 1952, 1953 and 1954.

b) These figures may be incomplete. The identified western European countries during this period were France and Italy in 1950; Austria, Finland, France and Italy in 1952; and Belgium, Finland, France, Italy and Greece in 1953 and 1954.

c) Figures prepared for the ECE's Coal Committee, seventy-seventh session, 21–24 September 1981.

d) Lower figures of 25.800 million tons in 1979 and 24.500 million tons in 1980 are given in *Rynki węglowe* 5/1982.

5.1 indicate. Five years later, they were four times as high; ten years later, over eight times as high and, by 1964, more than nine times as high as they had been at the end of the war. The increase in exports was particularly rapid towards western Europe where they appear to have been seven times as high in 1958 as they were in 1953, and almost eighteen times as high in 1963. Exports to the Centrally Planned Economies, by contrast, rose slightly more slowly than total exports and exports to Japan initially moved very much more slowly. But, in contrast to exports to both the Centrally Planned Economies and western Europe which tended to level out after 1964, exports to Japan pursued their expansion and reached their peak in 1975. Thereafter, they declined and were thus responsible, together with the fall in sales to the West, for the contraction in total exports which set in after 1977. The reduction in exports to both Japan and western Europe was associated with an extraordinarily rapid expansion of American and Australian sales of hard coal to both destinations.[3]

## II

## Prospects to 1990

The Soviet Union's production of solid fuels has thus stagnated since the middle of the 1970s; its output of hard coal actually declined in 1979 and 1980 and, as consumption has been maintained at some 95 per cent of production, so did exports which continued to fall in 1981. The outlook for both production and exports depends on the USSR's reserves of solid fuels and its ability to exploit them. Its reserves and their development are examined in the next few pages; plans and forecasts for output and exports in the next section.

## RESERVES AND THEIR DEVELOPMENT

It must first be said that the Soviet Union's reserves of coal are huge. According to its own estimates,[4] they amount to 6970 billion metric tons, 5700 billion tons of which are recoverable with present technology. Of the latter figure, however, over 3500 billion metric tons, or 60 per cent, are inferred reserves located in the Tugunska basin (estimated to have over 2000 billion metric tons) and in the Lena basin, (estimated to have over 1500 billion metric tons). Neither of these sites has yet been explored or is likely to be exploited in the near future. Measured reserves, (i.e., proved and probable) which

## Soviet Coal Exports

COAL EXPORTS
(MILLION METRIC TONS)

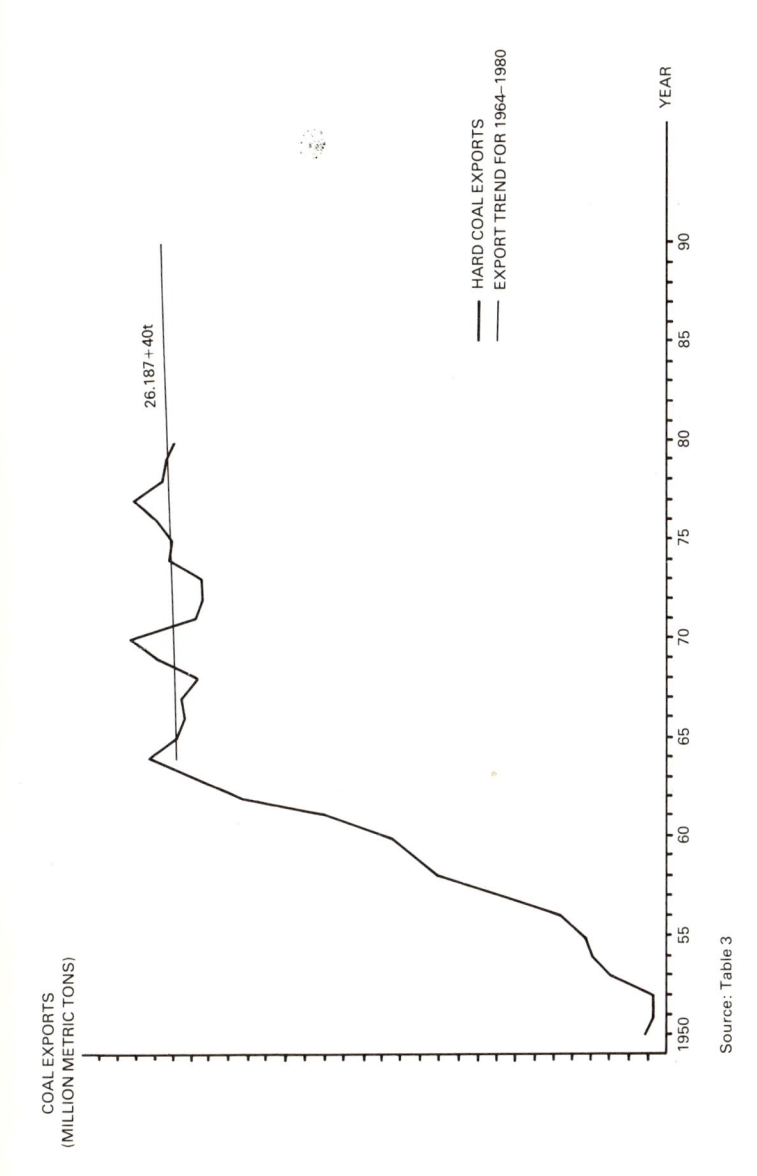

26.187 + 40t

—— HARD COAL EXPORTS
—— EXPORT TREND FOR 1964–1980

YEAR

Source: Table 3

FIGURE 5.1  Export Trend, 1950–1990

Table 5.4 The Direction of Soviet Hard Coal Exports, 1950–1980 (percentage distribution) (total exports = 100)

|      | Centrally Planned Economies | Western Europe | Japan | Other |
|------|---|---|---|---|
| 1950 | 5[a]  | 3[b]  | 5  | 87 |
| 1951 | 24[a] | 47[b] | —  | 29 |
| 1952 | 36[a] | 52[b] | 4  | 8  |
| 1953 | 72[a] | 16[b] | 7  | 5  |
| 1954 | 67[a] | 20[b] | 3  | 10 |
| 1955 | 54 | 40 | 2 | 4 |
| 1956 | 52 | 44 | 1 | 3 |
| 1957 | 64 | 30 | 4 | 2 |
| 1958 | 67 | 28 | 4 | 1 |
| 1959 | 65 | 31 | 3 | 1 |
| 1960 | 63 | 33 | 4 | — |
| 1961 | 64 | 29 | 5 | 2 |
| 1962 | 66 | 28 | 5 | 1 |
| 1963 | 61 | 34 | 4 | 1 |
| 1964 | 64 | 30 | 4 | 2 |
| 1965 | 64 | 29 | 5 | 2 |
| 1966 | 63 | 30 | 6 | 1 |
| 1967 | 59 | 29 | 9 | 3 |
| 1968 | 57 | 30 | 11 | 2 |
| 1969 | 55 | 30 | 12 | 3 |
| 1970 | 58 | 29 | 10 | 3 |
| 1971 | 61 | 27 | 10 | 2 |
| 1972 | 61 | 27 | 10 | 2 |
| 1973 | 59 | 27 | 12 | 2 |
| 1974 | 57 | 28 | 13 | 2 |
| 1975 | 58 | 27 | 13 | 2 |
| 1976 | 56 | 30 | 12 | 2 |
| 1977 | 56 | 30 | 11 | 3 |
| 1978 | 59 | 27 | 9 | 5 |
| 1979 | 60 | 26 | 9 | 5 |
| 1980 | 62[c] | 25[c] | 8[c] | 5[c] |

*Sources:* See Table 5.3

*Notes:* See Table 5.3.

serve as the basis for Soviet long-term planning amount to 255 billion tons.

Lower figures are published by the United Nations[5] which show the USSR's total reserves to amount to almost 4 billion metric tons and "known economic reserves in place" to have amounted to some 166 billion in 1971. The criterion for inclusion under this heading is not the technical feasibility but rather the economic profitability of exploitation suggesting that, with the rise in fuel prices since then, the estimate for these reserves errs on the low side. This being so, it seems fair to conclude that the Soviet Union has some 200 billion tons of proved and probable reserves most of which are profitable at present prices.[6]

The Soviet Union's chief hard coal basins are, in order of importance as producers: the Donets, the Kuznetsk, Karaganda, Perchora and South Yakutian. The Donets basin, the oldest, has been producing since the middle of the nineteenth century. Its measured reserves are, according to Soviet estimates, 40.4 billion tons.[7] But the rising costs of mining in the basin, owing to the need to build increasingly deep mines, has meant that production is stagnating at some 200 million tons per annum. The Donets basin, with the Kuznetsk and Pechora basins, has been the chief supplier of exports to date.

The Kuznetsk basin in western Siberia began to be exploited in the late 19th century near the Trans-Siberian railway. It is estimated to have 60 billion metric tons of reserves according to Soviet sources. In 1980 it was producing 141 million tons and, in contrast to the Donets basin, continued to expand powerfully until 1976. The Kuznetsk basin provides 15 per cent of Soviet hard coal exports.

Modern exploitation of the Karaganda basin began in the nineteen-thirties. Soviet estimates of its reserves are 7.6 billion metric tons: 48 million tons were produced there in 1980, most of which was for consumption in the area. Production has been rising very slowly since the middle of the 1970s.

The Pechora basin began to be mined in 1941. Its reserves are estimated to be 7.9 billion metric tons according to Soviet sources; it produced 28 million tons in 1980. Production has been rising gradually despite its location within the Arctic Circle and the presence of permafrost.

The South Yakutian basin in eastern Siberia, which has been producing for local needs since 1940 at least, has been developed on a large scale under the Soviet-Japanese agreement of June 1974 which provides for repayment of Japanese credits with coking coal deliveries. These are expected to begin in 1983 and will be shipped from a terminal in the Pacific port of Nakhodka which went into operation in December 1978 and has an initial capacity of 6.2 million tons a year. The reserves of the South Yakutian basin are estimated to be 2.6 billion tons and its production in 1980 amounted to 3 million tons.

In addition to these five hard coal basins, the USSR also mines the Ekibastuz coalfields in northern Kazakhstan which produce subbituminous coal of low heating value which the Soviets nevertheless class as hard coal. The Ekibastuz basin began to be exploited in the 1950s and its reserves are estimated to be 3.7 billion metric tons. Production in 1980 was 66 million tons and extraction is being expanded rapidly.

Finally, there is the Kansk-Achinsk lignite basin situated in southern Siberia which began to be exploited in 1940. This contains measured reserves of 73 billion tons, or two-thirds of all the lignite reserves of the Soviet Union. In 1980, it produced 35 million tons a year and plans are to raise this rapidly.

As this summary review of the chief coal basins indicates, the expansion of coal production is taking place essentially in northern Kazakhstan and Siberia. One of the rapidly developing coal-mining areas, moreover, is to become a substantial exporter. This is the South Yakutian basin which, in contrast to past practice, is to be devoted primarily to exports.

## TRANSPORT

The location of the basins marked out for rapid development does, however, raise the problem of transport. For, if we except the South Yakutian fields which are to supply Japan, the coal basins are up to 4,000 kilometres away from the west of the USSR where 75 per cent of Soviet industry is concentrated, and more than 4000 kilometres away from eastern and western Europe which are the two chief destinations of Soviet exports. The solution being tried out in the Ekibastuz and Kansk-Achinsk regions, where the difficulty is compounded by the poor quality of the coal, involves the construction of giant mine-mouth power stations to convert the fuel into electricity, which is then to be transported by cable westwards. However, this is likely to remain economic only so long as rail is the only means of transporting coal.[8]

Another mode of transport which is being considered and is

already in use between Donetsk and a port on the Black Sea is the slurry pipeline. This new technology for transporting coal has three components: first, the plant to prepare the liquid which grinds down the coal and mixes it with water to produce a coal slurry of about 50 per cent coal by weight; second, the pipeline and its pumping stations; and, third, the dewatering plant to separate the coal from the water once it has reached its destination. The slurry pipeline is thought to be significantly cheaper than coal transport by rail for large annual flows over distance of 2000 kilometres or more.[9]

Finally, a vast programme for the transformation of Siberian coal into gas and liquid was announced by the Novosti News Agency in June 1981. However, as the most economic method of producing gas from coal is to transport it to its point of consumption and to convert it there, the transformation of coal into gas does not solve the transport problem. On the other hand the cheapest method of converting coal into liquid is to do so at the mine-mouth and then to transport it by pipeline and ship. Such transport is not judged likely to play an important role until the real price of oil is two or three times its level at the beginning of 1981.[10]

No matter which way one looks at the solution to the transport problem associated with substantial development of the eastern coalfields, it will clearly require large investments above and beyond those needed for actual mining. Although the estimated amounts for both purposes are not known,[11] there is some evidence, already noted, that these are not being generated within the Soviet Union, so that production has ceased to expand. If the necessary finance is not to be made available domestically, it will have to come from the West. Soviet spokesmen and publications repeatedly emphasize the need for western co-operation in the case of coal and, as will be seen, certain production forecasts are already being made dependent on the conclusion of agreements with importers in the West. But what the previous discussion makes plain is that, in the absence of substantial domestic or foreign investment, the eastern coalfields will cease to develop, and the Soviet production of solid fuels continue to stagnate and may even contract.

## PRODUCTION AND EXPORT FORECASTS

Available plan figures and other forecasts seem to be based on two different assumptions concerning investment in the Soviet coal fields.

The 1981–85 plan, on the one hand, which initially put total coal production in 1985 at 770–800 million metric tons and then set it at 775 million tons,[12] foresees a modest increase in output of 8 per cent in 1985 over 1980. This compares with our own calculation, shown in Appendix A and based on the trend equation for 1970–1981, of 751.8 million metric tons for 1985, barely a 5 per cent increase over 1980.

The breakdown of the plan by coal basin is shown below in Table 5.5. It lists all the main basins described earlier plus the Padmoskovski basin in the Moscow region.

Table 5.5 1981–85 Production Plan broken down by Coal Basin

| Basin | 1980 | 1985 |
|---|---|---|
| Donets | 204 | 210 |
| Ekibastuz | 66 | 84 |
| Kansk-Achinsk | 35 | 48 |
| Karaganda | 48 | 50 |
| Kuznetsk | 141 | 154 |
| Padmoskovski | 25 | 20 |
| Pechora | 28 | 28 |
| South Yakutian | 3 | 12 |

Source: *Economicheskaia Gazeta*, February 1982, p. 1.

The eleventh Five-Year-Plan includes no figure for exports. This is consistent with Soviet practice which withholds the publication of plan figures for individual export products on account of the unpredictablity of sales abroad. Our own calculations, shown in Appendix A and based on the trend equation for 1964–1980 presented in Figure 5.1, show an imperceptible increase to 26.66 million metric tons in the export of hard coal.

On the other hand, the Soviet forecasts for 1990, expressed in millions of metric tons of coal equivalent and presented in Table 5.6, show a production level of 675 million tons in 1990, or almost a 40 per cent increase over 1980. This compares with our own calculation, shown in Appendix A and based on Table 5.2, of 591.7 million tons in 1990, or an increase of only 12.5 per cent over 1980. But, whereas our estimate makes no explicit assumption with respect to investment,

Table 5.6 The USSR's Coal Demand and Production (million tons of coal equivalent) (average annual growth: %/year)

|  | 1973 | 1980 | 1990 | 1973–80 | 1980–90 |
|---|---|---|---|---|---|
| Demand | 449 | 474 | 625 | 0.8 | 2.8 |
| Production | 469 | 483 | 675 | 0.4 | 3.4 |

Source: *Economic Bulletin for Europe*, vol. 33, no. 2, pp. 220–21.

the Soviet forecast is expressly premised on the conclusion of export and, hence, co-operation contracts.

This is reflected in the export forecasts based on the production and consumption forecasts in Table 5.6, which put net exports (exports minus imports) at between 50 and 90 million metric tons of coal equivalent in 1990.[13] Other predictions have been even more ambitious, indicating that Soviet solid fuel exports might well increase 3–4 times in the short term.[14] Both forecasts, however, seem to be expressions of wishful thinking.

As Appendix A shows, our own export estimate for hard coal in 1990 is only 26.86 million metric tons. If to this we add the 9 million tons of coking coal which are due to come on stream for export in 1983 as a result of co-operation between Japan and the USSR in the South Yakutian basin,[15] and the 6 million tons of coke which have been exported annually in the past few years, we reach a figure of some 42 million tons for exports of coal and coke in 1990. This, it will be appreciated, is significantly lower than either of the Soviet forecasts.

Thus, the Soviet plan figures, which show an 8 per cent increase in production between 1980 and 1985, as compared to not quite 3 per cent in the preceding five-year period, suggest some acceleration in investment but no major change in the investment policy pursued until now. Moreover, if consumption is to continue to increase at the same rate at least as production, as it has been doing, they do not imply any great increase in exports or in the quantity of Soviet coal made available to western markets.

The Soviet forecasts for 1990, by contrast, do suppose a major policy change in favour of massive investment in the coal industry and of reliance on western co-operation. However, although their partial realisation – and this is all that seems possible[16] – would imply a greater share of Soviet exports for the West and thus greater Soviet activity in western coal markets, it seems unlikely that the Soviet Union which at present exports 5 per cent of its output, will be exporting some 10 to 20 per cent of its production by 1990, as the Soviet forecasts suggest.

## Appendix A

### I Linear Extrapolation of Soviet Coal Production (million metric tons)

| Year | Estimated Production Plan | Plan |
|------|---------------------------|------|
| 1982 | 730.5 | 728[a] |
| 1983 | 737.6 | |
| 1984 | 744.7 | |
| 1985 | 751.8 | 775 |
| 1986 | 758.9 | |
| 1987 | 766.1 | |
| 1988 | 773.2 | |
| 1989 | 780.3 | |
| 1990 | 787.4 | |

a) *Planovoye Khoziastvo*, no. 1 (January 1982) p. 9.

### II. Linear Extrapolation of Soviet Coal Production (million metric tons of coal equivalent)

| Year | Estimated Production | Soviet forecast |
|------|---------------------|-----------------|
| 1980 | 525.8 | |
| 1981 | 532.4 | |
| 1982 | 539.0 | |
| 1983 | 545.6 | |
| 1984 | 552.2 | |
| 1985 | 558.8 | |
| 1986 | 565.4 | |
| 1987 | 571.9 | |
| 1988 | 578.5 | |
| 1989 | 585.1 | |
| 1990 | 591.7 | 675 |

III. Estimate of Soviet Coal Exports (million metric tons)

| Year | Estimated exports |
|------|-------------------|
| 1981 | 26.50 |
| 1982 | 26.54 |
| 1983 | 26.58 |
| 1984 | 26.62 |
| 1985 | 26.66 |
| 1986 | 26.70 |
| 1987 | 26.74 |
| 1988 | 26.78 |
| 1989 | 26.82 |
| 1990 | 26.86 |

# 6 The USSR and The International Aluminium Market

## Carmine Nappi

This chapter examines the role played by the Soviet Union in the world market for aluminium (including alumina and bauxite). It analyses the structure of Soviet industry for this metal and attempts to explain recent changes in Soviet trade position in the light of the more global strategy brought into play with the 10th Five-Year-Plan (1976–1980).

PRELIMINARIES ON COST AND TECHNOLOGY

There are usually three phases in the production of alumina into aluminium: mining the bauxite, producing alumina and finally the transformation of alumina into aluminium.

The term "bauxite" refers to an ore containing at least 40 per cent silica and which is economically suitable for the production of aluminium. Bauxite ores can be divided into three distinct groups corresponding to three different types of technological treatment: monohydrated bauxite (the bauxite of the USSR, as well as France, Greece, Hungary, Italy, Turkey, Yugoslavia and northern Asia) from which alumina is extracted using the European version of the Bayer process; trihydrated bauxite (found in Australia, Brazil, Ghana, Guinea, Guyana, Surinam and Sierra Leone) which is treated using the American version of the same process; and finally there is Jamaican or Caribbean bauxite which requires a synthesis of the European and North American processes.[1]

Bauxite is not the only alumina-bearing ore. Alumina can also be extracted from other ores such as alunite, nepheline, anorthosite or even from clays and shales.[2] These bauxite substitutes are characterized by lower alumina and higher silica content; this is a drawback since it reduces the level of bauxite's alumina yield and therefore increases production costs. The USSR possesses vast deposits of bauxite with low alumina content, nepheline, alunite and anorthosite. Those deposits have been exploited despite the relatively higher costs involved, because of the Soviet inclination to use locally available raw materials.

The great majority of bauxite reserves are located on the earth's surface at depths varying between 10 and 100 metres. Yet, in contrast to this fact, bauxite deposits at depths of 700 metres are now being mined in the USSR, while others at depths of from 300 to 400 metres are being worked in France, Hungary and Yugoslavia. The open pit deposits are much less costly to mine than underground ones and permit production flows more easily adjustable to demand fluctutations.

The second phase of aluminium metallurgy consists in separating the alumina from the other substances of which bauxite is composed. The production of a ton of alumina using Bayer's process developed in 1888 requires an average of 2 to 2.5 tons of bauxite.

The cost of transporting bauxite is considerably higher than that of transporting the alumina extracted from it. One would, thus, expect to find alumina plants located close to bauxite mines. But such was not the case in the past, when these plants were more likely to be found near aluminium smelters. Starting in the mid-60s this situation began to change. At first glance, this would seem to be a more rational strategy. However, it should be noted that moving (capital intensive) processing plants closer to mining sites may prove less profitable if the mines are located in remote areas requiring the construction of roads, housing, repair shops or even hydro-electric dams.

Finally, we should keep in mind that during the last few years, the search for economies of scale has stimulated considerable growth in the productive capacity of individual production units. The capacity of most recent plants exceeds the one-million-ton level while those being built towards the end of the 1960s fell in the 100–200 thousand range.

The last step in processing aluminium consists in separating the metal from its oxide. This is done by means of an electrolysis process requiring considerable energy inputs (16–17 thousand kwh per ton of aluminium produced). Energy accounts for more than 20 per cent of aluminium production costs.

The production of a ton of aluminium also requires about 2 tons of alumina, 4–8 pounds of fluorspar, cryolite, aluminium fluoride and between 10 and 12 man-hours.[3] The aluminium processing plants require tremendous investments if compared with averages for other industry groups.

## USSR AND WORLD ALUMINIUM PRODUCTION

Aluminium production is highly concentrated since the United States, USSR, Japan and Canada account for 60 per cent of total world output. Table 6.1 shows that the production pattern in the Soviet Union is no different from that in the United States, in Japan and in most industrialised European countries: its international market share keeps pace with the degree of transformation of the mineral. In 1979 Soviet production accounted for close to 16 per cent of the world aluminium output. This percentage stood at about 11 per cent for alumina and 7.4 per cent for bauxite (including alunite and nepheline). In 1979 the Soviet Union also held second place among the principal producers of aluminium (just behind the United States' 30 per cent mark) and third place on the list of alumina producing countries (behind Australia, 22 per cent, and the United States, 20 per cent). In the case of bauxite, only Australia, Guinea and Jamaica out-produced the Soviet Union.

While the Soviets' international market share remains stable at around 16 per cent for aluminium, the same does not hold for alumina and bauxite. During the last ten years, the drop has been 2 per cent for alumina and 3.3 per cent for bauxite. These are important characteristics to keep in mind if we want a proper understanding of the changes occurring in their trade pattern towards the second half of the 1970s. It should also be noted that these decreases were not limited to the Soviet Union; they affected the United States, France, Canada and Japan as well.

The international aluminium market was dislocated by major structural upheavals during the 1970s. These are the most important: Australia's unprecedented breakthrough doubled its percentage of alumina and bauxite production to the levels of 22 per cent and 31 per cent respectively (the end of the 1980s will see a replay of this feat in the production of the metal); the growing importance of Guinea whose share in world bauxite production has tripled to just under the 14 per cent level; the relative decline of bauxite and alumina production in those countries responsible for the creation of the International Bauxite Association (IBA), especially Jamaica, Guyana and Surinam, coupled with a rise in production in non-member countries such as Brazil; the destruction or scrapping of almost half of Japan's aluminium production capacity, rendered non-competitive by soaring energy costs.

## USSR AND WORLD ALUMINIUM CONSUMPTION

Because of its physical properties (light weight, low fusion point, tensile resistivity and conductivity), aluminium is much in demand in the container and packaging industry and in industries related to transportation, construction and electrical products. These industries use aluminium in all its many forms – ingots, plates, wires, rods – to manufacture a multitude of finished or semi-finished goods.

Table 6.2 shows consumption activities to be just as concentrated as those on the production side. The United States (29.5 per cent), the USSR (12 per cent), Japan (10.8 per cent) and the Federal Republic of Germany (6.7 per cent) together consume 60 per cent of the world's aluminium.

Between 1970 and 1980 market shares appear fairly stable, with only marginal variations in Europe, Africa and Oceania. The only notable change is the 5 per cent drop for the United States. This decrease is offset by a growth of consumption in Asia (especially in Taiwan and South Korea – included here among "others"), Brazil, Japan and China. Soviet consumption increased at a slightly slower pace than the overall rate of increase, causing its standing to slip from 13.3 per cent in 1970 to 12 per cent at the end of the decade. The drop looks steeper if only the second half of the 1970s is considered.

Finally, it is interesting to note that in 1980 the USSR's share in international aluminium consumption fell below its share in world production. Although this profile resembles that of Norway and Canada, it is quite unlike that of the other major producers (the United States, Japan or even Germany) which are without any net export potential. Observe further that the USSR, along with the Federal Republic of Germany, was one of the few aluminium producing countries to record a higher growth rate in production than in consumption during the 1970s.

Table 6.1 Geographical Distribution of the International Production of Bauxite (B), Alumina (A) and Aluminium (Al): 1970, 1975 and 1979 (in percentages)

|  | 1970 | | | 1975 | | | 1979 | | |
| --- | --- | --- | --- | --- | --- | --- | --- | --- | --- |
|  | B[b] | A | Al | B | A | Al | B | A[c] | Al |
| Europe[a] | 12.6 | 12.4 | 19.6 | 10.4 | 14.6 | 25.4 | 9.0 | 15.1 | 23.7 |
| Fed. Rep. of Germany | — | 3.6 | 3.0 | — | 4.7 | 5.3 | — | 5.0 | 4.9 |
| France | 5.0 | 4.7 | 3.7 | 3.4 | 4.1 | 3.0 | 2.2 | 4.0 | 2.6 |
| Greece | 3.8 | 1.5 | 0.9 | 3.9 | 1.8 | 1.1 | 3.3 | 1.6 | 0.9 |
| Norway | — | — | 5.7 | — | — | 4.7 | — | — | 4.4 |
| United Kingdom | — | 0.5 | 0.4 | — | 0.3 | 2.4 | — | 0.3 | 2.4 |
| Yugoslavia | 3.5 | 0.6 | 0.5 | 3.0 | 0.1 | 1.3 | 3.4 | 1.6 | 1.1 |
| Others | 0.3 | 1.5 | 5.4 | 0.1 | 3.6 | 7.6 | 0.1 | 2.6 | 7.4 |
| Africa | 5.4 | 2.9 | 1.6 | 11.4 | 2.4 | 2.1 | 14.9 | 2.0 | 2.6 |
| Ghana | 0.6 | — | 1.1 | 0.4 | — | 1.1 | 0.2 | — | 1.1 |
| Guinea | 4.1 | 2.9 | — | 10.0 | 2.4 | — | 13.9 | 2.0 | — |
| Others | 0.7 | — | 0.5 | 1.0 | — | 1.0 | 0.8 | — | 1.5 |
| Asia[a] | 6.3 | 7.8 | 9.1 | 4.4 | 7.6 | 11.0 | 4.1 | 7.7 | 9.6 |
| India | 2.3 | 1.5 | 1.6 | 1.4 | 1.3 | 1.3 | 2.2 | 1.6 | 1.4 |
| Japan | — | 6.1 | 7.1 | — | 5.9 | 8.0 | — | 5.7 | 6.6 |
| Others | 4.0 | 0.2 | 0.4 | 2.0 | 0.4 | 1.7 | 1.9 | 0.4 | 1.6 |
| America | 44.2 | 49.2 | 46.2 | 31.7 | 38.4 | 36.7 | 27.5 | 36.4 | 40.0 |
| Canada | — | 5.2 | 9.4 | — | 4.3 | 6.9 | — | 3.4 | 5.7 |
| Guyana | 7.3 | 1.5 | — | 5.0 | 1.1 | — | 3.8 | 0.8 | — |

| | | | | | | | | | |
|---|---|---|---|---|---|---|---|---|---|
| Others | 3.7 | 0.6 | 1.1 | 2.9 | 1.0 | 1.8 | 3.1 | 1.1 | 3.9 |
| Oceania | 15.3 | 10.2 | 2.0 | 27.5 | 19.3 | 2.6 | 31.3 | 22.0 | 2.8 |
| Australia | 15.3 | 10.2 | 2.0 | 27.5 | 19.3 | 1.7 | 31.3 | 22.0 | 1.8 |
| New Zealand | — | — | — | — | — | 0.9 | — | — | — |
| Total Western Countries | 83.8 | 82.5 | 78.5 | 85.4 | 82.3 | 77.8 | 86.8 | 83.2 | 78.7 |
| Eastern Countries | 16.2 | 17.5 | 21.5 | 14.6 | 17.7 | 22.2 | 13.2 | 16.8 | 21.3 |
| China | 0.8 | 1.3 | 1.3 | 1.2 | 1.5 | 1.4 | 1.7 | 1.5 | 2.4 |
| Czechoslovakia | — | 0.3 | 0.4 | — | 0.4 | 0.3 | — | 0.3 | 0.2 |
| Hungary | 3.3 | 2.1 | 0.6 | 3.6 | 2.8 | 0.6 | 3.4 | 2.5 | 0.5 |
| Poland | — | — | 1.0 | — | — | 0.8 | — | — | 0.6 |
| Romania | 1.3 | 0.9 | 1.0 | 1.0 | 1.6 | 1.6 | 0.7 | 1.6 | 1.4 |
| USSR[d] | 10.7 | 12.7 | 16.6 | 8.6 | 11.3 | 16.9 | 7.4 | 10.7 | 15.8 |
| Others | 0.1 | 0.2 | 0.6 | 0.2 | 0.1 | 0.6 | — | 0.2 | 0.4 |
| Total | 100.0 | 100.0 | 100.0 | 100.0 | 100.0 | 100.0 | 100.0 | 100.0 | 100.0 |
| Volume (in 10⁶ MT) | 60.6 | 21.2 | 10.3 | 76.3 | 26.6 | 12.7 | 88.0 | 30.8 | 15.2 |

Notes:
a) Excluding Eastern countries.
b) Data on bauxite production come from official sources which take no account of variations in composition or degree of humidity.
c) The data in this column are for the year 1978.
d) Data for the Soviet Union include not only bauxite but also other substances such as alunite and nepheline which contain alumina. Very low-grade bauxite is also included.

Source: Table derived from World Bureau of Metal Statistics, *World Metal Statistics*, London, various issues.

Table 6.2 Geographical Distribution of International Aluminium Consumption: 1970, 1975 and 1980 (in percentages)

|  | 1970 | 1975 | 1980 |
|---|---|---|---|
| Europe | 26.1 | 24.8 | 25.1 |
| Belgium | 1.8 | 1.6 | 1.5 |
| Spain | 1.3 | 1.9 | 1.8 |
| France | 4.1 | 3.5 | 3.8 |
| Italy | 2.8 | 2.4 | 3.0 |
| Fed. Rep. of Germany | 6.7 | 6.2 | 6.7 |
| United Kingdom | 4.0 | 3.5 | 2.6 |
| Others | 5.4 | 5.7 | 5.7 |
| Africa | 0.7 | 1.0 | 1.0 |
| Asia | 12.1 | 14.0 | 15.2 |
| India | 1.6 | 1.3 | 1.7 |
| Japan | 9.1 | 10.3 | 10.8 |
| Others | 0.4 | 2.4 | 2.7 |
| America | 39.2 | 34.9 | 35.4 |
| Brazil | 0.8 | 1.8 | 2.0 |
| Canada | 2.2 | 2.5 | 1.9 |
| United States | 34.9 | 28.8 | 29.5 |
| Mexico | 0.3 | 0.4 | 0.6 |
| Others | 1.0 | 1.4 | 1.4 |
| Oceania | 1.4 | 1.4 | 1.6 |
| Australia | 1.2 | 1.2 | 1.4 |
| New Zealand | 0.2 | 0.2 | 0.2 |
| Total Western Countries | 79.5 | 76.1 | 78.3 |
| Eastern Countries | 20.5 | 23.9 | 21.7 |
| Hungary | 0.9 | 1.5 | 1.1 |
| Poland | 1.2 | 1.2 | 1.0 |
| GDR | 1.6 | 1.8 | 1.5 |
| China | 1.8 | 2.8 | 3.7 |
| Romania | 0.4 | 1.1 | 0.9 |
| USSR | 13.3 | 13.9 | 12.0 |
| Czechoslovakia | 1.1 | 1.2 | 0.8 |
| Others | 0.2 | 0.4 | 0.7 |
| Total | 100.0 | 100.0 | 100.0 |
| Volume (in $10^6$ MT) | 9.9 | 11.3 | 15.5 |

*Source:* Table derived from World Bureau of Metal Statistics, *World Metal Statistics*, London, various issues.

## SOVIET UNION AS ALUMINIUM TRADER

During the 1975–80 period, international exports of primary aluminium accounted for 23 per cent of world metal production, trailing behind refined copper (29.4 per cent) but ahead of lead (17 per cent) or most other non-ferrous metals. In 1980, the flow of international aluminium exports almost reached the 4 million metric ton level. Table 6.3 provides further information on this flow. It lists the major exporting countries and outlines the evolution of their market shares during the past decade. As specifically concerns the Soviet Union, Table 6.3 allows us to measure its standing on international aluminium markets, its export/production ratio and the distribution of its export flows between the Eastern-bloc and Western countries.

Until 1975 (the last year for which we could find data in official sources) the Soviet Union exported large quantities of primary aluminium, keeping company with exporters such as Canada and Norway. Between 1972 and 1975 the Soviets were responsible for 15 per cent of world aluminium shipments. This figure was close to 20 per cent for Canada and about 16 per cent for Norway. Also note that the market shares of the last two countries show a downward trend. It is further apparent that the world exports are just as highly concentrated as the production and consumption sectors. In 1975 the three countries mentioned were responsible for 46 per cent of total world exports.

During the first half of the 1970s, the Soviet Union exported an average of about 500,000 Mt of aluminium, equalling 25 per cent of its production. During the same period, just under 75 per cent of Soviet exports (370,000 Mt) went to Eastern-bloc countries (in particular Hungary, East Germany, Czechoslovakia and Poland). Hungary alone imported 110,000 Mt in 1975 and probably close to 165,000 Mt in 1980.[4] The rest went to Western countries.

Since we do not have access to the Soviet totals for the second half of the 1970s, it is difficult to evaluate the export development during that period. But it is worth noting that Soviet exports to Western countries seem to have reached a ceiling in 1978; afterwards they decline in absolute terms. We should also point out here the fluctuations in the Soviet export/production ratio as related to Western countries. Between 1972 and 1975 the Soviets shipped 6 per cent of their primary aluminium production to the West. Between 1976 and 1978 this percentage climbed to 8 per cent and then fell to 5 per cent for the years 1979 and 1980. Is this slowdown in Soviet

Table 6.3 International Aluminium Trade: 1972 to 1980 (in $10^3$ MT)

### A) Major exporting countries

| Countries | 1972 | Rank | 1973 | 1974 | 1975 | Rank | 1976 | 1977 | 1978 | 1979 | 1980 | Rank |
|---|---|---|---|---|---|---|---|---|---|---|---|---|
| Canada | 698.7 | 1 | 698.5 | 681.5 | 509.2 | 1 | 507.5 | 655.3 | 862.6 | 550.0 | 784.7 | 1 |
| Norway | 536.8 | 2 | 576.1 | 554.5 | 451.5 | 3 | 561.8 | 555.3 | 630.1 | 565.3 | 521.2 | 3 |
| USSR | 455.4 | 3 | 518.3 | 528.7 | 502.4 | 2 | — | — | — | — | — | — |
| France | 165.4 | 4 | 183.6 | 179.8 | 163.8 | 6 | 149.2 | 165.8 | 166.4 | 157.6 | 177.4 | 7 |
| Holland | 153.8 | 5 | 193.7 | 294.0 | 264.2 | 4 | 290.4 | 316.2 | 294.4 | 359.4 | 365.3 | 4 |
| Ghana | 131.8 | 6 | 126.2 | 137.6 | 135.8 | 8 | 145.1 | 148.1 | 111.3 | 152.6 | 131.9 | 8 |
| United States | 100.8 | 7 | 211.1 | 188.7 | 168.7 | 5 | 138.6 | 88.9 | 102.4 | 163.3 | 604.7 | 2 |
| United Kingdom | 85.0 | 8 | 85.3 | 87.4 | 87.7 | 10 | 162.1 | 144.8 | 159.9 | 204.7 | 194.1 | 6 |
| Fed. Rep. of Germany | 85.0 | 9 | 104.6 | 174.5 | 159.7 | 7 | 281.4 | 199.1 | 271.6 | 247.9 | 223.7 | 5 |
| New Zealand | 65.0 | 10 | 91.4 | 81.7 | 91.1 | 9 | 108.1 | 121.8 | 132.8 | 129.1 | 33.8[b] | 9 |
| Others | 542.4 | | 593.4 | 676.8 | 637.9 | | — | — | — | — | — | |
| Total | 3020.4 | | 3382.2 | 3585.2 | 3172.0 | | 3097.3[a] | 3163.0[a] | 3543.3[a] | 3415.3[a] | 3735.3[a] | |

### B) USSR exports

| | 1972 | 1973 | 1974 | 1975 | 1976 | 1977 | 1978 | 1979 | 1980 |
|---|---|---|---|---|---|---|---|---|---|
| Export/production ratio | 24% | 26% | 25% | 23% | — | — | — | — | — |
| Exports to western countries | 123.0 | 134.8 | 133.5 | 125.6 | 156.6[c] | 182.4[c] | 210.8[c] | 154.5[c] | 96.0[c] |

Notes:
a) Totals based on latest information available at time of writing.
b) Note that in 1980 the production levels for Spain (106.7 Mt), Bahrain (68.5 Mt) and Argentina (66.8 Mt) were higher than that of New Zealand.
c) Since no official data exist for Soviet aluminium exports after 1975, the source used derives the statistical data presented here from official documents on western imports.

exports to Western countries merely circumstantial or does it herald deeper structural shifts in its foreign trade in aluminium? Since this question cannot be answered without some knowledge of the structure of the Soviet aluminium industry, we shall return to it later.

As for Soviet imports, they were marginal for aluminium, but not for bauxite and alumina. Table 6.4 outlines the evolution of alumina and bauxite imports for the 1964–1975 period and provides the country-of-origin breakdown.

It may be seen that, after modest beginnings, Soviet bauxite imports from Guinea increased rapidly to reach the level of almost 2 million metric tons in 1975, thus meeting more than 50 per cent of the Soviet imports of this ore. The remaining need was met by imports from Yugoslavia (27 per cent), Greece (18 per cent) and Turkey. The industrial compensation agreements signed since 1975 (by which the financing and construction of mines and plants are paid for in end-products) may slightly alter the general picture of Soviet bauxite supplies. In 1976, an agreement of this kind signed with Indonesia to develop the bauxite mines on the Island of Bintan gave the Soviet Union an additional supplier. The Soviets must also have increased their bauxite imports from Kindia in Guinea as mining activity reached its peak there and construction of the Nikolaev alumina plant on the Black Sea (for the processing of bauxite from Guinea and Yugoslavia) neared its completion.

Turning to alumina imports, we find that Hungary (40 per cent in 1975) has remained the major Soviet supplier since at least 1962 when its aluminium oxide began to feed Russia's Volgograd plant. The Soviets' remaining needs are met by imports from Jamaica, Guyana, Italy and a number of other countries. Here again, the picture has no doubt since been altered by the signing of industrial compensation agreements. In fact when the USSR lent a sum of $6 million to Turkey in 1976 for the construction of their Seydisehir complex, the terms of the loan stipulated that the sum would be partially repaid in alumina exports. And the two agreements signed with India (Vishakapatam and Korba) are even more far-reaching. The first case concerns an alumina plant completely financed ($400 million) by the Soviets and for which repayment is to be made entirely in alumina exports. In 1981 a basic agreement was also signed between Tsvetmetproexport and the Hellenic Bank for Industrial Development. The agreement concerns a feasibility study for the construction in northern Greece of an alumina plant which would use local bauxite and have an initial capacity of 600,000 Mt. The plant would use

Table 6.4 Soviet Bauxite and Alumina Imports: 1964-1975 (in 10³ MT)

A) *Bauxite imports*

| Origin | 1964 | 1965 | 1966 | 1967 | 1968 | 1969 | 1970 | 1971 | 1972 | 1973 | 1974 | 1975 |
|---|---|---|---|---|---|---|---|---|---|---|---|---|
| Greece | 449 | 481 | 427 | 430 | 457 | 529 | 615 | 526 | 441 | 635 | 503 | 611 |
| Yugoslavia |  | 124 | 360 | 647 | 721 | 827 | 814 | 600 | 794 | 690 | 664 | 947 |
| Turkey |  |  |  |  |  |  |  | 76 | 152 | 148 | 203 | 75 |
| Guinea |  |  |  |  | 55 | 44 | 119 | 211 | 328 | 253 | 1844 |
| Total | 449 | 605 | 787 | 1077 | 1233 | 1400 | 1548 | 1413 | 1714 | 1473 | 1623 | 3477 |

B) *Alumina imports*

|  | 1964 | 1965 | 1966 | 1967 | 1968 | 1969 | 1970 | 1971 | 1972 | 1973 | 1974 | 1975 |
|---|---|---|---|---|---|---|---|---|---|---|---|---|
| Hungary |  |  |  | 89 | 148 | 169 | 202 | 161 | 244 | 345 | 323 | 405 |
| Greece |  |  |  | 22 | 28 | 38 |  |  |  |  |  |  |
| United States |  |  |  | 53 | 194 | 354 | 291 | 447 | 243 | 206 | 85 | 114 |
| Jamaica |  |  |  |  |  |  |  | 20 |  | 79 | 143 | 169 |
| Trinidad |  |  |  |  |  |  |  |  | 160 |  |  |  |
| France |  |  |  |  | 18 | 29 |  |  |  |  |  |  |
| Guyana |  |  |  |  |  |  |  |  |  | 134 | 82 | 121 |
| Turkey |  |  |  |  |  |  |  |  |  | 62 | 127 | 38 |
| Italy |  |  |  |  |  |  |  |  |  | 26 | 51 | 76 |
| India |  |  |  |  |  |  |  |  |  |  |  | 47 |
| Others |  |  |  | 3 |  | 5 | 25 | 127 | 51 | 51 | 75 | 59 |
| Total |  |  |  | 167 | 388 | 595 | 518 | 755 | 698 | 903 | 886 | 1029 |

*Source:* Shabad, T. "Raw Material Problems of the Soviet Aluminium Industry," *Resources Policy*, vol. 2, no. 4 (1976): 232-233.

Soviet technology and funds while 75 per cent of its production would be absorbed by the USSR and other Eastern-bloc countries.[5]

In addition to these agreements, the USSR has concluded long-term supply contracts. The one signed in 1979 with Jamaica is among the most important. After long negotiations both short-term and long-term agreements have been finalised. The former cover the export of 50,000 tonnes/year of Jamaican alumina to the USSR over the 1980-83 period. The long-term contracts, which run from 1984, will cover the export of 250,000 tonnes/year to the Soviet Union. According to the *Mining Journal*, the new agreements will obviously require a significant increase in Jamaica's output of alumina as the government has indicated that the contracts will not affect supplies to its main western customers.[6,7]

## CONCENTRATION OF PRODUCTION ACTIVITIES

The international aluminium industry is not only characterized by its vast scope[8] but also displays a high degree of concentration in its production activities. The combined production capacity of the six largest western companies (Alcoa, Alcan, Pechiney-Ugine-Kuhlmann, Reynolds, Kaiser and Alusuisse) plus the Aluminium Division of USSR's ministry of Non-Ferrous Metals (Glavaluminium) equalled, in 1979, 11.7 million tons, the equivalent of 60 per cent of the world's aluminium production capacity.[9] Available information on the question of concentration of production activities confirms some of the aluminium industry's salient characteristics. First, the industry is highly concentrated but the degree of this concentration seems to be slowly diminishing. Secondly, the industry has been and remains highly integrated.[10]

## SOVIET ALUMINIUM INDUSTRY

After the discussion of the USSR's standing on the world aluminium market[11] we can take a closer look at the Soviet aluminium industry.

The Soviet aluminium industry is mainly concentrated in the eastern part of the country, with 70 per cent of total production coming from east of the Urals, in Siberia and central Asia. The industry exhibits a certain number of distinctive characteristics.[12] The first of these is that the countries' alumina producers are seldom supplied with high-quality bauxite (ore containing at least 52 per cent aluminium oxide and only 4 to 5 per cent silica). While in the rest of the world 95 per cent of the alumina produced is extracted from bauxite with low silica content, this percentage scarcely exceeds 50 per cent in Russia where low-yield bauxite, alunite and nepheline are still extensively used. This helps to explain Soviet interest in bauxite and alumina imports and the vigour of their prospecting efforts. (It has been estimated that in 1980 not even 43 per cent of Soviet alumina will be extracted from bauxite with low silica content.) Despite the higher processing costs involved, the Soviets are obstinate in the use of their domestic resources. This is perhaps consonant with a policy of self-sufficiency. However, it does not necessarily insure the best use of available resources when one considers the human and physical capital spent on discovering, modifying or adapting new processes for extracting alumina from low-yield bauxite, alunite and nepheline.

The Soviet aluminium industry is secondly characterized by a 40 per cent dependence on foreign alumina and high quality bauxite. In 1976, about 24 per cent of the Soviet aluminium was processed from high quality imported bauxite and more than 16 per cent from alumina which also derived from foreign sources. Corresponding percentages for domestic sources were 17.5 per cent for nepheline, 16.25 per cent for alunite, 15 per cent for low-silica bauxite and 11.25 per cent for bauxite with high silica content. In 1980, the Soviets were expected both to rely more heavily on domestic mineral inputs and to increase imports of high quality bauxite to the detriment of alumina.

Thirdly, the Soviet aluminium industry boasts sixteen smelters, six of which have an output capacity exceeding 200,000 Mt. Not only are these plants gigantic – the Bratsk plant has a 600,000 Mt capacity with the possibility of expanding to between 800,000 and 1,000,000 Mt; the Pavlodar plant has a 560,000 Mt potential while Sayan and Tadzik both reach the 500,000 Mt level – but they are also supplied with hydro-electric energy which is for the most part reliable and relatively cheap in the long term.[13]

By lowering total production costs through capitalization on economies of scale, low-cost energy and centralized research and development efforts, the Soviets have been able to counterbalance the higher costs imposed by the use of low-grade bauxite and non-bauxite deposits. This puts them in a position to attack western markets with confidence. Also, it is to be noted that, following the world trend, new Soviet plants are reverting to the use of prebaked carbon anodes and abandoning the Soderberg process despite considerable Soviet improvements of this technique.

The fourth salient point about the Soviet aluminium industry concerns its integration into western trade networks at the beginning of the 1970s after a rather long period of isolation. Until recently this had meant that the Soviets were shipping about 25 per cent of their exports to the West and importing more and more alumina and high-grade bauxite from industrialised and developing countries. The USSR thus also benefited from the advantages of international trade. (This brings to mind the Nikolaev alumina plant on the Black Sea whose entire operation relies on imported bauxite.) This integration has been further shown in the USSR's imports (especially from Pechiney) and its exports of technology to developing countries (Algeria, North Korea, Egypt, Guinea, India, Indonesia, Mexico, the Philippines, Turkey, etc.).[14] Soviet aid provided in the domain of technology has not only been technical (building infrastructure, installing systems for processing alunite into alumina, engineering projects, etc.) but also financial, with repayment of such aid to be made in end-products.

## NEW PATTERNS IN SOVIET TRADE IN ALUMINIUM

Due to low energy costs, concentration of research and development efforts, a rather well developed economic infrastructure and capitalization on economies of scale, the USSR has been in a position in the 1970s to export to western markets at competitive prices between 120,000 and 210,000 Mt/year of primary aluminium. These are exports of considerable value (the equivalent of the average output of a modern smelter) and this value continued to increase until the end of 1978. How are we to explain that these exports should drop in absolute terms in the years following this period?

We have the choice of several hypotheses. Some suggest that Soviet aluminium exports are dependent on the level of foreign exchange needed to finance net cereal imports. Others interpret the drop in Soviet exports of aluminium ingots as the expression of a political will to reduce the westward flow of high-energy-input ingots and gradually replace them with exports of semi-finished aluminium products.

The first of these hypotheses seems hard to defend. Such a supposition might be right for all raw materials exports of the USSR taken together but not for particular commodities one-by-one. The Soviets need foreign exchange not only to finance "net cereal imports" but also many other things including western technology purchases, industrial equipment imports, construction of gas pipelines and so on.

The second hypothesis deserves our closer attention especially in relation to the broader issue of increasing value-added in Soviet exports. In other words, why export the energy intensive aluminium ingots when the export of semi-products (with greater local value-added) can generate more foreign exchange and permit the import of a larger basket of products including those with a high degree of "packaged energy"? We have no precise quantitative data with which to test the hypothesis that Soviet central authorities decided to reduce exports of aluminium ingots because of their relatively weak value for the national economy and replace them with exports carrying greater value added. However, this hypothesis is corroborated by western commodity traders in very close contact with the Soviets. One of these is R. Kestenbaum, president of Gerald Metals SA, an important merchant consulted by Soviet authorities for their metal exports to western markets. During the first international aluminium congress held in Madrid in 1980, he stated:

> The other more or less common characteristic mentioned above is the importance of gross and net effectiveness, in terms of foreign exchange, in some of the decision-making processes affecting industrial developments and exports to the West. In other words, what will be the local cost, in terms of local currency and local employment and local well-being, of each dollar's worth of export earnings? This factor has greatly determined the change...in emphasis on exports of aluminium altogether as well as the change in emphasis on export of primary aluminium ingot into emphasis on export of semi-products wherever possible. It has been calculated that the net local cost of one dollar of exports (in constant dollar terms) in eastern aluminium-exporting countries has been reduced in local terms by 24 per cent between 1975 and 1980 and this has been due largely to the change in the materials being exported – namely, semi-products rather than ingot. This factor has also determined the reduction in total terms of aluminium export altogether, and a beginning of a concerted import pattern of aluminium into some of the socialist countries from the West. After all, energy costs are rising everywhere in the world, includ-

ing socialist countries, and why export expensive "packaged energy" when there are other more viable exports with which to pay for the "packaged energy" which can then be imported?[15]

To confirm his hypothesis, Kestenbaum looks to the fact that during the 1974–1979 period, while socialist countries as a whole increased their aluminium ingot production by 12 per cent, their exports to western countries fell by 18 per cent. This drop cannot be explained by a weakening of the demand in market-economy countries since their consumption rate increased by 12 per cent during the same period. Nor does the evolution of Soviet demand totally explain this reduction.

The last hypothesis is one of the most seductive among the reasons advanced to explain the sudden drop and change in pattern of Soviet aluminium exports to the West. However, we believe that it needs to be completed by a more political dimension. Faced with the progressive depletion of known reserves (reflected in the decrease in average ore content) and the waste of natural resources (since they fix purely quantitative objectives thus discouraging the rational development of mineral deposits), Soviet authorities moved to define a new global strategy. According to F. Gèze, this new strategy was first put into practice in the 10th Five-Year-Plan (1976–1980) and revolves around four main axes:
— increased efforts to economize on natural resources;
— increased use of western techniques to improve the productivity of new plants (remember that Pechiney is the chief supplier of technology to the Nikolaev alumina plant);
— further economic integration within the CMEA;
— cooperation with the Third World.

The last axis seems particularly interesting. Around it revolves not only sales of equipment or agreements for geological and mining projects,[16] but also increased imports from third-world countries. François Gèze does more than confirm the importance of the industrial compensation agreements mentioned above, he situates them in a very thought-provoking context:

> The most spectacular aspect of the new Soviet strategy, however, concerns the rapid growth of third-world imports for two types of mineral substances – bauxite and alumina, and phosphates – which the USSR already produces in large quantities.

The import formula chosen is generally that of industrial compensation where the construction of mines and plants is paid for in resulting product. A long-term supply contract is often the next step. In the last few years, the Soviet Union has signed at least five contracts of this type, with Guinea and Indonesia for bauxite, with Turkey (twice) and India for alumina... The 1978 agreement on phosphate development at Meskala in Morocco is the largest Moscow has ever signed with a third-world country... In this case, as with the bauxite and alumina agreements, the profitability or efficiency criteria seem to have won out over the principle of self-sufficiency at all costs. The fact is that for the moment the USSR finds it more economical to import these ores than to intensify the development of its own resources which are less rich and more difficult to retrieve... And, it would seem that the selective increase in the imports of third-world ores is aimed mainly at shoring up the USSR's export potential against erosion from internal problems. *The growth of phosphate and alumina imports is thus not so much a matter of satisfying internal demand (already covered by domestic production) as it is a means of retaining control of the eastern European economies through exports of fertilizer and aluminium.*[17]

If this analysis is correct, we are given another important explanation of the drop in Soviet exports of aluminium to western countries: the desire to foster or maintain the dependence of satellite countries on Soviet shipments of a metal so strategic to economic development.

## USSR: AN IMPORTER OF WESTERN ALUMINIUM IN THE FUTURE?

The USSR is the second largest producer of aluminium and it belongs among the top four producers of alumina and bauxite. During the 1970–1975 period, the Soviet Union (along with the Federal Republic of Germany) was one of the few aluminium-producing countries whose production growth rate exceeded that for consumption.

As a result of this production and consumption pattern the Soviets were able gradually to create a net export capacity. This was also facilitated by: availability of relatively cheap energy, centralization of research and development efforts, installation of economic infrastructures for the development of resources in its central and eastern regions, and capitalization on economies of scale.

Since these advantages amply counterbalanced the negative effects of high production costs occasioned by the use of low-yield bauxite, alunite and nepheline deposits, several analysts and western producers expressed fears of "dumping." The fear that western markets would be flooded with Soviet aluminium ingots was especially evident towards the end of 1978 when aluminium started to be traded on the London Metal Exchange. The Soviets' aluminium exports attained record levels that year. And their 210,000 Mt of exports – although of marginal impact when compared to world production and consumption – were deemed sufficient to destabilise the market and increase the instability of producer prices and profits. The attempt was then made to renegotiate the "Gentlemen's Agreement" reached at the beginning of the 1970s, which aimed at limiting and channelling such exports so as to minimize their effect on international prices.

These fears generally proved to be exaggerated. Soviet aluminium exports to the West not only experienced a sudden drop after 1978 but also underwent a change in composition, with semi-products gradually replacing aluminium ingots. We have suggested that this structural change can be mainly explained by the desire of central authorities to reduce the net cost of domestic exports – especially the energy cost packaged in ingots – and help promote the concentration of high-value-added activities in Soviet industry. However, in the Soviet Union economic factors are to a great extent inextricably linked to political concerns. We therefore believe that this hypothesis needs to be completed by a political one. It was then suggested that the Soviet Union started importing more and more alumina from developing countries and reduced its exports of aluminium ingots to the West in order to keep its eastern European allies dependent on Soviet shipments of a metal so essential to their economic development. In that sense, the USSR is simply exercising its "commodity power" in its trade relations with communist countries.

What future developments can we expect in this domain?... We believe that, although the evolution of communist-bloc production and consumption profiles should be closely watched, fears that the western market will be flooded with cheap Soviet metal will prove increasingly groundless. Based on the current trend in Soviet consumption and production patterns, we can expect quite the opposite. After being a net exporter of aluminium, the USSR is likely to become a net importer. This appears extremely plausible, considering construction delays on new electrolysis plants and eastern-bloc countries per capita consumption levels, which are sharply inferior to those of the leading western countries. In 1979 the average per capita consumption level in eastern European countries stood at 8.7 kg compared with 29.9 kg in the United States, 24.1 kg in Norway, 20.2 kg in the Federal Republic of Germany, 19.2 kg in Japan, 17.1 kg in Australia and 17.0 kg in Canada and Sweden.[18]

One way of raising the eastern bloc's per capita aluminium consumption would be to increase imports of aluminium ingots from the West. Will this solution be adopted? No one can answer this question without pretending to know the outcome of an internal conflict (be it ever so slight) between Soviet proponents of economic profitability and the system's unyielding advocates of self-sufficiency... We certainly make no claim to such knowledge.

# 7 The Role of the Soviet Union in Metals Markets: A Case Study of Copper, Manganese and Chromite

## Walter Labys

This chapter analyses the manoeuvrability of the Soviet Union in three strategic metals markets.[1] The approach taken is to adopt a recently proposed framework which interrelates market conditions, price formation, and market structure and power so as to draw implications regarding the role of the Soviet Union in the future performance of these markets.[2] The metals markets selected for analysis are those in which the Soviet Union can exert differing degrees of market power, from a lower degree for copper and a moderate degree for manganese to a higher degree for chromite. This chapter has been organised such that the above framework is applied to each of the metals in turn. The concluding emphasis in each section is on the form and extent of the commodity power that could be exercised: economic power which implies the maximization of economic benefits from trading, political power which implies a capacity to compel another country to modify its behaviour through its perception of what actions might take place, and strategic power which implies the strategic and economic impacts of actually executing the threat. In the final section comments are offered regarding problems posed by possible Soviet influences on the evaluation of both market structure and power.

## THE SOVIET METALS POSITION

There is no need to provide an overview on the Soviet position regarding its metals and minerals industry. Such surveys can be found, for example, in works by Sutulov (1973), Strishkov (1979 and 1980), Switucka (1979), and Jenson (1982).[3] Rather, I have focused specifically on the role of the three metals of interest in Soviet industrial growth and trade.

**Metals Production**

Copper, manganese and chromite are products of the Soviet mining industries and serve as inputs into a variety of ferrous and non-ferrous metal industries. These industries have lacked full growth potential because of delays in plant modernization, labour shortages and transportation problems. The slow development of advanced methods of mining, concentration, roasting, smelting and metal rolling has led to a substantial deficiency in non-ferrous metals.[4] To solve some of these problems, the Soviet Union has become dependent on metals technology from Western countries including the United States, France, Germany (FR), Sweden and Japan. The Eleventh Five-Year-Plan (1981–85) also has specific provisions to move the non-ferrous metals industries forward.

Among the 400 different minerals mined and processed in the Soviet Union, some 23 constitute the major metal industries. Among these, copper is the major non-ferrous metals industry, having produced some 125 million tons annually between 1976 and 1979. Manganese and chromite production is lower, the former averaging 9 million tons over the same period and the latter some 2 million tons. These lower figures underscore the importance of the Soviet Union in these markets. It is the world's leading producer of manganese ore and the second largest producer of chromite.

**Metals Trade**

The trade of metals is given a high priority in Soviet planning. Actual trading and contracting takes place through a state-trading organisation (STO) administered by the Ministry of Foreign Trade. The composition and direction of this trade, particularly to the CMEA countries, can be said to reflect the geopolitical interests of the Soviet

Union. Exports are also directed to help achieve an overall trade balance, even if some sales are made below world prices.

Soviet trading patterns are directed primarily to the CMEA countries and to a lesser amount to Western Europe. Refined copper exports are the second most important non-ferrous metal export. While primary aluminium exports amounted to some 560,000 tons in 1979, refined copper exports were 240,000 tons. Chromite and chrome exports were smaller at 750 tons and manganese exports were 1,250 tons.

**Metals Self-Sufficiency**

The Soviet Union has managed to attain self-sufficiency in metal supply, as compared to agriculture where a strong dependence on grain imports still exists.[5] Because of the planned nature of the economy, this means that domestic metals demand must be moved into line with the country's productive capacity. Where this capacity is in excess, such as for copper, exports are encouraged to gain hard currency. This currency constraint has not led the Soviet Union to trade extensively with developing countries, except where barter arrangements are possible. While this has limited its role in direct investment in these countries, the Soviets have entered into agreements where the objective is to increase state-owned minerals production.

The Soviet record in self-sufficiency is impressive; import dependency exists only for bauxite and aluminium, tin, fluorides, antimony, tungsten, barium and molybdenum. However, there have recently been signs that this situation may change. In the last two years exports of some minerals have declined. While the Soviet Union has been a source of supply to the West, it has increased its imports of metals and may eventually compete with the West for certain supplies.[6] Even though the Soviet Union exports titanium and vanadium, imports of these materials are increasing. In many cases, these increases in imports have taken place to maintain exports and thus trade ties to the CMEA countries.

Dependency of the West on the Soviet Union has centred on that country's major metal exports: chromite, manganese, platinum metals and gold. A problem could arise as lesser (quality) grades of ore are mined in the Soviet Union such as for chromite and manganese. Since many strategic metals can also be found in South Africa, one can understand why the Soviet Union as well as Cuba have decided to play a strong role in the geopolitics of that area.

## COPPER

**Market Conditions**

Soviet production of copper in 1978 amounted to 1.00 million tons of refined copper, 0.98 million tons of blister copper and 0.88 million tons of copper ore (copper content). Reverberatory smelting continues to be the main process for the smelting of blister copper.[7] The country also operates 40 concentrators with a total probable annual capacity of about 5 million tons of concentrates. Most copper mining is done by open pit methods with only a small portion (10 per cent) originating as a by-product of other metals mining.

The main copper ore regions are located in Central and Eastern Kazakhstan, the eastern slope of the Ural Mountains, Uzbekistan, the Transcaucasus, Eastern Siberia and Norilsk.[8] Kazakhstan has the position of being the main production centre of the USSR, containing about one-half of its total copper reserves in 1979. It possesses 48 known copper deposits, of which 19 (containing two-thirds of the Kazakhstan's reserves) are being mined. Principal areas of copper production include the Balkhash complex, the Irtysh complex and Aktyubinsk.

The Urals is the second largest copper producing region. Copper ore is surface-mined at Uchalinskiy, Sibayskiy, and Gayskiy, and deep-mined at Degtyarsk, Karabash, Gayskiy, Imeni III International and Levikhinskiy. Gross reserves of the Udokan deposit in Siberia, the third largest region, amount to about 1200 million tons of ore with an average copper content of 1.5 per cent (20 per cent oxides, 80 per cent sulphides). Plans are to develop this deposit between 1981–1990 and to produce 35 million tons per year of ore yielding a refined copper output of 400,000 tons per year. The Soviet Union has been negotiating with British, French, and Japanese companies for joint development of the Udokan deposit. At the same time, it has been assisting Mongolia in construction of the Erdenet copper-molybdenum complex and has offered assistance to India to consider the feasibility of establishing a copper operation there.

The overall goal of the Soviet Union in copper appears to be that of expanding production and exports considerably. Regarding the growth of production during the period 1965–1977, Table 7.1 reports increases as follows: copper ores and concentrates from 0.75 to 1.10 million tons (copper content), copper blister from 0.77 million tons to 1.44 million tons, and refined copper from 0.78 to 1.29 million tons.

There is also an attempt to modernize the industry in terms of mining efficiency and of improved recovery of metal and of by-products in smelting and refining. The Five-Year-Plan extending from 1975–1980 aimed at increasing primary copper output by 20–30 per cent over the 1975 level. If these targets are achieved, Soviet exportable surplus of refined copper could reach 400 thousand tons which would almost double the volume exported in 1975.[9] This would put some pressure on a world copper market which in recent times has been in a state of excess supply.

Consumption of copper in the Soviet Union takes place at each stage of its highly integrated copper system, culminating in industrial products. Growth rates of Soviet copper consumption in the past decade have been among the highest in the world, although not as high as in Japan. Although details on end-uses of refined copper are not available, experts believe that the bulk of it is directed to electrical construction and associated heavy electrical equipment.[10] This kind of activity is expected to remain important for some time to come, but it must eventually decline somewhat in relation to national product. In addition, Soviet plans for the expansion of aluminium production imply further substitution away from copper. The ratio index of refined copper consumption to GNP reached a peak of 10.8 in 1961, and similar to the trend in other industrialized countries this ratio has declined, reaching 9.8 in 1975.

The Soviet Union has not been a major exporter of copper. However, Table 7.2 shows that its exports of refined copper have doubled between 1966 and 1974. While the Soviets' main concern in the 1960s was to meet their growing domestic needs and to supply the requirements of the CMEA countries, they now have shifted their export interest to Western Europe as a means of gaining foreign exchange.[11] However, Western copper demand has slowed since 1974, mostly as a consequence of increasing copper inventories in that area as well as growing economic recession.

**Price Formation**

Most copper trade is in the form of refined metal, thus making the refined or wire bar price the most representative international price.[12] Accordingly, unrefined copper prices as well as prices of fabricated products are closely linked to the refined prices. All three forms of copper – concentrate, blister and refined – are sold mainly under bilateral sales contracts between a producer and a buyer.

Table 7.1 Comparison of the USSR and World Copper Market (thousands of metric tons)

| | 1965 | 1970 | 1971 | 1972 | 1973 | 1974 | 1975 | 1976 | 1977 | 1978 | 1979 |
|---|---|---|---|---|---|---|---|---|---|---|---|
| Exports (Ref) | | | | | | | | | | | |
| USSR | 93 | 123 | 174 | 202 | 238 | 248 | 205 | 220 | 220 | 240 | 240 |
| World | 2,057 | 2,558 | 2,572 | 2,748 | 2,862 | 3,167 | 2,835 | 2,953 | 3,006 | — | — |
| Production (Ore)[a] | | | | | | | | | | | |
| USSR | 848 | 694 | 749 | 806 | 849 | 898 | 927 | 968 | 830 | 865 | 885 |
| World | 6,081 | 7,302 | 7,318 | 8,054 | 8,633 | 8,853 | 8,138 | 9,034 | 7,661 | 7,557 | 7,607 |
| Production (Blis)[a] | | | | | | | | | | | |
| USSR | 848 | 694 | 749 | 806 | 849 | 898 | 927 | 968 | 935 | 955 | 980 |
| World | 6,686 | 7,426 | 7,413 | 8,146 | 8,725 | 8,875 | 8,571 | 8,980 | 8,029 | 7,924 | 8,035 |
| Production (Ref)[a] | | | | | | | | | | | |
| USSR | — | — | 715 | 767 | 806 | 855 | 880 | 922 | 950 | 980 | 1,000 |
| World | — | — | 7,565 | 8,390 | 8,778 | 9,198 | 8,654 | 9,151 | 8,537 | 8,707 | 8,883 |

| | | | | | | | | | | | | |
|---|---|---|---|---|---|---|---|---|---|---|---|---|
| Consumption (ore) | | | | | | | | | | | | |
| USSR | 750 | 925 | 990 | 1,030 | 1,060 | 1,060 | 1,100 | 1,130 | 1,100 | — | — | — |
| World | 5,100 | 6,300 | 6,370 | 7,010 | 7,290 | 7,550 | 7,270 | 7,670 | 7,790 | — | — | — |
| Consumption (Blis) | | | | | | | | | | | | |
| USSR | 770 | 1,075 | 1,150 | 1,225 | 1,300 | 1,350 | 1,400 | 1,420 | 1,440 | — | — | — |
| World | 5,510 | 6,810 | 6,820 | 7,500 | 8,020 | 8,220 | 7,740 | 8,210 | 8,300 | — | — | — |
| Consumption (Ref) | | | | | | | | | | | | |
| USSR | 783 | 950 | 985 | 1,030 | 1,100 | 1,100 | 1,220 | 1,250 | 1,290 | 1,290 | 1,360 | |
| World | 6,150 | 7,290 | 7,290 | 7,950 | 8,550 | 8,300 | 7,460 | 8,540 | 9,010 | 9,367 | 9,882 | |
| Imports (Ref) | | | | | | | | | | | | |
| USSR | 0.7 | 1.1 | 7.4 | 8.8 | 6.1 | 4.9 | 8.5 | 5.0 | 5.0 | — | — | |

[a]Production figures presented for comparison only. They do not equate with consumption and exports.

*Source:* L. L. Fischman (ed.), *World Mineral Trends and U.S. Supply Problems*, Resources for the Future, Washington, DC, 1981, and U.S. Bureau of Mines, *Mineral Yearbook*, various issues.

Table 7.2 Destinations of USSR Exports of Refined Copper[a] (metric tons)

|  | 1966 | 1967 | 1968 | 1969 | 1970 | 1971 | 1972 |
|---|---|---|---|---|---|---|---|
| Cuba | 700 | 600 | 500 | 600 | 600 | 601 | 600 |
| Belgium–Lux | — | — | — | — | — | — | — |
| Czechoslovakia | 27,400 | 28,400 | 32,400 | 37,800 | 35,800 | 37,000 | 35,200 |
| Finland | — | — | — | 2,000 | 2,020 | 2,040 | 2,041 |
| Germany, East | 42,900 | 41,600 | 43,800 | — | — | — | — |
| Germany, West | — | — | 5,400 | — | — | — | — |
| Hungary | 7,900 | 8,700 | 13,000 | 13,800 | 16,600 | 16,100 | 29,200 |
| Japan | — | — | — | — | — | — | — |
| Netherlands | — | 1,500 | 4,100 | 2,300 | 16,815 | 57,100 | 52,000 |
| Poland | 6,100 | 4,400 | 4,200 | 3,865 | 3,553 | 6,000 | 5,900 |
| Romania | 4,200 | 4,100 | 4,300 | 4,150 | 4,095 | 3,968 | 7,423 |
| Vietnam, North | 45 | 500 | 410 | — | — | — | — |
| Sweden | — | — | — | — | — | — | — |
| United Kingdom | — | 3,200 | — | — | — | — | — |
| Total Exports | 120,100 | 94,000 | 109,300 | 107,400 | 123,100 | 173,600 | 202,100 |
| Total Imports | 7,400 | 1,400 | 9,400 | 400 | 1,000 | 7,400 | 8,800 |

|  | 1973 | 1974 | 1975 | 1976 | 1977 | 1978 |
|---|---|---|---|---|---|---|
| Cuba | 1,100 | 1,140 | 1,200 | — | — | — |
| Belgium–Lux | 9,028 | 4,002 | 6,257 | 8,142 | 276 | — |
| Czechoslovakia | 37,743 | 38,705 | 38,746 | 41,000 | 37,000 | 39,000 |
| Finland | 5,061 | 5,001 | 5,003 | 5,150 | 4,943 | 5,005 |
| Germany, East | — | — | — | — | — | — |
| Germany, West | 18,861 | 11,934 | 12,481 | — | — | — |
| Hungary | 31,296 | 33,125 | 33,121 | 22,313 | 12,260 | 4,480 |
| Japan | 16,551 | 16,165 | 62 | — | — | — |
| Netherlands | 27,763 | 38,107 | 35,224 | 4,097 | 6,045 | 575 |
| Poland | 3,756 | — | 694 | 7,509 | 11,624 | 5,163 |
| Romania | 16,964 | 9,289 | 5,641 | 1,204 | — | — |
| Vietnam, North | — | — | — | — | — | — |
| Sweden | 5,492 | 9,981 | 8,124 | 2,545 | — | — |
| United Kingdom | 14,327 | 10,006 | 1,060 | 9,004 | 1,022 | — |
| Total Exports | 237,700 | 247,978 | 205,618 | 220,000 | 220,000 | 240,000 |
| Total Imports | 6,100 | 4,880 | 8,532 | — | — | — |

[a] Because of gaps in reporting data, column totals do not necessarily equal the sum of the entries.

*Source: Metal Bulletin Handbook,* London, various issues.

Copper sales contracts are similar to other commodity contracts in their specifications of quantities, grades, dates, and so forth. However, they differ in that they do not specify the actual sales price. The pricing clause normally is of a very general type such as "the seller's price at the time of delivery".

The bases for determining the refined price are the transactions on the London Metal Exchange (LME). Acceptance of LME prices by the trade results in a uniform price level for all sellers and buyers. With a neutral and uniform price determined separately from bilateral contract negotiations, there is in principle little possibility for the exporters or importers of copper to take any initiatives with regard to prices. Nonetheless, an increase in market shares by the Soviet Union and the CMEA countries could make it possible in practice for them to influence the LME prices to their advantage in the short term.[13] Physical turnover on the LME is limited, and a few well-timed sales or purchase orders could have a significant effect on price developments.

This sensitivity of the LME could provide the Soviet Union with the opportunity to increase LME prices systematically on the days they choose for pricing their copper sales. However, traders on the LME claim that concerted action of this kind is uncommon. An attempt to influence LME prices could, for instance, easily lead to retaliatory action of the same kind by other sellers or buyers. Awareness of the advantages of the LME as a neutral pricing medium may discourage such attempts.

**Market Structure and Power**

The supply side of the world copper market can be termed a homogeneous oligopoly with a large competitive fringe. There is a high concentration among copper producing firms, with the eight largest firms in mining accounting for 50 per cent of total capacity and in refining accounting for 44 per cent.[14] On the demand side, primary copper is absorbed mainly by the fabricating industry, which transforms the refined copper bars or cathodes into various shapes and in some cases processes them further still. None of the fabricators has a capacity approaching the largest units at the mining stage.

The structure of the world copper market is normally described in terms of the major multinational copper producers together with the major State-Trading Organisations (STOs).[15] Table 7.3 shows a

Table 7.3 Copper Production by Countries (in thousands of metric tons)

| Country | Mine Production | Smelter Production | Refined Production |
|---|---|---|---|
| USSR | 865 | 955 | 980 |
| USA | 1,358 | 1,869 | 1,869 |
| Chile | 1,036 | 427 | 749 |
| World | 7,557 | 7,327 | 7,968 |

*Note:* Primary and secondary production combined.
*Source:* US Bureau of Mines, 1978.

simplified form of market share analysis based on copper production only at the country level.

The above figures show that the Soviet Union lies somewhere between the United States and Chile in terms of its shares of world production based on 1978 figures. These shares, which average about 17 per cent across categories, are not large relative to that of the major multinational mining firms nor to the major developing countries as a group.

Any exercise of economic, political or strategic power by the Soviets in the copper market would depend on which of the three major copper power groups it might want to join. The first of these is the major privately-owned multinational mining companies. The second of these is the group of state-owned copper companies, some of which are located in developing countries. One recent source, Labys (1981), has estimated the proportion of private and state-owned companies in world production to be 61 per cent and 39 per cent respectively.[16]

A third major power group is the concentration of the major developing country producer within the Inter-governmental Council of Copper Exporting Countries (CIPEC).[17] The Council was established in 1967 by the largest of those developing country producers: Chile, Peru, Zaire, and Zambia. The membership of CIPEC undertook its first action to influence copper prices in late 1974. This action took the form of a 10 per cent joint reduction of copper exports followed by a further 5 per cent. In as far as such action has had no subsequent influence on price, one could argue that the sellers have failed to take advantage of their market power, by relegating price determination to an outside institution like the LME. However, there are a number of factors which have prevented the full realisation of price control by international cartels. For the case of copper-exporting developing countries, their dependence on copper is sufficiently strong that they would probably be forced to yield and accept inferior terms rather than to face the threat of a halt or reduction in trade flows.

Any action which the Soviet Union can take as part of one of these power groups would seem limited. Because the Soviets have opposed attempts at price and revenue stabilisation within UNCTAD for political reasons, it is unlikely that they would join a producer's cartel such as CIPEC. However, their interest in maximizing export incomes from all minerals including copper might cause them to support CIPEC's policies. Even then some conflicts of interest might still exist. The Soviet Union has displaced some of the developing-country copper exporters from the world market, and cooperation through CIPEC which would involve backing these same producers might be unlikely, especially since any form of market restriction would clearly not be in the interest of the Soviet Union. In the case of copper, the conclusion must be that the Soviet Union has little opportunity to exert political or strategic power in that market.

## MANGANESE

### Market Conditions

The Soviet manganese industry remains the largest in the world, producing some 9.1 million tons of the world total of 21.1 million tons in 1978. As shown in Table 7.4, this level of output represents a rapid growth rate from some 6.8 million tons in 1970 to 8.4 million tons in 1975. Most of this came from the Nikopo basin in the Ukraine, reportedly the largest deposit in the world.[18] The second largest producing area was the Chiatura basin in Georgia. Small amounts of manganese are also produced at the Dzhezdinsk and Atasuysk mines in Kazakhstan.

The Soviet Union is considered a consumer of manganese ore as well as of ferro-manganese. Consumption of the former has increased from 2.0 million tons in 1970 to 2.5 million tons in 1975, while consumption of the latter peaked at about 0.85 million tons in 1970, falling to 0.70 million in 1976. The rates of manganese ore consump-

Table 7.4 Comparison of the USSR and World Manganese (Ore) Market (Actual Weight, thousands of metric tons)

| | 1960 | 1970 | 1971 | 1972 | 1973 | 1974 | 1975 | 1976 | 1977 | 1978 |
|---|---|---|---|---|---|---|---|---|---|---|
| Exports | | | | | | | | | | |
| USSR | 973 | 1,200 | 1,400 | 1,300 | 1,300 | 1,482 | 1,411 | 1,342 | 1,352 | 1,186 |
| World | 6,126 | 9,810 | — | — | 10,789 | 12,260 | 12,022 | 11,582 | 9,069 | 8,815 |
| Imports | | | | | | | | | | |
| E. Europe | 732 | 884 | — | — | 1,277 | 1,381 | 1,383 | 1,369 | 2,363 | 1,470 |
| World | 6,054 | 9,180 | — | — | 11,226 | 11,891 | 11,520 | 10,921 | 10,086 | 8,706 |
| Production | | | | | | | | | | |
| USSR | 5,872 | 6,841 | 7,318 | 7,819 | 8,245 | 8,155 | 8,459 | 8,636 | 8,595 | 9,057 |
| World | 12,737 | 18,500 | 21,900 | 22,000 | 21,081 | 22,046 | 24,598 | 23,946 | 22,019 | 21,076 |
| Consumption[b] | | | | | | | | | | |
| USSR | 1,716 | 1,974 | 2,072 | 2,282 | 2,431 | 2,335 | 2,470 | 2,505 | 2,430 | — |
| World | 4,500 | 7,264 | 7,871 | 8,025 | 8,717 | 8,858 | 9,181 | 9,025 | — | — |
| Processing[c] | | | | | | | | | | |
| USSR | 592 | 850 | 731 | 730 | 745 | 831 | 829 | 701 | — | — |
| World | 2,588 | 4,162 | 4,037 | 3,984 | 4,533 | 4,924 | 4,450 | 4,367 | — | — |
| Unit Values[a] | | | | | | | | | | |
| USSR (fob) | 37.3 | 18.4 | — | — | 20.2 | 21.6 | 22.3 | 22.7 | 26.3 | 32.4 |
| World (fob) | 28.2 | 16.6 | — | — | 21.0 | 28.4 | 35.7 | 39.0 | 41.8 | 41.9 |

Key: a— $US per ton, b—Manganese Content, c—Ferro-manganese Consumption.

Source: "Review of Recent Developments in the World Market for Manganese: Statistical Annex," TD/B/IPC/Manganese/7/add. 1, UNCTAD, Geneva, 1980; L. L. Fischman (ed), *World Mineral Trends and U.S. Supply Problems*, Resources for the Future, Washington, D.C., 1981; and *Metal Statistics*, Metalgesellschaft, Hamburg, various issues.

tion and ferro-manganese production are important. If manganese ore were the sole input and little loss in processing existed, then this ratio would remain at about 0.80.[19] But manganese also has other uses such as in dry cell batteries or in steelmaking. Thus, this ratio has varied in the Soviet Union from a low of 2.20 in 1969 to a high of 2.57 in 1973 (latest available figure).

It should be noted that these consumption rates are perhaps the highest of any country. According to Charles River Associates (1976), even though the Soviet rate of manganese consumption per ton of steel produced has declined by approximately 40 per cent in the last two decades, the Soviets still use twice as much per ton of steel as the average for Western steel producers. This has been attributed to several factors:
1) The relatively low manganese content of their iron ores,
2) the relatively great abundance of their manganese ores,
3) the unusually high sulphur content of their cokes, and
4) the desired high manganese content of their pig iron.

Soviet exports of metallurgical grade manganese have not remained constant. According to Table 7.4, they have increased from 1.20 million tons in 1970 to 1.48 million tons in 1974, but more recently have declined to 1.19 million tons in 1978 and 1.25 million in 1979. Although the steel industries of the United States, Japan, and Western Europe depend heavily on manganese ore imports, their annual requirements are met by non-Soviet sources. It appears that increased domestic demand in the Soviet Union, together with less readily available good ore from domestic deposits could restrict their exports to their present destinations in CMEA countries. Nonetheless, presently rising manganese prices could provide them with an incentive to increase exports. As an example, discussions have been held with Union Carbide of the United States to construct a ferro-manganese plant at Nikopol which would be tied to US imports of Soviet ferro-manganese in spite of the already high non-MFN duty. In 1976 this duty added some 22.4 cents per long-ton unit to the delivered price of ore from communist countries.[20] This reflects the interest of Soviet planners in the higher value-added obtainable from ferro-manganese as compared to manganese exports.

**Price Formation**

There are no major markets where manganese prices are observed and formed. All manganese ore prices are negotiated by contract, depending on variable factors such as chemical analyses, freight rates, inclusion or exclusion of export and/or input duties, needs of the buyer, and the general availability of ores of the desired quality. While published quotations reflect general market conditions, the export unit values reported in Table 7.4 show Soviet f.o.b. prices increasing less rapidly since 1973 than that of the world average, probably due to their long-term commitments to CMEA countries.

**Market Structure and Power**

The production of manganese ore is dominated by the Soviet Union and the Republic of South Africa; the two countries possessed some 80 per cent of the world's available reserves in 1980.[21] Market concentration is also high at the production level. Given a world production level of 9.58 million tons (manganese content) in 1978, the Soviet Union and South Africa together accounted for 3.49 and 1.90 million short tons respectively. Three other countries can be counted as important in the world total: Gabon with 0.93, Brazil with 0.86 and Australia with 0.69 million tons.[22]

The possibilities for the Soviet Union to exercise economic, political or strategic market power depend on the behaviour of the other countries within the dominant share. According to Fischman (1980), only Brazil and South Africa figure between both leading world suppliers and world consumers of manganese ore.[23] The possibility that these countries, together with Gabon and India, could form a cartel has been given some credence by CRA (1976).[24] If these countries were to restrict supply and increase prices, the Soviets would be under little political pressure to restrain increased exports, an action which obviously would be in their economic interest. By being willing to collude at least on a tacit basis, they would accept such price leadership as a basis for increasing their Western market share.

However, evidence can be cited as to the unlikelihood of such a cartel. First, deep ocean nodules represent an alternative major potential source of manganese. Second, the likelihood of supply shortages in manganese and ferro-manganese through 1990 is very small. In particular, Fischman (1980), in presenting probabilities of world shortages in manganese and ferro-manganese supplies, has concluded that the possibilities of small or even large supply disruptions are negligible.[25]

Regarding the role of the Soviet Union in this outlook, Table 7.5 indicates that historically most of its exports have gone to CMEA

Table 7.5 Destinations of USSR Exports of Manganese (Ore) (thousands of metric tons)

| Chief Destinations: | 1966 | 1967 | 1968 | 1969 | 1970 | 1971 | 1972 | 1973 | 1974 | 1975 | 1976 | 1977 | 1978 |
|---|---|---|---|---|---|---|---|---|---|---|---|---|---|
| Bulgaria | — | — | — | — | — | 110 | 103 | 108 | 130 | 126 | 127 | 108 | 78 |
| Canada | — | — | — | — | — | — | — | 10 | 13 | — | — | — | — |
| Czechoslovakia | 149 | 186 | 177 | 150 | 153 | 252 | 265 | 331 | 329 | 341 | 356 | 320 | 373 |
| France | 116 | 65 | 99 | 89 | 109 | 99 | 93 | 9 | — | — | — | — | — |
| Germany, East | 198 | 216 | 108 | 177 | 175 | 193 | 172 | 165 | 150 | 179 | 185 | 186 | 170 |
| Japan | 106 | 100 | 107 | 50 | 96 | 111 | 96 | 38 | 194 | 112 | 75 | 110 | 19 |
| Korea, North | — | — | — | — | — | — | — | 21 | 21 | 20 | 20 | 11 | 20 |
| Norway | — | — | — | — | — | — | — | 52 | 65 | 57 | 5 | — | — |
| Poland | 317 | 304 | 318 | 364 | 365 | 360 | 417 | 465 | 495 | 484 | 482 | 502 | 446 |
| Sweden | — | — | — | 37 | 47 | 47 | 40 | 17 | 37 | 26 | 18 | 5 | — |
| United Kingdom | 134 | 104 | 71 | 44 | 42 | 27 | 12 | 14 | — | — | — | — | — |
| Yugoslavia | — | — | — | — | — | — | — | 19 | 26 | 30 | 26 | 34 | 17 |
| Total Exports | 1,218 | 1,250 | 1,150 | 1,197 | 1,200 | 1,400 | 1,300 | 1,300 | 1,482 | 1,411 | 1,342 | 1,352 | 1,186 |

Source: Metal Bulletin Handbook, London, various issues.

countries. But this trade pattern should not influence our perception of the role of the Soviets in the world manganese market. As Table 7.5 shows, their exports needed to balance the market have declined from some 1.48 million tons (actual weight) in 1974 to some 1.19 million tons in 1978. Since the imports of East European countries have risen to 1.47 million tons in 1978, this implies a greater competition for the world's available manganese. However, one past attempt by the Soviets to extend their commodity power from a political to a strategic nature has failed. The reduction of Soviet manganese supplies to the West during the Korean War had little effect on its availability.

This outcome emphasizes the ability of other producers such as South Africa and Australia to maintain the world's supply in the long run. In addition, Soviet importance in this regard may decline; Fischman (1980) notes that Soviet production may be more needed to support their own as well as CMEA ferro-manganese production and steelmaking.[26] This view tends to be supported by the relatively low levels of recent Soviet manganese reserve figures and by the nation's progressive exhaustion of higher grade ores.

## CHROMITE

### Market Conditions

The Soviet chromite industry is the second largest in the world. As shown in Table 7.6, production in 1978 amounted to some 2.30 million tons, up from 1.72 million tons in 1970. About 94 per cent of total Soviet chromite reserves are situated in Kazakhstan, with the balance in the Ural Mountains.[27] There are over 20 deposits in Aktyubinsk Oblast in western Kazakhstan. Molodezhneye, Millionnyy, and Almaz-Zhemchuzhina are the largest, with total gross reserves of some 60 million tons.

The Soviet Union consumes and exports both chromite and ferro-chromium. Consumption of chromite has increased from 0.29 million tons in 1970 to 0.61 million tons in 1977. Ferro-chromium consumption has risen from 35 thousand tons in 1970 to 113 thousand in 1976. This consumption is divided between 45 per cent in metal production, 32 per cent in refractors, and 23 per cent in chemical and other industries. While the ratio of chromite consumption to ferro-chromium production has followed a relatively constant trend downwards in most countries, the ratio has fluctuated more in the Soviet Union. It registered a low of 3.36 in 1962 and then jumped to 4.51 in 1970. Since then it has declined to 3.63 in 1974 (most recent available figure).[28]

Soviet exports of chromite (typically about 48 per cent $Cr_2O_3$) have declined in recent years, from some 1.20 million tons in 1970 to some 0.74 million tons in 1978. This decline has affected countries other than just the CMEA ones, as shown in Table 7.6. During 1970–1978, exports to non-CMEA countries decreased from 0.96 to 0.33 million tons, while they increased slightly to CMEA ones from 0.22 to 0.39 million tons.

**Price Formation**

As with the case of manganese, there are no major markets for chromite price determination. Chromite and ferro-chromium are imported by brokers or importers having foreign sources of supply, by direct negotiation with producers, or directly by consumers or processors from subsidiary companies or corporate interests. Prior to 1974, contracts were generally established on a one-year basis, but were switched to six-month contracts by Russian and Turkish suppliers to allow greater pricing flexibility during the period of rapid price advances in 1974–75.[29]

The relation between Soviet and world chromite prices at the import level is shown in Table 7.6. Soviet prices have grown faster than world prices, with a particularly strong increase having occurred between 1974 and 1975. The Soviet Union was the price leader in this case, encouraged by the strong demand derived from world stainless steel production. There were also problems of uncertainty about future supplies from Rhodesia, coupled with the possibility that the United States would reimpose its Rhodesian embargo. Since this price increase was also followed by Turkey, insufficient supplies were available to return prices to a competitive level. Even when world demand began to lessen, the Turks did not lower prices so as to increase their market share. Such a market experience implies that Soviet supply restraints can lead to a degree of price manipulation.

**Market Structure and Power**

The World's production of chromite is divided among some 23 countries. Among these countries accounting for a major portion of

Table 7.6 Comparison of USSR and World Chromite Market[a] (Actual Weight, thousands of Metric Tons)

| | 1965 | 1970 | 1971 | 1972 | 1973 | 1974 | 1975 | 1976 | 1977 | 1978 |
|---|---|---|---|---|---|---|---|---|---|---|
| Exports | | | | | | | | | | |
| USSR | — | 1,200 | 1,400 | 1,600 | 1,200 | 1,106 | 1,171 | 975 | 673 | 738 |
| World | | | | | | | | | | |
| Processing[b] | | | | | | | | | | |
| USSR | 74 | 35 | 38 | 54 | 76 | 98 | 112 | 113 | — | — |
| World | 668 | 932 | 929 | 898 | 1,172 | 1,332 | 1,146 | 1,244 | — | — |
| Consumption[c] | | | | | | | | | | |
| USSR | 349 | 286 | 361 | 390 | 366 | 421 | 472 | 570 | 613 | — |
| World | 2,280 | 3,039 | 2,943 | 2,926 | 3,371 | 3,505 | 3,669 | 3,800 | 3,900 | — |
| Production | | | | | | | | | | |
| USSR | 1,400 | 1,722 | 1,929 | 1,850 | 1,900 | 1,950 | 2,080 | 2,120 | 2,180 | 2,300 |
| World | — | 6,100 | 6,200 | 6,430 | 6,723 | 7,197 | 7,850 | 8,500 | 9,500 | 9,612 |
| Unit Values[d] | | | | | | | | | | |
| USSR | — | 64 | 77 | 73 | 58 | 69 | 155 | 291 | 283 | 220 |
| World | — | 60 | 62 | 62 | 53 | 54 | 125 | 150 | 141 | 132 |

*Key:* a. Many of the figures in this table are estimates. b. Chromium consumption. c. Chrome oxide content. d. Average value in $/long ton of $Cr_2O_3$ imported into the United States from the USSR and all sources.

*Source:* L. L. Fischman (ed), *World Mineral Trends and U.S. Supply Problems,* Resources for the Future, Washington, D.C., 1981; and *Metal Statistics,* Metalgeschellschaft, Hamburg, various issues.

the world total of 9.61 million tons reported for 1978 are the Soviet Union with 2.30 million tons, South Africa with 3.47 million tons, Albania with 1.10 million tons, Rhodesia with 0.53 million tons, the Philippines with 0.59 million tons, and Turkey with 0.41 million tons.[30] This gives the Soviet Union and Albania a market share of 35 per cent. Adding the other four countries increases the share to 87 per cent.

Although the portion under centrally controlled market economies is as high as 35 per cent, a large share of world production is still in the hands of private industry, held primarily by large mining and resource companies. While Soviet production is handled by a single State-Trading Organization, production in South Africa is distributed among 6 to 10 of its minerals companies. Among these, General Mining and Barlow Rand account for approximately 60 per cent of total production.

The possibilities for the Soviet Union to exercise economic, political or strategic commodity power depend on the actions taken by other countries. According to a CRA (1976) study, the mineral policies of the South African government have reflected a view that encourages its producers to exploit market power.[31] This has taken the form of allowing collusion privately and tacitly among its major mining firms and with producers in other countries. Although South Africa intends to increase chromite production substantially and has shown little interest to collude with the USSR and Turkey, the Soviets could exercise their market power and increase their profits considerably by taking advantage of their growing market share. Fischman (1980), for example, does attach a moderate to high probability to the likelihood of a possible shortage of chromium supplies to the United States for one reason or another.[32]

The importance of Rhodesia despite South Africa reserves stems from Rhodesian chromite being of better quality for metallurgical purposes. This situation could be considerably worsened by political instability in South Africa. Already the declining exports of the Soviet Union to the West have caused concern. To some extent, the consequences of their behaviour will be dampened only as long as South Africa is able to boost its production of chromite and ferro-chromium.

Apart from the possibility of Rhodesian supplies being reduced to the West because of political instability, the Soviets can repeat their market restricting activities of the past. It is possible that even Turkey might enter a restrictive arrangement if it were to its advantage. The

Soviet Union was able to more than double the price of its chromite exports in 1975 in part because of the uncertainty in the world market, as mentioned above. While this reflects taking advantage of economic power, and threats of Soviet supply disruption reflect political power, there does not appear to be a chance of strategic power. In neither World War I, nor World War II, nor the Korean conflict was any participant's war effort significantly hampered by the lack of chrome.

## CONCLUSIONS

Let me conclude by focusing on several important aspects of Soviet metals trade that have emerged from this analysis of the copper, manganese and chromite industries. To begin with, the need for Western technology to improve the productivity of these industries implies that trade may expand rather than diminish. Even though foreign investment is not possible, the Soviet Union has expressed an interest in compensation agreements in which technology and hard currencies are traded for access to minerals supply. Limitations to such expansion are MFN tariff provision in Western countries as well as Western hesitancy to become too dependent on the Soviet Union.

Where such dependence might increase, there are two ways in which the Soviets can impose strategic pressure on Western needs for copper, chromite and manganese. First, any monopolistic position held by the USSR can be advantaged. As witnessed in the case of chromite, the Soviet Union, together with Turkey, managed to increase prices substantially in 1975. However, the concentration of these three metals markets has declined since the 1960s. While the United States, the Soviet Union and Germany (FR) were responsible for a little over one-half of the chromite consumption in 1970, this share declined to about one-third by 1976. Japan, South Africa, and other countries have now become important consumers.

Secondly, and related to the first, are the short-term supply contingency risks that result from concentration of supply in areas subject to politically instigated supply disruptions. These risks have been shown to be higher for chromite and ferro-chromium than for manganese and ferro-manganese. They arise because sources of supply other than those of the Soviets are located in Southern Africa where the Soviets have recently increased their efforts to destabilise the existing governments.

These supply issues also affect the growth of domestic processing facilities. Primary metals are needed to feed these facilities in the United States as well as in Western Europe. If the USSR increases its imports, begins to decrease its exports, and competes for available chromite and manganese, this will drive prices up and reduce metal availability to the West. With higher energy costs in the West required to produce the processed ferro-metals, these industries could suffer a decline. Such a situation could become more serious should Western strategic stockpiles reach low levels.

The Soviet Union could also influence metals price movements, not only by the exercise of its economic power mentioned above, but also by engaging in transactions on a market such as copper where price instability is already typical. The economic costs imparted by such an intervention are high. Apart from upsetting purchase patterns, such instability could distort decisions not only to expand capacity but also to reduce or to expand production.

Finally, the potential of the USSR to exercise political and strategic power seems less, particularly for copper and manganese. Some political power might be exercised in restraining supplies of chromite, but this depends on whether supplies from other producers are simultaneously reduced. The possibility of exercising strategic power in chromite does not seem to be present to any substantial degree.

# 8 The Soviet Impact on World Trade in Gold and Platinum

Michael Kaser

SOVIET SECRECY

The bounty of Nature is not taken without human cost. The miners of coal and ores who made possible the Industrial Revolution suffered tragic losses in Europe and North America, and even today, despite great improvements in industrial safety throughout the world, natural resources have still to be won at the expense of life and limb.[1] But the toll levied by Stalin's exploitation of gold and platinum beggars the record of the capitalist system, and has yet to be revealed in all its enormity.[2]

The regime for Kolyma gold and Norilsk platinum was punitive during only twenty years (1937–56); the Soviet government no longer needs remote sub-Arctic regions to which to draft political suspects in their hundreds of thousands, but it still badly needs precious metals, above all gold, to earn the currency to buy grain and Western technology. No independent evaluation of the economic viability of gold and platinum exports can be made in the absence of factual information from the USSR, for neither cost nor output statistics of any non-ferrous metal have been published since the Second World War in absolute quantities (though some index-numbers have been issued) and the foreign trade returns on any non-ferrous metals were suppressed from 1977 – on gold forty years earlier! Data on individual deposits, mines and refineries are still to be found, notably in the journal of the Ministry of Non-Ferrous Metallurgy of the USSR, *Tsvetnye metally* (which is published in English in cover-to-cover translation), but within censorship constraints designed to conceal all output and much unit-cost data; the transmission to any unauthorized person of information on the production of non-ferrous metals is a criminal offence under Soviet law.[3] Even the arrival of Soviet bullion is veiled by Western customs authorities to protect commercial secrecy. The USSR switched the bulk of its gold sales from London to Zurich in the early 1970s in order to gain secrecy; the UK authorities responded by suppressing the relevant returns, but in 1980 a Swiss tax on gold weakened the attraction of Zurich. Although they made concessions on the tax, the Swiss authorities later that year allowed imports to be revealed, frightening Soviet sellers to the point at which both the Swiss and British became still more secretive in 1981.[4] Actual deliveries are rendered more obscure by the Soviet practice of buying as well as selling,[5] and net bullion transactions with CMEA states are further complicated by gold production in Mongolia and Romania and by substantial dealing by the Hungarian National Bank.[6] Rather than attempt to identify individual country sales, one standard source, the annual booklets entitled *Gold* (followed by the year) of Consolidated Gold Fields, presents only net transactions with all CMEA members, China, and North Korea.[7]

For many years the Soviet government was not even willing publicly to admit that its State Bank sold bullion; since it has never released its balance of payments,[8] such reticence is not made explicit. But an article commemorating the Bank's sixtieth anniversary in 1981, by its President, at length did set out its policy, though by no means squarely:

The spontaneity characterizing capitalist markets not infrequently brings from time to time variations from plan of Soviet deliveries intended to pay for imports. In such circumstances, the USSR as a gold-producing country can utilize the sale of gold in order to enlarge imports, in particular to surmount disproportions evoked by unforeseen circumstances.

Heavy selling of gold in 1982, when the gold price was extremely low, showed that it was the "spontaneity" of Soviet agriculture – a fourth poor harvest in succession was in prospect – that has been an important incentive to dispose of bullion for hard currency and to keep Western observers guessing on the production and reserves behind such sales.

## ESTIMATES OF PRODUCTION

The aim of national self-sufficiency in non-ferrous metals was formulated by the Soviet authorities as early as January 1925, and metals with a high value-to-weight ratio (of which gold and platinum are salient examples) were seen as justifying the costs of opening up virgin territory from which – once the infrastructure was installed – commodities with a lower ratio could be extracted. At the start of the first Five-Year-Plan (1928–32) Stalin described to the Director of Glavzoloto (the Chief Administration for the Gold and Platinum Industry founded in September 1927) his policy for "our outlying regions of Russia. At the beginning we will mine gold, then gradually change over to the mining and working of other minerals, such as coal and iron."[9] A sudden policy-change – the year 1929 is characterized in Soviet historiography as "the Year of the Great Turn" – engineered by Stalin transformed both the demand and the supply conditions for gold. The "Great Turn" was from the Communist Party's encouragement by voluntary and gradual means of farm cooperatives (within the semi-market economy of Lenin's New Economic Policy) to coerced collectivization (under a "command economy," wherein resources were to be mobilized primarily for investment). Collectivization and the drive for "heavy" industry would – and did – reduce the export availability of grain, which until then had been the main Soviet (and prerevolutionary Russian) exportable. The economy's demand for gold was thus immediately enhanced as a substantive earner of foreign exchange. Complementing such "demand-side" considerations, there was a sudden availability of prisoners. The virtual civil war whereby collectivization was enforced not only killed (or allowed to die) perhaps five millions, but imprisoned an estimated 3.5 million recalcitrant peasants. The lives of "class enemies" were cheap and they could be conveniently and usefully set to work in regions from which escape was scarcely feasible.[10]

A much greater effort was deployed to produce gold than platinum and the discussion in this study concentrates on the former. Both Kolyma between 1931 and 1957 and Norilsk between 1935 and 1957 were operated by agencies of the security forces (NKVD, from 1946 MVD).

Statistics of gold mining ceased to be published after 1928 and of gold reserves after 1935. Soviet concealment was so effective that the Vice-President of the United States, Henry Wallace, could visit

Magadan and the mining zone in 1944, as a wartime Allied leader, and (publicly at least) report no sign of prison labour.[11] Very high estimates of output were conveyed by prisoners after the Second World War[12] – mostly foreigners of Allied or neutral nationality who had been caught up in Stalin's prewar purges.[13] Thus a group of Poles released in 1947 put the peak prewar output of the Kolyma fields at 400 tonnes, dropping to 250 in 1943–4 and reaching 300 by 1946.[14] Two émigré economists were notable in perceiving the exaggeration in the global estimates made,[15] but prisoners' reports were not systematically perused for their mine-by-mine information until the present writer was commissioned for a detailed study by Consolidated Gold Fields.[16] The estimates of others, extrapolated from the very high levels, had, meanwhile, put output at as much as 240 tonnes in 1960 and 500 tonnes in 1969; none, surprisingly, made allowance for a fall in output following the mass release of political prisoners around 1956.[17]

The closure of the forced-labour mining camps was the key development to which the United States Central Intelligence Agency (CIA) tied its much lower series of gold production estimates in a press release of 1964 – a range of 135 to 155 tonnes. Rumours have not been denied that the real source for the startling new figure was Oleg Penkovsky, the sole high-level spy (later caught and executed for treason) who is known to have worked for British intelligence in Moscow. The CIA (and with it the United States Bureau of Mines)[18] reduced its estimates in 1978 (almost certainly because it believed progress at Muruntau had not been as fast as had been thought previously) – working the series back a lower (but not uniformly lower) level. It raised its estimates in 1980, but did not make public its reasons for the changes either down or up.

Estimates in Table 8.1, from the present writer's paper for the Association of American Geographers,[19] have also passed through three phases. The first was based largely on press and radio reports on individual gold fields and on statements in Soviet textbooks of economic geography. Commissioned by Consolidated Gold Fields, it was published in 1971.[20] That corporation arranged for him to be joined by a gold-mining engineer, David Dowie, in a re-examination of the published evidence and with the latter's assessment of the output of individual fields from reports of the equipment available in each. The results were made available in 1974.[21] Both he and researchers at Consolidated Gold Fields separately began further in-depth studies in 1979 and the present writer's analysis was

Table 8.1 Author's Estimates of Soviet Gold Production by Field, 1970–1990

|  | Tonnes 1970 | 1980 | 1981 | 1990 Projection |
|---|---|---|---|---|
| Severovostokzoloto (North East Gold Production Association) | 82 | 85 | 83 | 72 |
| Primorzoloto (Maritime Territory Gold Production Association) | 14 | 17 | 17 | 22 |
| Yakutzoloto (Yakut Gold Production Association) | 40 | 49 | 50 | 68 |
| Zabaikalzoloto (Transbaikalian Gold Production Association) | 17 | 28 | 28 | 43 |
| Lenzoloto (Lena Gold Production Association) | 15 | 16 | 16 | 18 |
| Other Siberian Producers | 13 | 14 | 13 | 10 |
| By-product gold | 48 | 61 | 63 | 91 |
| Main-product gold in Kazakhstan | 9 | 11 | 11 | 13 |
| Central Asian producers | 16 | 44 | 47 | 94 |
| Kirgiz | — | — |  | 5 |
| Tadzhik | 1 | 1 |  | 4 |
| Uzbek | 15 | 43 |  | 85 |
| Uralzoloto (Urals Gold Production Association) | 9 | 11 | 11 | 13 |
| Armzoloto | 1 | 9 | 9 | 20 |
| Other | — | — | — | 5 |
|  | 264 | 345 | 348 | 469 |

*Source:* M. Kaser, "Gold" in R. Jensen, T. Shabad and A. Wright (eds), *Soviet Natural Resources and the World Economy* (Chicago: Chicago University Press, 1982), chapter 24.

completed in early 1981. Consolidated Gold Fields had published segments of most of its results by 1981,[22] but there was nothing in the latest annual instalment.[23] They had nevertheless settled upon a single figure (in place of a range previously published) for production. Both investigations concede that the Dowie-Kaser series overstated output by attributing output efficiencies per installation which, while correct for Western practice, were more than would be feasible under such Soviet operational conditions as interruptions of power and materials supply, inadequate availability of spare parts and repair services, rigorous climate and the absence of profit incentives to maximize utilization. The present writer, furthermore, had double-counted the output of private prospecting teams; when more information about their activity was published, notably in a 1975 decree encouraging their work, it seemed almost certain that their output (estimated at 27 tonnes) was comprehended in the output of the state enterprise to which they were under contract.

The three sets of estimates are now within a range of 17 per cent of each other. Consolidated Gold Fields formulated a range of 280 to 350 tonnes for 1977–8 but settled on some 300 tonnes in a report discussing 1976–78.[24] The CIA showed 307 tonnes for 1979, the latest year for which it has revealed its estimates,[25] and the present writer 336 for that year, 345 for 1980, and 348 tonnes for 1981.[26]

The mining of platinum has not attracted the same attention as that of gold,[27] but has been subject to the same Soviet secrecy and was undertaken also with forced labour in Stalin's day. Construction of the present-day Norilsk Mining-Metallurgical Combine, named after A.P. Zavenyagin,[28] was begun in 1935; the first coal and nickel were extracted the following year, but platinum metals were a later product. The release of prisoners in 1954–6 must have brought a fall in output throughout its range; transferred to the Ministry of Non-Ferrous Metallurgy *in toto* (plant, public utilities, railway and river-port at Dudinka), a major expansion programme was launched in 1961. Currently Norilsk produces three-quarters of Soviet platinum (and even a little by-product gold). Soviet reserves, according to the US Bureau of Mines in 1977, are "adequate to maintain current production for many years, with increased exports".[29]

Only one estimate, apparently agreed by all parties, is made in the West of Soviet output of platinum-group metals. The same output is shown by the US Bureau of Mines in Washington,[30] Metallgesellschaft AG in Frankfurt[31] and the Institute of Geological Studies in London;[32] the conversion of metric weights into troy ounces in the standard commercial yearbook seems to have been effected with spurious accuracy.[33] The consensus is that Soviet output passed the 100-tonne mark in 1979, having risen by nearly one-quarter in a mere four years (82 tonnes in 1975).[34]

## THE SOVIET MARKET POSITION

The USSR is the world's second largest producer of gold, ranking well behind South Africa, but divides nearly all world output of platinum about equally with that country. Excluding production in China, Mongolia, North Korea and Romania, and minor output elsewhere in communist countries, the worldwide mining total for 1981 was 1,310 tonnes, of which South Africa supplied 50.2 per cent and the USSR 26.6 per cent; platinum-group metals aggregated in 1980 212 tonnes, of which the USSR contributed 47.6 per cent and South Africa 45.3 per cent.[35] Canada is in third place for each metal, producing in the years stated 50 tonnes of gold (3.8 per cent of world output) and 13 tonnes of the platinum group (6.1 per cent). Smaller producers in Africa (40 tonnes), in Latin America (96 tonnes), in Asia and in Oceania (each 35 tonnes), with a little from Europe, constituted the other gold producers, but platinum producers outside the "big three" were negligible.

Tables 8.2 and 8.3 compare output and trade for gold and platinum respectively. The Soviet share of the former has risen from 24.5 per cent in 1975 to 26.6 per cent in 1981 and of the latter from 46.1 per

Table 8.2 Production and trade in gold, 1975–1981

| Output | 1975 | 1976 | 1977 | 1978 | 1979 | 1980 | 1981 |
|---|---|---|---|---|---|---|---|
| World[a] | 1,262 | 1,291 | 1,295 | 1,306 | 1,296 | 1,288 | 1,310 |
| South Africa | 713 | 713 | 700 | 706 | 705 | 675 | 656 |
| Soviet Union | 309 | 322 | 325 | 331 | 336 | 345 | 348 |
| *Soviet disposals* | | | | | | | |
| Sales to West | 141 | 326 | 400 | 407 | 229 | 50 | 280 |
| Other disposals (net) | 50 | 52 | 54 | 56 | 58 | 60 | 62 |
| Net change in reserves | +118 | −56 | −129 | −132 | +49 | +235 | +6 |

[a]Excluding communist countries other than the USSR.

*Source:* L. du Boulay *et al., Gold 1982* (London: Consolidated Gold Fields, 1982), p. 16, and Kaser, op. cit., Table 18.

*Note:* All Soviet figures are estimates within a substantial margin of error.

Table 8.3 Production and trade in platinum-group metals, 1975–1980

| Output | 1975 | 1976 | Tonnes 1977 | 1978 | 1979 | 1980 |
|---|---|---|---|---|---|---|
| World | 178 | 186 | 196 | 197 | 202 | 212 |
| South Africa | 81 | 84 | 89 | 89 | 94 | 96 |
| Soviet Union | 82 | 87 | 90 | 95 | 100 | 101 |
| Canada | 12 | 13 | 14 | 11 | 6 | 13 |
| *Exports* | | | | | | |
| South Africa | 58 | 68 | 70 | 81 | 99 | 90 |
| Soviet Union | 56 | 81 | 79 | 74 | 87 | 46 |
| Canada | 16 | 14 | 14 | 12 | 6 | 13 |

*Source:* Output from p. 184, exports from p. 195 of *World Mineral Statistics, 1976–80* (London: HMSO, 1982); same series to 1979 in troy oz. in *Metal Bulletin Handbook, 1981* (London: Metal Bulletin, 1981), pp. 413–19.

cent in 1975 to 45.3 per cent in 1980. In terms of gold bullion exports, South Africa ranks first (543 tonnes in 1981), with the USSR second (at around 280 tonnes); each made further sales in newly-minted coins – krugerrands and chervontsy respectively. Soviet exports are, however, subject to significantly differing estimation, of which Table 8.4 sets out the principal series. The writer's series, as shown in Table 8.2, as far as 1978 draw upon discussions with knowledgeable observers, for 1979 and 1980 are those of the Union des Banques Suisses, but also confirmed by informed circles; that for 1981 is rather below estimates current within the London bullion market.[36] All series imply (after allowing for domestic uses and some occasional sales to East Europe net of deliveries from Mongolia) that reserves had to be drawn upon in 1976, 1977 and 1978, that reserves were substantially increased in 1980 and by a small amount in 1979; and that in 1981 reserves seem to have been virtually untouched – new production covering all disposals.

Estimates of disposals are crucial to linking output and reserve series with the last data published by the Soviet authorities before the Second World War. The writer's examination of each gold field, using particularly prisoners' testimony, helped to furnish production estimates to which index-numbers of regional outputs (sporadically published in Soviet sources) could be related and afforded a con-

Table 8.4 Alternative Estimates of Soviet Gold Sales to the West, 1974–1981

Tonnes

| Source | Declared coverage | 1974 | 1975 | 1976 | 1977 | 1978 | 1979 | 1980 | 1981 |
|---|---|---|---|---|---|---|---|---|---|
| 1) | Net Western imports from communist countries | 220 | 149 | 412 | 401 | 410 | 199 | 90 | 283 |
| 2) | Gross Soviet and East European sales to West | 150 | 150 | 350 | 450 | 450 | 280 | 90 | 200–300 |
| 3) | Soviet sales on international markets | 220 | 150 | 300 | 401–10 | 410–30 | 200–50 | 110–50 | — |

*Sources:* 1) Du Boulay *et al.*, op. cit., p. 15 (i.e. the latest Consolidated Gold Fields estimate); 2) United Nations, *Economic Survey of Europe in 1981* (New York: United Nations, 1982), p. 311 (i.e. the Bank of International Settlements series); 3) Anita Tiraspolsky, "L'Or soviétique: production et ventes," *Le Courrier des Pays de l'Est*, 247 (1981), p. 51 (citing for 1974–7 S. G. Schoppe, "Changes in the Function of Gold within the Soviet Foreign Trade System since 1945–46," *Soviet and Eastern European Foreign Trade*, XV (1979), pp. 60–95).

sistency check with estimates of the United States Mint, which purported to be very precise, at least until 1938 (rounded estimates were given for 1939 and 1940).[37] Annual figures were thus compiled back to 1936, for the first day of which Soviet gold reserves were last published. The CIA has made known its estimates of reserves for years beginning with 1960[38] – another fact which is said to be due to Penkovsky – and the writer tied together the two reserve magnitudes with his output series by estimates of domestic consumption and external disposals. Reserves of the USSR State Bank rose from 247 tonnes at the end of 1935 to 2,270 at the end of 1960. The total reserve at the first date cannot be definitely quoted because some gold was held directly by the Commissariat of Finance, but if it was of the order of 350 tonnes the net increment over those 25 years was 1920 tonnes. The increment may be assumed to have resulted from the excess of production over disposals, although seizures of bullion during and after the Second World War must be borne in mind. The one accretion other than by domestic extraction which is well known was the gold stock of the Spanish Republican government (510 tonnes) which was received by the USSR Commissariat of Finance on 2 November 1936.[39] Disposals for domestic industrial use are estimated at an annual minimum average of 6 tonnes during 1936–50 and 11 tonnes in 1951–60 (virtually only in chemical and electrical engineering and photography, since the jewellery industry – chiefly wedding rings and official decorations – was probably supplied only with recycled gold) or 200 tonnes as a minimum. Sales abroad must have been small between 1936 and 1953.

Khrushchev once claimed that he could not understand why Stalin kept stockpiling gold and it was his administration which initiated renewed selling for convertible currency. Between 1953 and 1960 sales were 1,281 tonnes and some deliveries of bullion were made in payment for wartime supplies by the Allies. Five tonnes were aboard HMS *Edinburgh* when it was sunk by German submarine U456 on 30 April 1942 on convoy duty from Murmansk;[40] further research could reveal what other bullion was shipped to the Allies but as most Allied deliveries to the USSR after that date were Lease-Lend a maximum estimate is made of 25 tonnes. Together the draw-down during 1936–60 must have been no less than 1,506 tonnes. To satisfy a net increment in reserves of 1920 tonnes, the addition of 510 tonnes of Spanish gold and that draw-down, output must have been 2915 tonnes. The present writer's estimates of output for 1940–50 plus those of the US Mint for 1936–9 cumulate to 3282 tonnes. The CIA soon afterwards increased its estimate of the gold reserve by some 100 tonnes so that the excess of cumulated production over known minimal uses seems to be of the order of 270 tonnes, or approximately 10 tonnes a year over the 25 years between estimates of gold reserves. In the earliest year for which they are available in their latest form (1965) the CIA estimates are 28 tonnes below the present writer's.

The importance of these relatively small divergences is that the lower the output the more reserves have to be drawn down in order to supply (known) gold sales. The CIA does not state how much it allows for disposals other than as sales to the West, but in those years during which no such sales were made, a comparison of its reserve increments with outputs shows that non-Western disposals were estimated within a range of 37 to 71 tonnes. The present writer applies a deduction from output rising from 50 tonnes in 1975 to 62 in 1981 in order to indicate (Table 8.2) that only in three years, 1976–8, did sales to the West cause a draw-down on reserves.

Stocks of platinum, on the other hand, are not in any published estimate, but a comparison of estimates of output and exports to the West in Table 8.3 shows that the latter constituted 68 per cent of Soviet production in 1975 and 87 per cent in 1979. Export volumes for 1979 are as follows, in troy oz.:

| | | |
|---|---|---|
| France | 20,200 | |
| FRG | 50,951 | |
| Japan | | |
| platinum | 266,642 | |
| palladium | 723,722 | |
| rhodium | 18,135 | |
| Netherlands | 2,294 | |
| Switzerland | 104,715 | |
| UK | — | (65,394 in 1976) |
| United States | | |
| palladium | 581,434 | |
| rhodium | 17,310 | |
| ruthenium | 47,958 | |

Total for countries listed   1,833,361 (= 57.024 tonnes)

The USSR is the largest producer and exporter of platinum-group metals, supplying a quarter of imports by market economies of platinum and over half of palladium and rhodium.

## SOVIET PRICING

Large though its share is in world production and trade of both gold and platinum, the Soviet Union is not a long-run price-maker in international markets. The long-run supply constraints are based on South Africa for both metals and in the short-run demand factors – in the case of gold much of it speculative – are paramount. There is a contrast between the two metals in formation of the "standard price": a highly variable twice-daily setting in London, sensitive to every change, for gold and a much stickier South African (Rustenburg) price for platinum, which can remain nominal (with no buyers at that price) for substantial periods while deals are being conducted at a lower price.

The USSR is rendered still more a price-taker for precious metals by selling not as a regular export item (as do South Africa and Canada) but as its balance of payments requires. Table 8.5 identifies the decisive variables of the current balance other than receipts from sales of gold (largely determined by the visible balance since invisibles tend to be in equilibrium) and borrowing from abroad.

The current deficits incurred between 1975 and 1978 (due to the need to buy grain after the very bad harvest of 1975 – worse than in 1972 – cumulated on a rising trend of buying Western equipment) were jointly met by gold sales and borrowing. The price of gold influenced the choice between bullion and borrowing in that gold sales had a higher share of the combined receipts from both when it was high (and when, to complete the criteria, interest rates were also high enough to be a disincentive to borrow). In such circumstances it is not possible to predict Soviet selling behaviour to a given price without also postulating its balance-of-trade experience and external credit conditions. There is, moreover, a "policy factor" tending towards reliance or independence from the West – there was a shift from reliance towards self-sufficiency in 1978, which seems to have been enhanced in 1981.

Soviet sales of gold in the second half of the 1970s peaked in 1978 and of platinum in 1979, but market conditions would have evoked a continuance of sales through to 1980, after which sharp price declines would have indicated a reversal. Thus, the London price (expressed in dollars per troy ounce at the average sterling-to-dollar exchange rate) deflated by the index of UK import prices was for gold 3.2 times in 1979 and 3.4 times in 1980 its 1975 price and for platinum 1.4 and 1.5 times respectively. Yet (as Table 2 shows) the USSR exported for

Table 8.5 Estimates of the Soviet Hard-Currency Balance of Payments, 1970–1980

|  | *Millions of dollars* Current account | | | Capital account | |
|---|---|---|---|---|---|
|  | Balance excluding gold | Gold sales | Total | Gross borrowing abroad | Net total |
| 1970 | 22 | — | 22 | 291 | 266 |
| 1971 | 81 | 79 | 160 | 288 | 227 |
| 1972 | −967 | 380 | −587 | 602 | −77 |
| 1973 | 251 | 900 | 1151 | 1340 | 522 |
| 1974 | 836 | 1178 | 2014 | 1426 | 386 |
| 1975 | −5439 | 725 | −4714 | 5408 | 5694 |
| 1976 | −4300 | 1369 | −2931 | 4694 | 2952 |
| 1977 | −1620 | 1618 | 2 | 1777 | 1917 |
| 1978 | −2206 | 2673 | 467 | 1785 | 173 |
| 1979 | 600 | 2200 | 2800 | −2900 | −2100 |
| 1980 | 2220 | 1800 | 4020 | — | — |

*Source:* 1970–78 from P. G. Ericson and R. S. Miller, 'Soviet Foreign Economic Behavior: a Balance of Payments Perspective' in US Congress Joint Economic Committee, *Soviet Economy in a Time of Change*, Vol. 2 (Washington: USGPO, 1979), p. 212; 1979 from F. Lemoine, 'La Balance des paiements des pays de l'Est en 1978 et 1979', *Le Courrier des Pays de L'Est*, 274 (1981): 9; 1980 from C. Beaucourt, 'La Balance des paiements courants de l'URSS à l'horizon 1985', ibid. 259 (1982): 35.

hard currency 68 per cent of the year's output of gold in 1978 but only 14 per cent in 1979 and 93 per cent of its platinum output in 1978 but only 46 per cent in 1980. The USSR raised its gold sales in 1981 to perhaps 80 per cent of its output even though the price fell by one-third during the year; judging by press reports, platinum sales also seem to have increased even though its price fell by a quarter during the year.

The Soviet domestic retail price has been rapidly pushed upwards. The standard quotation for 14 carat gold (583) octupled from 5.65 roubles per gram in April 1969 to 45 roubles per gram in December 1981 – each leap in the state-determined price being by such large amounts as 50 and 60 per cent. At its peak of $850 an ounce on 21

January 1980, the world price had seen an even greater rise (it was 20.7 times the $41.13 average of 1969) but the average of 1981 ($459.85) was in fact not much greater a multiple of 1969 (11 times) than the Soviet retail price. Because, of course, other Soviet prices have been almost constant (a mere 4 per cent rise 1969–81 in state shop prices) whereas Western retail prices have greatly risen, the relative retail price of gold has risen much more in the USSR. At the official exchange rate (0.745 to the $) the 1981 price would have been $60.40 per gram (for 14 carat gold), but the factor employed within CMEA to convert non-commercial to commercial roubles (2.3 Soviet roubles to CMEA's transferable roubles) yields $26.30 ($816 per oz. or $1,400 for 1,000 fineness), a price more appropriate for comparison.

The transfer price between state enterprises of gold for industrial use was 3.80 roubles per gram (14 carats) in the July 1967 wholesale price lists, which ostensibly was not revised in the non-ferrous metal group until January 1982, but the possibility of unannounced changes must be considerable. Nevertheless the 1967 price should have represented the costs of production (labour, materials and a 6 per cent charge for capital) and at 118.20 roubles per oz. (for 14 carat metal) was (at 0.90 to the $) $131.30 in 1967 prices, which applying an inflator of dollar prices over the 14 years, would represent $384.70 for 14 carats or $660 for 1,000 fineness in 1981 prices;[41] production costs will certainly have increased over that period and hence the evidence is that the USSR on the evidence of costs converted at the official exchange rate is making a domestic loss on foreign sales. This could be among the reasons which have led the USSR to mint the chervonets since 1976 because the premium on legal tender coins diminishes such loss.

No corresponding retail or wholesale prices could be found for platinum but the overall conclusion for gold, that the USSR does not sell on a strictly commercial basis, is not unlikely to apply also to platinum. The need for earning foreign exchange is the prime consideration for selling either metal, and output is large enough (reserves of gold are between four and five years current output) for sales to be effected as and when required – the quantity sold being enlarged when the price declines.

Patently the USSR has an interest that its own sales minimize downward pressure on price, subject to the objective that the required revenue be earned by a combination of volume and price in the plan year. When the gold price was on an upward trend in the

1970s, the USSR authorities, at least on some occasions, restrained their sales within any one year when the price rise slackened (their own sales, of course, often initiating the weakening). During the sharp down-swing of the early 1980s, they also held off the market to attenuate the fall: thus in early 1982, they put it about that they had made no sales at all for a stated period in a clear attempt to hold the price steadier.

Such commercial acumen is no more than normal and does not affect the underlying function of Soviet gold (and probably platinum) sales to provide hard currency whenever the Soviet balance of payments requires. It seems premature to conclude – as does Consolidated Gold Fields latest examination – that "sales from Russia should be regarded in much the same way as those from other major mine producer."[42] The "policy factor" of a centrally planned economy remains the overriding influence on Soviet trade in precious metal.

## MARKETING TACTICS

Commercial considerations in implementing whatever strategy is decided under such a policy would dictate consultation on tactics with the other principal producer and exporter of both metals, South Africa, as was for a time the case with respect to diamonds, in which the two countries are also thrown together by their natural endowment, and remains the case for karakul pelts, of which Soviet Central Asia and Namibia are the world's main producers. Allegations of such collusion have been particularly frequent since 1980, when a senior representative of South African gold interests was seen in Moscow (it was the topic of a BBC TV *Panorama* on 6 April 1981).

The modalities of selling in each country differ in that (as the governor of the Reserve Bank of South Africa responsible for gold marketing strategy put it)[43] South Africa provides the "hard core" of the world's gold supply and the USSR "plays it at the top". Consultation on when to sell would integrate those strategies. Both countries have diversified their outlets in recent years. Both traditionally sold only through London and Zurich, but as noted above, the USSR abandoned the former for much of the 1970s. South Africa from 1976 began making sales in Frankfurt (as had the USSR earlier but only in small quantities) and in the United States, and, soon after, the USSR began direct disposals in Kuwait and Tokyo, as South

Africa has in Paris and Hong Kong. The principal channel of the USSR State Bank remains, however, the Wozchod Handelsbank, its wholly-owned subsidiary in Zurich.

## THE SOVIET DILEMMA

The economic and political factors which led the USSR, half a century ago, to compensate the deficit incurred by buying Western equipment and technology differ in each respect from those now obtained. Then, the USSR switched from grain export to grain self-sufficiency; from 1963 (the year of the first grain purchases in North America, paid for by gold sales), the USSR has shifted from grain self-sufficiency to grain import. Then, the extraction of gold was exclusively labour-intensive, working placers with the most primitive tools;[44] now, it is increasingly capital-intensive as lodes come to dominate (either open-cast in Central Asia or deep reefs in Siberia and the Far East) and the infrastructure needed for operations in remote and harsh regions. Then, there were huge numbers of labourers for whom Stalin had to find prison work; now, the government faces a severe labour shortage and has to offer wage incentives as an inducement to work in unpleasant climates and conditions.

On any of the measures of cost as reflected in the Soviet domestic price of gold, sales at the world price of the first half of 1982 must be unprofitable, judged as a commercial transaction. But, as seems apparent from the insensitivity of sales to the world price, decisions are not commercial. The USSR planning authorities at first determine their import needs and then draw up the receipts which have to be earned to satisfy them. Among those receipts is the sale of gold and the most that can be said is that, given whatever may be chosen as import requirements (part of what has been termed the 'policy factor'), it is the size of other receipts – export earnings or borrowing – that determine the offer of gold. Two recent studies have demonstrated that reasonable projections of earnings and of grain and machinery imports do not exhibit any unmanageable visible deficits by 1985. Desai restricts her projections to grain requirements under a variety of assumptions[45] and Beaucourt puts all current purchases and sales into hers.[46] The latter sets potential annual gold sales to 1985 at between 275 and 330 tonnes annually and projects prices at the 1979 and at the 1980 averages (respectively $307 and $612 per oz.). Only under her most 'extreme' scenario of continuing bad harvests and poor hydrocarbon export receipts does even the lower of her balance-of-payments projections require gold sales. Time will tell, but the greatest uncertainty must attach to all attempts to assess the future Soviet impact on the world market for gold and platinum.

# 9 The Soviet Impact on International Trade in Asbestos

Petr Hanel

## INTRODUCTION

The central part of this chapter is concerned with the patterns of Soviet trade in asbestos and their impact on market structure, market power and price formation. Very little reliable data concerning Soviet production, consumption and trade of asbestos are available. Due to the lack of Soviet foreign trade statistics on asbestos the data from importing countries have been used. Moreover, much of the information presented below has been obtained from industry experts who answered our questionnaires.

Asbestos is a name applied to a number of naturally fibrous minerals. The principal variety is chrysotile, other commercial varieties are amosite and crocidolite.

Chrysotile accounts for about 95 per cent of world production and, unless stated otherwise, this paper is concerned with chrysotile. The principal deposits of chrysotile are in the Soviet Union and Canada and in smaller quantities also in China, Australia and Italy.

Chrysotile is graded and grouped into one of seven categories according to fibre length. Most of the categories are divided into several subgroups to comprise the commercial specifications. Asbestos is a highly differentiated product. One producer alone offers its customers 420 grades of fibre in 1,320 different forms.

A detailed breakdown of asbestos consumption by use shows that asbestos-cement products (sheets, roofing materials and pipes) account for more than half of total consumption in the US and for more than two-thirds in the rest of the world. Two other construction related materials, floor tiles and non-asbestos cement roofing, account for another 20–25 per cent of total consumption.

## SOVIET PRODUCTION AND CONSUMPTION

Table 9.1 gives some indication of Soviet importance in the world production of asbestos.[1] The table shows that during the late 1970s the USSR accounted for more than 45 per cent of world production, followed by Canada, South Africa and China.

Over the last three decades Soviet production of asbestos has been growing at a higher rate than the world output. This trend should continue in the near future as new mining capacities are brought into production in the USSR.

The asbestos industry was one of the few mineral industries existing in pre-Revolutionary Russia. Asbestos, mainly long fibres used for the manufacture of textile products, was mined in the Urals in the Bashenovsk and Nebolshikh Kolichestvakh regions. Since the advent of the Soviet regime other deposits have been discovered and opened (in the 1960s) at Tuva and at Dshetygarinskoe in Kazakhstan, as well those of Kiembaevskoe in the Southern Urals, Molodezhnoe in the Zabaikal north of Chita (long-fibred asbestos). Discovered, but so far awaiting development, are extensive deposits at Bugetsaysk in Kazakhstan.[2]

Table 9.2 gives details of production at individual sites. Recently the major investment project at the Kiembai was undertaken as a joint venture of COMECON countries; in exchange for their participation member states will be receiving a part of the production of the new complex. The project's first stage (250-thousand-ton yearly capacity) was completed in November 1979 and 130 thousand tons were produced in 1980. The output will be shared among the COMECON members in proportion to their contribution. From 1981 on, some 170 thousand tons are expected to be supplied annually to the participating countries for 12 years or more. According to the latest *Mining Annual Review*,[3] the second stage of the Kiembai complex was put into operation in December 1980. However, in industry circles it is believed that in 1981, contrary to published reports, regular production of the project's first stage did not reach the 250-thousand-ton target level. Aside from this development of new mining capacities there is a programme of modernization of the older mines.

Notwithstanding the overall trend, there are indications that the Soviet production of asbestos decreased markedly in 1979 and did not attain the levels planned.[4] This hypothesis seems to be supported[5] by the very low export figures for 1979 (see below). In spite of production volumes, the Soviets have not as yet succeeded in obtaining a sufficient variety of fibre lengths. The exchange programme between Canadian and Soviet asbestos producers assured the Soviets access to Canadian technology, equipment and know-how and is believed to have contributed to the improvement in quality of Soviet asbestos and to its increased acceptability in the international market.

Asbestos is not recycled and stockpiling is negligible. Consequently, annual world consumption of asbestos tends to be approximately the same as annual world production. World consumption of asbestos is thought to be in the range of 5.57 million tons. The USSR is by far the biggest consumer. The latest estimates of its total consumption vary considerably, reaching from 1.5 million tons (estimates based on data used for Table 9.1) to 2.2 million tons. Our conservative estimate is based on more recent data and therefore likely to be more accurate.

The exact data for the Soviet Union's pattern of asbestos use are not available. Given the prevalence of the USSR's consumption in world consumption, the Soviet pattern of consumption is closer to the world pattern than that of the United States (see Table 9.3). The first category specified in Table 9.3 contains long fibre chrysotile (the major end-use products include textiles, woven linings and electrical and high pressure insulation materials). The second category includes chrysotile, amosite and crocidolite fibre and is used for asbestos-cement (A-C) pipes, sheets and moulded products, and asbestos papers for brake linings and gaskets. The third category – short fibre – is used in linings and as a filler in coatings, plastics and floor tiles.

Table 9.3 shows that, in 1974, the latest period for which such detailed data are available, Eastern Europe was already the biggest consumer of asbestos in the world. Building materials account for more than three-quarters of the total consumption of asbestos in the USSR and Eastern Europe. The vigorous growth of the construction industry was absorbing an increasing proportion of the total production of asbestos. Consequently, the growth rate of apparent Soviet asbestos consumption (18 per cent per year) exceeded the rate of growth of its total production (14 per cent per year). These total figures are however of limited interest because the various categories of asbestos are not easily substitutable. A comparison of the demand

Table 9.1  The Soviet Share in World Production of Asbestos: 1953–1990 (in thousand metric tons)

| Year | Production Capacity World t | Production Capacity USSR t | Production Capacity Share % | Production World t | Production USSR t | Production Share % | Exports World t | Exports USSR[a] t | Exports Share % | Apparent consumption USSR t |
|---|---|---|---|---|---|---|---|---|---|---|
| 1953 | n.a. | n.a. | n.a. | 1419 | 272 | 19.2 | | | | 851 |
| 1962 | n.a. | n.a. | n.a. | 2742 | 998 | 36.0 | | 146 | | 536 |
| 1965 | n.a. | n.a. | n.a. | 3146 | 785 | 27.5 | | 248 | | 681 |
| 1970 | n.a. | | | 3444 | 1066 | 31.0 | | 385 | | 719 |
| 1971 | n.a. | | | 3581 | 1152 | 32.2 | | 433 | | 787 |
| 1972 | n.a. | | | 3794 | 1220 | 32.3 | | 433 | | 831 |
| 1973 | n.a. | | | 4171 | 1280 | 30.7 | 2756[c] | 499 | 16.3 | 832 |
| 1974 | 4596 | 1482 | 32 | 4115 | 1360 | 33.0 | 2736[c] | 528 | 19.3 | 1282 |
| 1975 | | | | 4139 | 1896 | 45.8 | 2606 | 613 | 23.5 | 1220 |
| 1976 | | 2200 | | 5085 | 1850[h] | 45.0 | 3041[d] | 630[h] | 20.7 | 1300 |
| 1977 | | | | 5221 | 1900[h] | 46.0 | 2621[d] | 600[h] | 22.8 | 1345 |
| 1978 | 5705 | 2600 | 46 | 5178 | 1945[h] | 47.0 | 2931[d] | 600[h] | 20.4 | 1570 |
| 1979 | 5715 | 2600 | 46 | 5278 | 2020[h] | 46.8 | | 450[h] | | 1550 |
| 1980 | 6575 | 2800 | (43) | | 2150[h] | | | 600[h] | | |
| 1981 | | 3250 | | | (3265)[b] | | | (634)[g] | | |
| 1985 | 7296 | 3000–3500 | (41–48) | 5500–6100[f] | (4140)[b] | | | (771)[g] | | |
| 1990 | | | | | (4800)[e] | | | | | |

Notes:
a) *Statistical Yearbook 1976, Member Countries CMEA*, (coinciding with Roskill (1978)).

b) *Asbestos*, 78/12/00 p. 49.
c) Our estimate = world export excl. USSR from Roskill, 1976 plus USSR's exports from (a) and/or detailed import figures from Roskill.
d) USSR's exports to COMECON countries were estimated from table 5 and added to Roskill figures to obtain total exports of USSR and of the world.
e) Information from Canadian Dept. of Ind. and Trade.
f) *Asbestos* – Dec. 1979, p. 14.
g) Projections – *Asbestos*, Dec. 1978, p. 40.
h) Latest figures from *Mining Annual Review*, June 1981.

*Sources:* Capacity, US Bureau of Mines, 1979, 1980. World production, US Bureau of Mines, 1980 (1970–1979); Roskill, 1980 p. 12 (1962–1965). Exports, US Bureau of Mines p. 9 (1978).

Table 9.2 USSR: Asbestos Production by Principal Mines and Mills, 1968–1990

| Mine and Mill | Location | 1968[a] | 1975[a] | 1977 | 1978 | 1979 | 1985 | 1990 |
|---|---|---|---|---|---|---|---|---|
| Uralasbest | Asbest, Sverdlovsk, Urals | n.a. | 1133 | — | 1240[b] | 1270[b] | n.a. | 2000 |
| Dzhetygara | Kustanay Oblast, Kazakhstan | 270 | 326 | 640 | 640[b] | 640[b] | 1145 | 1145 |
| Tuvaasbest | Aktourak, Krasnoyarsk, Tuva ASSR | 26 | 186 | — | — | 110[b] | 200 | 200 |
| Kiembai | Orenburg Oblast, southern Urals | 0 | — | — | — | 130[b] | 500 | 500 |
| Moldojnaja | | — | — | — | — | — | 200 | 200 |
| Total (Categories 1 to 6) | | 1200 | 1646 | 2400 | | | 4800 | 4800 |

*Source:* a) *Asbestos*, December 1977; b) *Mining Annual Review*, 1981.

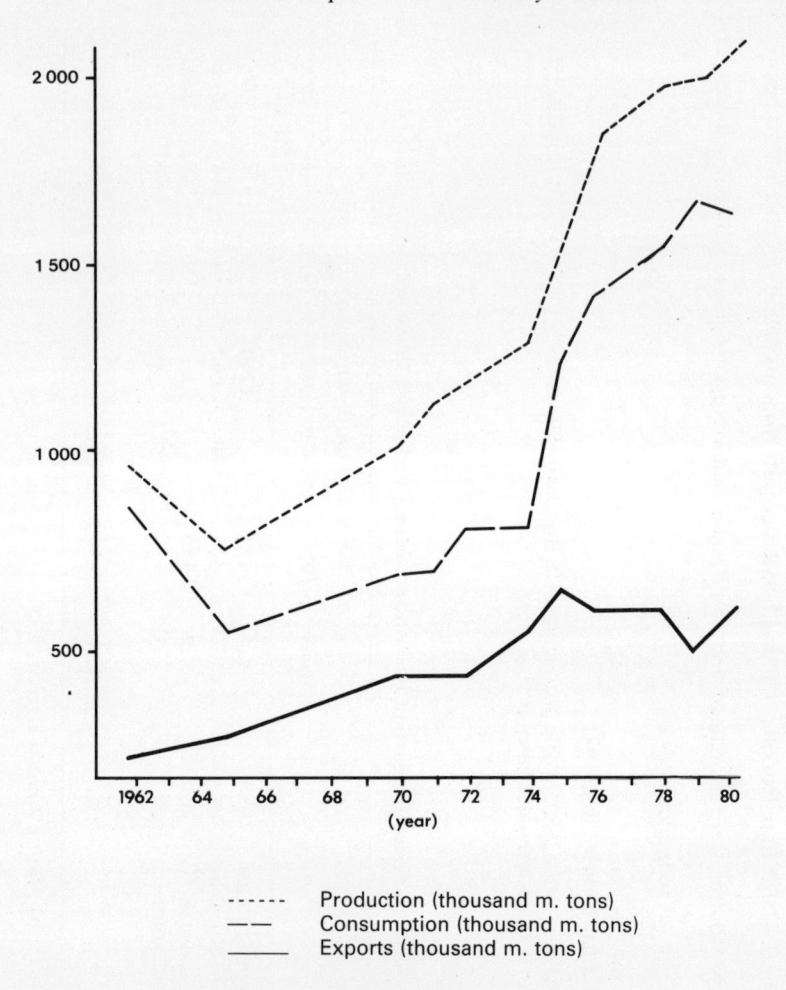

FIGURE 9.1  The Evolution of Soviet Production, Consumption and Exports of Asbestos

- - - - - Production (thousand m. tons)
— — Consumption (thousand m. tons)
——— Exports (thousand m. tons)

and production patterns by category of fibre shows that up to 1974 at least, Eastern Europe had to import longer fibres (12 per cent of the total consumption of category 2 and 80 per cent of category 1) from outside of the COMECON.[6] The composition of the consumption and production of asbestos by category reveals that the USSR's position as a leading producer is in fact more fragile than the total production figure might suggest.

Table 9.3 World Consumption of Asbestos in 1974 (thousands of metric tons and (%))

| Region | Category 1 t | % | Category 2 t | % | Category 3 t | % | Category 4 t | % | Total t |
|---|---|---|---|---|---|---|---|---|---|
| Canada & US | 29 | (3) | 335 | (40) | 417 | (50) | 48 | (6) | 830 |
| Western Europe | 23 | (2) | 567 | (52) | 453 | (42) | 45 | (4) | 1088 |
| Eastern Europe[a] | 27 | (2) | 750 | (60) | 440 | (35) | 32[b] | (3) | 1247[b] |
| Japan | 5 | (1) | 181 | (54) | 141 | (42) | 9 | (3) | 336 |
| World total | 97 | (2) | 2331 | (55) | 1623 | (39) | 123 | (3) | 4204 |

*Notes:*
a) Eastern Europe contains USSR and Centrally Planned Economies.
b) The Soviet production of fibres of group 8 and 9 used as soil additive has not been included in the table.
c) Category 1 contains long fibre chrysotile (groups 1, 2 and 3 of the Canadian classification). Category 2 includes chrysotile, amosite and crocidolite fibres (groups 4 and 5). Category 3 contains short fibres (groups 6 and 7). Category 4 contains the shortest fibres (groups 8 and 9).

*Source:* Sorès Inc. & A.D. Little.

## SOVIET EXPORTS OF ASBESTOS

The geographic concentration of asbestos deposits in a very few countries and the universal demand for the mineral's unique characteristics explain why it is so extensively traded on international markets. The leading exporter is Canada (60 per cent), followed by the Soviet Union (19 per cent) and South Africa (13 per cent). The principal importers are the US (20 per cent), followed by Japan, West Germany, France and the U.K.

Both the total production and exports of Soviet asbestos have been growing in absolute terms and are likely to continue to do so in the future. During the 1960s, Soviet exports grew faster than production so that by the early 1970s the Soviets were exporting almost forty per cent of their asbestos production. Less than half of their exports were absorbed by Other Centrally Planned Economies.

The pattern of growth observed in the 1960s was reversed during the last decade. In spite of an impressive increase in Soviet asbestos production (which more than doubled during the 1970s), exports increased at a slower pace until 1975 when they benefited from the temporary reduction of Canadian exports, to reach the overall high of 613 thousand tons. This is also the last year (at the time of writing) for which Soviet data on exports of asbestos are available. Information collected from importing countries indicates that the record figure of 1975 exports was probably not repeated in subsequent years.[7]

The COMECON countries received on the average above 40 per cent of total Soviet asbestos exports up to the mid-1970s (the sporadically available figures for more recent years (Table 9.4) are not sufficient to complete the picture but they do not show any sign of a dramatic downturn). It thus seems that the Soviet Union, as a loyal ally, continued to place high priority on satisfying the growing needs of other socialist countries. To assess the implications of this assumption, the 6-year-trend (1970–1976) of Soviet exports to other COMECON countries was projected for the years 1977–1980 (for which no import data to COMECON countries are yet available) and is indicated in parentheses in Table 9.4. Should this scenario be true, then the COMECON would be absorbing an increasing proportion of total Soviet exports. The dependence of COMECON countries on Soviet asbestos varies from country to country. Judging from available figures it would appear that the COMECON countries depended on Soviet asbestos for more than two-thirds of total consumption.

The following ten countries, listed in order of decreasing tonnage of imported USSR asbestos, accounted in 1977 for over eighty per cent of Soviet asbestos exports to non-communist countries: Japan, Yugoslavia, West Germany, France, India, Belgium & Luxembourg, Italy, Spain, the United States and the United Kingdom. Together, they imported forty per cent of the world asbestos production and accounted for well over sixty per cent of world trade. With the exceptions of the United Kingdom and United States which imported negligible quantities of asbestos from the Soviet Union, some of these countries relied heavily on supply of Soviet asbestos. Table 9.5 shows the share of exports supplied to this group of importing countries by the USSR and the other two major exporters, Canada and South Africa.

The dependence on Soviet asbestos varies significantly among countries. Yugoslavia and India imported two-thirds of their total imports of asbestos from the USSR. Among the industrial countries of Western Europe, France imported more than one-third of its total imports of asbestos from the USSR, other countries import much less. In absolute terms, Japan constitutes an important export

Table 9.4 Soviet Exports of Asbestos to COMECON Countries (thousand tons)

| | 1970 | 1971 | 1972 | 1973 | 1974[a] | 1975[a] | 1976 | 1977 | 1978 | 1979 |
|---|---|---|---|---|---|---|---|---|---|---|
| Bulgaria[c] | 21.2 | 22.8 | 19.7 | 30.6 | 32.6 | 28.8 | — | — | — | — |
| Cuba[c] | 9.5 | 10.8 | 12.3 | 12.0 | 14.0 | 8.8 | — | — | 17.0 | 20.0[e] |
| Czechoslovakia | 20.4 | 21.7 | 20.9 | 21.7 | 28.0 | 31.2 | 28.4 | 33.8 | 32.7 | 20.[e] |
| East Ger.[c] | 43.1 | 43.7 | 48.7 | 44.0 | 44.7 | 59.4 | — | — | — | — |
| Hungary[c] | 13.9 | 16.3 | 16.8 | 18.9 | 26.0 | 27.9 | 31.2 | 36.7 | 33.2 | 23.4 |
| Poland | 26.8 | 43.2 | 58.8 | 63.9 | 74.9 | 76.2 | 70.2 | 55.3 | 61.6 | 45.2 |
| Romania[d] | 19.0 | 20.2 | 19.7 | 22.2 | 21.7 | 34.3 | — | — | 17.0 | 17.0[e] |
| Total | 154.9 | 178.70 | 196.9 | 213.3 | 217.9 | 266.6 | 275[b] | (294)[f] | (313)[f] | (333)[f] |

Sources:
a) Roskill, 1980
b) Canadian Government, Dept. of Ind. Trade and Commerce.
c) *Industrial Minerals*, June 1975.
d) Author's estimate for 1970, for the rest the same as (c)
e) *Soviet Business and Trade*, various issues, 1979.
f) Author's estimates – extrapolations of the trend (1970–1975)

Table 9.5 Imports of Asbestos by the Group of Ten Principal Importers[a] and Evolution of the Market Shares Held by South African, Canadian and Soviet Exports

| Year | World (t) | (index) | S.A. (%) | CA (%) | USSR (%) | Total (%) Share |
|---|---|---|---|---|---|---|
| 1962 | 1260343 | 78  | 18.6 | 71.9 | 6.4  | 96.9 |
| 1965 | 1445829 | 90  | 17.4 | 68.4 | 9.2  | 95.0 |
| 1970 | 1609817 | 100 | 15.7 | 66.5 | 9.1  | 91.3 |
| 1971 | 1573719 | 98  | 16.9 | 66.1 | 12.0 | 95   |
| 1972 | 1760618 | 109 | 15.6 | 68.4 | 10.0 | 94   |
| 1973 | 2048813 | 127 | 10.6 | 67.9 | 8.8  | 88   |
| 1974 | 2085252 | 129 | 13.9 | 67.7 | 11.2 | 92.8 |
| 1975 | 1790226 | 111 | 17.6 | 58.7 | 15.4 | 91.7 |
| 1976 | 1939844 | 120 | 14.5 | 65.0 | 13.6 | 93.1 |
| 1977 | 1840530 | 114 | 14.3 | 64.8 | 14.6 | 93.7 |
| 1978 | 1671170 | 104 | 14.2 | 68.4 | 10.9 | 93.5 |
| 1979 | 1755391 | 109 | 15.6 | 68.4 | 9.1  | 93.1 |

*Note:* [a]France, W. Germany, Belgium & Lux., Spain, Italy, U.K., Yugoslavia, India, U.S.A.

*Source:* Calculated from U.N. Commodity trade statistics (SITC 276.4).

market; up to 1977 it was the first importer of Soviet asbestos, though the Soviet share of Japan's imports of asbestos exceeded the 25 per cent mark only once, in 1975, due to the disruption of Canadian production and exports.

Owing to the significant differences among importing countries with respect to their reliance on Soviet asbestos, the evolution of market shares held by the USSR, Canada and South Africa is shown separately for the group of West European importers, Japan, and India in Figure 9.2.

## USSR AND ASBESTOS PRICES

Asbestos commands a different price depending on grades. Chrysotile, which constitutes by far the most important variety of asbestos, is producer-priced. Canada, maintaining a dominant position on the

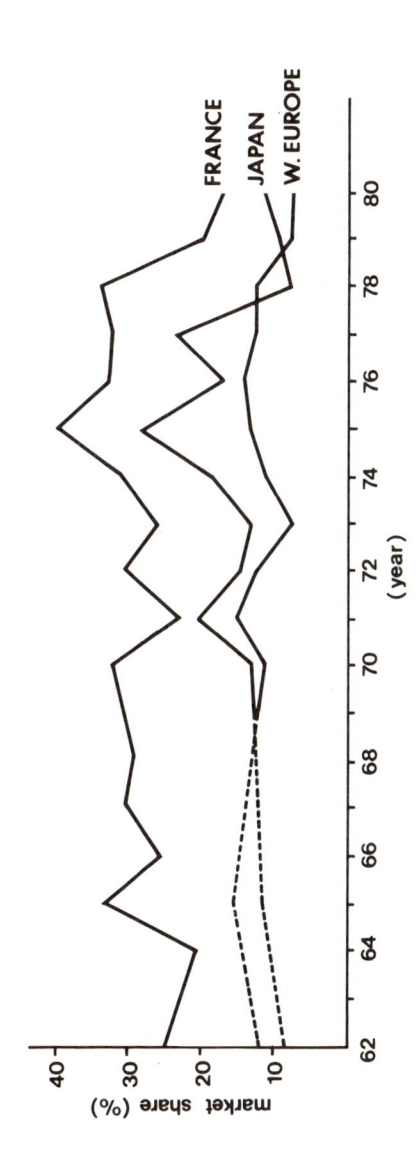

FIGURE 9.2 Evolution of USSR's Share of Asbestos Market

market, is a price leader.[8] While North American prices are being regularly published, there is no direct public information on the prices contracted by the South African and Soviet exporters.

The following discussion will be concerned with the observed unit value of exports (i.e. $/metric ton) which can be regarded as an average price p, of varous categories $p = \Sigma p_i x_i / \Sigma x_i$, when $p_i$ is the price of the category i, and $x_i$ is the quantity of category i. The use of this weighted average price for intertemporal comparisons implies that the grade composition of each country's asbestos exports did not change over time. This is a realistic assumption for short-term comparisons, since the structure of exports reflects the composition of output. Besides, it is a well-known fact that the Soviet Union produces and exports mainly the shorter fibres (groups 5 and 6) owing to the shortage of longer fibres.[9] In general, within each category, the quality of Soviet asbestos has so far been lower than that of comparable Canadian and South African products.

The observed unit values of total asbestos imports will be treated in the following analysis as a synonym for the weighted average price described above. The price trend in the US[10] shows that until 1974 the relative stability of asbestos prices, characteristic of a mature oligopolistic industry, resulted in an actual decline of the asbestos price in constant dollars. The energy crisis and the temporary acute shortage of Canadian asbestos in 1975 led to substantial price increases which slowed down at the end of the 1970s owing to the decline in overall demand. The prices for imported asbestos in Western Europe and in Japan, India and Yugoslavia were showing a similar pattern of remarkable price stability up until 1973/4, followed by a sudden upsurge. Figures 9.3, a, b, c show the evolution of prices for individual regions and countries.

The detailed composition of imports by grades not being available, no attempt can be made to identify the degree to which observed evolution of price differentials reflects changes in the composition of total asbestos imports for each market. Assuming that the composition of imports did not change dramatically, it is possible to examine the evolution of the relative price of Soviet and Canadian asbestos on each import market.[11]

The relative price of Soviet and Canadian asbestos $P_u/P_c$ imported to Western Europe shows a sharply increasing trend (4 per cent/ year), beginning in the early 1970s so that in 1978 the prices were virtually identical. Evolution of the relative price ($P_u/P_c$) in Japan follows a similar pattern but the increase was more gradual and started in the 1960s. The relative price fluctuated on both markets starting with an upsurge in 1973 when the Russians, apparently taking advantage of the strong demand, attempted to increase revenues from asbestos exports to earn as much foreign exchange as possible to help pay for record imports of grain. A similar upsurge in Soviet asbestos prices occurred in 1975, again coinciding with record grain imports. This time, however, the situation on the asbestos market offered a more likely explanation for the price increase; there was an acute shortage of asbestos due to the disruption of production in Canada. This situation favoured the Russians who, in the face of additional demand, raised both their prices and their market share practically everywhere. This contrasts sharply with the experience of 1973, when the price increase cost the Russians part of their market share and, as a result, their revenues dropped by ten per cent, indicating that the demand for Soviet asbestos was at that time relatively price-elastic.[12] An attempt can be made to test statistically the hypothesis that Soviet asbestos prices are raised in periods of increased grain importation. This can be done by regressing the yearly observations of the price of Soviet asbestos in France (the most important importer of Soviet asbestos) on the annual imports of grain by the USSR. These two variables do in fact show a significant positive correlation:

$$P_u = 108.3 + 4.35 \text{ M} \qquad R^2 = 0.34$$
$$(2.66)$$
$$(F = 7.09) \text{ signif.} = 0.02$$

A less significant positive correlation also exists between the standardized residual of the price variable from the linear time trend and the standardized residual of the imports of cereals and their trend.[13]

The empirical tests suggest that in times of need for foreign currency the Soviets attempted to raise prices rather than to increase the volume of asbestos sales.[14]

In contrast to the upward trend of the relative price ($P_u/P_c$) observed on the markets of industrialised capitalist countries, the relative price shows a downward trend in India and Yugoslavia – two countries having special relationships with Russia. Aside from a political explanation – which is not altogether unlikely since Russia has often been willing to trade economic losses for political gains – the other possible reason could be that long-term bilateral contracts were negotiated with fixed prices or in barter terms, similar to those

186  The Soviet Impact on Commodity Markets

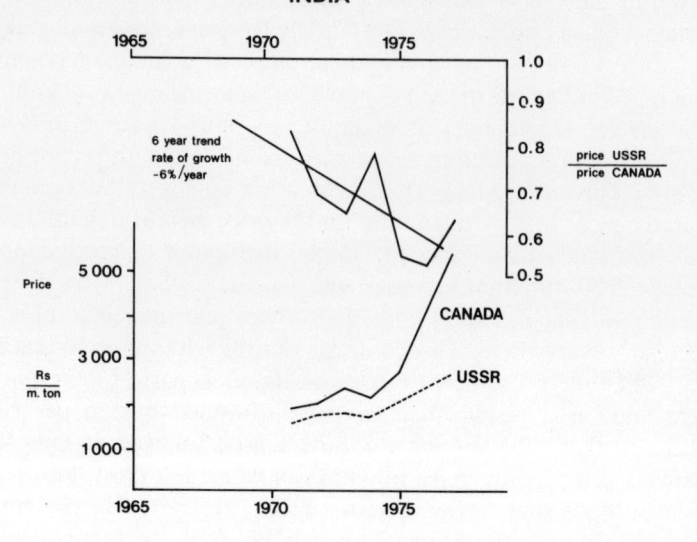

**INDIA**

(a) Source: Roskill, 1976, 1980

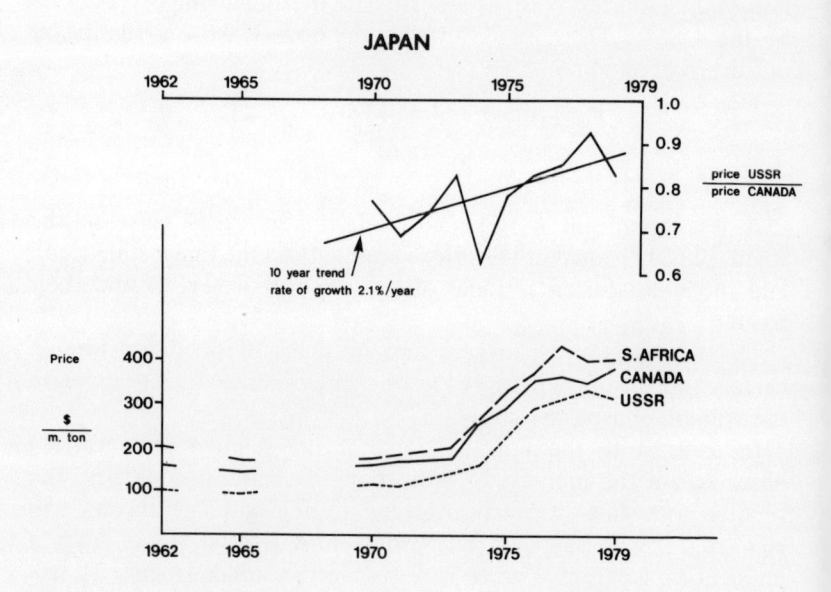

**JAPAN**

(b) Source: Roskill, 1976, 1980

FIGURE 9.3  The Evolution of Import Prices

**WESTERN EUROPE (6)**

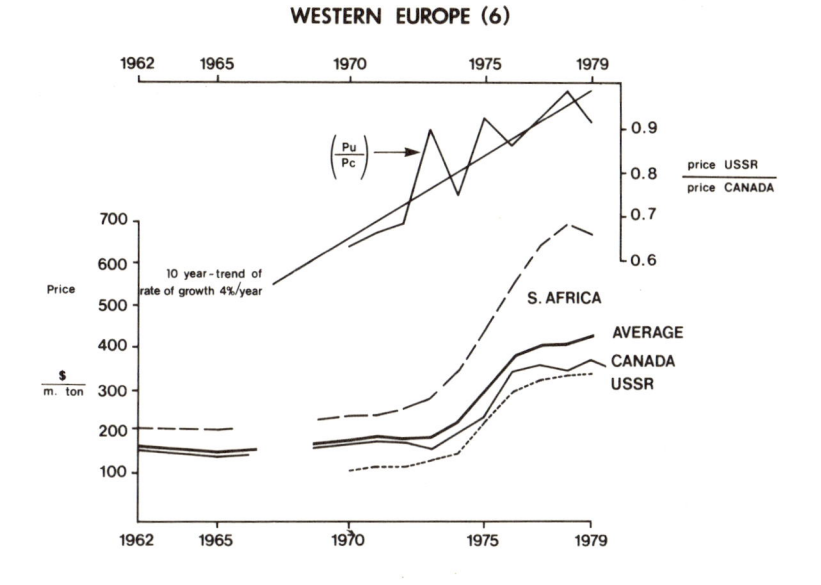

[Figure: price and price-ratio chart for Western Europe, 1962–1979, showing S. AFRICA, AVERAGE, CANADA, USSR prices ($/m. ton) and the ratio price USSR / price CANADA; 10-year trend of rate of growth 4%/year indicated.]

(c)   Source : Roskill, 1976, 1980

FIGURE 9.3   (continued)

Russia has with COMECON countries. Finally, another possible explanation for the downward trend of relative prices in India and Yugoslavia could be that the relative prices reflect changes in the quality of Russian asbestos, the better grades being shipped increasingly to the West. This is probably happening but only to a limited extent. In any case, according to industry experts, the quality of Soviet asbestos shipped to Western Europe remains inferior to the Canadian product.

## THE IMPACT OF SOVIET COMPETITION ON THE INTERNATIONAL ASBESTOS MARKET

The three principal exporters dominate the international market to such an extent that the gains of any one among them are likely to be at the expense of the other two. Owing to its unique kind and quality, South African asbestos is not so exposed to Russian competition as are Canadian types for which Soviet grades are close substitutes.

Therefore, the USSR's past gains on the market were mostly made at the expense of Canadian exports; this is reflected by the significant negative correlation between the variations of the market share of Canada and the USSR both on the Western European market and in Japan.

*In W. Europe* (12 observations):

$(E_u/E_i)_t = 30.9 - 0.32 \ (E_c/E_i)_t$ $\qquad R^2 = 0.49$

$\qquad\qquad\qquad (2.4)$ $\qquad\qquad\qquad$ (F = 5.76) signif. = 0.05

*In Japan* (18 observations):

$(E_u/E_i)_t = 34.6 - 0.42 \ (E_c/E_i)_t$ $\qquad R^2 = 0.46$

$\qquad\qquad\qquad (3.2)^{***}$ $\qquad\qquad\qquad$ (F = 10.4) signif. = 0.01

The symbols $E_{u,c}$ indicate exports to the given market by the USSR and Canada (as the case may be); $E_i$, total exports to the given market or country and t, the year. The Western European sample covers 1962, 1965 and 1970 to 1979; the Japanese: all years from 1962 to 1979.

The regression results clearly show a pattern of substitution between Canadian and Soviet exports on both the Western European and Japanese markets. On the other hand, results not reproduced here show that Soviet exports do not exert any influence on the evolution of the market share held by South Africa. What is then the impact of Soviet prices on the market?

In the case of close substitutes, the quantities sold may be expected to increase when the relative price declines and vice versa. In the simplest linear specification, the price/quantity relationship may be tested by estimating:

$$(E_u/E_c)_t = a - b \ (P_u/P_c)_t$$

where the symbols $E_{u,c}$ indicate once again exports of asbestos (quantity) by the USSR and Canada respectively. $P_u$ and $P_c$ are the prices (unit values) of Soviet and Canadian asbestos and t is the year (1962–1980).

In order to minimize the problems of measurement it was thought preferable to concentrate on national import markets. France and Japan, the principal importers of Soviet asbestos, were the logical choice for this test.

The regression was estimated in two slightly different versions; in the case of France, both gave results corresponding to the theoretical expectation. The first relates prices and shares of Soviet and Canadian exports. The second relates the Soviet share in total French imports of asbestos to the relative price of Soviet and Canadian exports.

As expected, the regression coefficient is negative in both cases and can be thought of as a rough approximation of the cross-elasticity of substitution between Soviet and Canadian exports.[15] The results indicate that a certain proportion of the variance of the ratio between Soviet and Canadian exports of asbestos to France (or in the second case of the Soviet share of total French imports of asbestos) can be explained by the movement of relative prices.

Delivery problems are common when dealing with Russian asbestos exporters and it must be recognised that they present a serious handicap which even lower Soviet prices often can not overcome.[16] It can therefore be assumed that along with the variation of the relative prices, variations in Soviet asbestos output also help to explain the observed evolution of asbestos exports. When Soviet exports to France are regressed on Soviet production and on the relative price of asbestos this hypothesis is not contradicted. The coefficient associated with the output is significant at 10 per cent only, but the significance of the relative price is enhanced in this formulation:

$$(E_u)_t^F = 100{,}872 + 6.3 \text{ OUT} - 116{,}529 \, (P_u/P_c)_t^F$$

$$(1.4) \qquad\qquad (-3.4)$$

$R^2 = 0.57$ (F = 7.0) signif. = 0.01

Attempts to regress the French imports of Soviet asbestos on the time variables and on demand indicators, such as France's industrial production index or its index of the construction activity, failed to give significant results.

An attempt to regress the Soviet share of the Japanese market or the relative price failed to give statistically significant results. According to the majority of experts, the Soviet Union does charge different prices to different customers; our attempt to test this assertion statistically failed to give conclusive results.

To conclude, there is some evidence that relative prices played a limited role in shaping the competition on France's asbestos market. This tentative conclusion could probably be extended to some other importing countries of Western Europe and it is also supported by the opinion of experts who believe that prices on the continent would probably be higher than they are today if the Soviet asbestos were not on the market.

## OUTLOOK

Given the differences in the pattern of demand for asbestos, the prospects for evolution of demand are different for the US and Western European countries on the one hand and for Eastern Europe including the Soviet Union on the other hand. Slow demographic growth and the growing concern regarding the harmful effects for asbestos in Western countries are likely to result in zero growth of demand of asbestos. The US Bureau of Mines[17] forecasts the average rate of growth to year 2000 in the range between −2 per cent/year and +1.8 per cent/year.

The demand for asbestos in the rest of the world is growing faster than in the US, and owing to the future construction potential of developing countries, it is estimated to continue to increase at the rate of 4.5 per cent/year for the next twenty years. Should problems prevent an increase in general living standards in the rest of the world, the consumption of asbestos would grow at only 3.6 per cent/year. Table 9.6 summarises the forecasted scenario for the US and the USSR as well as for the world as a whole.

The forecasts depend, of course, on the underlying assumptions and on the time period used to estimate the rate of growth to be extrapolated to the future. The extrapolations used by the US Bureau of Mines and the author's extrapolation of the apparent consumption shown in note b, Table 9.6, are both based on a ten-year trend. Under this assumption, future Soviet production should be sufficient to cover internal consumption and leave approximately one million metric tons of asbestos for exports, i.e. 16 per cent of Soviet production in the year 2000. The excess of Soviet production over Soviet internal demand is likely to be almost entirely absorbed by Soviet exports to other COMECON members, leaving only 250 thousand metric tons for exports outside COMECON in the year 2000. This is, however, an optimistic scenario.

The ten-year trend hides the fact that in the last five years the rate of growth of Soviet production, high as it has been, was clearly slower than the growth of apparent Soviet consumption. Extrapolation of the five-year trend (1974–1978) would result in the USSR becoming a net importer of asbestos in the 1990s.

Owing to delayed production increases and continuing commitments to COMECON countries, it is likely that the Soviets will in the future decrease their exports outside the COMECON bloc.[18]

Although the Soviet Union is the leading producer of asbestos, its

Table 9.6 Summary of Forecasts of US and Rest of World Asbestos Demand (thousand metric tons)

| | 1978 | 2000 Forecast range low | high | Probable 1990 | 2000 | Probable Average annual growth rate 1978–2000 (%) |
|---|---|---|---|---|---|---|
| United States | | | | | | |
| total | 619 | 397 | 920 | 620 | 620 | –0– |
| cumulative | | 10 884 | 16 867 | 7 440 | 13 640 | — |
| USSR[a] | | | | | | |
| total | 1 834 | 3 995 | 5 835[b] | 3 112 | 4 833 | 4.5 |
| cumulative | | 60 009 | 74 079 | 28 376 | 66 619 | |
| World | | | | | | |
| total | 5 154 | 10 203 | 15 340 | 8 340 | 12 607 | 4.1 |
| cumulative | | 163 955 | 209 876 | 80 873 | 186 121 | |

Notes:
a) The forecast for the USSR and COMECON was calculated by the author applying the "rest of the world" rates to the 1978 consumption.
b) Extrapolation of the observed apparent consumption of the USSR over the period 1970–78 gives the forecasted consumption for 2000 as 5516 thousand metric tons, i.e. close to the high range forecast based on the growth rate 5.4 per cent/year, used by the US Bureau of Mines.

Source: US Bureau of Mines, Asbestos, 1980

impact on the market in non-communist countries has been limited. Soviet exports probably moderated to some extent price increases which would otherwise have taken place in periods of strong demand. Given the likelihood of a slow growth in future demand for asbestos and the continuing export capacity of Canadian and South African producers, it is unlikely that Soviet market power would increase notably.

The political impact of asbestos exports has been limited to the COMECON countries, but has, perhaps also to a lesser degree, affected some developing countries close to the USSR. As with many other raw materials, the socialist countries depend almost entirely upon the Soviet Union for their supply of asbestos. The ongoing integration within the COMECON makes it increasingly difficult for the resource-poor member countries to generate revenues in convertible currencies which would make it possible for them to seek alternative supply sources. The privileged position of the dominant supplier certainly confers on the USSR a wide margin of economic and political leverage. The fact that asbestos is but one of the many resources over which the USSR can exercise such discretionary power surely enhances her supremacy over the COMECON states.

CONCLUSION

In the mid-1970s, the Soviet Union became the first producer of asbestos, it is also by far the first consumer of this very differentiated mineral. Soviet production capacity is being expanded and is likely to continue to be expanded in the future whereas future expansion possibilities elsewhere in the world appear to be more limited.

Although the COMECON taken as a whole is a net exporter of asbestos, most countries outside the Soviet Union have to import some special categories of asbestos. The categories of asbestos exported by the Soviet Union are quite common and in fact mostly of lower quality than comparable products from Canada or from South Africa. Soviet exports of asbestos appear to be a closer substitute for Canadian exports than for the South African ones. Accordingly, when the Russians lower their price in relation to the price of Canadian asbestos, the share of Soviet exports on the importing markets have a tendency to increase and vice versa.

As far as the pattern and motivation underlying pricing of Soviet asbestos are concerned, the observed pattern suggests that prices were raised in years of large grain imports; the statistical test does not reject this hypothesis. The data however show that at least in one instance, in the period 1972–73, the price increase led to a decrease in export revenues apparently owing to elasticity of demand for Soviet asbestos.

Regarding the prospects for the asbestos industry in the future, there is little doubt that the relative importance of the Soviet Union as the first producer will go unchallenged for many years to come. However, because it is also the most formidable consumer of its own asbestos and because the demand both in the Soviet Union and in other COMECON countries will continue to grow faster than in the Western countries, most of the Soviet asbestos will be needed to cover intra-COMECON needs. Russia plans to allocate some twenty per cent of its future production to exports, almost half of which will go to other communist countries and only seven to ten per cent will find its way into the market economies. The demand of developing countries for asbestos will be growing in proportion to the growth of construction activity there, as the negative impact of the potential health hazards on demand for asbestos will be less important there than in the industrialised countries.

The Soviet Union is likely to stay in its traditional markets but to decrease somewhat their share in the long run. The Soviets' continuing presence on western markets will enable them to attempt, from time to time, to increase their prices in order to improve their balance of payments. In order to succeed in this goal the USSR needs to improve further the quality of its asbestos; hence a need for Western technology.

By decreasing their demand for asbestos through limitation of its use and through a continuing search for new substitutes, Western countries are likely to become, in the future, still less dependent on Soviet asbestos than they have been in the past. As for the COMECON countries, their dependence on Soviet asbestos is likely to grow, as the world market becomes tighter, and prices of asbestos from non-Communist sources rise above those fixed by long-term bilateral agreements concluded within the COMECON.

# 10 The Soviet Union in International Grain Markets

M.M. Kostecki

SOVIET GRAIN TRADE PATTERN

The position of the USSR in the world grain economy has been quite unique during the last decade. On the one hand, Soviet purchases of foreign grain accounted for a very important share of world grain imports and reflected a significant dependence of the USSR on foreign grain supplies. On the other hand, the Soviet Union has been one of the major grain producers and has remained a significant grain exporter. Table 10.1 provides some indication as to the relative importance of the USSR in the world grain market and in grain production.

These data from the late 1970s show the Soviet Union to be the second largest grain importer, the third largest grain producer and the sixth major grain exporter. The Soviet grain trading monopoly EXPORTKHLEB handled export or import transactions covering about 12 per cent of internationally-traded grain. That share was even more significant in the case of maize and wheat – two grains accounting for the bulk of Soviet grain purchases abroad. This high concentration, coupled with the grain trading monopoly, places the USSR among the major factors determining world market conditions.

The pattern of Soviet grain trade has varied markedly over the last three decades, in terms of both the Soviets' net trading position and the types of grain traded. With the exception of two years (1963/64 and 1965/66), the USSR was a net exporter of grain during the 1950s and the 1960s. At that time net Soviet grain exports were comparable in volume to those of Australia. And the USSR was frequently

Table 10.1 Major Grain Producers and Traders – (1974–1978 averages)

| Exporters | a % | b % | Producers | a % | b % | Importers | a % | b % |
|---|---|---|---|---|---|---|---|---|
| USA | 47.8 | 47.8 | USA | 17.2 | 17.2 | Japan | 12.4 | 12.4 |
| Canada | 10.0 | 57.8 | China | 17.1 | 34.3 | USSR | 9.3 | 21.7 |
| France | 8.5 | 66.3 | USSR | 13.2 | 47.5 | China | 5.1 | 26.8 |
| Argentina | 7.1 | 73.4 | India | 8.8 | 56.3 | Italy | 4.9 | 31.7 |
| Australia | 6.6 | 80.0 | Canada | 2.7 | 59.0 | UK | 4.8 | 36.5 |
| USSR | 2.7 | 82.7 | France | 2.5 | 61.5 | Netherlands | 4.4 | 40.9 |
| Thailand | 2.3 | 85.0 | Brazil | 1.9 | 63.4 | Germany Fed. | 4.2 | 45.1 |
| Netherlands | 2.2 | 87.2 | Indonesia | 1.8 | 65.2 | Poland | 3.3 | 48.4 |
| South Africa | 1.6 | 88.8 | Argentina | 1.7 | 66.9 | Belgium-Lux. | 3.0 | 51.4 |
| Germany Fed. | 1.3 | 90.1 | Turkey | 1.5 | 68.4 | Spain | 2.8 | 54.2 |

*Notes:*
a) Country World Share (%)
b) Cumulated World Share (%)

*Sources:* FAO *Trade Yearbook*, Vol. 30 1976, Vol. 32 1978. FAO *Production Yearbook*, Vol. 30 1976, Vol. 32 1978.

viewed as, potentially, a major competitor of the United States and Canada in international grain markets.[1] During those years, the Soviets also showed concern for the stabilisation of world grain prices and participated in several international wheat agreements as a wheat exporting country. The USSR preferred to retain that status in subsequent agreements even though its net trading position in wheat has since changed considerably.[2]

The Soviet Union intensified its purchases of foreign grain from the early 1970s on and became a consistent net grain importer. The data referring to Soviet grain exports, imports, production and net trading position are included in Table 10.2. They indicate that from 1971/72 on, Soviet grain imports markedly exceeded grain exports. This was true for the totals of grain traded even though the net export position was maintained in the case of wheat in 1971/72, 1973/74 and the following year. The changing pattern of the Soviets' net trading position coincided with important modifications of their grain imports by type of grain. As indicated in Table 10.3, wheat was the major grain imported by the USSR during the 1960s.

Table 10.2 Soviet Production and Trade of Grain, 1956/57–1980/81 (million metric tons)[a]

| Year beginning July | Production | Imports | Exports | Net[b] |
|---|---|---|---|---|
| 1956/57 | 125.0 | 0.9 | 5.4 | −4.5 |
| 1957/58 | 102.6 | 1.5 | 6.2 | −4.7 |
| 1958/59 | 134.7 | 1.7 | 7.7 | −6.0 |
| 1959/60 | 119.5 | 1.0 | 6.8 | −5.8 |
| 1960/61 | 125.5 | 0.8 | 7.0 | −6.2 |
| 1961/62 | 130.8 | 0.8 | 8.4 | −7.6 |
| 1962/63 | 140.2 | 0.6 | 8.3 | −7.7 |
| 1963/64 | 107.5 | 10.4 | 4.7 | +5.7 |
| 1964/65 | 152.1 | 2.6 | 4.3 | −1.7 |
| 1965/66 | 121.1 | 9.0 | 5.2 | +3.7 |
| 1966/67 | 171.2 | 3.9 | 5.3 | −1.4 |
| 1967/68 | 147.9 | 2.3 | 6.4 | −4.1 |
| 1968/69 | 169.5 | 1.2 | 7.4 | −6.2 |
| 1969/70 | 162.4 | 1.8 | 7.6 | −5.8 |
| 1970/71 | 186.8 | 1.3 | 8.5 | −7.2 |
| 1971/72 | 181.2 | 8.3 | 6.9 | +1.4 |
| 1972/73 | 168.2 | 22.8 | 1.8 | +21.0 |
| 1973/74 | 222.5 | 11.3 | 6.1 | +5.2 |
| 1974/75 | 195.7 | 5.7 | 5.3 | +0.4 |
| 1975/76 | 140.1 | 26.1 | 0.7 | +25.4 |
| 1976/77 | 223.8 | 11.0 | 3.3 | +7.7 |
| 1977/78 | 195.7 | 18.9 | 2.3 | +16.8 |
| 1978/79[c] | 237.0 | 15.6 | 2.8 | +12.8 |
| 1979/80[c] | 179.0 | 31.0 | 0.8 | +29.7 |
| 1980/81[d] | 185.0 | 31.0 | 1.0 | +30.0 |

*Notes:*
a) Rounded to the nearest million tons, except for production and trade data. Thus, totals may not tally due to rounding.
b) Minus indicates net exports.
c) Preliminary for trade.
d) Forecast.

*Source:* USDA, Supplement 1 to Document WAS-23, Washington, D.C., October 1980 p. 31.

Table 10.3 Composition of Soviet Grain Imports by Type of Grain, 1960–1979 (per cent)

| Grain | 1960–1964 | 1965–1969 | 1970–1974 | 1975–1979 |
|---|---|---|---|---|
| Wheat | 88.9 | 87.2 | 58.2 | 43.6 |
| Maize | 0.9 | 5.8 | 25.6 | 48.4 |
| Other grains | 10.2 | 7.0 | 16.2 | 8.0 |

*Source:* FAO, *Trade Yearbook*, various issues.

In the mid-1970s imports of feed grains made very strong gains and now account for a larger share of Soviet grain imports than wheat.

The Soviet grain trade followed a very erratic pattern in the 1960s and the 1970s. Significant year-to-year variations in volumes of total grain imports and exports could be observed (see Figure 10.1). Moreover, as might have been expected, changes in import volumes countered changes in export volumes. Imports varied significantly both for wheat (which is mainly food grain) and coarse grains. In relative terms, Soviet grain imports would seem to have been more subject to instability than Soviet grain production. The coefficient of variation for Soviet wheat imports (1964–78) is 95 per cent as compared with 16 per cent for Soviet wheat output.[3] The coefficient is also much higher for the Soviet imports than for imports by some other major wheat buyers. (Note, for example, that the coefficient of variation of China's wheat imports is only 35 per cent as compared with 19 per cent for China's wheat output.)

One can also observe wide variations of Soviet imports from particular grain supplying countries. These year-to-year shifts of Soviet grain purchases among alternative sources of supply also increased the trade instability resulting from fluctuations in total imports (see below).

A trend analysis of the Soviet imports of wheat and coarse grain (1960–79) gives the following results:

| Type of Imports | Time Derivatives | Standard Errors[a] |
|---|---|---|
| Wheat | 424.7 | 139.3 |
| Coarse Grain | 748.4 | 123.7 |

[a] These imply a 1 per cent level of statistical significance.

198　　　　*The Soviet Impact on Commodity Markets*

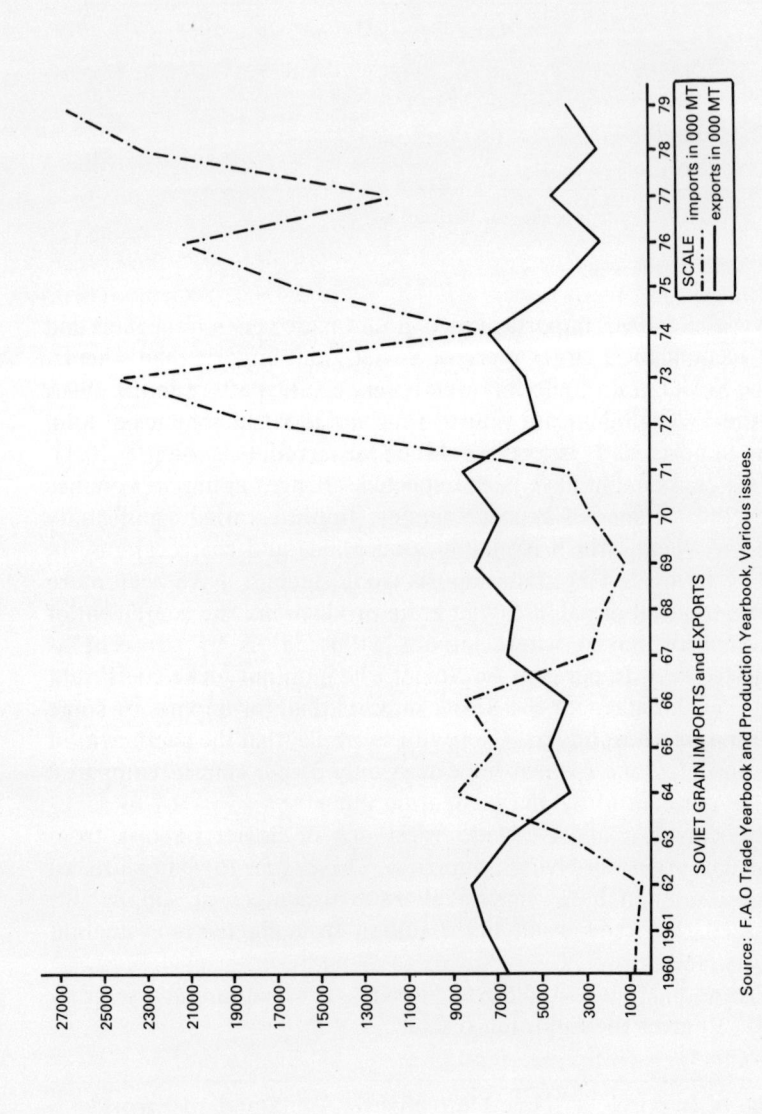

Figure 10.1　Soviet Grain Imports and Exports

Source: F.A.O Trade Yearbook and Production Yearbook, Various issues.

The time derivatives given above, measuring the average annual rate of import growth, clearly show that Soviet imports of coarse grain (in volume) have been increasing much faster than Soviet wheat imports.

An analogous trend analysis conducted for Soviet grain exports gives statistically insignificant results.

The Soviet Union's major grain suppliers have been the United States, Canada, Australia and Argentina and the USSR has been a leading export market for the countries concerned. (Appendix 1 indicates the values of Soviet grain imports by country of origin.) In purchases from these countries, the Soviet Union has used long-term agreements to cover a substantial part of import requirements. This is one of the few areas in which the USSR has used such agreements when importing from the market economies. During the last decade the United States, Australia and Argentina made gains in their relative market shares in Soviet grain markets mainly to the detriment of Canada. This has been due to two major factors.

First, while Canada's exports are mostly comprised of wheat, Soviet wheat imports have been increasing more slowly than its coarse grain imports. Secondly, the results of a constant market share analysis also show that Canada's relative share in the Soviet wheat market has slipped considerably.[4] However, the partial US grain embargo on shipments to the Soviet Union imposed in January 1980 increased the shares in the Soviet grain market held by exporters other than the United States. Large quantities of US grain were sold during the embargo to countries which normally purchase grain from other sources, thereby permitting these sources to supply grain to the Soviet Union.[5]

A country's reliance on foreign markets or sources of supply may have important economic and political implications. It influences the trader's bargaining power. In the case of an essential good, such as grain, it also gives some indication as to the scope for using trade to exercise political pressure. Several indicators of Soviet dependence on the major grain exporters and vice versa are presented in Table 10.4.

It may be seen that the three major grain exporters (US, Canada and Australia) together relied less on the Soviet Union as a foreign market than the USSR relied on them as a source of supply. This is true not only in terms of the relative import and export shares but also in terms of producers' and consumers' dependence on the trade flows considered. Indeed, the three exporting countries alone accounted for more than 85 per cent of foreign grain supplies to the

Table 10.4 Dependence on Grain Trade: USSR and Major Exporters (average for 1976/7–1978/9 – in percentages)

| Coefficient | Exporter USA | Canada | Australia | Argentina | EEC | USA Canada Australia | World |
|---|---|---|---|---|---|---|---|
| Grain Exports to the USSR Total Grain Exports | 12.4 | 10.0 | 2.6 | 10.1 | 1.8 | 11.0 | 9.4 |
| Grain Exports to the USSR Total Exports to the USSR | 49.0 | 49.0 | 9.2 | 55.6 | 0.3 | 44.3 | 7.9 |
| Grain Exports to the USSR Total Grain Production | 3.9 | 4.2 | 1.6 | 5.7 | 0.1 | 3.6 | 1.3 |
| Grain Exports to the USSR Soviet Grain Imports | 71.0 | 12.3 | 2.0 | 10.0 | 1.4 | 85.3 | 100. |
| Grain Exports to the USSR Soviet Grain Utilisation | 9.2 | 1.6 | 0.2 | 1.3 | 0.1 | 11.0 | 12.3 |

Sources: USDA, *Foreign Agriculture Circular: Grains*; various issues. IMF, *Direction of Trade*, 1980 (for total exports to USSR). FAO, *Trade Yearbook*, 1979 (for grain prices)

USSR, whereas the Soviet Union purchased only 11 per cent of the three countries' total grain exports. Moreover, every ninth bushel of grain consumed in the USSR originated either in North America or Australia, whereas the Soviet imports accounted for less than 4 per cent of these countries' average production. Thus to all appearances, if the grain trade in question were (hypothetically) stopped, the Soviets would probably find it more painful to survive than the grain producers concerned to operate without access to the Soviet market. The more so because the USSR shows an important deficit in international trade of agricultural food products since the early 1970s.[6] Grain has also been a dominant feature on the list of the market economies' exports to the USSR. For the USA, Canada and Argentina grain exports accounted for about half the total exports to the Soviet Union. In the late 1970s, grain purchases constituted about 10 per cent of total Soviet imports from the Western market economies. Since the major grain exporting countries do not necessarily share Soviet views on foreign policy, an essential good such as grain remains a most obvious candidate for linking East-West trade with East-West politics through use of "grain power".

Soviet grain exports have been traditionally mostly directed to the COMECON countries. But during recent years Soviet grain exports have accounted for almost all of Mongolia's grain needs, covered about 80 per cent of Cuba's grain imports and 80 per cent of the foreign grain purchases of Vietnam and North Korea.[8] The USSR's grain exports (mostly wheat) constituted, as well, a significant factor in the grain supplies of several East European countries (including Poland).

Note, however, that the Soviet export commitments were frequently met by re-exports. A portion of Cuba's grain requirements was covered by Canadian grain shipments, with bills being sent directly to Moscow. A considerable share of the Soviet grain sales in the 1970s does not appear to be straight commercial transactions aimed at generating foreign exchange. The volume of Soviet grain exports has been strongly influenced by domestic grain availabilities in the USSR (see below). Note, however, that the Soviets frequently met a sizable part of their commitments to allied countries even in years of poor Soviet crops such as 1963/64 and 1972/73.

## SOVIET GRAIN ECONOMY AND GRAIN TRADE

The grain trade patterns outlined above require explanation. These include the factors accounting for the variability in Soviet grain trade, the simultaneous imports and exports of grain and the levels and relative importance of the trade concerned.

The following discussion will be organised under two headings: (i) structural trade and (ii) cyclical trade. By structural imports are meant those purchases of foreign grain which fill the gap between average production and utilisation. Cyclical imports are imports to compensate for fluctuations in the domestic availability of grain.

**Structural Imports**

Soviet policy regarding grain trade falls into three distinct periods. First, during Stalin's era (till 1953) the Soviets exported grain to acquire badly needed foreign exchange even in periods of poor crops and insufficient availability of grain for human consumption. During the second period extending till the early 1970s, adequate supplies of grains for human consumption were assured and belt tightening was put into effect mainly through the livestock sector. From the early 1970s on, new emphasis was placed on expanding livestock and milk production.[9]

Soviet grain production has been rapidly increasing during the last two decades (see Appendix 2). However, the data on grain utilisation (Table 10.5) show that the Soviet utilisation of grain (particularly feed grain) has been rising even more rapidly. Feed grain accounts presently for more than half of total grain utilisation in the USSR. This trend obviously resulted in the rapid increase of feed grain imports – especially corn (see Appendix 3). However, it also had an important impact on the Soviet purchases of foreign wheat. High quality foreign wheat bought to satisfy some of the domestic food requirements considerably increased the availability of lower quality Soviet grain for the livestock industry.

Development of Soviet livestock, motivated by the political promises of the authorities to improve the average Soviet diet has been the major determinant of the growth in structural grain imports.

Regression analyses performed for the 1956/57 – 1980/81 period show that Soviet grain imports increase as grain utilisation for feed rises (Appendix 4; equations (i), (ii) and (v)). The rising trend in the Soviet utilisation of feed grain is likely to continue. If the promise of more high quality meat and dairy consumption goes unfulfilled it might result in serious worker unrest – a particularly dangerous course for the Soviet leadership.

In spite of its dynamic growth, Soviet grain output is frequently

Table 10.5  Utilisation of Grain in the Soviet Union, 1966/67–1980/81[a]
(million metric tons)

| Year beginning July 1 | Feed | Food | Dockage Waste | Seed | Industrial | Total |
|---|---|---|---|---|---|---|
| 1956/57 | 33 | 42 | 12 | 18 | 3 | 108 |
| 1957/58 | 34 | 43 | 10 | 18 | 3 | 109 |
| 1958/59 | 39 | 43 | 13 | 18 | 3 | 117 |
| 1959/60 | 40 | 43 | 12 | 18 | 3 | 116 |
| 1960/61 | 41 | 42 | 13 | 20 | 3 | 118 |
| 1961/62 | 45 | 44 | 13 | 21 | 3 | 126 |
| 1962/63 | 43 | 48 | 14 | 23 | 2 | 130 |
| 1963/64 | 32 | 47 | 5 | 23 | 2 | 110 |
| 1964/65 | 44 | 45 | 17 | 22 | 3 | 130 |
| 1965/66 | 56 | 44 | 12 | 24 | 3 | 139 |
| 1966/67 | 60 | 44 | 14 | 24 | 3 | 144 |
| 1967/68 | 64 | 44 | 12 | 24 | 3 | 146 |
| 1968/69 | 72 | 44 | 17 | 25 | 3 | 160 |
| 1969/70 | 83 | 45 | 23 | 23 | 3 | 177 |
| 1970/71 | 92 | 45 | 22 | 25 | 3 | 188 |
| 1971/72 | 93 | 45 | 13 | 27 | 3 | 181 |
| 1972/73 | 98 | 45 | 15 | 26 | 3 | 187 |
| 1973/74 | 105 | 45 | 33 | 27 | 3 | 214 |
| 1974/75 | 107 | 45 | 23 | 28 | 3 | 206 |
| 1975/76 | 89 | 45 | 14 | 28 | 3 | 180 |
| 1976/77 | 112 | 45 | 31 | 29 | 3 | 221 |
| 1977/78 | 122 | 45 | 29 | 28 | 4 | 228 |
| 1978/79[b] | 125 | 46 | 28 | 28 | 4 | 231 |
| 1979/80[b] | 126 | 46 | 22 | 28 | 4 | 226 |
| 1980/81[c] | 110 | 47 | 28 | 28 | 4 | 217 |

*Notes:*
a) Rounded to the nearest million tons, except for production and trade data. Thus, totals may not tally due to rounding.
b) Preliminary data.
c) Forecast.

*Source:* USDA, *Supplement to Document WAS-23*, Washington, D.C., October 1980, p. 21.

considered too low given the resources employed.[10] The Soviets clearly mobilised important resources in the seventies to accelerate the increase in domestic grain production. (Note, for example that in 1974–1975 about 27 per cent of total Soviet investments was devoted to agriculture.)[11] Nevertheless, Soviet grain productivity remained low. This has been variously blamed on inappropriate farming practices, insufficient mechanisation and irrigation and ill-conceived organisation of the Soviet agricultural system, etc...

The partial US grain embargo against the USSR has certainly nourished the Soviet resolve to become self-sufficient in grain.[12] It is, however, unlikely that any major progress in that respect can be accomplished before 1985.

The Soviet structural grain imports are also motivated by problems with grain logistics within the USSR. First of all, the Soviets lose considerable quantities of grain in dockage and that waste has considerably increased since the mid-1960s (see Table 10.5). Secondly, the recurring transport bottlenecks hamper interregional distribution of grain.[13] A large portion of Soviet wheat imports takes place because it is a cheaper way to supply the northern Soviet cities than moving grain within the Soviet Union.

All of the aforementioned forces, combined with the increase in population and per capita income, contribute to the existence of an important structural gap between grain utilisation and domestic availability of grain in the USSR. This gap is not likely to be closed during the coming decade and, if no major change in East-West relations takes place, the Soviets will continue to buy Western grain in the foreseeable future.

**Cyclical Imports**

Variability in domestic grain production is generally considered the main cause of the erratic pattern of Soviet grain imports.[14] Soviet grain production has in fact varied considerably on a year-to-year basis and such fluctuations have certainly had their influence on Soviet import programmes.

This erratic pattern of Soviet grain production could have a particularly strong impact on trade flows given the problems involving the interregional distribution of Soviet grain, domestic price rigidities and relatively small stockpiling capacities. Moreover the Soviet authorities have been very reluctant to use price mechanisms to deal with national and/or regional grain shortages. The Soviets consider it economically and organisationally cheaper to obtain extra grain through imports than to use price mechanisms to deal with *ad hoc* shortages. Note that Soviet grain prices may have as well an important impact on the structural imports of grain. Soviet domestic prices for grain are set below international prices, expanding import needs above the free trade level. There is little initiative to increase domestic grain production in state farms that continue to rely on subsidies.

Furthermore, even if the domestic target price is allowed to adjust periodically to the world market price to reduce imports the system is still likely to follow an erratic trade pattern. A central planning body fixes its prices *ex ante,* whereas the real equilibrium prices may only be known *ex post*. Divergencies between the two are likely to appear and *ad hoc* adjustments through foreign trade are required to deal with shortages or surpluses at home. The last point is particularly relevant to the urban food distribution system relying on fixed and subsidised consumer prices.

A regression test has been conducted to examine the relationship between the deviation from the grain production trend (as the explicatory variable) and the deviation from the grain import trend (see Appendix 4; equation VI). The results of the test thus confirm the validity of the production argument in explaining the year-to-year variations of Soviet grain imports. (See also Figure 10.2.)

## INTERNATIONAL GRAIN PRICES AND THE USSR

The impact of the Soviet grain trade on international grain prices and vice versa is difficult to evaluate in general terms. First, the nature and the intensity of the relationship in question varied considerably over time, depending on changing Soviet agricultural policies, trade policies and international market conditions, etc. Secondly, the evidence in question is scarce and difficult to separate from the other determinants of international prices and Soviet grain trade levels.

The issue involves two broad ranges of somewhat different problems. The first refers to international prices in the short-run and is mainly concerned with the link between the large year-to-year variability in Soviet grain imports and the corresponding variability in international grain prices. The second is mostly concerned with the implications of the expanding Soviet import programmes for long-

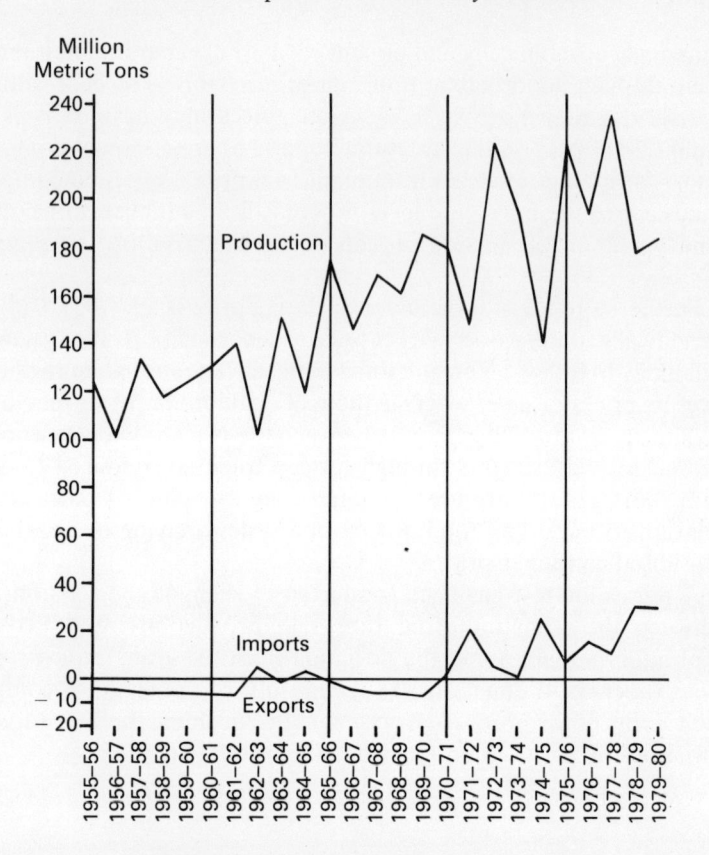

Source: U.S.D.A. Foreign Agricultural Circular

FIGURE 10.2  Soviet Grain Production and Imports 1955/56–1979/80

term prices in international grain markets and the impact of the long-term price trend on Soviet grain imports.

**Long-Term Perspective**

The Soviet grain import programme expanded during the seventies in spite of rising international grain prices.

This probably means that in spite of price increases in international markets, it was more rational for the Russians to import grain (and so to improve the average diet and free resources for elsewhere in the economy) rather than to aim at self-sufficiency. The Soviets are potentially capable of becoming self-sufficient in grain though probably at great cost. Consequently, the theory of comparative advantage is likely to provide the most appropriate analytical framework to explain Soviet behaviour.

One possibly simple way of looking at the problem is to consider the prices of Soviet grain imports relative to the unit value of Soviet total exports. The changes of this variable during the 1970s are presented in Figure 10.3.

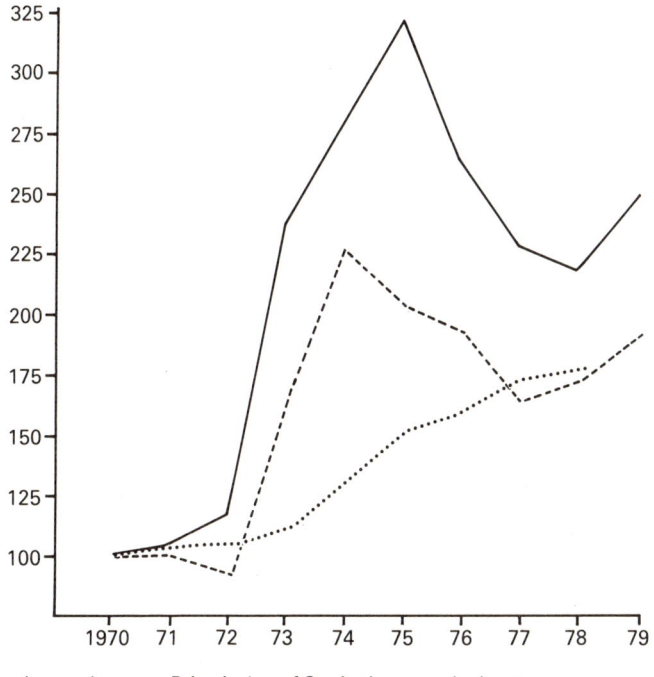

Legend: ——— Price index of Soviet imported wheat
------ Price index of Soviet imported maize
·········· Index of unit value of Soviet exports

Source: *Commodity Trade and Price Trends,* World Bank 1979 edition and United Nations, *Yearbook of International Trade Statistics* volume 1, special table G

Note: Wheat: Yearly arithmetic mean of U.S no 1 soft red winter FOB Atlantic ports and Canadian no 1 western red spring basis in store, Thunder Bay
Maize: US no 2 yellow at Gulf ports

FIGURE 10.3 Evolution of Soviet Terms of Trade (1970=100)

The Soviets bought particularly significant quantities of coarse grain (mainly maize) in the first and the last three years of the 1970s when the terms of trade were evolving to their advantage. Note also that the two peak years of Soviet wheat imports (1972/73 and 1975/76) were confronted with contrasting year-to-year trends in international prices. In the first period prices were on a strong upswing, in the second period a strong tendency towards lower price levels may be observed.

It is very difficult to make any guess as to the future programmes of Soviet grain imports, particularly after the 1980 partial US embargo on grain sales to the USSR and with the increasing tensions in US-Soviet relations following 1981/82 events in Poland. An effort to increase the Soviet self-reliance in grain clearly motivated several high-level agricultural planning decisions taken at the beginning of 1980.[15] Note that this might be due not only to the obvious political reasons but also to price considerations. The embargo in question forced the Soviets to pay higher prices for foreign grain due to the increased cost of market operations and to other considerations of a speculative nature.[16]

The future position of the USSR as an importer of grain may be also influenced by the evolution of the relative prices of wheat and corn. Soviet imports of wheat shot up in 1979/80 and remained high in 1981.[17] However, this movement seems to be mostly motivated by the desire to compensate for grain shortages resulting from the US embargo. Obviously, the Soviet grain imports of the 1970s had some long-term effect on international grain prices. *Ceteris paribus*, these prices would not have risen so high without Soviet purchases. Nevertheless any general conclusion in that respect is of a highly speculative character since the major exporters could reasonably have been expected to limit quantities of grain in international markets had the Soviets failed to buy.

**Short-Term Perspective**

The Soviets are frequently blamed for much of the year-to-year price variability in international grain markets. It would thus be pertinent to see whether any more general pattern of Soviet impact on international grain prices might be indentified.

To examine the issue, first-order differences in international grain prices have been regressed on first-order differences in Soviet grain imports. The test has been conducted for the 1961–79 period for wheat and maize separately. The results of the test are as follows:

(1) WPRICEDIF = −17.213 + 0.0196 WIMPDIF

$R^2 = 0.23$

(2) MPRICEDIF = 46.997 + 0.0087 MIMPDIF

$R^2 = 0.53$

This means that changes in Soviet wheat imports account for 23 per cent of the annual variations in international wheat prices (with the model being significant at the 1 per cent level). The regression model for maize (model 2) makes an even stronger case with 53 per cent of the variance in world maize prices accounted for by changes in the Soviet maize imports. The results of the above regression analysis thus side with the hypothesis that the Soviet Union was responsible for much of the annual price fluctuation in international grain markets during the 1960s and 1970s.

The Soviet influence was particularly strongly felt in 1972/73 when the major grain exporters (including the CWB) failed to anticipate the enormous Soviet demand for foreign grain (especially wheat). EXPORTKHLEB bought, at that time, huge quantities of foreign grains at very low prices (partly benefiting from exporter's subsidies) and was held responsible for a considerable rise in international prices.[18] Note, however, that international grain prices continued to rise in the following crop years even though the Soviets *did not* purchase important grain quantities. Moreover, in 1975/76 when the EXPORTKHLEB's grain imports exceeded the 1972/73 record level by 25 per cent, international prices were lower in February and March 1976 than the year before when the Soviets bought much less grain.

Since the Soviet purchases represent only one among many determinants of world-price levels for grain in the short-run, it is practically impossible to isolate the Soviet impact. Nevertheless, it is apparent that from the early 1970s on, the Soviets were strongly inclined to conduct important grain purchases in periods of weak domestic crop with little regard to the stability of international grain prices and international availabilities of grain.

Indeed, for reasons such as domestic price rigidities, small grain stocks, problems in interregional distribution, etc., it may be suggested that the USSR would tend to make up for domestic grain shortages resulting from sudden falls of output by increasing grain imports and reducing grain exports. It has been shown that there is an inverse relation between Soviet grain imports and Soviet grain exports ($R^2 = 0.81$; see Appendix 5 equations i, ii and iv).

## CONCLUSIONS

During the last two decades, the USSR has begun to assume a new position in the world grain trade. In times past, the Soviets have been viewed as a major potential competitor in grain export markets. However, in the mid-1960s and especially during the 1970s there appeared a clear trend in the rising volumes of Soviet grain imports (especially coarse grains).

This increasing importance of the USSR as a buyer in the international grain market coincided with the reinforcement of the erratic pattern of its grain trade.

Such a trade pattern stems from complex rationales which defy any single factor explanation. Nevertheless, several key elements of the Soviet agricultural system clearly exert a dominant influence on the trade flows in question.

On the basis of direct and indirect inferences from statistical analyses, this study sides with the view that the increase of Soviet livestock during the 1970s has been the single most valid domestic determinant of the rising grain import programme. The impact of this factor has been reinforced by the rigidity of domestic grain prices, low productivity in the Soviet grain economy and poor grain logistics.

The study also confirms the responsiveness of Soviet grain imports to the year-to-year fluctuations of the domestic grain output. The production argument appears to be a major explicatory element of the erratic pattern in Soviet grain imports.

The statistical test and qualitative analysis presented above enable us to side with the view that Soviet grain imports had a very considerable impact on international wheat and maize prices both in the long and short run. The extent of that influence varied widely from year to year. It has, however, been very significant for the past two decades overall and is likely to continue in the mid and late 1980s.

As a buyer the USSR has approached the international grain market basically without discriminating among sources of supply on political grounds. This apolitical businesslike attitude was in harmony with the fact that the Soviets rely more heavily on foreign grain than do Western grain economies on the Soviet market. Thus whatever "commodity power" this situation affords is in the hands of the major grain exporters rather than the Soviet Union's. Yet the West has made little use of such "grain power" as it may reasonably be supposed to possess; even President Carter's embargo was very limited and only timidly implemented. This restraint holds no mystery. There exist several major constraints on the use of "grain power". The foremost is the powerful farmer lobby's opposition to policies it fears might reduce incomes. Other constraints involve the lack of a common political will among the major grain exporters or an unwillingness to pay the economic price for the use of "grain power".

Paradoxically enough, if anyone may be said to benefit from "commodity power" in international grain markets it is the Soviet Union. Since the USSR is an important grain supplier to several of its political allies it can use Western grain to make them even more dependent.

Table A-1 USSR Imports of Grain by Country of Origin, July/June 1970/71–1979/80

| Commodity & Country | 1970/71 | 1971/72 | 1972/73 | 1973/74 | 1974/75 | 1975/76 | 1976/77 | 1977/78 | 1978/79 | 1979/80[a] |
|---|---|---|---|---|---|---|---|---|---|---|
| | | | | | | Million metric tons | | | | |
| Wheat | | | | | | | | | | |
| US[b] | — | — | 9.5 | 2.7 | 1.0 | 4.0 | 2.9 | 3.3 | 2.9 | 3.9 |
| Canada | .3 | 2.8 | 4.2 | 1.6 | .3 | 3.2 | 1.2 | 1.7 | 2.0 | 2.1 |
| Australia | — | .5 | .9 | .1 | .8 | 1.2 | .4 | .3 | .1 | 2.7 |
| Argentina | — | .1 | — | — | .7 | 1.2 | .1 | 1.1 | — | 2.0 |
| EC | — | .1 | .7 | .1 | — | — | — | — | — | .6 |
| Others | .2 | — | .3 | .1 | — | .4 | — | .2 | .1 | .6 |
| Total | .5 | 3.5 | 15.6 | 4.5 | 2.5 | 10.1 | 4.6 | 6.7 | 5.1 | 11.4 |
| Coarse Grains | | | | | | | | | | |
| US[b] | — | 2.9 | 4.2 | 5.2 | 1.3 | 9.9 | 4.5 | 9.2 | 8.3 | 11.4 |
| Canada | — | .2 | .9 | .2 | — | 1.3 | .2 | .2 | .1 | 1.3 |
| Australia | — | — | — | 0 | .1 | .8 | .1 | — | — | 1.3 |
| Argentina | — | .1 | .1 | .3 | 1.1 | .2 | .2 | 1.6 | 1.4 | 3.0 |
| EC | — | — | 1.2 | .5 | .1 | .5 | .2 | .2 | .2 | .2 |
| Others | .3 | 1.1 | .5 | .2 | .1 | 2.6 | .3 | .6 | — | 1.3 |
| Total | .3 | 4.3 | 6.9 | 6.4 | 2.7 | 15.6 | 5.7 | 11.7 | 10.0 | 18.6 |

|  |  |  |  |  |  |  |  |  |  |
|---|---|---|---|---|---|---|---|---|---|
| Total |  |  |  |  |  |  |  |  |  |
| US[b] | — | 2.9 | 13.7 | 7.9 | 2.7 | 13.9 | 7.4 | 12.5 | 11.2 | 15.3 |
| Canada | .3 | 3.0 | 5.1 | 1.8 | — | 4.5 | 1.4 | 1.9 | 2.1 | 3.4 |
| Australia | — | .5 | .9 | .1 | .9 | 2.0 | .5 | .3 | .1 | 4.0 |
| Argentina | — | .1 | .1 | .3 | 1.8 | 1.4 | .3 | 2.7 | 1.4 | 5.1 |
| EC | — | .1 | 1.9 | .5 | .1 | .5 | .2 | .2 | .2 | .8 |
| Others | .5 | 1.2 | .8 | .3 | .1 | 3.0 | .3 | .8 | .1 | 1.9 |
| Total[c] | .8 | 7.8 | 22.5 | 10.9 | 5.2 | 25.7 | 10.3 | 18.4 | 15.1 | 30.5 |

— Denotes less than 50,000 tons.

*Notes:*
a) Preliminary.
b) US exports based upon Export Sales data, which normally include transshipments whereas Census data may not.
c) Totals may not add due to rounding. Excludes rice and pulses.

*Source:* USDA Supplement 1 to Document WAS-23, Washington, D.C., October 1980, p. 29.

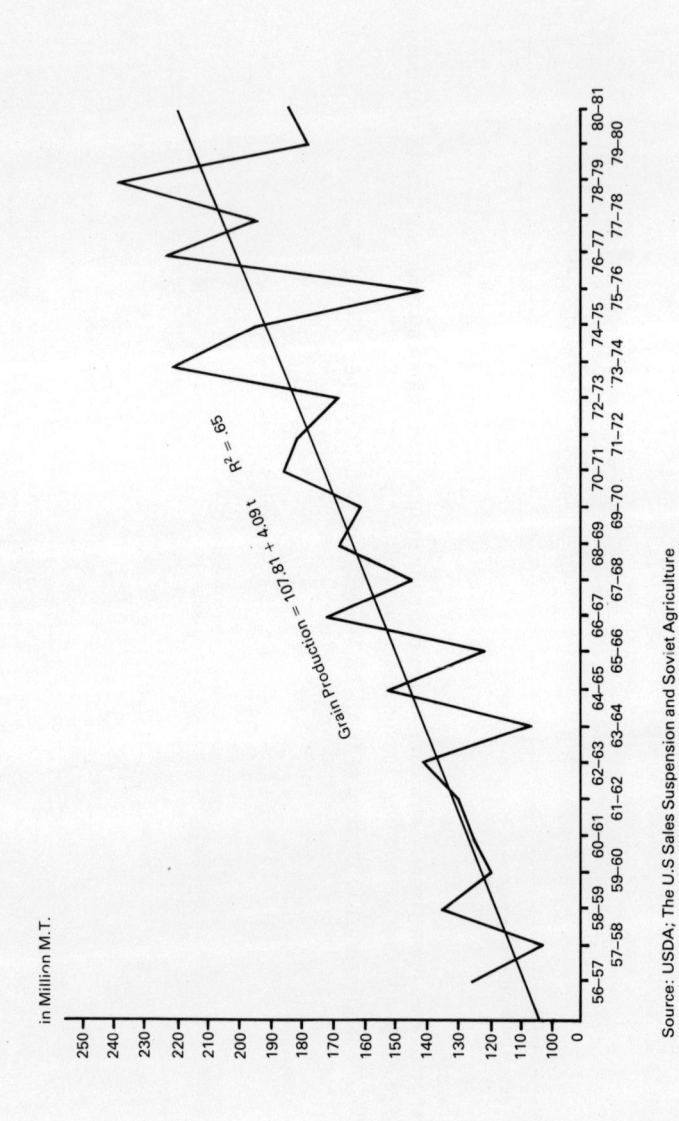

FIGURE A-1 Trend of Soviet Grain Production, 1956/57 – 1980/81

Grain Production = 107.81 + 4.09 t    $R^2 = .65$

Source: USDA; The U.S Sales Suspension and Soviet Agriculture

*The Soviet Union in International Grain Markets* 215

COARSE GRAINS IMPORTS = −3660 + 748.4t
$R^2 = .65$

Source: F.A.O, Trade Yearbook, Various issues.

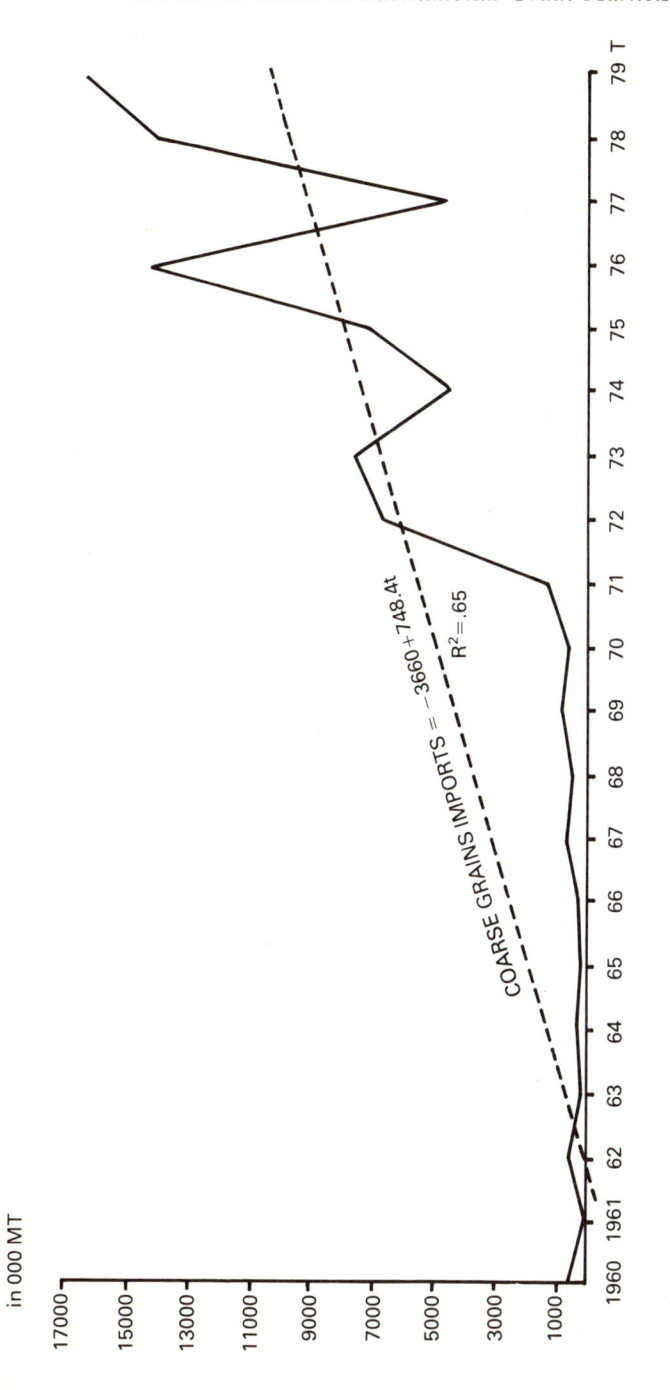

FIGURE A–2  Trend of Coarse Grains Imports over Time, 1960–1979

FIGURE A-3  Trend of Wheat Imports over Time, 1960-1979

Source: F.A.O, Trade Yearbook, Various issues.

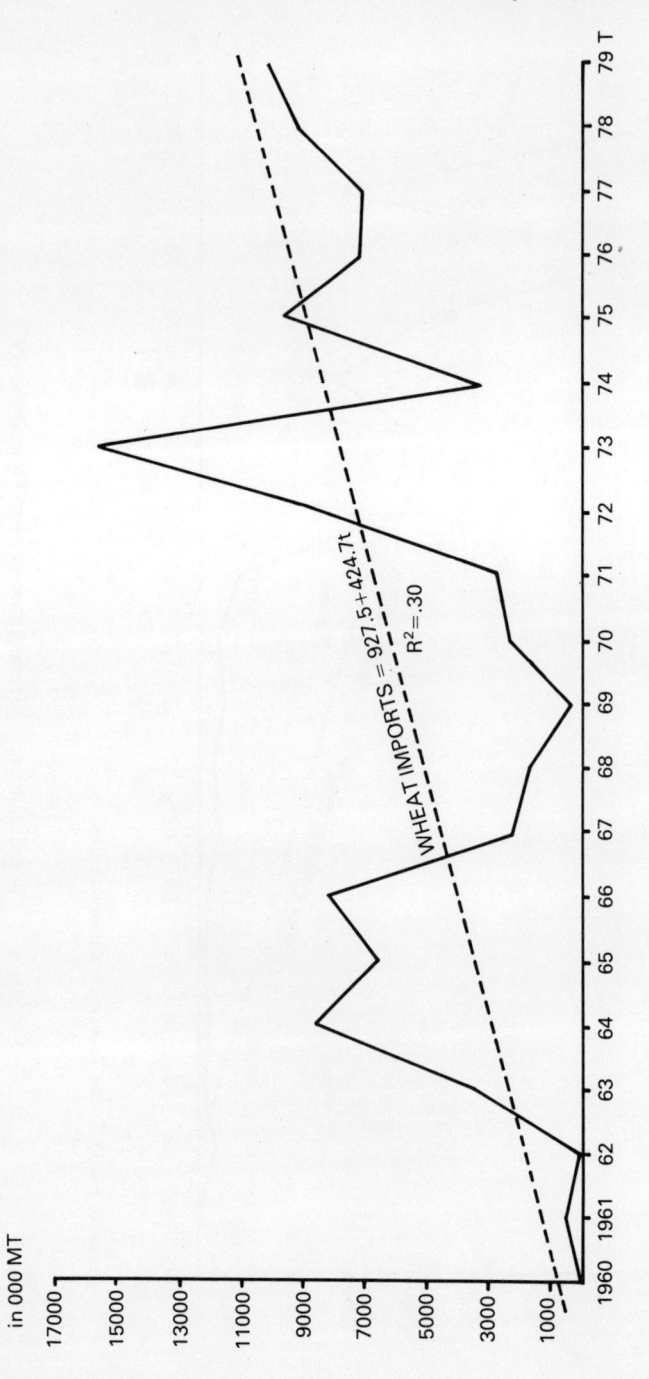

WHEAT IMPORTS = 927.5 + 424.7t
$R^2 = .30$

## Expected Determinants of Grain Imports — Regression Results (1956/57 – 1980/81)

(i)     GRAIMP =    11.253 − 2.238 GRAEXP + 0.1241 FEED − 0.127 DEVIAT
                             (2.92)** (−5.70)**      (4.46)**        (−3.42)**
                                         $R^2 = 0.90$

(ii)     GRAIMP =    18.937 − 3.026 GRAEXP + 0.0761 FEED
                                  (4.95)* (−7.79)**       (2.59)*
                                             $R^2 = 0.85$

(iii)     GRAIMP =    26.902 − 3.464 GRAEXP − 4.388 DEVIAT
                                   (12.39)**    (9.05)**        (−1.00)
                                            $R^2 = 0.81$

(iv)     GRAIMP =    27.656 − 3.609 GRAEXP
                                  (13.59)** (−10.19)**
                                          $R^2 = 0.81$

(v)     GRAIMP =    −6.683 + 0.20835 FEED
                                 (−1.81)     (4.59)**
                                          $R^2 = 0.45$

(vi)     DEVIATIMP =    −0.5128 − 0.164 DEVIAT
                                      (−0.53)     (−3.50)**
                                                $R^2 = 0.34$

(vii)     DEVIATIMP =    −0.8844 + 0.1389 DEVPRICE
                                       (−0.79)      (2.00)*
                                                  $R^2 = 0.12$

*List of Symbols:*
GRAIMP:     Grain imports (million metric tons)
GRAEXP:     Grain exports (million metric tons)
FEED:     Grain utilisation for feed (million metric tons)
DEVIAT:     Deviation from the grain production trend
DEVIATIMP:     Deviation from the grain import trend
DEVPRICE:     Deviation from the price trend

*Note:*     **     Significant at 1%
             *     Significant at 5%

*Source:*     Data compiled from USDA Doc. WAS–23 (Supplement) October 1980.

# 11 The USSR as a Major Factor in International Cotton Markets

Lewis A. Fischer*

INTRODUCTION

World cotton production experienced relatively small changes in the 1970s. The six largest producers now provide about 75 per cent of aggregate world output.

There have been however significant differences in the quality of the product. Generally speaking, medium- and short-staple cotton constitutes the bulk of the Soviet crop: as a prominent expert of Soviet agriculture observed "one encounters in the Soviet Union a great many verbal and written complaints that farms produce large quantities of short-staple cotton and very often the long-stapled product is not as long as indicated by the statistics."[1] The very coarse short-fibred Asiatic variety is grown in India and Pakistan, and their influence on the market is marginal. Egypt is the world's largest producer of extra-long and long-staple cotton and holds a prominent market position in international relations.

WORLD PRODUCTION CONSUMPTION AND TRADE IN COTTON

**Production**

Cotton is one of the very few commodities the output of which exceeded the Five-Year-Plans of the 1970s. Table 11.1, while reflect-

* The author is indebted to Professor Karl-Eugene Wadekin for his thoughtful comments on this paper.

Table 11.1 Cotton: Production Trend in the Largest Producer Countries

|  | Average 1972/73–1974/75 (1000 metric tons) | Average 1978/79–1980/81 (1000 metric tons) | Change % |
|---|---|---|---|
| World | 13,824 | 13,793 | None |
| USA | 2 773 | 2 658 | −4.2 |
| USSR | 2 490 | 2 833 | +13.8 |
| China | 2 385 | 2 334 | −2 |
| India | 1 218 | 1 350 | +10.8 |

Source: *Cotton-World Statistics,* Vol. 34, No. 9, April 1981, International Cotton Advisory Committee, pp. 24–25.

ing the production trend in the four largest producing countries, indicates that the Soviet Union achieved an almost 14 per cent growth. On the other hand, production declined in both the United States and the People's Republic of China.

The Soviet cotton area advanced eight per cent from 1973/74 throughout 1980/81 and reached 3.1 million hectares. That compares with 5.3 million hectares in the US. Yield average increased as well. The latter was credited in a Soviet statement as being because of "wide-ranging utilisation of chemicals and fertilizers, amelioration of soil conditions, application of improved systems of crop rotation and hectarage expansion under such wilt resistant varieties of cotton as Tashkent 1 and Tashkent 3."[2]

Recently one of two Soviet scientists attributed the achievement to efficient organisation and management:

> In the USSR cotton production is oriented towards the specialization and concentration of the industry on the basis of interfarm cooperation and agro-industrial integration, as well as the steady improvement of labour organization, production, management, i.e. the establishment of specialized agrocomplexes for seedcotton production, procurement and primary commercial processing.[3]

The crucial factor is however that USSR cotton is grown only on irrigation land. The provision of irrigation water to cotton farms at no charge is essential in both yield development and the cost structure. It represents a very significant subsidy provided by the government to the producers. Maintaining high output and special incomes on the cotton growing state farms and collectives as well as supporting the huge cotton factories in Tashkent and in many other Asian locations strengthen the political power of the Soviet Union in those areas. When the Russians combined into a single unit the three Uzbek states, they taught the hitherto nomad population to grow cotton, sugar-beets and other crops as a basis for their settlement. The vast Central Asian irrigation scheme is the foundation of the cotton industry. Authorities have been considering charging cotton growers for water; however, for obvious political reasons such a change is not forthcoming in the foreseeable future. There are plans to divert the flow of two great Siberian rivers to irrigate new agricultural land. That would reduce by 20 per cent the fresh water flow into the Arctic Ocean. It would however provide vital irrigation to millions of cotton acres in Kazakhstan and fortify the Soviet presence. But it seems that the Soviet planners have dismissed the possibility of expansion: the 1981–85 Five-Year-Plan foresees a slight decline of the cotton crop for the Plan period.

The difference in both methods of production and data on production costs is so great that a realistic comparison with the US is not possible. In the United States the prime goal of the farm industry has been to meet the requirements of the textile industry for fibre type. This has been achieved, and now US breeders are working on new varieties which should be wilt resistant and early maturing. The Soviet breeders' aim is to improve the quality of the product with particular attention to uniform staple length suitable to mechanised cultivation, particularly harvesting. Presently 25 varieties are grown in the Soviet Union of which ten are the choice of Soviet researchers and relatively long staple.

Seed cotton harvesting is 55 per cent mechanised in the USSR. In contrast, already in 1972 slightly over 99 per cent of the total US crop was picked or harvested by machines.

In summary, cotton production is a very important sector of Soviet agriculture. The government provides a great deal of overt and disguised subsidies and is likely to sustain a policy of incentives particularly in terms of quality research. It has been estimated that nearly a third of irrigation water is annually lost by seepage and evaporation and a lot of irrigated land falls out of production by salification. Thus, USSR cotton acreage is likely to be stabilised around three million hectares.

## Consumption

There has been a major increase in the consumption of synthetic fibres over the past fifteen years. Consequently, cotton's share in world-wide fibre consumption has fallen. Nevertheless, due to the rising demand for textiles – particularly in developing countries – the absolute quantity of cotton consumed has risen during the past decade. As shown by the material embodied in Table 11.2 world cotton consumption increased by eight per cent during the 1970s. The pattern of consumption differs considerably from region to region: it decreased in North America and Western Europe by 15 and 8 per cent respectively while it increased by 11 per cent in Asia and Oceania. Cotton use in the socialist countries continued to grow. The rate of increase in the People's Republic of China accounted for 19 per cent, in the Soviet Union for 5 per cent and Eastern Europe for 2 per cent. Developing countries' (excluding China) consumption has also increased by six per cent. Governments in both India and Pakistan stimulate cotton consumption. Cotton is apparently benefiting from the rising prices of man-made fibre which are now 50 per cent higher than cotton. The overall textile picture does not appear to be optimistic in Japan and consumption decreased over time. Cotton textile activity has slowed down in the member countries of the European Community. The sharpest decline occurred in the United Kingdom where consumption in 1977/78 was 415,000 bales, decreased to 402,000 in 1979 and the International Cotton Advisory Committee projects 250,000 bales for 1980/81. Generally speaking, cotton consumption in the highly industrialised countries either declined or stagnated during the last decade. With some insignificant regional deviations, the same trend prevailed in the consumption of man-made fibres.

## International Trade

As indicated by the material in Table 11.3, over the past five years the United States has captured about 30 per cent and the USSR about 20 per cent of the world's cotton export market. Since the other half is scattered over medium and small suppliers the two countries share an oligopoly on the international scene. The specifics of this development differ however very significantly: world total export increased by a negligible 3 per cent, USA export by 41 per cent and USSR

Table 11.2 World Cotton Consumption 1971/72–1980/81

(1000 metric tons)

| | 71–72 | 72–73 | 73–74 | 74–75 | 75–76 | 76–77 | 77–78 | 78–79 | Preliminary 79–80 | Estimate 80–81 |
|---|---|---|---|---|---|---|---|---|---|---|
| North America | | | | | | | | | | |
| Canada | 79 | 74 | 70 | 51 | 56 | 48 | 52 | 56 | 59 | 56 |
| Mexico | 163 | 173 | 180 | 178 | 181 | 165 | 160 | 165 | 165 | 168 |
| US | 1743 | 1691 | 1626 | 1276 | 1583 | 1453 | 1412 | 1382 | 1421 | 1301 |
| Total | 2037 | 1990 | 1933 | 1567 | 1885 | 1734 | 1689 | 1672 | 1713 | n.a. |
| South America | | | | | | | | | | |
| Brazil | 325 | 369 | 379 | 390 | 423 | 433 | 490 | 531 | 575 | 596 |
| Total | 619 | 658 | 712 | 677 | 711 | 737 | 794 | 838 | 886 | n.a. |
| Western Europe | | | | | | | | | | |
| France | 235 | 231 | 234 | 202 | 203 | 208 | 184 | 179 | 184 | 173 |
| Germany F.R. | 240 | 233 | 238 | 209 | 222 | 209 | 176 | 169 | 173 | 173 |
| Italy | 200 | 187 | 195 | 180 | 195 | 200 | 182 | 212 | 228 | 217 |
| Total | 1403 | 1394 | 1403 | 1277 | 1332 | 1364 | 1233 | 1287 | 1360 | n.a. |

| | | | | | | | | | | | |
|---|---|---|---|---|---|---|---|---|---|---|---|
| Eastern Europe | | | | | | | | | | | |
| Czechoslovakia | 108 | 108 | 112 | 113 | 114 | 115 | 117 | 117 | 119 | n.a. | |
| Total | 596 | 599 | 601 | 585 | 594 | 596 | 602 | 610 | 628 | 618 | |
| USSR | 1843 | 1843 | 1865 | 1886 | 1897 | 1897 | 1908 | 1930 | 1951 | 1962 | |
| Asia and Oceania | | | | | | | | | | | |
| China P.R. | 2298 | 2450 | 2602 | 2558 | 2320 | 2472 | 2624 | 2797 | 2949 | 2992 | |
| China (Taiwan) | 132 | 115 | 156 | 160 | 210 | 217 | 199 | 217 | 250 | 249 | |
| India | 1193 | 1236 | 1272 | 1254 | 1323 | 1193 | 1153 | 1225 | 1279 | 1323 | |
| Pakistan | 438 | 539 | 539 | 438 | 466 | 390 | 412 | 434 | 444 | 449 | |
| Turkey | 184 | 220 | 210 | 262 | 295 | 317 | 297 | 304 | 267 | 293 | |
| Total | 5749 | 6143 | 6454 | 6160 | 6318 | 6281 | 6405 | 6826 | 7139 | n.a. | |
| Africa | | | | | | | | | | | |
| Egypt | 210 | 217 | 223 | 221 | 232 | 249 | 265 | 282 | 295 | 304 | |
| Total | 456 | 482 | 514 | 518 | 540 | 560 | 565 | 604 | 631 | n.a. | |
| World Total | 12703 | 13109 | 13482 | 12670 | 13277 | 13169 | 13196 | 13767 | 14308 | 14202 | |

Source: *Cotton World Statistics*, Quarterly Bull. of ICAT, Jan. 1981. *Cotton Monthly Review of World Situation*, ICAT, Vol. 34, no. 6 (Part I).

Table 11.3 Exports of Cotton: World and Major Exporting Countries 1971/72–1979/80
(1000 metric tons)

| Exporting Country | 71–72 | 72–73 | 73–74 | 74–75 | 75–76 | 76–77 | 77–78 | 78–79 | 79–80 |
|---|---|---|---|---|---|---|---|---|---|
| World Total | 4095.0 | 4604.9 | 4201.0 | 3744.1 | 4062.3 | 3801.6 | 4060.9 | 4256.0 | 5000.0 |
| United States | 737.1 | 1154.8 | 1333.2 | 854.7 | 720.9 | 1041.6 | 1194.0 | 1345.6 | 2009.3 |
| % of World | 18.0 | 25.1 | 31.7 | 22.8 | 17.7 | 27.4 | 29.4 | 31.6 | 40.2 |
| USSR | 650.5 | 726.3 | 737.2 | 802.2 | 878.1 | 971.4 | 856.4 | 791.4 | 823.9 |
| % of World | 15.9 | 15.8 | 17.5 | 21.4 | 21.6 | 25.6 | 21.1 | 18.6 | 16.5 |
| South America | 427.8 | 403.9 | 277.4 | 233.5 | 315.6 | 267.8 | 276.4 | 246.0 | 262.8 |
| % of World | 10.5 | 8.8 | 6.6 | 6.2 | 7.8 | 7.1 | 6.8 | 5.8 | 5.3 |
| Asia and Oceania | 907.2 | 879.0 | 602.8 | 684.3 | 1013.2 | 516.0 | 672.5 | 645.1 | 775.7 |
| % of World | 22.2 | 19.1 | 14.4 | 18.3 | 25.0 | 13.6 | 16.6 | 15.2 | 15.5 |
| Africa | 881.2 | 956.2 | 810.2 | 628.7 | 703.1 | 593.8 | 559.8 | 650.6 | 683.9 |
| % of World | 21.5 | 20.8 | 19.3 | 16.8 | 17.3 | 15.6 | 13.8 | 15.3 | 13.4 |

Source: Cotton World Statistics, ICAC, Vol. 34 (1981) No. 9, pp. 34–35.

exports by 16.8 per cent (calculated on three-year averages). This trend is strengthened by diminishing export volume in other major exporting countries. Exports in both South America and Africa diminished by 29 per cent each. Egypt and Sudan in Africa, Brazil and Peru in South America recorded significant setbacks. In Asia, Turkey's export decreased from an annual average of 292,000 metric tons in 1971/72–1973/74 to 202,000 metric tons by 1977/78–1979/80. In the same period Iranian exports dwindled from 107,000 to 58,000 metric tons.

The distribution of world imports is shown in Table 11.4.

The salient feature is the spectacular increase of purchases by Asian countries. For many years Japan absorbed about half of the total Asian imports; but its share accounted for only 28.6 per cent by 1979/80, still representing the respectable volume of 716,000 metric tons. Despite a large domestic production, the People's Republic of China became an important buyer; its purchase in 1979/80 is an estimated 824,000 metric tons, the largest of any single country. The constant growth of the textile industries in South Korea, Malaysia and Singapore called for augmented supplies of cotton over the last decade.

Western Europe's imports have also declined. Most of the decline occurred in the Economic Community as European textile industries became less competitive with those of Asia, reflecting – among other things – rising relative labour costs and the acquisition by Asian countries of fairly simple technology. This, plus a continuing shift into man-made fibres, reduced the need for raw cotton.

Figures 11.1 and 11.2 illustrate the international trade in the 1970s.

**Exports**

USSR cotton exports into other than COMECON countries in the 1950s and 1960s remained under 100,000 metric tons, thus their impact on the world market was marginal. The Soviet Union dominated and still dominates the COMECON markets: it supplied 60 per cent of the East European market in 1965–69 and 75 per cent in 1976. As an example in 1977/78 through 1979/80 Poland received 80 per cent of its cotton imports from the USSR; in Hungary Soviet cotton accounted for 55 per cent and so on. The US sold moderate quantities to the Socialist Bloc. A 3-year credit of $10 million to Poland was announced in 1977 and a similar credit for $5 million to Romania to finance purchases of US cotton.

Table 11.4 Imports of Cotton: World and Major Importing Countries 1971/72–1979/80
(1000 metric tons)

| Country | 71–72 | 72–73 | 73–74 | 74–75 | 75–76 | 76–77 | 77–78 | 78–79 | 79–80 |
|---|---|---|---|---|---|---|---|---|---|
| World Total | 4001.9 | 4522.2 | 4394.7 | 3757.5 | 4209.7 | 3887.8 | 4325.2 | 4409.2 | 5024.2 |
| North America | 119.7 | 105.1 | 110.8 | 85.8 | 111.2 | 92.3 | 88.6 | 95.7 | 105.6 |
| % of World | 3.0 | 2.3 | 2.5 | 2.3 | 2.6 | 2.4 | 2.0 | 2.2 | 2.1 |
| S. America | 72.5 | 55.5 | 63.0 | 53.3 | 32.8 | 36.4 | 44.7 | 54.4 | 36.1 |
| % of World | 1.8 | 1.2 | 1.4 | 1.4 | 0.8 | 0.9 | 1.0 | 1.2 | 0.7 |
| W. Europe | 1290.5 | 1453.2 | 1246.6 | 1144.2 | 1288.5 | 1149.8 | 1204.1 | 1127.9 | 1240.4 |
| % of World | 32.2 | 32.1 | 28.4 | 30.5 | 30.6 | 29.6 | 27.8 | 25.6 | 24.7 |
| France | 234.8 | 255.8 | 231.6 | 216.6 | 242.2 | 208.1 | 213.8 | 175.2 | 204.5 |
| Germany F.R. | 240.5 | 260.0 | 197.7 | 230.7 | 226.6 | 193.6 | 210.7 | 177.4 | 193.2 |
| Italy | 197.7 | 194.3 | 202.7 | 168.5 | 192.8 | 190.4 | 187.1 | 222.0 | 243.5 |
| Portugal | 108.4 | 140.7 | 120.6 | 87.6 | 109.1 | 100.4 | 115.6 | 103.2 | 130.5 |
| U.K. | 128.6 | 167.0 | 122.1 | 103.9 | 126.6 | 100.4 | 109.7 | 93.7 | 88.0 |
| Yugoslavia | 61.8 | 103.6 | 108.4 | 70.0 | 111.7 | 93.2 | 134.4 | 105.2 | 105.2 |
| E. Europe | 559.8 | 577.0 | 579.2 | 612.8 | 570.2 | 593.4 | 597.0 | 608.9 | 616.9 |
| % of World | 14.0 | 12.8 | 13.2 | 16.3 | 13.5 | 15.3 | 13.8 | 13.9 | 12.3 |
| Czechoslovakia | 106.2 | 106.2 | 114.9 | 117.1 | 108.4 | 114.9 | 117.0 | 119.3 | 125.8 |
| USSR | 162.6 | 130.1 | 140.9 | 140.9 | 119.3 | 97.6 | 65.0 | 86.7 | 54.2 |
| % of World | 4.1 | 2.9 | 2.6 | 3.7 | 2.8 | 2.5 | 1.5 | 2.0 | 1.1 |
| Asia & Oceania | 1718.7 | 2110.2 | 2158.5 | 1627.3 | 2022.1 | 1825.3 | 2241.6 | 2355.1 | 2905.1 |
| % of World | 42.9 | 46.7 | 49.1 | 43.3 | 48.0 | 46.9 | 51.8 | 53.4 | 57.8 |
| Africa | 78.1 | 91.1 | 95.7 | 93.2 | 65.5 | 93.0 | 84.2 | 80.5 | 65.9 |
| % of World | 2.0 | 2.0 | 2.2 | 2.5 | 1.6 | 2.4 | 1.9 | 1.8 | 1.3 |

Source: *Cotton World Statistics*, Quarterly Bulletin of ICAC, April 1981.

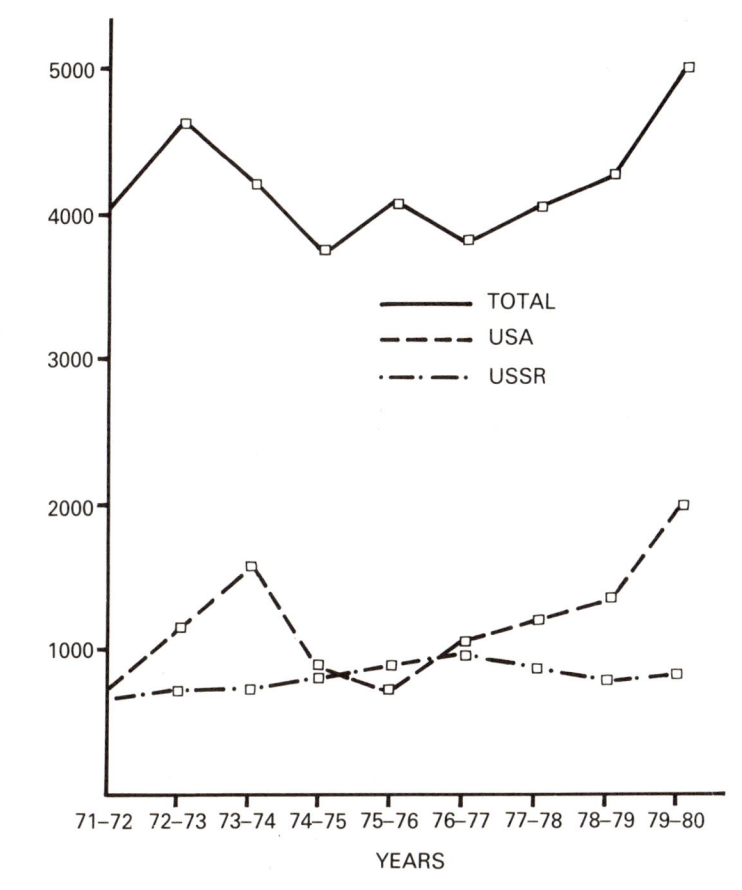

FIGURE 11.1  Exports of Cotton, 1971/72 to 1979/80

Most remarkable was the gradual growth in Soviet exports to Western Europe in the 1970s. Only 6 per cent of Western Europe's cotton imports came from the Soviet Union during 1965/66–1969/70, compared with 14 per cent from the United States and 80 per cent from other countries. By 1976/77, the Soviet percentage had risen to 25 per cent while the US share had dropped to 12 per cent and the proportion from other countries had fallen to 63 per cent. For the last three years (1977/78 through 1979/80) the average market share of the Soviet Union was 20 per cent and that of the United States 10 per cent. Nearly half of France's cotton imports in 1975/76 and over one-third in the average of the last five years were of Soviet origin.

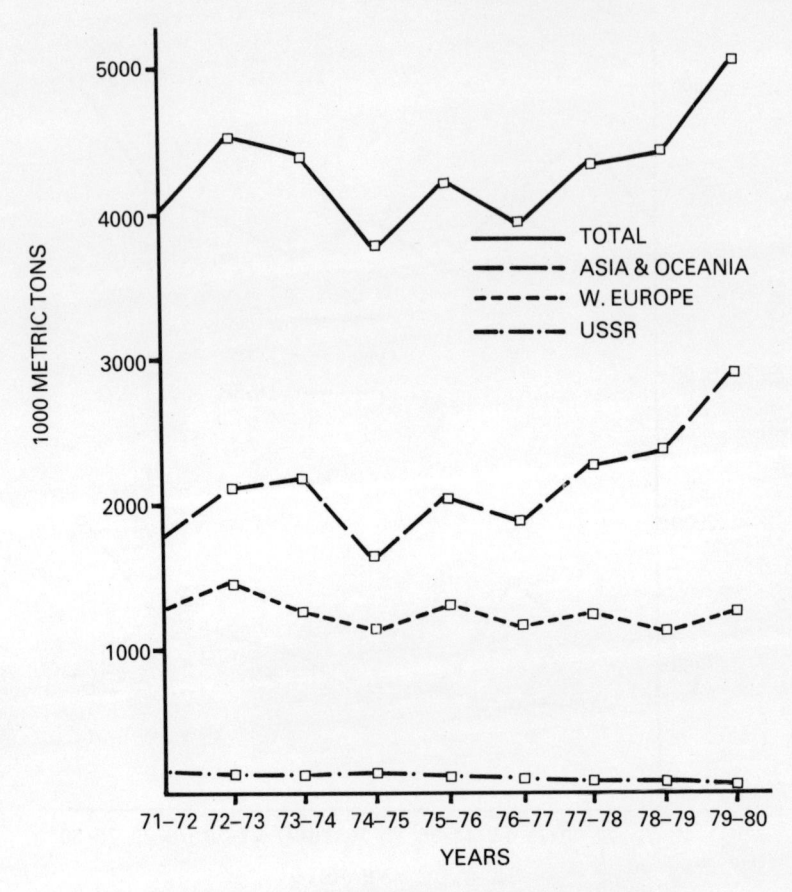

FIGURE 11.2  Imports of Cotton, 1971/72 to 1979/80

Soviet exports to Yugoslavia, considered here to be in Western Europe, totalled 68,000 metric tons in 1977, double those in 1974. In 1977/78–1979/80 Soviet cotton accounted for 61 per cent of total Yugoslav imports.

Japan has also become a major market for Soviet cotton. Its share in Japanese cotton imports climbed from 7 per cent in 1965–69 to 16 per cent in 1976 and averaged 12 per cent in 1977/78–1979/80, while the US share accounted for 36 per cent.

Table 11.5 is the overview and Table 11.6 is a synopsis of Soviet export development. Evolution in the Soviet exports of cotton by destination is summarised in Figure 11.3.

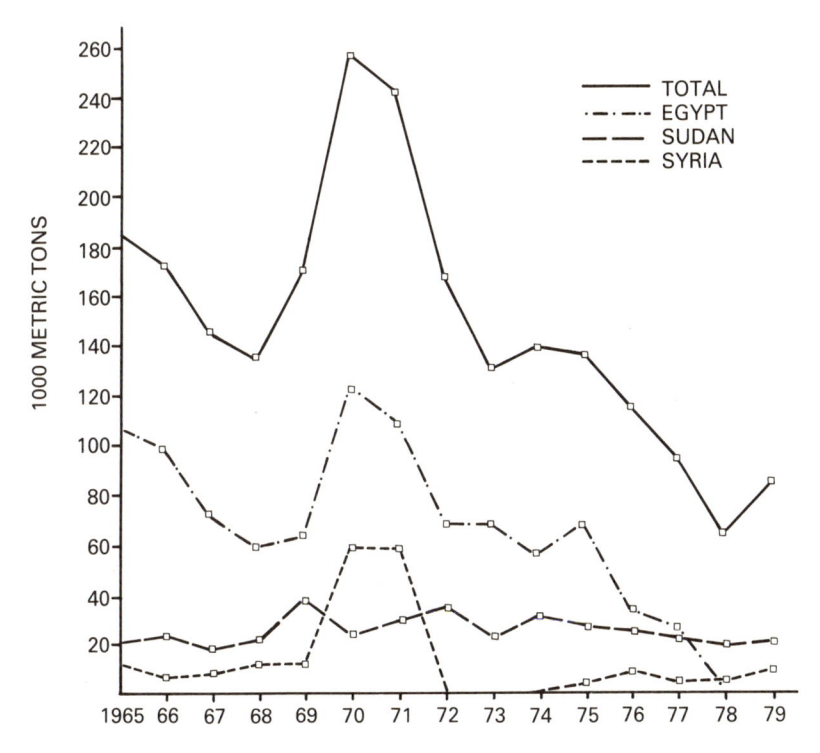

FIGURE 11.3  Imports of Cotton into the USSR: Selected Major Suppliers, 1965–1979

## Imports

Table 11.7 reveals that Egypt has been the Soviet Union's main cotton supplier over the 1960s and early 1970s. The Soviet textile industry needed the high quality, extra long staple cotton as the modernisation of the industry progressed. The annual tonnage of imports to the Soviet Union is economically less important than the quantity suggests. According to reports from Cairo, the Soviets also used to re-export Egyptian cotton to the West in exchange for hard currency. In 1977 President Sadat decided to suspend cotton shipments to the USSR. According to a Soviet report "Egyptian papers claimed that Soviet textile factories would shut down since their operation depends on Egyptian cotton." A Russian agronomist, V. Krasichko, had disproved the theory that high quality, fine-staple

Table 11.5 Export of Cotton from USSR, by Country of Destination, Calendar Years, 1965–1979 (1,000 metric tons)

| Destination | 1965 | 1966 | 1967 | 1968 | 1969 | 1970 | 1971 | 1972 | 1973 | 1974 | 1975 | 1976 | 1977 | 1978 | 1979 |
|---|---|---|---|---|---|---|---|---|---|---|---|---|---|---|---|
| Eastern Europe | | | | | | | | | | | | | | | |
| Bulgaria | 31.2 | 38.7 | 30.8 | 36.1 | 37.7 | 46.6 | 39.5 | 44.4 | 48.4 | 49.6 | 42.2 | 37.9 | 51.1 | 41.1 | 42.8 |
| Czechoslovakia | 63.9 | 60.5 | 55.2 | 69.8 | 46.6 | 71.9 | 60.5 | 61.0 | 59.6 | 73.6 | 65.7 | 61.3 | 66.5 | 66.6 | 61.6 |
| Germany, D.R. | 85.5 | 82.8 | 79.0 | 78.3 | 69.7 | 98.4 | 83.4 | 81.8 | 78.4 | 89.9 | 90.3 | 76.8 | 92.4 | 80.5 | 79.2 |
| Hungary | 40.3 | 38.4 | 40.5 | 45.2 | 29.8 | 49.8 | 36.0 | 43.1 | 38.2 | 45.0 | 53.1 | 40.7 | 48.6 | 49.6 | 49.9 |
| Poland | 79.5 | 90.0 | 75.8 | 80.7 | 75.6 | 103.0 | 104.4 | 95.8 | 90.0 | 114.3 | 112.2 | 105.1 | 136.1 | 126.6 | 109.0 |
| Romania | 29.9 | 30.2 | 31.4 | 29.5 | 27.6 | 32.8 | 33.4 | 28.4 | 30.5 | 26.8 | 31.4 | 39.3 | 63.1 | 51.6 | 34.8 |
| Total | 330.3 | 340.6 | 312.7 | 339.6 | 287.0 | 402.5 | 357.2 | 354.5 | 345.1 | 399.2 | 394.9 | 361.1 | 457.8 | 416.0 | 376.5 |
| Cuba | 16.5 | 13.2 | 13.8 | 16.9 | 13.4 | 16.7 | 19.1 | 17.4 | 18.7 | 22.4 | 20.9 | 28.4 | 30.2 | 29.6 | 28.7 |
| Korea, DPR | 10.2 | 9.7 | 10.1 | 13.2 | 10.1 | 11.6 | 11.5 | 7.9 | 7.1 | 8.2 | 6.1 | 4.5 | 4.0 | 4.0 | 4.3 |
| Vietnam, DR | 2.0 | 0 | 3.0 | 3.0 | 3.0 | 3.0 | 3.0 | 2.9 | 1.9 | 5.5 | 7.0 | 22.0 | 26.7 | 28.2 | 43.4 |
| Total | 28.7 | 22.9 | 26.9 | 33.1 | 26.5 | 31.3 | 33.6 | 28.2 | 27.7 | 36.1 | 34.0 | 54.9 | 60.9 | 61.8 | 76.4 |
| Western Europe | | | | | | | | | | | | | | | |
| Belgium | 0.5 | 4.8 | 5.6 | 4.9 | 1.6 | 0 | 3.4 | 3.4 | 13.9 | 8.9 | 3.4 | 5.7 | 6.1 | 3.2 | 5.2 |
| France | 13.3 | 14.7 | 14.4 | 7.9 | 9.8 | 3.8 | 25.3 | 43.8 | 62.0 | 51.0 | 91.1 | 127.6 | 99.0 | 96.1 | 75.2 |
| Germany, FR | 19.5 | 17.9 | 17.8 | 10.5 | 12.0 | 3.5 | 9.4 | 10.7 | 24.1 | 15.6 | 26.0 | 35.8 | 32.6 | 24.1 | 18.2 |
| Italy | 7.9 | 16.1 | 16.3 | 4.8 | 10.4 | 2.6 | 2.9 | 14.4 | 5.1 | 3.5 | 12.4 | 18.8 | 17.2 | 5.0 | 7.0 |
| Netherlands | 1.5 | 1.9 | 2.2 | 1.2 | 0 | 0 | 1.1 | 0.7 | 6.2 | 2.8 | 0.6 | 4.2 | 4.0 | 5.1 | 2.5 |
| United Kingdom | 14.3 | 19.2 | 14.8 | 14.9 | 12.8 | 3.1 | 11.7 | 20.2 | 32.6 | 25.3 | 27.5 | 32.1 | 22.9 | 19.6 | 19.0 |
| Total, EC | 57.0 | 74.6 | 71.1 | 44.2 | 46.6 | 13.0 | 53.8 | 93.2 | 143.9 | 107.1 | 163.4 | 229.5 | 181.8 | 153.1 | 127.1 |

|  |  |  |  |  |  |  |  |  |  |  |  |  |  |
|---|---|---|---|---|---|---|---|---|---|---|---|---|---|
| Austria | 6.4 | 6.0 | 3.1 | 3.2 | 2.3 | 1.5 | 0.9 | 6.6 | 5.5 | 2.4 | 2.6 | 5.5 | 11.3 | 7.5 | 5.3 |
| Finland | 12.2 | 12.6 | 13.0 | 11.7 | 10.6 | 13.5 | 9.5 | 11.2 | 10.6 | 5.5 | 6.2 | 10.8 | 8.9 | 6.4 | 9.3 |
| Switzerland | 0.2 | 0.6 | 0.9 | (1/) | (1/) | (1/) | (1/) | (1/) | (1/) | (1/) | (1/) | (1/) | (1/) | (1/) | (1/) |
| Yugoslavia | 0 | 5.2 | 17.3 | 24.4 | 15.1 | 21.2 | 14.6 | 33.0 | 35.6 | 29.7 | 45.1 | 63.9 | 68.4 | 66.8 | 55.1 |
| Total, all W.E. | 75.8 | 99.0 | 105.4 | 83.5 | 74.6 | 49.2 | 78.8 | 144.0 | 195.6 | 144.7 | 218.8 | 318.5 | 280.5 | 233.8 | 196.8 |
| Japan | 13.5 | 30.6 | 66.7 | 81.3 | 55.6 | 28.7 | 68.5 | 112.7 | 117.7 | 130.8 | 103.7 | 91.7 |  | 85.7 | 82.0 |
| Other |  |  |  |  |  |  |  |  |  |  |  |  |  |  |  |
| Algeria | 0 | 1.0 | 1.0 | (1/) | (1/) | (1/) | (1/) | 3.0 | 1.0 | 2.9 | 3.0 | 5.0 | 0 | — |
| Bangladesh | 0 | 0 | 0 | 0 | 0 | 0 | 5.8 | 14.0 | 9.2 | 12.1 | 7.6 | 6.5 | 5.0 | 6.5 |
| Canada | 9.4 | 11.6 | 27.5 | 14.5 | 5.3 | 0.9 | 0 | 0 | 1.3 | 1.2 | 0.4 | 4.2 | 0 | 0 | — |
| Others | 0 | 0 | 0.2 | 2.4 | 3.3 | 3.9 | 8.7 | 7.0 | 23.9 | 16.5 | 33.8 | 36.9 | 51.0 | 16.2 | 11.9 |
| Total | 457.7 | 507.8 | 534.4 | 554.4 | 452.3 | 516.5 | 546.8 | 652.2 | 728.3 | 738.7 | 800.2 | 877.9 | 972.9 | 857.8 | 789.1 |

1/ Less than 500 metric tons, if any.

*Source: 1978–79: Cotton World Statistics, ICAC, p. 137.*

Table 11.6  Distribution of Soviet Cotton Exports by Regions 1965/69–1975/79

|  | 1965/69 | 1975/79 |
|---|---|---|
|  | per cent of total exports ||
| Communist Countries[a] | 70 | 53 |
| Western Europe (incl. Yugoslavia) | 17 | 29 |
| Japan | 10 | 8 |
| Others | 3 | 10 |
| Total | 100 | 100 |

[a]Includes Bulgaria, Czechoslovakia, East Germany, Hungary, Poland, Romania, Cuba, North Korea, Vietnam.

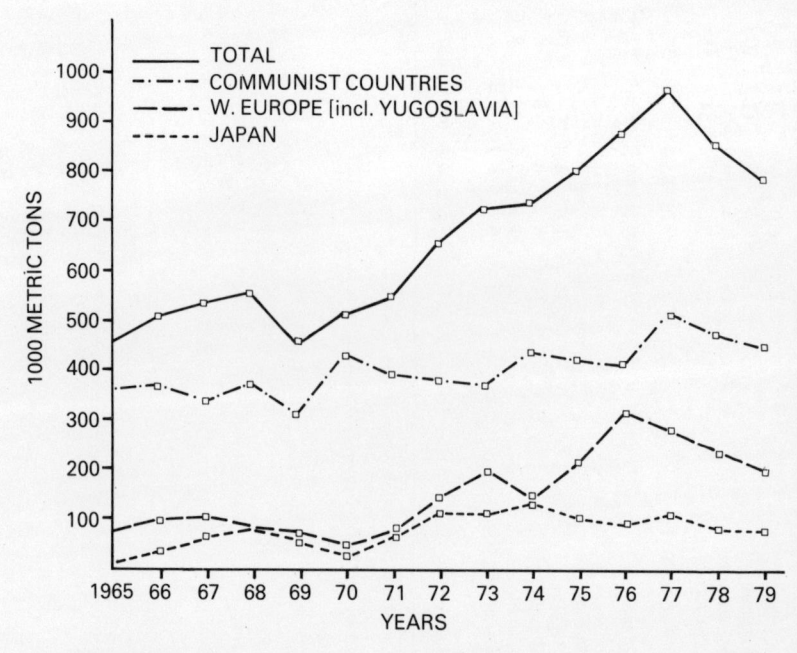

FIGURE 11.4  Export of Cotton from USSR by destination 1965–1979

Table 11.7 Imports of Cotton into USSR by Country of Origin, Calendar Years, 1965–1979 (1,000 metric tons)

| Country of Origin | 1965 | 1966 | 1967 | 1968 | 1969 | 1970 | 1971 | 1972 | 1973 | 1974 | 1975 | 1976 | 1977 | 1978 | 1979 |
|---|---|---|---|---|---|---|---|---|---|---|---|---|---|---|---|
| Africa |  |  |  |  |  |  |  |  |  |  |  |  |  |  |  |
| Egypt | 107.1 | 98.5 | 71.4 | 59.5 | 64.1 | 122.7 | 108.3 | 69.0 | 67.8 | 56.6 | 68.5 | 34.9 | 27.1 | 0 | — |
| Mali | 1.0 | 1.0 | 1.9 | 1.5 | 1.5 | 1.6 | 2.0 | 1.0 | — | — | 0 | 0 | a | 0 | — |
| Morocco | 0.7 | 0.8 | 1.0 | 0.7 | 1.9 | a | 0 | 0 | — | — | 0 | 0 | a | 0 | — |
| Somali | 0.1 | 0 | 0.1 | 0 | 0 | 0.2 | 0 | 0 | — | — | 0 | 0 | a | a | — |
| Sudan | 11.8 | 7.0 | 8.8 | 12.9 | 13.0 | 59.5 | 59.9 | 1.5 | a | a | 4.3 | 9.6 | 5.0 | 5.4 | 9.6 |
| Tanzania | 0 | 0.1 | 0 | 0 | 0 | 0 | 0 | 0 | a | a | 0 | 0 | a | n.a. | n.a. |
| Uganda | 0 | 0.3 | 0.7 | 0.7 | 0 | 1.2 | 0 | 0 | a | a | a | 0 | a | 0 | — |
| Total | 120.7 | 107.7 | 83.9 | 75.3 | 79.5 | 185.2 | 170.2 | 71.5 | 67.8 | 56.6 | 72.8 | 44.5 | 32.1 | 5.4 | 9.6 |
| Western Hemisphere |  |  |  |  |  |  |  |  |  |  |  |  |  |  |  |
| Brazil | 12.1 | 14.9 | 8.0 | 3.5 | 5.2 | 0.8 | 0 | 0 | 9.9 | a | a | 0 | a | 0 | — |
| Asia |  |  |  |  |  |  |  |  |  |  |  |  |  |  |  |
| Afghanistan | 14.2 | 9.1 | 10.7 | 6.6 | 2.5 | 3.5 | 5.5 | 8.0 | 8.9 | 17.0 | 11.7 | 14.6 | 16.7 | 17.6 | 23.3 |
| Iran | 7.1 | 6.4 | 11.2 | 13.7 | 24.8 | 20.3 | 21.5 | 24.5 | 14.0 | 17.5 | 16.8 | 22.1 | 21.1 | 19.9 | 24.0 |
| Iraq | 0.5 | 0.3 | 0.2 | 0.5 | 0.8 | 0.4 | 1.0 | 0 | a | a | a | a | a | 0 | — |
| Pakistan | 1.0 | 2.0 | 5.2 | 4.6 | 7.7 | 11.4 | 6.1 | 10.5 | 2.0 | 3.0 | 3.0 | a | a | 0 | — |
| Syria | 21.3 | 23.5 | 18.4 | 22.5 | 39.0 | 23.7 | 30.1 | 35.0 | 24.0 | 31.0 | 27.2 | 26.4 | 22.9 | 19.2 | 22.0 |
| Turkey | 0.5 | 1.0 | 2.0 | 2.3 | 2.8 | 1.8 | 7.5 | 7.7 | a | a | a | 1.0 | 1.6 | 2.9 | 2.2 |
| Yemen | 0.5 | 1.4 | 0 | 0.8 | 0.2 | a | 0 | 0 | a | a | a | a | a | n.a. | n.a. |
| Total | 45.1 | 43.7 | 47.7 | 51.0 | 77.8 | 61.1 | 71.7 | 85.7 | 48.9 | 68.5 | 58.7 | 63.1 | 62.3 | 59.6 | 71.5 |
| Greece | 4.9 | 6.4 | 4.9 | 7.0 | 8.0 | 10.5 | 0.8 | 9.4 | a | 11.7 | 1.4 | 3.7 | 0 | 0 | — |
| Others | 0.1 | 0 | 0 | 0 | 0 | 0.1 | 0 | 0.1 | 4.1 | 3.3 | 3.9 | 5.2 | 0 | 0 | 4.4 |
| Total | 182.9 | 172.7 | 144.5 | 136.8 | 170.5 | 257.7 | 242.7 | 166.7 | 130.7 | 140.1 | 136.8 | 116.5 | 94.4 | 65.0 | 85.6 |

a. Less than 500 metric tons, if any.

*Source:* Compiled from *Foreign Trade of the USSR.* 1978–79 from: *Cotton World Statistics,* ICAC, pp. 137.

cotton can grow only in the conditions of Egypt. He stressed that Soviet varieties of fine-staple cotton were already grown in the Soviet Central Asian Republic of Tradzhikistan, which produced 250,000 metric tons in 1977.

**Price Policy**

The material embodied in Table 11.8 indicates the Soviet government's price policy is aimed at acquiring a larger part of the non-Communist market. The quotations have been kept below the US prices particularly in the last three years or so. In this context the following statement of the USDA is illustrative:

> Unit values of cotton shipped to France were well below unit values of cotton shipped to West Germany and Japan, and well below world prices. This might mean special concessions in the price of cotton or exchange rates to France. The low unit values may be why Soviet cotton exports to France expanded so rapidly, and why there have been reports that other West European countries could purchase Soviet cotton at lower prices from French merchants than by buying directly from the USSR.[4]

Table 11.8 Cotton Prices in Selected Countries CIF North Europe Quotations[a] ($US)

|  | US Memphis | Mexico | USSR | Egypt Giza 67 | Menouf Giza 68 |
|---|---|---|---|---|---|
| 1976–77 | 82.33 | 82.55 | 81.95 | 142.06 | 158.21 |
| 1977–78 | 64.74 | 68.47 | 65.38 | n.a. | 133.28 |
| 1978–79 | 76.25 | 75.99 | 77.92 | n.a. | 150.80 |
| 1979–80 | 87.49 | 85.86 | 85.89 | 136.37 | 153.05 |
| 1980–81 |  |  |  |  |  |
| August | 102.31 | 96.94 | 94.94 | 135.25 | 152.65 |
| December | 106.00 | 100.50 | 96.19 | 139.38 | 157.96 |
| March | 100.25 | 93.12 | 92.38 | 137.85 | 156.22 |

[a] When not otherwise indicated, prices refer to Strict Middling 1–1/16″ basis.

Source: Cotton World Statistics, ICAC, Vol. 34 No. 6 (1981): 38–39.

## Cotton Power

Cotton is a prominent earner of the foreign currency the Soviet needs to cover imports. In the ten years included in Table 11.9 the USSR paid for 53 per cent of its grain imports with incomes from cotton exports. In four of those ten years export values equalled or surpassed the values of grain imports. That makes the financial significance of cotton evident.

Table 11.9 Value of Cotton Exports and Grain Imports, Soviet Union: 1970–1979 (in million roubles)

| Calendar Year 1 | Cotton Exports 2 | Grain Imports 3 | Col. 2 as a % of Col. 3 |
|---|---|---|---|
| 1970 | 339 | 117 | 289 |
| 1971 | 360 | 190 | 190 |
| 1972 | 430 | 732 | 59 |
| 1973 | 470 | 1147 | 41 |
| 1974 | 640 | 526 | 121 |
| 1975 | 660 | 1923 | 34 |
| 1976 | 762 | 2232 | 34 |
| 1977 | 1009 | 1028 | 98 |
| 1978 | 836 | 1655 | 51 |
| 1979 | 798 | 2254 | 45 |
| Total | 6304 | 11804 | av. 53 |

*Source:* Base data (Col 2 and 3) obtained from USDA, Cotton Division, FAS, Washington, D.C., August 1981.

The socio-economic aspect of the very expensive irrigation system has been stressed. Data on per unit cost in Soviet literature are vague. In the 1960s Khrushchév gave a figure of 2,600 roubles as the capital cost of irrigation per hectare.[5] Under-utilization, salinity and swampiness cause very high maintenance costs which call for constant investment. Not even estimates can be made on the amounts involved. Yet, securing a relatively high standard of life for a potentially hostile, non-Russian population the Soviet Union established a strong political power. Following the interpretation of Professor Labys this is the pattern of a "negative power". Accordingly, if cotton prices fell severely on the world market the Soviets would have to increase the subsidies to the producing regions which are already uneconomic.[6]

Soviet cotton marketing in COMECON countries is an interesting combination of political and marketing power. Trade between the USSR and the COMECON occurs in the form of bilateral transactions. Due to their political power the Soviets dominate the market, determine the prices and practically exclude competition. Accordingly, the political power of the USSR secures for Soviet cotton an almost unrestricted market power in the COMECON.

It seems that the USSR failed to establish a market power in Western Europe. Soviet sales to France declined in the early 1980s and the United States' share increased while other suppliers gained a substantial part of the market as well.

# Notes

CHAPTER ONE  SOVIET COMMODITY POWER

1. For an extended theoretical discussion of the factors affecting such influence, see A.O. Hirschman, *National Power and the Structure of Foreign Trade* (Berkeley: University of California Press, 1969), especially pp. 13–52.
2. See for instance J. Quigley, *The Soviet Foreign Trade Monopoly* (Columbus, Ohio: State University Press, 1974), pp. 103–107, 127; L.J. Brainard, "Soviet Foreign Trade Planning" in US Congress, Joint Economic Committee, *Soviet Economy in a New Perspective* (Washington: Government Printing Office, 1976), pp. 695–708.
3. See for instance L.L. Fischman, *World Mineral Trends and US Supply Problems* (Washington D.C., Resources for the Future, 1981), pp. 483–489; US Department of Interior, Bureau of Mines, *Minerals Yearbook Preprints: Platinum–Group Metals* (Washington: Government Printing Office, 1979); US Department of Interior, Bureau of Mines, *Minerals Yearbook Preprints: Chromium* (Washington: Government Printing Office, 1979).
4. Federal Trade Commission, Report to the Subcommittee on Small Business, US Senate, *The International Petroleum Cartel* (Washington: Government Printing Office), pp. 124–125.
5. Compiled in Charles River Associates, "An Economic Analysis of the Aluminum Industry," Cambridge, Mass., 1971, Table 3 and 4, pp. 3–50, xeroxed, based on yearbooks of American Bureau of Metal Statistics, US Bureau of Mines, and W.R. Skinner.
6. Raymond Vernon and Brain Levy, "State-Owned Enterprises in the World Economy: The case of Iron Ore," in Leroy P. Jones (ed.) *Public Enterprise in Less-Developed Countries: Multidisciplinary Perspectives* (Cambridge, Mass.: Cambridge University Press, forthcoming).
7. Zuhayr Mikdashi, *The International Politics of National Resources* (Ithaca N.Y.:Cornell University Press, 1976), p. 121; and Zuhayr Mikdashi, *A Comparative Analysis of Selected Mineral Exporting Industries* (Vienna: OPEC), xeroxed, pp. 13–15 and 134–135.
8. See for instance Marshall Goldman, *The Enigma of Soviet Petroleum* (London: George Allen and Unwin, 1980), pp. 68–69, 83; and A.J. Klinghoffer, *The Soviet Union and International Oil Politics* (New York: Columbia University Press, 1977), pp. 66–68.
9. S.D. Krasner, *Defending the National Interest* (Princeton N.J.: Princeton University Press, 1979), pp. 120–121; C.D. Goodwin (ed.), *Energy Policy*

*in Perspective* (Washington D.C.: Brookings Institute, 1981), pp. 116–117.
10. S.D. Krasner, *Defending the National Interest,* pp. 186–188, 238; Mira Wilkins, *The Maturing of Multinational Enterprise* (Cambridge, Mass.: Harvard University Press, 1974), pp. 367–368. Also Ingram, *Expropriation of US Property in South America* (New York: Praeger, 1974), pp. 93–94.
11. Krasner, *Defending the National Interest*, pp. 227, 234, 241; P.E. Sigmund, *Multinationals in Latin America* (Madison, Wisc.: University of Wisconsin Press, 1980), p. 153; Mikdashi, *The International Politics of National Resources*, p. 113. Also G.M. Ingram, *Expropriation of US Property in South America*, p.321.
12. S. Moment, "Long Term Associations of Developing Countries with Consumers of Bauxite, Alumina and Aluminum," United Nations Industrial Development Organization, Vienna, 1978, pp. 24–36.
13. R.B. Stobaugh, "The Oil Companies in Crisis" in Raymond Vernon (ed.), *The Oil Crisis* (New York: W.W. Norton, 1976), pp. 186–188; Commission of the European Community, "Report by the Commission on the Behaviour of the Oil Companies in the Community during the period from October 1973–March 1974," Brussels, 1974, p. 162.
14. Mikdashi, *International Politics of Natural Resources,* pp. 82–117, 187, 232–233.
15. For a description of the Aramco formula for determining output, see M.A. Adelman, *The World Petroleum Market* (Baltimore, Md.: Johns Hopkins University Press, 1972, published for Resources for the Future), pp. 85–89. And for a description of prewar aluminum consortia formulas for determining output see Charles River Associates, "Economic Analysis of the Aluminum Industry," pp. 3–24. In the postwar period, overlapping joint ventures have provided an informal means of pooling information and maintaining desired price and supply policies.

CHAPTER TWO LONG-TERM COMMODITY AGREEMENTS

1. V.S. Patalichev's speech of June 12, 1964 was published in the Soviet monthly *Foreign Trade* 7 (1964). See also Lavigne, "L'URSS à la conférence mondiale sur le commerce et le développement," *Le Courrier des pays de l'Est* 13 (1964): 31.
2. UNCTAD TD (IV)/GG/1, May 11, 1976, *Commodities: Ways and Means of Normalizing the Development of World Commodity Markets.*
3. *Ibid.*
4. A. Ivanov and V. Polezhaev, "U.N. Conference on a Common Fund for Commodities," *Foreign Trade* 10 (1977): 41.
5. UNCTAD TD/B/AC31/CRP2, February 1, 1980 (Original in Russian), p.5.
6. UNCTAD, 1976, op. cit.
7. *Ibid.*
8. A. Ivanov and V. Polezhaev, "Urgent Problem of International Trade in Primary Materials," *Foreign Trade* 5 (1976): 45–46.

9. V. Polezhaev, "International Commodity Agreements. Some Problems in their Functioning," *Commerce extérieur* 8 (1981): 35.
10. V. Polezhaev, "International Wheat Agreement," *Foreign Trade* 10 (1980): 37.
11. *Financial Times*, August 13, 1981.
12. For instance the USSR exported 1.1 million tonnes in 1971, imported 800,000 tonnes in 1972, 1 million in 1973; exported 100,000 tonnes in 1974, and from then on appeared constantly as importer, again with huge fluctuations (1 million tonnes in 1977, 60,000 tonnes in 1978). See: P.F. Raugel, *L'accord international sur le sucre et le marché mondial des produits édulcorants*, Paris: Université de Paris I, 1980, p.225.
13. Soviet authors are quite accurate in describing the operation of the sugar market. But they fail to mention, be it even incidentally, the role of the socialist countries on this market. See: J. Shavartsshtein and E. Heifich, "Sugar Market and its Prospects," *Foreign Trade* 1 (1974).
14. Statement of group D (socialist countries) at the 4th Session of the Conference negotiating the creation of a Common Fund, UNCTAD, TD/IPC/CONF/26, October 6, 1980.
15. A. Dimitriev, "The Basic Problems of Today's Rubber Market," *Foreign Trade* 8 (1980): 51. As usual in the matter of ICAs, the reader of Dimitriev's article would never imagine that the USSR is a member of the Agreement.
16. The same violent critique of the USA is to be found in A. Kireyeva, "World Capitalist Cotton Market," *Foreign Trade* 7 (1980).

CHAPTER THREE EXPORTS OF PRIMARY COMMODITIES

1. Using the Appendix tables, the NRP sectors are defined to include fuels, non-food raw materials, grain and flour and other food.
2. The numbers in parentheses indicate the percentage share of the commodity in total Soviet exports in 1976. The source used is: E.A. Hewett, *Soviet Primary Product Exports to CMEA and the West*, Association of American Geographers, Project on Soviet Natural Resources in the World Economy, no. 9 (May 1979).
3. There was a similar discussion in the 1950s. The interested reader may wish to refer to the work of Menderhausen, Holzman and Wiles, to name just a few examples.
4. See, for example: E.A. Hewett, *Foreign Trade Prices in the Council for Mutual Economic Assistance* (Cambridge: Cambridge University Press, 1974), p. 111,
5. This interpretation of the difference between NBTT and GBTT is given for example, by: J. Vanous, *Soviet and Eastern European Foreign Trade in the 1970s: A Quantitative Assessment*, US Congress, Joint Economic Committee, Part 2 (Washington, D.C.: Government Printing Office, 1981), p. 702 and it arises in the context of barter trade as in the case of CMEA trade.
6. See: E.A. Hewett, 'The Impact of the World Economic Crisis on Intra-CMEA Trade' in *The Impact of International Economic Disturb-*

ances on the Soviet Union and Eastern Europe: Transmission and Response, (eds.) L.D. Tyson and E. Neuberger (Oxford: Pergamon Press, 1980), p. 333. In contrast, GBTT would seem to be less suitable for market-type economies since changes in GBTT may reflect less price movements than changes in the balance of payments, and even capital movements. On this point see C.P. Kindleberger, *International Economics*, 4th ed. (Homewood, Illinois: Richard D. Irwin, Inc., 1968), p. 74.

7. This concept of terms of trade may be useful in assessing the distribution of gains resulting from changes in productivity at home and abroad. For a discussion of this point and related issues see: Kindleberger, *International Economics*, pp. 75–76 and J. Spraos, "The Theory of Deteriorating Terms of Trade Revisited," *Greek Economic Review*, vol. 1, no. 2 (1979): 15–42.
8. However, see Hewett, *Foreign Trade Prices*, pp. 113–114 when he justifies the use of NBTT for the period of the 1960s.
9. The following points which refer to gains from trade under conditions of market disequilibria are credited to: ibid., p. 112.
10. ITT are sometimes called "capacity to import." For more details see: Kindleberger, *International Economics*, p. 74.
11. See: Hewett (1980a) for a discussion of the relationship between the Fischer Price Index and the Fischer Unit Value Index as well as for discussion on the relationship between the Paasche and Laspeyres indices.
12. Thus, some of the information may now be provided in value terms, but not the volumes as in the past, while other information may be missing completely. For example, the value and volume entries in the official Soviet statistics in 1977 were reduced by some 50 per cent. The volume data on such important commodities as petroleum, gas, ores and wheat are missing completely.
13. This point is made: K.Dyba, *Ceskoslovenské Unejsi Ekonomické Vztahy* (Prague: Academia, 1980).
14. His choice of an adjustment factor of 1.01–1.03 per annum applied to unit values of machinery and equipment and industrial consumer goods is arbitrary. In contrast, it has been recently suggested by Treml (1981) that the *average* adjustment for quality should be 40 per cent(?), i.e. using a factor of 1.4 for inferior quality only.
15. The proportions of Soviet trade settled in hard currencies are not known. The only related evidence available came from Hungarian sources about Hungarian trade. Using these sources, Kohn and Lang – M.J. Kohn and N.R. Lang, *The Intra-CMEA Foreign Trade System: Major Price Changes, Little Reform*, US Congress, Joint Economic Committee (Washington, D.C.: Government Printing Office, 1977), p. 145 – estimated the share of hard-currency trade with socialist countries as 70 per cent of exports to "socialist" countries for the period 1971–1975 and Hewett, *The Impact of World Crisis*, p. 337 refers to "15 per cent" for more recent years.
16. These points are made and discussed in detail in E.A. Hewett, "The Foreign Sector in the Soviet Economy: Developments since 1980 and Possibilities to 2000," paper presented at *The Conference on the Soviet*

*Economy Towards the Year 2000*, Airlie House, 23–25 October, 1980, particularly in the Appendix.

17. These data together with Hewett's reestimation of the official Soviet indices for total trade are shown in Table 3.8 above (columns A and B respectively).
18. See discussion in Section 2 on the difference between NBTT and GBTT.
19. Hewett computed another set of Soviet NBTT, volume and unit value indices in trade with CMEA and reported in: Hewett, 'Impact of World Crisis', pp. 327–332. These indices are also disaggregated by commodity groups. We shall refer here in detail only to his 'Foreign Sector' which provides a comparison between CMEA and the West while his 'Impact of World Crisis' does not.
20. Another explanation was suggested by Rosefielde who uses estimates of terms of trade from: M.J. Kohn, *Developments in Soviet-Eastern European Terms of Trade, 1971–1975*, US Congress, Joint Economic Committee (Washington, D.C.: Government Printing Office, 1976) and Kohn and Lang, *The Intra-CMEA Foreign Trade System*. He suggests that the principal factor affecting Soviet terms of trade with non-socialist countries was a reduction in the share of oil total exports in that area. He bases this argument on the claim that the share declined from 53 per cent to 39 per cent and (the petroleum) export growth to the West was only 2.2 per cent. Rosefielde (1980) p. 155. However, his argument does not seem to be supported by empirical evidence provided elsewhere. See, for example: E.E. Jack, J.R. Lee and H.H. Lent, *Outlook for Soviet Energy*, US Congress, Joint Economic Committee (Washington, D.C.: Government Printing Office, 1976), p. 475, Appendix, Table 1 and Kohn, *Developments,* p. 141, footnote 14.
21. Vanous explains the deterioration of Soviet NBTT with OCPEs and LDCs by rapid increases of Soviet import prices of Cuban sugar from 1973 on (Cuban sugar accounts for 40–55 per cent of the Soviet imports from OCPE) and by higher proportion of fuels and non-food raw materials in Soviet imports from LDCs than in Soviet exports to LDCs. See: Vanous (1980) p. 70.
22. On this point see also the discussion in Section 3 above.
23. The price negotiations for 1975 were conducted on the basis of average WMP of the years 1972, 1973 and 1974 and the price negotiations for each year in the period 1976–1980 were based on average of WMP of each preceding five-year period. For a historical account of the introduction of sliding formula see for example: Kohn, *Developments*.
24. For example, Vanous' export index to MDCs and LDCs increases in 1975 while both Hewett and Dietz estimate decline in the Soviet aggregate export UVI for the West.
25. This argument could be narrowed down even further since among "fuels" it was predominantly *oil* prices which were responsible for the improvement in terms of trade. According to Kohn's estimates, the Soviet terms of trade with CMEA would have hardly improved in 1975 if the USSR was not an exporter of oil. See: Kohn, *Developments*, p. 140. See also discussion to Table 3.7 below and Section 5.

26. The rather different estimates shown in Table 3.4 are not useful in this respect because of the inclusion in "the West" of LCDs and, needless to say, Vanous' data seem in this respect more plausible.
27. The distinction corresponds to statistical groups 2 and 5 according to the Soviet trade classification (i.e. B.T.N.). For details see: Hewett, *Soviet Primary Exports to CMEA*.
28. For more details see *UN Monthly Bulletin of Statistics*, June 1978, pp. viii–liv (quoted in Hewett (1980), p. 324).
29. For a brief analysis of factors determining the expansion and slowdown in the growth of East-West trade as well as for the outlook for East-West trade see: L.J. Brainard, *Eastern Europe's Uncertain Future: the Outlook for East-West Trade and Finance*, US Congress, Joint Economic Committee (Washington, D.C.: Government Printing Office, 1981).
30. GBTT are not reported in Table 3.7 but can be easily computed. The comparable figures for 1977 for overall GBTT are as follows:

|      | Hewett A | Hewett B | Vanous |
|------|----------|----------|--------|
| 1977 | 108.6    | 112.6    | 115.7  |
| 1978 | 118.5    | 124.2    | NA     |

31. Hewett computed another set of UVI, NBTT and GBTT (using Fischer ideal indices) with *CMEA* in: Hewett, 'Impact of World Crisis', which are roughly consistent with Vanous' data except for GBTT for 1974. Hewett's indices are as follows:

|      | NBTT | GBTT |
|------|------|------|
| 1971 | 110  | 102  |
| 1972 | 100  | 114  |
| 1973 | 98   | 107  |
| 1974 | 100  | 99   |
| 1975 | 115  | 112  |
| 1976 | 114  | 109  |

32. For more details, see Section 2 above.
33. In view of (considerable) price differences between the CMEA and world market, an issue to which we shall return below, it could be argued that the official trade returns are distorted and that data on trade with CMEA countries are not comparable with the relevant data on trade with MDCs. For this reason it may be better to use adjusted data, such as those complied by Vanous which allow for price differences between both markets.
34. Strictly speaking, the windfall gains as defined here take trade volumes as given and attribute changes in windfall gains (i.e. changes in import capacity) due to changes in prices only. This may be a rather restrictive assumption since the change in relative product prices, which the change in terms of trade implies, may lead in the real world to trade diversions.
35. Rosefielde (1980) suggested the gains were in fact smaller. However, since it is not clear how his estimates were arrived at, it is not possible to

assess and compare them with our findings. The latter are, on the other hand, consistent with similar estimates of Hewett, 'Impact of World Crisis'.
36. See Hewett, 'Foreign Sector'. He computes separate estimates for the windfall gains due to improved terms of trade to obtain US$14,256 mil., a result which is quite consistent with our own estimates.
37. Ibid.
38. The available evidence suggests that the price realignment in the intra-CMEA trade has been imcomplete; not only did the absolute prices differ but there continue to be significant deviations in relative prices in terms of relative world prices. See for example: R. Dietz, *Price Changes in Trade with CMEA and the Rest of the World since 1975*, US Congress, Joint Economic Committee (Washington, D.C. Government Printing Office, 1979) and J. Vanous and M. Marrese, "Implicit Subsidies in Soviet Trade with Eastern Europe," discussion paper no. 80–32, Vancouver, B.C.: University of British Columbia, September 1980.
39. In theory, it is possible to obtain higher prices for machinery in the intra-CMEA trade provided the products are of higher quality. This explanation is obviously implausible for sudden changes in prices such as the one quoted here. Obviously more empirical research is needed in this context.
40. A small proportion of intra-CMEA trade is settled in convertible currencies. On this, see, for example: Kohn and Lang, *Intra-CMEA Foreign Trade System*, pp. 144–149.
41. Clearly, domestic (output) expansion which generates increasing claims on imports would still be accompanied by direct (administrative) import controls. However, what is being distinguished in the present case are import controls which are or which are not accompanied by domestic output expansion.
42. His argument is based on a very simple econometric model in which the Soviet primary product shipments to CMEA are a function of CMEA demand and hard-currency balance of trade (with a four period distributed lag). The Soviet primary product shipments to the West are simply a function of hard-currency balance of trade which is further adjusted for a time trend. Finally, the Soviet primary product shipments to other countries depend only on hard-currency balance of trade (again with a 4-period distributed lag). Thus, with the exception of CMEA, demand factors are excluded and, generally, so are all relevant supply factors. Needless to say, however, that a rather similar argument was made by Hanson who tested the proposition that the share of technology in total imports from the West depends on imports of food. See: P. Hanson, *International Technology Transfers from the West to the USSR*, US Congress, Joint Economic Committee (Washington, D.C.: Government Printing Office, 1976), p. 795.
43. Similar shifts took place before without any impetus of changes in terms of trade. See also: R. Portes, "Effect of the World Crisis on the East European Economies," discussion paper no. 70, London: Birkbeck College, January 1980.
44. For more details see: Z. Drabek, "Western Embodied Technology and

its Sectoral Impact on East European Exports to the West," mimeo for OECD, 1981 and Z. Drabek and J. Slater, "Methodology of Data Compilation on Flows of Embodied Technology on East-West Trade," mimeo for OECD, 1981.

CHAPTER FOUR THE SOVIET UNION AND WORLD TRADE IN OIL AND GAS

1. M.I. Goldman, *The Enigma of Soviet Petroleum: Half-Full or Half-Empty?* (London: George Allen and Unwin, 1980) Chapter 2 provides a readable account of this period.
2. The volume of crude oil and oil product exports in 1939 was 0.5 mmt, as reported in *Vneshniaia Torgovlia SSSR, 1918–1966.* The output figure of 31.1 is from *Narodnoe Khoziaistvo SSSR, 1922–72.* World oil exports have been estimated at 130 mmt in 1939, based upon information in L.M. Fanning, *Foreign Oil and the Free World* (New York: McGraw-Hill Book Co. Inc., 1954), p.340 and p.362. The United States exported 26 mmt, or 20 per cent of world exports of oil, in 1939.
3. See R.W. Campbell, *The Economics of Soviet Oil and Gas* (Baltimore: Johns Hopkins Press, 1968), pp. 1–22.
4. *Narodnoe Khoziaistvo SSSR.*
5. The development of the Soviet-East European energy relationship is analysed in J.B. Hannigan and C.H. McMillan, *The Energy Factor in Soviet-East European Relations,* Report No. 18, East-West Commercial Relations Series, Institute of Soviet and East European Studies, Carleton University, Ottawa, September 1981.
6. See Hannigan and McMillan, "CMEA Trade and Cooperation with the Third World in the Energy Sector," in NATO-Economics Directorate, ed., *CMEA: Energy 1980–1990* (London: Macmillan forthcoming), Table 3, for details of Soviet oil exports to the Third World.
7. See ibid., for further discussion of Soviet oil imports.
8. The multilateral accounting of the CMEA's International Bank for Economic Cooperation does not significantly alter this fact. See J.M. Van Brabant, *East European Cooperation: The Role of Money and Finance* (New York: Praeger, 1977).
9. While the prices of Soviet oil exports to CMEA countries are "based" on a lagged, moving average of world market prices, they have in fact diverged significantly from the latter, and in 1979 the price of Soviet crude to these countries was on average about 25 per cent below the market price of Arabian light crude. Moreover, these exports are paid for through clearing accounts under the terms of bilateral trade agreements. Above-plan exports to CMEA countries, and some oil exports to other socialist and developing countries are made on terms equalling or approaching those set by the world market, but these exports are marginal.
10. T. Barten'ev and Iu Komissarov, *SSSR – Finlandia: Orientiry Sotrudnichestva* (Moscow: Izdatel'stvo Politicheskoi Literatury, 1978), p. 65ff.
11. "V/O Sojuznefteexport's 50th Anniversary," *Foreign Trade USSR,* No. 5 (1981): 30.

## Notes

12. See J.E. Hartshorn, *Politics and World Oil Economics* (New York: Praeger, 1967) pp. 234–36 and Sutton, Vol. 1 (1968): 40-43 for two concise accounts of the Soviet oil "offensives" and the reaction of the Western oil majors.
13. Goldman, *op. cit*, pp. 88–89 cites evidence that the USSR at this time encouraged the Arab States to embargo shipments of their oil to the Western countries, while taking advantage of the embargo to expand its own exports.
14. See Hannigan and McMillan, "CMEA Trade..."
15. See B. Das Gupta, "Soviet Oil and the Third World," in D. Naygar (ed.) *Economic Relations between Socialist Countries and the Third World* (New Jersey: Allensheld, Osmun and Co. Publishers, Inc., 1977), pp. 105–142 and P.R. Odell, *Oil and World Power* (Harmondsworth: Penguin, 1979), pp. 65–68.
16. The Central Intelligence Agency (National Foreign Assessment Center) in its first report, *Prospects for Soviet Oil Production*, ER77–10270, April, 1977, predicted that Soviet oil production would peak at between 11–12 million barrels/day (mb/d) in the late 1970s or early 1980s, and steadily decline thereafter to 8–10 mb/d by 1985. In a separate report released about the same time (*The International Energy Situation: Outlook to 1985* ER77–10240U, April 1977) the CIA estimated that as a result, the USSR and Eastern Europe would, in 1985, be net importers of 3.5 to 4.5 mb/d.
17. See John P. Hardt, "Overview", in Joint Economic Committee, Congress of the United States, *Energy in Soviet Policy*, 1981, pp. 3–18; and M.I. Goldman, op. cit., chapter 8.
18. The new position shifts the previous 1985 production forecast to 1990, and modifies the USSR's projected oil import requirements.
19. The US Defense Intelligence Agency predicts that Soviet oil production will not decline during the 1980s. Output will instead "rise slowly through 1985, level off during the late 1980s, and then increase again after 1990." "Statement of Major General Richard X. Larkin and Edward M. Collins, Defense Intelligence Agency, before the Joint Economic Committee, Subcommittee on International Trade, Finance and Security Economics," July 8, 1981.
20. See J.P. Stern, "Western Forecasts of Soviet and East European Energy over the Next Two Decades (1980–2000)," in Joint Economic Committee, Congress of the United States, *Energy in Soviet Policy* (Washington, D.C.: Government Printing Office, 1981), p. 30, Table 5.
21. Two factors come into play here. First, production of substitute fuels will probably not be great enough to modify significantly the demand for oil. See L. Dienes, "Energy Conservation in the USSR," in Joint Economic Committee, Congress of the United States, *Energy in Soviet Policy* (Washington, D.C.: Government Printing Office, 1981), pp. 105–108. Second, the Soviet Union has been unable during the 1970s to lower the annual growth rate in apparent oil consumption below the annual growth rate in national income (see Appendix). In other words, the Soviet Union has not been notably successful to date in conserving oil.

22. See A. Bergson, "Soviet Economic Slowdown and the 1981–85 Plan," *Problems of Communism*, Vol. XXX, No. 3 (May-June, 1981): 24–26 and P. Hanson "Economic Constraints on Soviet Policies in the 1980s," *International Affairs* (Winter 1980/81): 21–42.
23. See J.B. Hannigan and C.H. McMillan, *The Energy Factor in Soviet-East European Relations*, Report No. 18, East-West Commercial Relations Series, Institute of Soviet and East European Studies, Carleton University, Ottawa, September 1981, for an evaluation of Kosygin's remarks on fuels exports to Eastern Europe in the 1981–85 period.
24. The reserve figure is crucial to any forecast of the Soviet potential to maintain or increase production. Western estimates of Soviet proved oil reserves vary from a low of 30–35 billion barrels (CIA, *Prospects*...ER77-10270), to a high of 150 billion barrels (Petrostudies Company. *Soviet Proved Oil Reserves, 1946–1980* (Malmo Sweden: Petrostudies, 1979). Soviet production potential is further clouded by differing opinions on the possibilities for new discoveries. The US Defense Intelligence Agency foresees that the discovery and testing of reserves in the established oil-bearing provides of the USSR will be enough to maintain current levels of production beyond 1990. Other analysts (e.g. J.P. Riva, "Soviet Petroleum Prospects: a Western Geologist's View," in Joint Economic Committee, *op.cit. pp.* 120–126) contend that only a major discovery in the very near future will permit present levels of production to be maintained, and attach a low probability to such a discovery.
25. In contrast to the experience of OPEC countries, associated gas has not played a major role in the longer-term development of the Soviet gas industry. In 1980, only about one-tenth of Soviet output was believed to be associate gas (J. Segal, "Growing Strength of the USSR – World Survey on Natural Gas," *Petroleum Economist* (August, 1981): 339).
26. See Hannigan and McMillan, *The Soviet Energy Stake in Afghanistan and Iran: Rationale and Risk of National Gas Imports*, Report No. 16, East-West Commercial Relations Series, Institute of Soviet and East European Studies, Carleton University, Ottawa, September 1981, for an analysis of the Soviet rationale behind natural gas imports and an account of recent events affecting the arrangements. Imports under the agreement with Iran were disrupted by the Iranian revolution in 1979 and ceased altogether in April, 1980.
27. Some LNG deliveries were made to Poland before the major pipeline links were established. See D. Park, *Oil and Gas in Comecon Countries* (London: Kogan Page, 1979).
28. Segal, *op.cit.*, Business Eastern Europe (July 17, 1981): 232.
29. The first Soviet exports of natural gas by pipeline were to Poland in 1944. S.A. Orudzjev, *Gazovaia Promyshelennost'po Puti Progressa* (Moscow: Nedra, 1976), p. 127.
30. The format is described and analysed in Hannigan and McMillan, "Joint Investment in Resource Development: Sectoral Approaches to Socialist Integration," in Joint Economic Committee, Congress of the United States, *East European Economic Assessment, Part 2 – Regional Assessments* (Washington, D.C.: Government Printing Office, 1981), pp. 259–295.

31. See J.B. Hannigan, *The Orenburg Natural Gas Project and Fuels-Energy Balances in Eastern Europe*, Report No. 13, East-West Commercial Relations Series, Institute of Soviet and East European Studies, Carleton University, Ottawa, July 1980, for an account of the Orenburg natural gas project and its effect on East European fuels-energy balances.
32. One CMEA country, Czechoslovakia, through which the Soviet gas was to be piped to Western Europe, was also to receive deliveries under the agreement. See Hannigan and McMillan, *Soviet Energy Stake...*
33. The Soviet Union has been dealing bilaterally with gas utilities, equipment suppliers and banks in the FRG, France, Italy, Austria, Belgium and the Netherlands. There has also been mention of Switzerland as a possible participant.
34. Based upon figures for world trade in natural gas in *Petroleum Economist* (august 1981):337.
35. This calculation assumes total West European gas consumption of around 400 bcm in 1990, with local supply accounting for 70 percent of total demand. See F. Muller, "Implications for the West, Including Defence, of CMEA Energy Prospects," in NATO-Economics Directorate, ed., *CMEA: Energy 1980–1990* (London: Macmillan, forthcoming) and "Gas Supply/Demand Gap Forecast for Western Europe", *Oil and Gas Journal* (August 14, 1978), pp. 31–36.
36. The nominal value of hard-currency earnings from oil and gas exports may well increase as the result of increased gas exports and rising gas prices, even if the volume of oil exports to hard-currency markets falls rapidly in the early 1980s.
37. Given prospective trends in world energy exports, it seems unlikely that the international price of natural gas will rise sufficiently more rapidly than the prices of oil and oil products in the years ahead. See J. Segal and F.E. Niering, "Special Report on World Natural Gas Pricing," *Petroleum Economist* (September, 1980): 373–378 for an excellent discussion of price trends and the factors determining them.
38. See Das Gupta, op.cit. and Goldman, op.cit.
39. Cf., H.E. Meyer, "Why We Should Worry About the Soviet Energy Crunch", *Fortune* (February 25, 1980): 82–88.
40. J.T. Jensen, "World Natural Gas Reserves and the Potential for Gas Trade," in R. Mabro, ed., *World Energy Issues and Policies* (Oxford University Press, 1980), pp. 43–69.
41. Ibid., p. 49.
42. Hannigan and McMillan, *The Energy Factor...* and *The Soviet-West European Relationship in Oil and Gas: Dependence or Interdependence?* East-West Commercial Relations Series, Institute of Soviet and East European Studies (Carleton University, Ottawa 1981).

CHAPTER FIVE SOVIET COAL EXPORTS

1. Primary coal production in the United States amounted to some 559.5 million metric tons.
2. Figures prepared for the ECE's Coal Committee, seventy-seventh session, 21–24 September 1981.

3. In 1980, American sales of hard coal to western Europe about doubled. Data prepared for the ECE's Coal Committee, seventy-seventh session, 21–24 September, 1981.
4. Made in 1968 and cited in Leslie Dienes and Theodore Shabad, *The Soviet Energy System; Resource Use and Policies* (New York: John Wiley & Sons, 1979), p. 105.
5. *United Nations' Statistical Yearbook 1978* (New York: United Nations) p. 184.
6. The Economic Commission for Europe cites a figure of 183 billion tons of coal equivalent for the reserves of the USSR. *Economic Bulletin for Europe*, vol. 33, no. 2, p. 220.
7. The figures for the reserves of the various coal basins are taken from Dienes and Shabad, op. cit. p. 106, the figures for output in 1980 from *Ekonomicheskaia Gazeta*, no. 7 (February 1982): 7.
8. *Economic Bulletin for Europe*, vol. 33, no. 2, p. 302.
9. Ibid., p. 301.
10. Ibid., p. 302.
11. Figures prepared for the ECE show a total figure for capital investment in coal mining, including ancillary activities such as the building of power plants, of Rbls. 1,484.10 million in 1979. This suggests that the rise of 10 per cent in total coal output for plan-period 1981–85 could mean an increase in investment of some Rbl. 150 million. See *Capital Formation and Cost of Production in the European Coal Industry in 1979*, ECE, Coal Committee, Group of Experts on Coal Statistics, May 1981.
12. *Pravda*, 19 November, 1981, p. 2.
13. *Economic Bulletin for Europe*, vol. 33, no. 2, p. 302.
14. Estimate communicated to the Second Session of the Senior Advisors on Energy (ECE), 1980 by the delegation of the USSR.
15. The capacity of the South Yakutian basin by 1983 is to be 13 million tons of coal, of which 9 million tons coking coal and 4 million tons of steam coal. Dienes and Shabad, op. cit., p. 115.
16. In addition to the South Yakutian project already well under way, there seems to be only one other project seriously envisaged, and this is at the discussion stage. It is an ambitious coal-liquefaction scheme between the Federal Republic of Germany and the USSR which may be partially paid for by the export of synfuel to Germany.

CHAPTER SIX THE USSR AND THE INTERNATIONAL ALUMINIUM MARKET

1. The European Bayer process permits production of higher quality alumina and requires lower levels of energy consumption. The American Bayer process deals with a simpler material and therefore requires less investments than those for other processes. But it also has its disadvantages since pure trihydrated bauxite reserves are limited. The European Bayer is more adaptable to both monohydrated and trihydrated bauxites, except that the latter must contain at least 10 to 15 per cent monohydrated bauxite and be free of quartz.
2. The reader interested in further study of processes for producing alumina from non-bauxite sources is referred to E.W. Greig and M.J. Adams,

"Non-bauxite sources of alumina," *World Aluminium Survey* (London: Metal Bulletin Ltd., 1977), pp. 73–82.
3. See also:
C. Nappi, *Commodity Market Controls: An Historical Review* (Lexington, Mass.: Lexington Books, 1979), chap. 8.
Oppenheimer & Co., *Aluminium Industry Report: Mid-Year Survey of Free World Primary Aluminium Capacity: 1974–1979* (New York: Metals Review, September 1974).
J.W. Stamper and H.F. Kurtz, "Aluminium," *Mineral Facts and Problems* US Bureau of Mines, Bulletin no. 667 (Washington: Government Printing Office, 1975), pp. 37–66.
4. I.D. Stankovich, *The Aluminium Industry in the Soviet Union* (London: Metal Bulletin Ltd., 1978), p. 50.
5. The reader interested in further information about this USSR-Greece agreement is referred to *Engineering and Mining Journal* vol. 182, no. 5, (May 1981): 12.
6. *Mining Journal* (November 2, 1979): 377. We should note that a few sections of the contracts between Jamaica and some eastern countries have been since then modified. Thus, the USSR replaced the 250,000 MT/year of alumina imports by 1,000,000 MT/year of bauxite imports. Algeria postponed the construction of its first aluminium smelter and therefore is no longer interested in the imports of 150,000 MT/year of alumina as from 1984. See: *Engineering and Mining Journal* Vol. 182, no. 7 (July 1981): 135.
Note that according to *Metals Week* (June 29, 1981), Jamaica is losing $57 for every metric ton sold to USSR. The loss can be explained as follows: since there has been no increase in Jamaican output of alumina, this country is buying alumina from Alcan or Alcoa at $218/MT and selling it to the USSR under contract for $205/MT. This $13/MT difference, plus $44/MT to ship alumina to the Soviet Union makes a loss of $57/MT.
7. In 1978 Jamaican alumina exports were divided as follows: United States (576,000 MT), United Kingdom (545,000 MT), Canada and Norway (314,000 MT each).
8. Stamper and Kurtz, "Aluminium", pp. 38–39.
9. According to a US Bureau of Mines publication (*Primary Aluminium Plants Worldwide,* Washington, June 30th, 1979), world aluminium capacity of production was equal in 1979 to 19.2 million short tons divided as follows: 3.2 million ST for the USSR, 2.1 million ST for Alcoa, 1.8 million ST for Alcan, 1.2 million ST each for Kaiser and Reynolds, 1.3 million ST for P.U.K. and 0.8 million ST for Alusuisse.
10. See:
Charles River Associates Inc., *Policy Implications of Producer Country Supply Restrictions: the World Aluminium – Bauxite Market* (Cambridge, Massachusetts: 1977), pp. 72–75–77.
Charles River Associates Inc., *An Economic Analysis of the Aluminium Industry* (Cambridge, Massachusetts: March 1971).
Metal Bulletin Ltd., *World Aluminium Survey* (London, England: 1977), pp. 109–123.

US Bureau of Mines, *Primary Aluminium Plants Worldwide*. Division of Nonferrous Metals (Washington, D.C.: June 30, 1979).
11. The reader interested in a more complete analysis of the international aluminium market is referred to: Charles River Associates Inc., *An Economic Analysis of the Aluminium Industry* (Cambridge, Massachusetts: March 1971).
Charles River Associates Inc., *Policy Implications of Producer Country Supply Restrictions: the World Aluminium – Bauxite Market* (Cambridge, Massachusetts: 1977).
Nappi, 1979, chap. 8, pp. 121–143.
12. Stankovich, *The Aluminium Industry*
T. Shabad, "Raw Material Problems of the Soviet Aluminium Industry," *Resources Policy*, v. 2, no. 4 (December 1976): 222–234.
13. Stankovich, *The Aluminium Industry*, table 5, pp. 35–44.
14. See also:
Stankovich, *The Aluminium Industry*, table 10, pp. 52–59 and "Mining Investment 1981: an Update and Review of Capital Projects Taking Shape Around the World," *Engineering and Mining Journal* Vol. 182, no. 1 (January 1981): 59–81.
15. R. Kestenbaum, "The Aluminium Industry in the Communist Bloc," in *Proceedings of the Metal Bulletin's First International Aluminium Congress, September 29 – October 1, 1980* (Madrid). Edited by Norman Connell and assisted by Patricia Lloyd. (London: Metal Bulletin Ltd., 1981), Session IV, p. V(2).
16. F. Gèze mentions that agreements of this type have been concluded with at least 30 developing countries, where the USSR was maintaining more than 6,000 experts. Twenty-one of these agreements were between African countries, on one side, and the USSR or Romania on the other.
F. Gèze, "L'USSR et les règles du jeu," *Le Monde Diplomatique*, vol. 28, no. 324 (March 1981): 11.
17. Translated from Gèze, 1981, p. 12 (the text is not underlined in the original version). Note that Hungary is no longer happy about the agreement reached in 1962 with the USSR concerning the transformation in that country of their alumina into aluminium. The interested reader is referred to M. Tompa, "La Hongrie relance son industrie de l'aluminium," *Le Courrier des Pays de l'Est*, no. 224 (December 1978).
18. Kestenbaum, 1981, p. V(4)
The Aluminium Association Inc., *Aluminium Statistical Review 1979* (Washington: The Aluminium Association Inc., 1980), p. 57.

CHAPTER SEVEN THE ROLE OF THE SOVIET UNION IN METAL MARKETS
1. Because of the difficulties of obtaining valid original sources of minerals data on the USSR, the data employed in this study are instead estimates from best available sources. This chapter thus represents a general overview rather than a scientific document.
2. The framework for analysing market structure, power, and price formation in commodity markets can be found in W.C. Labys, *Market*

# Notes

*Structure, Bargaining Power and Resource Price Formation* (Lexington, Mass., Lexington Books, 1980).
3. V. V. Strishkov, "The Mineral Industry of the USSR," in *Minerals Yearbook* (Washington, D.C.: US Bureau of Mines, 1979); Strishkov, V.V., "Soviet Union," *Mining Annual Review* (London: Mining Journal, 1980), pp. 579–605; N.W. Switucha, "COMECON's Mineral Development Potential and its Implications for Canada," M.R. no. 183, Energy, Mines and Resources, Canada, Ottawa, 1974; A. Sutulov, *Mineral Resources and the Economy of the USSR* (New York: McGraw-Hill, 1973); and R. Johnson, *Soviet Natural Resources in the World Economy* (Chicago: University of Chicago Press, 1982).
4. Strishkov, 1980, op. cit., p. 579.
5. S. D. Strauss, "Mineral Self-Sufficiency: The Contrast Between the Soviet Union and the United States," *Mining Congress Journal* (1979): 51.
6. H. E. Meyer, "Russia's Sudden Reach for Raw Materials," *Fortune* (July 28, 1980): 43–44.
7. J. H. Jolly, "Copper" in *Minerals Yearbook, 1979* (Washington, D.C.: US Bureau of Mines, 1979).
8. Reserve levels and their locations appear from Strishkov, 1979, op. cit., pp. 29–31.
9. Switucha, op. cit., p. 54.
10. L. L. Fischman, *World Mineral Trends and U.S. Supply Problems* (Washington, D.C.: Resources for the Future, 1981), p. 189.
11. Switucha, op. cit., p. 53.
12. This discussion is based on the more complete description of copper price formation found in Labys, op. cit., pp. 98–100.
13. This analysis is based on W.C. Labys, "Role of State Trading in International Minerals Markets," in M. M. Kostecki (ed.), *State Trading in Market Economics* (London: Macmillan Press, 1982).
14. Labys, 1980, op. cit., p. 87.
15. A more complete description of the role of multinational mining firms in the world copper market structure can be found in Labys, ibid., pp. 75–92.
16. Labys, 1980, ibid., pp. 75–92.
17. Ibid.
18. Reserve levels and their locations are from Strishkov, 1979, op. cit., pp. 36–37.
19. Fischman, op. cit., p. 55.
20. Switucha, op. cit., p. 53.
21. G.L. De Huff, "Manganese", in *Minerals Yearbook, 1979* (Washington, D.C.: US Bureau of Mines, 1979), p. 12.
22. G.L. DeHuff and T.S. Jones, "Manganese," in *Minerals Facts and Problems, 1980* (Washington, D.C.: US Bureau of Mines, 1980), p. 2.
23. Fischman, op. cit., p. 494.
24. Charles River Associates. "Policy Implications of Producer Country Supply Restrictions: The World Manganese Market," Prepared for the US Dept. of Commerce, Cambridge, Mass., 1976.
25. Fischman, op. cit., p. 500.

26. Ibid.
27. Reserve levels and their location are from Strishkov, 1976, op. cit., p. 28.
28. Fischman, op. cit., p. 490.
29. M. McCarthy, "The Future of the Chromium Industry," M.S. Thesis, College of Mineral and Energy Resources, West Virginia University, Morgantown, 1981.
30. N.A. Matthews, and J.L. Morning, "Chromium," in *Minerals Yearbook, 1979* (Washington, D.C.: US Bureau of Mines, 1979), p. 12.
31. Charles River Associates, "Policy Implications of Producer Country Supply Restriction in the World of Chromite Market," Prepared for the US Dept. of Commerce, Cambridge, Mass., 1976.
32. Meyer, loc. cit.

CHAPTER EIGHT THE SOVIET IMPACT ON WORLD TRADE IN GOLD AND PLATINUM

1. Like all CMEA member-states save one, the USSR publishes no statistics classifying occupational deaths, accidents or disease by branch of activity. The exception is Poland, where, during its brief public presence, Solidarity forced data on such mortality into the open; but mining was not separately given *(Mały rocznik statystyczny 1981*, pp. 52–3, cited in a note on the new facts by Michael Ellman and Batara Simatupang, '*Odnowa* in Statistics', *Soviet Studies* XXXIV (1982): 112). Industrial diseases and causes of death are available for Hungary for the population as a whole, but not by occupation.
2. Even at the height of de-Stalinization when Khrushchev was General Secretary of the Communist Party, little denunciation of the bestial conditions of Kolyma (still less of Norilsk) actually figured in the legal press – perhaps the most outspoken was in *Literaturnaya gazeta*, 4 April 1964. Our knowledge comes from *samizdat, tamizdat* and Western publications; the most thorough of the latter is Robert Conquest, *Kolyma: The Arctic Death Camps* (London: Macmillan, 1978).
3. Statute in *Vedomosti Verkhovnogo Soveta*, No. 1, 1959; commentary in V. D. Menshagin et al., *Sovetskoe ugolovnoe pravo: Osobennaya chast'* (Moscow: Izdatel'stvo Moskovskogo Universiteta, 1971), p. 33. For these references I am indebted to Professor Bernard Rudden of the University of Oxford.
4. David Marsh, "Shift in Bullion Trade away from Zurich to London," *Financial Times*, 20 November 1981.
5. David Marsh, "Russia and South Africa. Gold; The Game Hots Up," ibid., 26 October 1981.
6. The Bank held $2,433 mlm in gold and securities on 31 December 1981 (National Bank of Hungary, *Information Memorandum: $400 mlm Term Loan*, April 1981, p. 30); it valued gold at $226 per oz. If all the reserve was gold it was 145 tonnes.
7. See "Net Trade with Communist Sector" in Louise du Boulay et al., *Gold 1982* (London: Consolidated Gold Fields, 1982), p. 15.
8. Regular estimates are, however, made by United States government agencies and are published through the Joint Economic Committee of

the US Congress and the Congressional Reference Service (see source to Table 5).
9. V. Alkhimov, 'Krupneyshiy iz krupneyshikh' *Pravda*, 3 October 1981.
10. Transport to the Magadan region was by sea during the ice-free season or by air; the number of prisoners who escaped over a thousand miles of trackless *taiga* was trivial.
11. Henry A. Wallace, *Soviet Asia Mission* (New York: Reynal and Hitchcock, 1946). Subsequent reports by released prisoners showed that they were confined within their hutments throughout his stay and that the watchtowers and fences were temporarily dismantled. The secret police chief, executed immediately after Stalin's death for his atrocities, was represented as "chairman of the local-government authority."
12. For example, a Swiss, Elinor Lipper: *Eleven Years in Soviet Prison Camps* (London: Hollis and Carter, 1951).
13. Alexander Solzhenitsyn, *The Gulag Archipelago*, 3 vols. (London: Collins, 1973, 1975 and 1978).
14. S. Mora (pseudonym of K. Zamorski), *Kolyma: Gold and Forced Labour in the USSR* (Washington, D.C.: Foundation for Foreign Affairs, 1949), p. 10.
15. N. Jasny, "Labour and Output in Soviet Concentration Camps," *Journal of Political Economy* 59 (1951): 405–19; S. Swianiewicz, *Forced Labour and Economic Development* (London: Oxford University Press, 1965), p. 292.
16. Circulated by that corporation in mimeograph: with David Dowie, 'A Methodological Study of the Production of Primary Gold by the Soviet Union' (1974). The most valuable of the reports was by a Russian escapee, Vladimir Petrov, first published as *Soviet Gold* in 1949, but more recently available as *Escape from the Future* (Bloomington, Indiana: Indiana University Press, 1973). The writer appreciatively acknowledges correspondence with Dr Petrov, senior staff member of the Institute for Sino-Soviet Studies of the George Washington University.
17. The various estimates 1932–69 were collated by D. Stelzl, "Aspekte der Produktion des Verkaufs und der Reserven von Gold in den Osteuropaischen Ländern," *Jahrbuch der Wirtschaft Osteuropas* 4 (1973), pp. 406–7.
18. Its *Mining Annual Review* excludes by-product gold and is hence not directly comparable with the CIA series which includes it. Thus the 1978 issues showed 245 tonnes against the CIA, in its *Handbook of Economic Statistics 1978* (Washington, D.C.: USGPO, 1978), 270 tonnes.
19. Sources and workings of the present description of the Soviet gold industry will shortly be published by the writer in R. Jensen, T. Shabad and A. Wright (eds.), *Soviet Natural Resources and the World Economy* (Chicago: Chicago University Press).
20. In D. Lloyd-Jacobs, P. Fells, *et al.*, *Gold 1971* (New York: Walker, 1971), pp. 146–216.
21. Dowie and Kaser, as cited in note 16. It estimates Romania's output at 2 tonnes, China's at 6, North Korea's at 5, with small production in Bulgaria, Czechoslovakia, the GDR, Hungary, and Kampuchea (none of which is here included in Table 8.2).

22. David Potts et al., *Gold 1981* (London: Consolidated Gold Fields, 1981).
23. Du Boulay, op. cit. Miss du Boulay, in response to an enquiry by the present writer, said that Consolidated Gold Fields would continue to work on the subject of Soviet production and would anticipate publishing any conclusions that appeared to be of general interest in its annual survey of the gold market.
24. Potts, op. cit., p. 21. *World Mineral Statistics, 1975–79* (London: HMSO, 1981), p. 82, increased its estimate for 1979 to 300 tonnes, against 250 for 1975–78.
25. President Reagan appointed a new Director of the CIA, who ordered the publication of Agency estimates to cease.
26. The present writer's field-by-field analysis ends in 1980; the estimate for 1981 is the same as that for 1980 plus an increment for the full-year operation of the Mardzhanbulak mill-refinery, which started up in June 1980; no further field examination could be made for 1981.
27. Norilsk rates seven entries in the index to Vol. 2 and ten in Vol. 3 of Solzhenitsyn, op. cit., whereas Kolyma has respectively forty-six and nine. Paul Lydolph's comprehensive *Geography of the USSR* makes no mention of platinum in early editions (New York: Wiley, 1964, 1970) and only one in the latest (Elkhart Lake, Wisc.: Misty Valley Publishing, 1979), but has ample coverage of gold.
28. Described by Solzhenitsyn, op. cit., Vol. 2, as 'an out-and-out beast' (p. 517), he took charge in 1938 and had the rank of Deputy Minister of the NKVD/MVD. When he was made, with many Norilsk personnel, Hero of Socialist Labour in 1949, the official citations unwittingly revealed the extent of the MVD involvement in the project. Zavenyagin headed the Soviet nuclear-weapons programme (as Minister of Medium Engineering) from 1955 (Deputy Minister from 1953) but he died in December the next year. Norilsk was also the scene of a major prisoners' mutiny in 1953 (Solzhenitsyn, op. cit., Vol. 3, p. 280).
29. *Minerals Yearbook 1974*, Vol. III (Washington, D.C.: USGPO, 1977), p. 956.
30. Ibid.
31. *Metal Statistics 1969–1979* (Frankfurt-am-Main: Metallgesellschaft, 1980, p. 60).
32. *World Mineral Statistics 1974–78* (London: HMSO, 1980), pp. 172–3. The latest edition (ibid., 1976–80 (London: HMSO, 1982), p. 184, revises preliminary figures for the previous year.
33. *Metal Bulletin Handbook 1980* (London: *Metal Bulletin*, 1980), p. 498.
34. *World Mineral Statistics, 1975–79* (London: HMSO, 1981), p. 179.
35. Non-communist countries' output of gold from Du Boulay, op. cit., p. 16, and Soviet from the present writer's estimate in Table 8.1; platinum output from *World Mineral Statistics*, as cited in Table 8.3.
36. Sue Cameron and Anthony Robinson, "Soviet Union Sells Gas-oil to Raise Hard Currency", *Financial Times*, 29 January 1982, quoted these as 199 tonnes in 1979, 90 in 1980, and over 300 in 1981.
37. The Mint's estimates are reproduced in Harry Schwartz, *Russia's Soviet Economy* (Englewood Cliffs, N.J.: Prentice-Hall, 1954), second ed., p. 484.

38. *USSR Long-Range Prospects for Hard Currency Trade* (Washington, D.C.: CIA, 1975), Table 1, provided a first estimate of reserves for 1961–74. Revised estimates from 1966 appeared in CIA, *Handbook of Economic Statistics 1978*, op. cit., p. 49; M. Lavigne, "L'Or des Scythes et l'étalon-or," *Diogène* (January-June 1978): 40, cites end-year reserves as 1,446 in 1950, 1,953 in 1956, and 1,038 in 1965, which seems to be the CIA's revised estimate for 1966.
39. Angel Vinas Martin, *El Oro de Moscu* (Barcelona: Ediciones Grijalbo, 1979), states that 510.1 tonnes (equivalent to 460.5 tonnes of fine gold) were sent by the Republican government in ingots and in sixteen different national coinages. I am grateful to Mr Charles Power (St Antony's College, Oxford) for investigating this source for me.
40. All but 10 per cent of the bullion was salvaged in 1981 (45 per cent went to the salvage firm, 37 per cent to the Soviet government, and 18 per cent to the UK government).
41. Index of United States Wholesale Prices, IMF, *International Financial Statistics,* May 1976, p. 383, and June 1982, p. 422 (293 in 1981, 1967 = 100).
42. Du Boulay, op. cit., p. 27.
43. Dr Chris Stals, cited by Marsh (reference in note 5), which is also the source for some of the information on the diversification of direct bullion dealings by the two countries.
44. All forced-labour projects were designed to use only labour. Solzhenitsyn describes how the revetments, the lock gates, and even the wheelbarrows had to be made from locally-cut timber in the building of the White Sea Canal. Prisoners' reports tell the same story for Kolyma: virtually only transport and generating equipment were brought in from elsewhere. The objective was to permit concentration of capital goods on the prime objectives of the Five-Year-Plans.
45. P. Desai, "Soviet Grain and Wheat Import Demands in 1981–85," *American Journal of Agricultural Economics* 64 (1982): 312–22.
46. C. Beaucourt, "La balance des paiements courants de l'URSS à l'horizon 1985," *Le Courrier des pays de l'Est* (1982): 3–49.

CHAPTER NINE THE SOVIET IMPACT ON INTERNATIONAL TRADE IN ASBESTOS

1. World production has been growing very slowly or even decreasing since 1976, depending which data sources are consulted. Cf. figures in Table 6 and Table 8 in Roskill Information Services Ltd., *The Economics of Asbestos*, 3rd ed. (London: 1980) p. 12 and p. 14 and figures in Table 1: US Bureau of Mines, *Asbestos, A Chapter from Mineral Facts and Problems*, (Washington, D.C.: US Government Printing Office, 1980).
2. A brief account of the history of asbestos mining and production is presented in "Some reflections on the mineral industry in Russia," *Industrial Minerals* (July, 1970): 46–47 and *Industrial Minerals* (Jan. 1970): 23.
3. "The Soviet Union," *Mining Annual Review* (June 1981): 27–28.
4. Kazuo Ogawa, "Soviet Economic Trends and Chemical Industry," *Chemical Economy and Engineering Review* (Oct. 1980): 26.

5. A hint to production problems is given in the *Mining Annual Review* (1980): 132.
6. Tables for 1970 show the same pattern regarding Category 1 and Category 2 balance of Eastern Europe. Sorès & A.D. Little, *Etude des possibilités de fabrication des produits d'amiante au Québec* (Montréal: 1977).
7. The estimates for Soviet export in the period 1975–80 vary but none of them suggests that the high level of exports reached in 1975–76 was exceeded in the subsequent years. There remains however some confusion whether the record level of exports was reached in 1975 (613 thousand tons) or, as the latest issue of *Mining Annual Review* (1981) reports, 1976 (630 thousand tons). Figures for later years show a reduction in exports. The downturn of Soviet exports has apparently not been limited to the 1978–1979 period but continued in 1980. For example the import figures of France for 1980 show that while the overall imports of asbestos declined by 4 per cent compared to the previous year, the imports of Soviet asbestos decreased by 15 per cent so that their share of the market in 1980 was only 17.7 per cent, a decline of 2 per cent from the already very low 20 per cent in 1979.
8. See: Roskill, p. 101.
9. In an attempt to keep the composition of their exports of asbestos well balanced, Soviet exporters go as far as to tie sales of longer fibres to the purchases of sufficient quantities of short fibres.
10. See US, Bureau of Mines, *Asbestos 1980*, Table 7.
11. The evolution of the relative prices of Soviet and South African asbestos is less interesting because Soviet exports appear to be mainly in competition with Canadian exports.
12. Assuming that there was no shift in the demand for Soviet asbestos from 1972–73, the observed prices $P_{72} = \$127/t$, $p_{73} = \$147/t$, and quantities $Q_{72} = 89 \times 10^3$ t, $Q_{73} = 69 \times 10^3$ t, would indicate an average price elasticity of demand for Soviet asbestos in the six countries being in 1972/3 close to $e = -1.4$. This is of course only one observation and therefore a tentative indication only.
13. $(P-P)_u = 0.342 \ (M-M) \ R^{-2} = 0.12 \ F = 2.26 \ \text{sig.} = 0.1$
    (1.50)
14. An alternative explanation of the observed price/quantity relationship could be simply that the USSR did not produce enough asbestos in 1973 to satisfy her customers; her exports to W. Europe and to Japan indeed dropped from 1972 to 1973 so that the price might have gone up as a consequence of this shortage. Then of course the question would be why did Russian shortages of asbestos for export to the West coincide with shortages of grain. The hypothesis of intentional price manipulation appears more plausible.

The widely held belief in the industry is that the Russians did and will continue to supply at least a certain quantity of asbestos to Western markets even in periods of acute domestic shortage. This policy of "open door" to Western markets allegedly enabled them to dump desired quantities of asbestos on the market in times of need for foreign exchange.

15. It can be demonstrated that the observed points (quantity/price combinations) will underestimate the true elasticity of substitution in periods of increasing demand and overestimate it in periods of decreasing demand.
16. Private communication with one of the industry experts.
17. US, Bureau of Mines, *Asbestos 1980*.
18. According to declarations of Soviet officials visiting Canada, eighty per cent of Soviet production is earmarked for internal use. "Visite officielle d'une délégation soviétique de l'amiante chez les producteurs québécois," *Bulletin* (nov. déc. 1972): 2–3.

*General references*

US, Bureau of Mines, *Mineral Industries of Eastern Europe and the USSR* (Washington, D.C.: US Government Printing Office May 1978).

US, Bureau of Mines, *Asbestos, Minerals Yearbook* (Washington, D.C.: US Government Printing Ofice 1977, 1980).

*Statistical Yearbook, Member countries of the Council of Mutual Economic Assistance, 1976.* (Moscow: Statistika).

CHAPTER TEN THE SOVIET UNION IN INTERNATIONAL GRAIN MARKETS

1. D. Gale Johnson, *The Soviet Impact on World Grain Trade* (Washington, D.C.: The British North American Committee, 1977) p. 5.
2. See chapter by Marie Lavigne.
3. Coefficient of variation (V) measures relative deviation and has been calculated according to the formula:

$$V = \frac{X_i - \bar{X}}{\delta} 100\% = \frac{\text{Absolute deviation}}{\text{Standard deviation}} 100\%$$

4. Paul Reithmuller and Shelley Luxton, "Changing World Trade Patterns in Wheat: 1966/67 to 1977/78," *Australian Quarterly Review of the Rural Economy* vol. 2, no. 4 (November 1980): 385–391.
5. Clifton B. Luttrell, "The Russian Grain Embargo: Dubious Success," *Review of Federal Reserve Bank of St. Louis* vol. 62, no. 7 (August/September 1980): 1–8.
6. A.M. Emel'janov (ed.) *Kompleksnaja Programma Razvitija Sel'skogo Chozjajstwa v Dejstvii* (Moscow, 1977), pp. 271–274.
7. See for example: R.T. Maddock, "The Economic and Political Characteristics of Food as a Diplomatic Weapon," *Journal of Agricultural Economics* vol. 29, no. 1 (January 1978): 31–41. Peter Wallensteen, "Scarce Goods as Political Weapons: The Case of Food," *Journal of Peace Research* vol. 13, no. 4 (1976): 277–298.
   Ray D. Laird, "Grain as a Foreign Policy Tool in Dealing with Soviets: A Contingency Plan," *Policy Studies Journal* vol. 6, no. 4 (September 1978): 533–537.
8. E. Antal, "Le Commerce extérieur agro-alimentaire des pays du CAEM," *Problémes Economiques* no. 1701 (December 1980;: 27.

9. D. Gale Johnson, op. cit.
10. See, for example, Basile Kerblay, "Les enseignements de l'expérience soviétique d'agriculture collectiviste," *Revue d'Etudes Comparatives Est-Ouest* vol. 10, no. 3 (1979): 7–30.
11. D. Gale Johnson, op. cit., p. 14.
12. *The Wall Street Journal*, February 26, 1981.
13. OECD, *Examen des politiques agricoles, 1977* (Paris, 1978): 92–97.
14. *Review of the World Wheat Situation*, London, International Wheat Council, 1976/77, pp. 77–85.
15. *The Wall Street Journal*, February 26, 1981.
16. USDA, *Foreign Agricultural Economic Report*, various issues in 1980.
17. *The New York Times*, March 15, 1981.
18. In 1972 the Soviets set off a chain of events in world grain markets which resulted in explosive price increases, see: Albert Eckstein and Dale Heien, "The 1973 Food Price Inflation," *American Journal of Agricultural Economics* vol. 60, no. 2 (May 1978): 186–194.
19. Source: FAO, *Trade Yearbook*, various issues (for Soviet imports) World Bank, *Commodity Trade and Price Trends* (The US and Canadian prices are averaged for wheat, for maize the US prices are used).

CHAPTER ELEVEN THE USSR AS A MAJOR FACTOR IN INTERNATIONAL COTTON MARKET

1. Professor E.K. Wadekin to the author.
2. USDA, *US Team Reports on Soviet Cotton Production and Trade*, FAS-M-277, June 1977, p. 1.
3. Nazarenko, U., "Technological Factors of Cereal, Potato and Cotton Production," Collaborative Paper, International Institute for Applied Systems Analysis, Laxenburg, Austria, 1981, p. 22.
4. USDA, Foreign Agriculture Circular, *Cotton* (August 1978): 6.
5. Volin, L., *A Century of Russian Agriculture* (Harvard University Press, 1970), p. 373.
6. Professor W. Labys to the author.

# Selected Bibliography

## VOLUMES

ADELMAN, Morris, A. *The World Petroleum Market.* Baltimore, Md: Johns Hopkins University Press, 1972. xviii, 438 p.

BARTEN'EV, T. and KOMISSAROV, I., *SSSR – Finlandia: Orientiry Sotrudnichestva.* Moscow: Izdatel'stvo Politicheskoi Literatury, 1978.

VAN BRABANT, J.M., *East European Cooperation: The Role of Money and Finance.* (New York; Praeger, 1977).

BRAINARD, L.J. *Eastern Europe's Uncertain Future: The Outlook for East-West Trade and Finance.* US Congress. Joint Economic Committee. Washington, D.C.: Government Printing Office, 1981.

CAMPBELL, Robert W. *The Economics of Soviet Oil and Gas.* Baltimore, Johns Hopkins University Press, 1968. xv, 279.

CONQUEST, Robert. *Kolyma: The Arctic Death Camps.* London, Macmillan, 1978. 256 p.

DIENES, Leslie & SHABAD, Theodore. *The Soviet Energy System; Resource Use and Policies.* New York, Wiley, 1979. vii, 298 p. (Scripta series in geography)

DIETZ, R. *Price Changes in Soviet-Trade with CMEA and the Rest of the World since 1975.* US Congress. Joint Economic Committee. Washington, D.C.: Government Printing Office, 1979.

DU BOULAY, Louise et al. (eds). *Gold 1982.* London, Consolidated Gold Fields, 1982.

DYBA, K. *Ceskoslovenské Vnejsi Ekonomické Vztahy.* Prague: Academia, 1980.

EMEL'JANOV, A.M. (ed.) *Kompleksnaja Programma Razvitija Sel'skogo Chozjajstwa v Dejstvii.* Moscow, 1977.

FANNING, L.M. *Foreign Oil and the Free World.* New York: McGraw-Hill Book Co. Inc., 1954.

FISCHMAN, Leonard L. *World Mineral Trends and US Supply Problems.* Washington, D.C., Resources for the Future, 1981. xxxiv, 535 p. (Research Paper; R–20)

GOLDMAN, Marshall I. *The Enigma of Soviet Petroleum.* London, George Allen and Unwin, 1980.

GOODWIN, C.D. (ed.), *Energy Policy in Perspective.* Washington, D.C.: Brookings Institution, 1981.

HANSON, P. *International Technology Transfer from the West to the USSR.* US Congress. Joint Economy Committee. Washington, D.C.: Government Printing Office, 1976.

HARTSHORN, J.E. *Politics and World Oil Economics.* New York: Praeger, 1967.

HEWETT, Edward A. *Foreign Trade Prices in the Council for Mutual Economic Assistance.* Cambridge, Cambridge University Press, 1974. xii, 196 p. (Soviet and East European Studies).

HIRSCHMAN, Albert O. *National Power and the Structure of Foreign Trade.* 2nd ed. Berkeley, University of California Press, 1969. xiv, 170 p. Publications of the Bureau of Business and Economic Research, University of California.

INGRAM, G.M. *Expropriation of U.S. Property in South America.* New York: Praeger, 1974.

JACK, E.E., LEE, J.R. and LENT, H.H. *Outlook for Soviet Energy.* US Congress. Joint Economic Committee. Washington, D.C.: Government Printing Office, 1976.

JENSEN, R., SHABAD, T., WRIGHT, A. (eds) *Soviet Natural Resources and the World Economy.* Chicago, University of Chicago Press, 1982.

JOHNSON, Gale D. *The Soviet Impact on World Grain Trade.* London, British-North American Committee, x, 62 p.

JOHNSON, R. *Soviet Natural Resources in the World Economy* Chicago: University of Chicago Press, 1982.

KINDLEBERGER, C.P. *International Economics.* Fourth edition. Homewood, Illinois: Richard D. Irwin, Inc., 1968.

KLINGHOFFER, Arthur J. *The Soviet Union and International Oil Politics.* New York, Columbia University Press, 1977. ix, 389 p.

KOHN, M.J. *Developments in Soviet-Eastern European Terms of Trade: 1971–1975.* US Congress. Joint Economic Committee. Washington, D.C.: Government Printing Office, 1976.

KOHN, M.J. *Soviet-Eastern European Economic Relations: 1975–1978.* Volume 1. US Congress. Joint Economic Committee. Washington, D.C.: Government Printing Office, 1979.

KOHN, M.J. and LANG, N.R. *The Intra-CMEA Foreign Trade System: Major Price Changes, Little Reform.* US Congress. Joint Economic Committee. Washington, D.C.: Government Printing Office, 1977.

KOSTECKI, M. *East-West Trade and the GATT System.* London, Macmillan Press (For Trade Policy Research Centre), 1979.

KOSTECKI, M. (ed.) *State Trading in International Markets: Theory and Practice of Industrialized and Developing Countries.* London, Macmillan Press, 1982.

KRASNER, S.D. *Defending the National Interest.* Princeton, N.Y.: Princeton University Press, 1979.

LABYS, Walter C. *Market Structure Bargaining Power and Resource Price Formation.* Lexington, Mass., Lexington Books, 1979. xiv, 238 p.

LLOYD-JACOBS, P. Fells, et al., *Gold 1971,* New York: Walker, 1971.

LYDOLPH, Paul. *Geography of the USSR.* Elkhart Lake, Wisc.: Misty Valley Publishing, 1979.

MENSHAGIN, V.D. et al., *Sovietskoe ugolovnoe pravo: Osobennaya chast',* Moscow: Izdatel'stvo Moskovskogo Universiteta, 1971.

MIKDASHI, Zuhayr. *The International Politics of Natural Resources.* Ithaca, Cornell University Press, 1976.

NAPPI, Carmine. *Commodity Market Controls:* an historical review. Lexington, Mass., Lexington Books, 1979. xi, 199 p.
ODELL, P.R. *Oil and World Power,* Harmondsworth: Penguin, 1979.
PARK, D. *Oil and Gas in Comecon Countries.* London: Kogan Page, 1979.
QUIGLEY, John B. *The Soviet Foreign Trade Monopoly;* Institutions and Laws. Columbus, Ohio State University Press, 1974. ix, 256 p.
SCHWARTZ, Harry. *Russia's Soviet Economy.* 2nd ed. Englewood Cliffs, N.J., Prentice-Hall, 1954. xx, 682 p.
SIGMUND, P.E. *Multinationals in Latin America.* Madison, Wisc.: University of Wisconsin Press, 1980.
SUTULOV, Alexander. *Mineral Resources and the Economy of the USSR.* New York, Engineering & Mining Journal, 1973. 192 p.
STANKOVICH, I.D. *The Aluminium Industry in the Soviet Union.* London, Metal Bulletin Ltd. 1978.
SWIANIEWICZ, S. *Forced Labour and Economic Development;* an Enquiry into the Experience of Soviet Industrialization. London, Oxford University Press, 1965. ix, 321 p.
TYSON, Laura D. and NEUBERGER, Egon (eds). *The Impact of International Economic Disturbances on the Soviet Union and Eastern Europe.* Transmission and response. Oxford, Pergamon Press, 1980. viii, 493 p. (Pergamon Policy Studies on International Politics).
VANOUS, J. *Soviet and Eastern European Foreign Trade in the 1970s: A Quantitative Assessment.* Part 2. US Congress. Joint Economic Committee. Washington, D.C.: Government Printing Office, 1981 (a).
VANOUS, J. *Eastern European and Soviet Fuel Trade: 1970–1985.* Part 2. US Congess. Joint Economic Committee. Washington, D.C.: Government Printing Office, 1981(b).
VOLIN, Lazar. *A Century of Russian Agriculture:* from Alexander II to Khrushchev. Cambridge, Mass.: Harvard University Press, 1970. viii, 644 p. (Russian Research Centre Studies, no. 63)
WILKINS, Mira. *The Maturing of Multinational Enterprise.* Cambridge, Mass.: Harvard University Press, 1974.
ZAMORSKI, Kazimierz. *Kolyma: Gold and Forced Labour in the USSR.* (by Sylvester Mora–pseud.), Washington, D.C. Foundation for Foreign Affairs. 1949. vi, 66 p. (Foundation pamphlet, no. 7)

## ARTICLES AND CHAPTERS

ANTAL, E. "Le commerce extérieur agro-alimentaire des pays du CAEM". in *Problèmes Economiques,* no. 1701, 10 December 1980. pp. 25–32.
BEAUCOURT, C. "La Balance des paiements courants de l'URSS à l'horizon 1985," *Le Courrier des pays de l'Est.* (1982): 3–49.
BERGSON, A. "Soviet Economic Slowdown and the 1981–85 Plan," *Problems of Communism,* Vol. XXX, No. 3 (May-June, 1981): 24–36.
BRAINARD, L.J. "Soviet Foreign Trade Planning" in U.S. Congress, Joint Economic Committee, *Soviet Economy in a New Perspective* (Washington: Government Printing Office, 1976), pp. 695–708.

CHVARTSCHTEIN, I. & KHEIFTCH, E. "Le marché du sucre et les perspectives de son développement", in *Commerce Extérieur* (URSS), no. 1, 1974. pp. 44–53.

DAS GUPTA, B. "Soviet Oil and the Third World," in D. Naygar (ed.) *Economic Relations between Socialist Countries and the Third World* (New Jersey: Allensheld, Osmun and Co. Publishers, Inc., 1977), pp. 105–142.

DEHUFT F., GILBERT L. & JONES, Thomas S. "Manganese", United States. Bureau of Mines. *Mineral Facts and Problems.* 1980 ed. Washington, D.C., United States Department of the Interior, 1980. pp. 549–562.

DESAI, Padma. "Soviet Grain and Wheat Import Demands in 1981–85", in *American Journal of Agricultural Economics,* v. 64, no. 2, May 1982. pp. 312–322.

DIENES, L. "Energy Conservation in the USSR," in Joint Economic Committee, Congress of the United States, *Energy in Soviet Policy* (Washington, D.C.: Government Printing Office, 1981), pp. 105–108.

DIMITRIEV, A. "The Basic Problems of Today's Rubber Market," *Foreign Trade* 8 (1980): 51.

ECKSTEIN, Albert and HEIEN, Dale. "The 1973 Food Price Inflation," *American Journal of Agricultural Economics,* vol. 60, no. 2 (May 1978): 186–194.

ELLMAN, Michel and SIMATUPANG Batara. '*Odnowa* in Statistics', *Soviet Studies* XXXIV (1982): 112.

GREIG, E.W. and ADAMS, M.J. "Non-bauxite sources of alumina," *World Aluminium Survey* (London: Metal Bulletin Ltd., 1977), pp. 73–82.

HANNIGAN, John and MCMILLAN, Carl. "CMEA Trade and Cooperation with the Third World in the Energy Sector," in NATO-Economics Directorate (ed.), *CMEA: Energy 1980–1990* (London: Macmillan forthcoming).

HANSON, P. "Economic Constraints on Soviet Policies in 1980s," *International Affairs* (Winter 1980/81): 21–42.

HANSON, P. "Foreign Economic Relations", in Brown, A. & Kaser, M.C. (eds). *Soviet Policy in the 1980s.* London, Macmillan.

HARDT, John P. "Overview", in Joint Economic Committee, Congress of the United States, *Energy in Soviet Policy,* 1981, pp. 3–18.

HEWETT, E.A. "Soviet Primary Product Exports to CMEA and the West", in Association of American Geographers, *Project on Soviet Natural Resources in the World Economy.* Washington, AAG, 1979. (Discussion paper – Association of American Geographers, no. 9).

HEWETT, E.A. The Impact of the World Economic Crisis on Intra-CMEA Trade. In *The Impact of International Economic Disturbance on the Soviet Union and Eastern Europe: Transmission and Response.* Edited by L.D. Tyson and E. Neuberger. Oxford: Pergamon Press, 1980 (a).

IVANOV, A. and POLEZHAEV, V. "Problèmes du commerce international des matières premières: actualité et recherche d'une solution", in *Commerce Extérieur* (URSS), no. 5, 1976. pp. 40–46.

IVANOV, A. and POLEZHAEV, V. "U.N. Conference on a Common Fund for Commodities," *Foreign Trade* 10 (1977): 41.

IVANOV, A. and POLEZHAEV, V. "La Conférence des Nations Unies sur un Fonds Commun des produits de base", in *Commerce Extérieur* (URSS),

no. 10, 1977. pp. 36–41.
JASNY, Naum. "Labour and Output in Soviet Concentration Camps", in *Journal of Political Economy*, v. 59, no. 5, October 1951. pp. 405–419.
JENSEN, J.T. "World Natural Gas Reserves and the Potential for Gas Trade," in R. Mabro, ed., *World Energy Issues and Policies*, Oxford: Oxford University Press, 1980.
KERBLAY, Basile. "Les enseignements de l'expérience soviétique d'agriculture collectiviste", in *Revue d'Etudes Comparatives Est-Ouest*, v. 10, no. 3, 1979. pp. 7–30.
KESTENBAUM, R. "The Aluminum Industry in the Communist Bloc", in *Proceedings of the Metal Bulletin's First International Aluminium Congress, September 29 – October 1, 1980* (Madrid). Edited by Norman Connell and assisted by Patricia Lloyd. London, Metal Bulletin Ltd, 1981.
KIREYEVA, A. "World Capitalists Cotton Market", in *Foreign Trade* (USSR), no. 7, 1980.
KOSTECKI, M. "State Trading in Foreign Trade of the Mixed Economies: Review", *Economia Internazionale*, vol. XXXV, no. 2, 1982. pp. 1–18.
KOSTECKI, M., "Canada's Grain Trade with the Soviet Union and China", *Canadian Journal of Agricultural Economics*, vol. 30, no. 2, July 1982.
LABYS, Walter C. "Role of State Trading in International Mineral Markets", in Kostecki, M.M. (ed.) *State Trading in International Markets:* Theory and Practice of Industrialized and Developing Countries. London, Macmillan Press, 1982. pp. 78–102.
LAIRD, Ray D. "Grain as a Foreign Policy Tool in Dealing with Soviets: a Contingency Plan", in *Policy Studies Journal*, v. 6, no. 4, 1977. pp. 533–537.
LUTTRELL, Clifton B. "The Russian Grain Embargo: Dubious success", in *Federal Reserve Bank of St. Louis Review*, v. 62, no. 7, August/September 1980. pp. 1–8.
MADDOCK, R.T. "The Economic and Political Characteristics of Food as a Diplomatic Weapon", in *Journal of Agricultural Economics*, v. 29, no. 1, January 1978. pp. 31–41.
Cf., MEYER, H.E. "Why We Should Worry About the Soviet Energy Crunch", *Fortune* (February 25, 1980): 82–88.
MEYER, H.E. "Russia's Sudden Reach for Raw Materials", in *Fortune*, July 28, 1980. pp. 43–44.
OGAWA, Kazuo. "Soviet Economic Trends and Chemical Industry," *Chemical Economy and Engineering Review*, Oct. 1980: 26.
POLEZHAEV, Valentine. "L'accord international sur le blé", in *Commerce Extérieur* (USSR), no. 10, 1980. pp. 32–37.
POLEZHAEV, Valentine. "Accords Internationaux sur les produits de base – quelques problèmes de fonctionnement", in *Commerce Extérieur* (URSS), no. 8, 1981. pp. 28–35, 40.
RIETHMULLER, Paul and LUXTON, Shelley. "Changing World Trade Patterns in Wheat: 1966/67 to 1977/78," *Australian Quarterly Review of the Rural Economy*, vol. 2, no. 4 (November 1980): 385–391.
SEGAL, Jeffrey. "Growing Strength of the USSR – World Survey on Natural Gas", in *Petroleum Economist*, v. 48, no. 8, August 1981. pp. 335–339.
SHABAD, T. "Raw Material Problems of the Soviet Aluminium Industry", in

*Resources Policy*, v. 2, no. 4, December 1976. pp. 222–234.

SPRAOS, J. "The Theory of Deteriorating Terms of Trade Revisited." *Greek Economic Review*, Vol. 1, no. 2 (1979).

STAMPER J.W. and KURTZ, H.F. "Aluminium," *Mineral Facts and Problems* US Bureau of Mines, Bulletin no. 667 (Washington, D.C.: Government Printing Office, 1975), pp. 37–66.

STELZL, D. "Aspekte der Produktion des Verkaufs und der Reserven von Gold in den Osteuropäischen Ländern", in *Jahrbuch der Wirtschaft Osteuropas*, vol. 4, 1973.

STERN, J.P. "Western Forecasts of Soviet and East European Energy over the Next Two Decades (1980–2000)", in Joint Economic Committee, Congress of the United States, *Energy in Soviet Policy* (Washington, D.C.: Government Printing Office, 1981).

STOBAUGH, R.B. "The Oil Companies in Crisis," in Raymond Vernon (ed.), *The Oil Crisis* (New York: W.W. Norton, 1976), pp. 186–188.

STRAUSS, S.D. "Mineral Self-Sufficiency: The Contrast between the Soviet Union and the United States", in *Mining Congress Journal*, 1979.

STRISHKOV, V.V. "The Mineral Industry of the USSR," in *Minerals Yearbook* (Washington, D.C.: US Bureau of Mines, 1979).

STRISHKOV, V.V. "Soviet Union," *Mining Annual Review* (London: Mining Journal, 1980), pp. 579–605.

TIRASPOLSKY, A. "Les Termes de l'Echange des pays de l'Est de 1970 à 1977." *Le Courrier des Pays de l'Est;* C.E.D.U.C.E.E. no. 218 (Mai 1978).

VERNON, Raymond & LEVY, Brian. "State-Owned Enterprises in the World Economy: the Case of Iron Ore", in Leroy, P. Jones (ed.) *Public Enterprise in Less-Developed Countries:* Multidisciplinary Perspectives. Cambridge, Mass., Cambridge University Press, 1981.

WALLENSTEEN, Peter. "Scarce Goods as Political Weapons: the case of food", in *Journal of Peace Research*, v. 13, no. 4, 1976. pp. 277–298.

# DISCUSSION PAPERS

DOHAN, M. *Volume, Price and Terms of Trade Indices of Soviet Foreign Trade 1913–1938.* In *Two Studies in Soviet Terms of Trade 1918–1970.* Studies in East European and Soviet Planning, Development and Trade, no. 21. Bloomington, Indiana: Indiana University, International Development Research Center, November 1973.

DRABEK, Z. "The Heckscher-Ohlin Model and Centrally-Planned Foreign Trade". Discussion paper no. 80–15. Vancouver, B.C.: University of British Columbia, 1980.

DRABEK, Z. "Western Embodied Technology and its Sectoral Impact on East European Exports to the West." Mimeo, for OECD, 1981.

DRABEK, Z. and SLATER, J. "Methodology of Data Compilation on Flows of Embodied Technology on East-West Trade." Mimeo, for OECD, 1981.

HANNIGAN, J.B. & MCMILLAN, C.H. *The Energy Factor in Soviet-East European Relations.* Ottawa, Institute of Soviet and East European

Studies, Carleton University, 1981. (East-West Commercial Relations Series Report; no. 18).
HEWETT, E.A. "The Foreign Sector in the Soviet Economy: Developments since 1960 and Possibilities to 2000." Paper presented at *The Conference on the Soviet Economy Towards the Year 2000*, Arlie House, 23–25 October 1980(b).
MARER, Paul. *Postwar Pricing and Price Patterns in Socialist Foreign Trade* (1946–1971). Bloomington, International Development Research Centre, Indiana University, 1979. iv, 102 p. (IDRC Report, no. 1)
MCCARTHY, M. "The Future of the Chromium Industry," M.S. Thesis, College of Mineral and Energy Resources, West Virginia University, Morgantown, 1981.
MIKDASHI, Zuhayr. *A Comparative Analysis of Selected Mineral Exporting Industries* (Vienna: OPEC) xeroxed, pp. 13–15 and 134–135.
PORTES, R. "Effect of the World Crisis on the East European Economies." Discussion paper no. 70. London: Birkbeck College, January 1980.
RAUGEL, P.F. *L'accord international sur le sucre et le marché mondial des produits édulcorants*, Paris: Université de Paris I, 1980, p. 225.
STANKOVSKY, J. *Ost-West-Handel 1980 und Aussichten 1981.* Forschungsbericht no. 68 Vienna: Wiener Institut für Internationale Wirtschaftsvergleiche, April 1981.
SWITUCHA, N.W. "COMECON's Mineral Development Potential and its Implications for Canada," M.R. no. 183, Energy, Mines and Resources, Canada, Ottawa, 1979.
VANOUS, J. and MARRESE, M. *Implicit Subsidies in Soviet Trade with Eastern Europe.* Discussion paper no. 80-32. Vancouver, B.C.: University of British Columbia, September 1980.

DOCUMENTS

The Central Intelligence Agency, *The International Energy Situation: Outlook to 1985* ER77–1024OU, April 1977.
The Central Intelligence Agency (National Foreign Assessment Center), *Prospects for Soviet Oil Production*, ER77–10270, April, 1977.
Charles River Associates. *An Economic Analysis of the Aluminium Industry.* Cambridge, Mass., 1971.
Charles River Associates. "Policy Implications of Producer Country Supply Restrictions: The World Manganese Market." Prepared for the US Dept. of Commerce, Cambridge, Mass., 1976.
Charles River Associates. *Policy Implications of Producer Country Supply Restrictions: the World Aluminium – Bauxite Market* (Cambridge, Massachusetts: 1977).
Commission of the European Community, "Report by the Commission on the Behaviour of the Oil Companies in the Community during the period from October 1973–March 1974," Brussels, 1974, p. 162.
– FAO, Production Yearbook, Vol. 30 1976, Vol. 32 1978.
– FAO, Trade Yearbook, Vol. 30 1976, Vol. 32 1978.

Oppenheimer & Co., *Aluminium Industry Report: Mid-Year Survey of Free World Primary Aluminium Capacity: 1974–1979* (New York: Metals Review, September 1974).

Petrostudies Company. *Soviet Proved Oil Reserves, 1946–1980* (Malmo Sweden: Petrostudies, 1979).

Roskill Information Services Ltd., *The Economics of Asbestos*. London: 1980.

United Nations. *Economic Bulletin of Europe*. Vol. 31, no. 1, 1978.

United Nations. *Capital Formation and Cost of Production in the European Coal Industry in 1979*, ECE, Coal Committee, Group of Experts on Coal Statistics, May 1981.

J.E.C (1976): US Congress. Joint Economic Committee. *Soviet Economy in a New Perspective*: Washington D.C.: US Government Printing Office, 1976.

J.E.C. (1977): US Congress. Joint Economic Committee. *East European Economies Post-Helsinki*. Washington, D.C.: US Government Printing Office, 1977.

J.E.C. (1979): US Congress. Joint Economic Committee. *Soviet Economy in a Time of Change*. Washington, D.C.: US Government Printing Office, 1979.

J.E.C. (1981): US Congress. Joint Economic Committee. *East European Economic Assessment*. Washington, D.C.: US Government Printing Office, 1981.

J.E.C. (1981)(b): US Congress. Joint Economic Committee. *Energy in Soviet Policy*. Washington, D.C.: US Government Printing Office, 1981.

US Department of Interior, Bureau of Mines, *Minerals Yearbook Preprints: Chromium* (Washington, D.C.: Government Printing Office, 1979).

Federal Trade Commission, Report to the Subcommittee on Small Business, US Senate, *The International Petroleum Cartel* (Washington D.C.: Government Printing Office), pp. 124–125.

USSR's Ministry of Trade, *Vneshniaia Torgovlia SSSR*. Moscow, various issues.

# Index

Afghanistan  86, 87
Agricultural products  44
Albania  153
Algeria  92
All-Union Foreign-Trade
  Association  77
Alumina  116, 117, 119, 120, 125, 126, 132
Aluminium consumption  119, 122, 133–34
Aluminium exports  123, 129, 131, 133, 137
Aluminium imports  125, 132–34, 137
Aluminium industry  12, 127–29
Aluminium market  116–34
Aluminium processing
  technology  116–18
Aluminium production  118–19, 120, 127
Aluminium products  129
Aluminium smelters  128
Aluminium trading  123–27, 129–32
Amosite  173, 175
Antimony  137
Arab oil embargo  78
Argentina  21, 199
Asbestos  11; use of term  173
Asbestos-cement products  173, 175
Asbestos consumption  173, 175–79
Asbestos demand forecasts  191
Asbestos demand prospects  190–92
Asbestos deposits  179
Asbestos exports  179–82, 184, 192
Asbestos imports  182, 189
Asbestos industry  174, 193
Asbestos market  187–89
Asbestos prices  182–87
Asbestos production  174–79
Atasuysk mine  145
Australia  116, 118, 134, 148, 150, 199
Austria  79, 87, 88

Baku oil fields  70
Bananas  15
Bangladesh  25
Bargaining position  7
Bargaining strengths and weaknesses  10
Barium  137
Barlow Rand  153
Bauxite  13, 116–20, 125, 126, 128, 132, 133, 137
Bayer process  116
Belgium  76, 77, 180
Bilateral balancing agreements  105
Bilateral clearing agreements  76
Bintan  125
Bolivia  13
Brazil  116, 119, 148
Buffer stocks  19, 24
Buffer system  19
Building materials  175

Canada  11, 118, 119, 123, 134, 162, 180, 182, 184, 185, 187, 188, 189, 192, 195, 199, 201
Central planning  50
Centralizing controls  6
Centrally planned economies (CPEs)  30, 45, 50
Charles River Associates  147, 148, 153
Chile  144
China  18, 25, 119, 219, 221, 225
Chromite  7, 135, 136, 150–55
Chromite exports  137, 154
Chromite industry  150
Chromite market conditions  150–52
Chromite market structure and
  power  151–54
Chromite price formation  151
Chromium  10
Chrysotile  173, 175, 182
Citrus fruit  15

# Index

Coal basins  109, 112
Coal consumption  101
Coal exports  27, 54, 100–15
Coal policy changes  101
Coal production  100–1, 111–15
Coal reserves  101, 106–10
Coal slurry pipeline  111
Coal transformation to gas  111
Coal transport  110–11
Cocoa  17, 22
Coffee  17, 21
Collectivization  158
COMECON  3–5, 23, 174, 178, 180, 187, 190, 192, 193, 201, 225, 236
Commodity prices  19
Common Fund  23
Compensation agreements  87, 93
Consolidated Gold Fields  159–61
Copper  13, 15, 24
Copper consumption  139
Copper exports  137, 142
Copper market  135–45, 154, 155
Copper price formation  139–43
Copper production  138, 144
Copper sales contracts  143
Cotton  11, 15, 17, 24
Cotton consumption  221, 222
Cotton exports  221, 224, 225, 227–30, 232, 235
Cotton fibres  27
Cotton imports  225, 226, 228–35
Cotton market  218–36
Cotton power  235–36
Cotton production  218
Council for Mutual Economic Assistance (CMEA)  10, 18, 19, 24, 32, 33, 35, 38, 44, 45, 49–60, 71, 76, 78, 82–88, 91, 95–97, 136, 137, 139, 143, 147–51, 169
Crocidolite  173, 175
Cuba  8, 10, 23, 71, 137, 201
Czechoslovakia  87, 123

Dalnafta  77
Deficit trade  56, 57
Deflationary movements  7
Denmark  77, 79
Developing countries  15, 17, 19, 26, 38, 44, 45, 49, 55–58, 66, 71, 79, 91, 129
DFN  77
Disequilibrium  56
Donets basin  109
Double Factoral Terms of Trade (DFTT)  29
Dowie, David  159
Druzhba pipeline  77
Dzhezdinsk mine  145

East Germany  123
Eastern Europe  8, 21, 23, 25, 71, 84, 87, 92, 93, 96, 163, 175, 178, 190, 201, 221
Economic subsidisation  4
*Edinburgh* HMS  165
EEC  18, 22, 221, 225
Ekibastuz coalfields  110
Euronafta  77
Export costs  29
Export performance  56
Export prices  27, 28, 29, 33, 38, 39, 43, 44, 54
Export volume  28, 30
EXPORTKHLEB  194, 209
Exports  9, 12, 26–27, 29, 44, 45, 46, 57, 59; *see also* Aluminium; Asbestos; Chromite; Copper; Cotton; Grain; Manganese; Natural gas; Oil

Ferro-chromium  150, 151, 154
Ferro-manganese  147, 148, 154
Finland  71, 76, 77
Fischer Price Index (FPI)  31
Five-year-plan  82, 83, 84, 95, 112, 131, 136, 139, 158, 218
Flour  27
Fluorides  137
Food  27, 44
Foreign trade gap  59
Foreign trade relations  17
France  15, 76, 116, 117, 118, 136, 180, 188, 189
Fuels  43, 45, 59, 76

Gabon  148
Gas. *See* Natural gas
General Agreement on Tariffs and Trade  8
General Mining  153
Germany  10, 77
Gèze, F.  131
Ghana  116
GNP  59
Gold  11, 137, 156–72
    production estimates  158–61
    secrecy concerning  156–57
Gold financing  57
Gold market position  162–66
Gold marketing tactics  170
Gold mining  158–59
Gold prices  167–70
Gold production estimates  160
Gold reserves  158, 166
Gold sales  164, 167, 171, 172
Grain  7, 8, 9, 27, 156, 158, 171

## Index

Grain economy 194, 201–5
Grain embargo 199, 204
Grain exports 195, 198, 199, 209
Grain imports 194–99, 202–12, 215, 217
Grain markets 194–211, 206
Grain power 210, 11
Grain prices 195, 205–10
   long-term perspective 206–8
   short-term perspective 208–9
Grain production 194–96, 202, 204
Grain sales 208
Grain shortages 209
Grain trade
   cyclical imports 204–5
   structural imports 202–4
Grain trade dependence 200
Grain trade pattern 194–205
Grain utilisation 203, 204
'Great Turn' 158
Greece 116, 125
Gross Barter Terms of Trade (GBTT) 28, 29, 31, 45, 49, 50, 53
Gross national product 6
Group D 18
Guinea 116, 118, 125, 132
Guyana 116, 119, 125

Hard-currency earnings 84, 90
Hard-currency exports 78
Hard-currency markets 76, 79, 84, 94, 96
Hungary 21, 89, 116, 117
Hydrocarbon exports 94
Hydrocarbons 68

Import prices 27, 28, 30, 33, 39, 44
Import volume 28
Import 9, 17, 27, 29, 45, 51, 54, 56, 57, 132–34; *see also* Asbestos; Cotton; Grain; Natural gas
Income Terms of Trade (ITT) 30, 51
India 125, 132, 180, 185, 186, 187, 218
Indices of terms of trade; *see* Trade terms indices
Indonesia 13, 125, 132
Inflationary movements 7, 38, 44
Integrated Programme for Commodities (IPC) 20–25
Inter-governmental Council of Copper Exporting Countries (CIPEC) 144–45
International Bauxite Association 119
International Cocoa Agreement 22
International Commodity Agreements (ICAs) 15–25
International economic relations 6–14

International economic system 6
International Sugar Agreement 22–23
International Tin Agreement 21
Iran 13, 78, 86–89
Iraq 78
Iron ore 12, 13, 25, 27
Italy 77, 87, 88, 116, 125, 180
Izmir group 24

Jamaica 118, 119, 125, 127
Japan 12, 76, 106, 109, 110, 118, 119, 134, 136, 147, 154, 180, 182, 184, 186, 188, 228
Jute 25

Kansk-Achinsk lignite basin 110
Karaganda basin 109
Khrushchev 165, 235
Kiembai project 174
Kindia 125
Kolyma 156, 158, 159
Kosygin, Premier 83
Kuwait 68
Kuznetsk basin 109

Laspeyres Price Index (LPI) 31
Latin America 21
Lead 15
Lena Basin 106
Less-developed countries; *see* Developing countries
LNG 87, 92
Logs 27
London Metal Exchange 133, 143
Long-term commodity agreements 15–25
Luxembourg 180

Maize 194, 208, 210
Malaysia 225
Manganese 7, 25, 135–37, 154, 155
Manganese consumption 147
Manganese exports 149
Manganese market 145–50
   structure and power of 148–50
Manganese price formation 147–48
Manila Declaration 18
Mannesmann 88
Market structure 11–14
Market type economies (MTEs) 30, 50, 59
Metals 44
Metals markets 135–55
Metals position overview 136–37
Metals production 136

# Index

Metals self-sufficiency 137
Metals trade 136–37
Mexico 13
Middle East 86, 91
Molybdenum 137
Money supply 7
Mongolia 18
More Developed Countries (MDCs) 26, 27, 38, 44, 45, 49, 51, 55–58, 64
Mossadeq affair 13
MTN 154
Multilateral commodity agreements 15–20
Multinational companies 12–14, 17

Nafta 77
Nafta B 77
Nafta (It) 77
Nakhodka 110
Natural gas 27, 54, 57, 68–97
Natural gas exports 68, 86, 88, 89, 93, 94
Natural gas pipeline 5, 87
Natural gas prices 93
Natural gas reserves 85
Natural gas trade 90–94
Natural gas transport 92
Natural resource products (NRPs) 26, 38, 39, 42–44, 54, 58
Natural rubber 24
Neftekhimpromexport 87
Net Barter Terms of Trade (NBTT) 28–31, 35, 38, 45, 49–51, 53, 55–59
Netherlands 68, 76, 88, 89, 90
Nikolaev alumina plant 125, 129
Nikopo basin 145
Non-ferrous metals 12, 13, 27, 136, 156–58
Norilsk 156, 158, 161
North America 76
North Star project 87
Norway 119, 123, 134

Oil and oil products 8, 12, 13, 57, 68–97; see also Petroleum
Oil embargo 78
Oil exports 26, 68, 70–78, 83, 84, 94–97
Oil markets 77–85
Oil offensives 78
Oil prices 26, 78
Oil production 98, 99
Oil trade 90–94
Oil transport 92
OPEC 26, 78, 82, 91, 92, 96, 97
Ores 44

Other Centrally Planned Economies (OCPE) 38, 49, 55, 56, 58, 62

Paasche Price Index (PPI) 31
Packaged energy 130–31
Pakistan 218, 221
Palladium 166
Patolichev, V.S. 15
Pechora basin 109
Penkovsky, Oleg 159
Peru 13, 24
Petroleum 7, 15, 27, 54, 68–70, 72, 76
Petroleum products 27, 54
Philippines 153
Phosphate 25
Phosphate imports 132
Platinum 7, 10, 137, 156–72
  production estimates 158–61
Platinum market position 162–66
Platinum mining 161
Platinum prices 167–70
Platinium reserves 166
Platinium sales 167
Poland 21, 24, 57, 84, 87, 123, 225
Political behaviour effects 8
Political commodity power 3
Politics and trade 8–9
Price changes 42
Price elasticities 7
Price explosion 26
Price increases 8, 38, 44
Price indices 33
Price stabilisation 19
Price-stabilising agreements 15

Quantity indices 48, 49

Raw materials 10, 11, 19
Rhodesia 151, 153
Rhodium 166
Rolled ferrous metals 27
Romania 17, 18, 71, 89, 225
Rubber 17
Ruhrgas 88

Sampling procedures 33
Saudi Arabia 68
Sawn timber 27
"77" group 16, 18
Seydisehir complex 125
Sierra Leone 116
Single Factoral Terms of Trade (SFTT) 29, 30
Sliding price formula 39, 45
Soderberg process 129

# Index

Soft-currency markets 95
Sojuzgazexport 87
Sojuznefteexport 77
Solid fuels 102, 103, 106, 111
South Africa 11, 137, 148, 150, 153, 154, 162, 170, 180, 184, 187, 192
South Korea 119, 225
South Yakutian basin 109, 110
Southern Rhodesia 8
Sovoil 77
Soyuz pipeline 88
Spain 180
Special Drawing Rights (SDRs) 51, 53
State Committee for Foreign Economic Relations 87
Statistical criteria 32
Statistical problems 31–33
Strategic blackmail 3
Strategic commodity power 3
Substitution effect 59
Sugar 10, 17, 18, 20, 22–23
Suomen Petrooli 77
Surinam 116, 119
Surplus trade 56
Sweden 76, 77, 134, 36

Taiwan 119
Tea 25
Teboil 77
Technical progress 32
Terms of trade; *see* Trade terms
Textile industry 220
Third World; *see* Developing countries
Timber 25
Tin 12, 17, 21, 137
Titanium 137
Trade controls 9
Trade data provision 32
Trade gains 10–11, 27–30, 35, 50
Trade imbalances 55, 56
Trade prices 51
Trade returns 32, 35
Trade statistics 33, 34
Trade terms 33, 35–55
Trade terms computation 31–33
Trade terms indices 33, 36

Transitgas 87
Tsvetmetproexport 125
Tugunska basin 106
Tungsten 137
Tungsten Committee 25
Turkey 116, 125, 132, 153, 154

UDI 38
UNCTAD 15–18, 20, 23, 145
Unit value indices 32, 33, 40, 46
United kingdom 76, 77, 180, 221
United States 8, 11, 12, 13, 68, 76, 118, 119, 136, 144, 147, 154, 155, 180, 195, 199, 204, 219, 220, 227
United States Central Intelligence Agency (CIA( 82, 83, 85, 159, 161, 165, 166

Vanadium 137
Vegetable oil 15
Vietnam 71
Vneshnyaya Torgovlya Sovyetsogo Soyuza (VTSS) 33
Volga-Urals oil fields 70, 77
Volgograd plant 125

Wallace, Henry 158
West Germany 76, 87–89, 119, 132, 134, 136, 154, 180
Western Europe 8, 76, 77, 79, 87–90, 92, 93, 147, 184, 187, 188, 190, 225, 227, 228
Western Siberia 68, 70, 77, 84
Western technology 58, 59, 156, 171
Wheat' 20, 194, 197, 208, 210, 216
Wheat agreements 195
Windfall gains 50–54
World commodity markets 55–58
World market prices (WMP) 39, 58

Yakutia project 87
Yamal pipeline 89
Yugoslavia 71, 116, 117, 125, 180, 185, 187, 228

Zavenyagin, A. P. 161
Zinc 15